THE CONTRASTING ECONOMIES ∾ A Study

of Modern Economic Systems

LYNN TURGEON *HOFSTRA COLLEGE*

Allyn and Bacon, Inc. ∾ Boston

© *Copyright 1963 by Allyn and Bacon, Inc.*
150 Tremont Street, Boston

All rights reserved. No part of this book may be
reproduced in any form, by mimeograph or any other means,
without permission in writing from the publishers.

Library of Congress Catalog Card Number: 63-13825

Printed in the United States of America

First printing .... *April, 1963*

Second printing ...... *March, 1964*

330. 109
T936c

Preface

In a world permeated with uncertainties, one near certainty is becoming evident: "growthmanship" is occupying an increasingly important place in our national thinking as the sixties progress. The source of this increasing preoccupation with our own rate of economic growth is not difficult to perceive. It is the inexorable ascent of the economy of the USSR and, as a corollary, the competitive image we in the United States must present to the more underdeveloped areas of the world.

Most of the participants in the discussion over relative rates of economic growth have thus far engaged in something resembling a "numbers game." The first move in this game is the establishment of the current relative position of the United States and Soviet economies. For this purpose, we must estimate the annual output of goods and services produced by the two economic complexes. The findings here will depend to some extent on the inclusiveness of the measure of the "pie" as well as the relative importance assigned to the different components of the total product. Depending on the yardstick and relative weights employed, we find that the Soviet economy turns out anywhere from 30 to 50 per cent as many goods and services as ours does.

The next step in our latest national pastime is to project future rates of growth for the two systems, partly on the basis of the past record. Projections of Soviet economic development are comparatively easy to make. Since the Soviet economy develops unfettered by either lack of effective demand or "favorable" investment opportunities, we can predict with a relatively small margin of error where the Soviet economy will be in 10 or even 20 years. To some extent, the Soviet rate of growth will be in-

305007

fluenced by changes in Russian international commitments, but in general we can predict that their total product will grow by about six or seven per cent annually, or by between 80 and 100 per cent during the present decade.[1]

When we come to projecting our own rate of economic growth, the picture is less clear. Persuasive arguments can be advanced to support either an acceleration or a retardation of the historic three per cent average annual increase in our gross national product. Perhaps the safest guess would be to assume a continuation of this historic long term growth rate. To some extent, our future growth will also depend on changes in our international commitments. But it seems unlikely that our rate of growth can significantly exceed one-half of the growth rate achieved by the Soviet economy.

The outcome of the game seems inescapable. The total products of the two systems are converging, and it is only a question of time before the present world pre-eminence of our economy will disappear. Optimistic players will find our economic superiority continuing at least until the end of the century, while our pessimists will probably reach the conclusion that the eclipse will occur as early as the seventies.

We could undoubtedly spend considerable time and effort analyzing the various factors which might influence the speed with which the existing gap between the economies of the two major coexisting powers will be reduced or eventually eliminated. But in this connection, we would most certainly have to know such important variables as the projected magnitude of the expenditures for the military establishments and economic assistance programs of both the United States and the USSR, neither of which can be anticipated with any degree of accuracy.

[1] A monumental study of Soviet national income by Professor Abram Bergson of Harvard estimates that the Soviet total product has been growing over the past decade at an annual rate of 7.5 per cent. The new Twenty-Year Plan covering the next two decades anticipates a somewhat faster rate of overall growth in the sixties (9.6%) largely because of some grandiose expectations for their agricultural sector. During the seventies, however, the projected rate of overall growth of 7.2% is similar to that of the past decade.

As a result, it would seem that we might profitably concede at the outset that the Soviet economy—particularly in view of its vast mineral wealth and considerably larger population—will eventually surpass ours in certain important respects. But instead of worrying too much about *when* and in what sense an eclipse will take place, we shall attempt to investigate the questions of *how* and *why* this event will probably transpire. In other words, we will focus our attention primarily on an examination of the contrasting sources and limitations of relative growth as well as the underlying nature of the economic expansion being achieved under the two systems.

The following material has been developed for teaching a course in contemporary economic systems at Hofstra College. When I began teaching in 1957, I inherited a one-semester economics course entitled "Captialism and Its Alternatives," designed primarily for Business Division students having some background in economic principles. Shortly thereafter, the launching of Sputnik generated somewhat greater student interest in the Soviet Union generally, with the result that more non-economics majors in the various social sciences began registering for the course.

At an early stage, it became clear that the traditional encyclopedic texts for courses in comparative economic systems—dealing as they do with over-technical theoretical controversies or isolated and somewhat disconnected sections on different economies—left something to be desired for our purposes. On the other hand, a one-semester course concentrating solely on the operations of the Soviet economy, for which a number of fine texts and collections of readings have already appeared, seemed rather esoteric for our requirements.[2] As a result, I have attempted to synthesize these

[2] Two collections of readings stand out: Franklyn D. Holzman, *Readings on the Soviet Economy,* Rand McNally, Chicago, 1961 and Morris Bornstein and Daniel R. Fusfeld, *The Soviet Economy: A Book of Readings,* Richard D. Irwin, Homewood, Illinois, 1962. Both collections rely heavily on reprinting papers originally submitted by panelists appearing before the Subcommittee on Economic Statistics of the Joint Economic Committee, and published in three parts under the title, *Comparisons of the United States and Soviet Economies,* U.S. Government Printing Office, Washington, 1959. The lists of recommended readings at the end of

two approaches by writing a non-technical text suitable for a course in contemporary economic systems, with *emphasis* on the Soviet economy, contrasting its institutions, operations, and developments with our own.

In writing this book, I have benefited greatly from the questions most frequently raised by students in my classes, and my greatest debt of gratitude is to them. I am also especially grateful to Drs. Dorothy Douglas and Murray Yanowitch—both of whom used my preliminary notes in their teaching of comparative systems at Hofstra, and contributed valuable suggestions. Others who have read and commented on all or parts of the manuscript include: Marvin Lee, Jack Minkoff, Sayre Schatz, Leo Kaplan, and my wife, Livia. Finally, a special note of appreciation is in order for Arnold Miller, one of my former students, who collected price data in the USSR with dedication, compiled a glossary of terms, and indexed this volume.

LYNN TURGEON

Chapters III through XII are asterisked to indicate materials contained in the two collections of readings.

Contents

The Contrasting Economies

I ∾ Introduction

A STUDENT OF COMPARATIVE ECONOMIC SYSTEMS is confronted today with a vast array of national economies ranging all the way from something which might be called "modified capitalism" on the right to imperfect or developing communism on the left. Between the economies of the United States and the USSR—our right and left prototypes at the extremes of the array—our student finds many "mixed" systems. On the right side, he finds capitalist-oriented economies committed primarily to investment and production for private profit, but with varying proportions of government ownership and social welfare activities. On the left, our student finds a growing number of noncapitalist-oriented economies, all ostensibly dedicated to investment and production for someone's eventual use, yet still containing residual capitalist enclaves of varying significance.

Were our student to attempt a study of the individual characteristics of each of our contemporary national economies, he would have his life's work cut out for him. Fortunately such a detailed study seems unnecessary. Most of the essential things that we have to say about comparative economic systems can be discussed in the context of either of our two prototypes, the modified, well-developed capitalist system of the United States, or the developing communist economy of the USSR. Occasionally we may wish to examine a particular economic institution or development outside the economy of either the United States or the USSR, but in general we shall be examining institutions and developments in the economies of the two major coexisting powers.

Although all contemporary economic systems must solve certain basic problems arising from conditions of scarcity, the methods used may vary considerably. We shall approach our study of capitalist and noncapitalist-oriented economies by examining the methods by which basic problems get solved in the United States and the USSR. For example, we shall be attempting to answer such questions as the following: How are the nation's savings mobilized and how are investment decisions made? How is agricultural produce extracted under the two systems? How is the distribution of goods and services effected? By what mechanism is an adequate labor force assured? How and to what extent are labor incentives employed? How are relative prices and over-all price movements determined? What management problems are there and how are they handled in the two systems? How is government revenue raised and for what purposes is it spent? What role does foreign trade play in the two types of economies? What applicability do the developmental experiences of the United States and USSR have for the newly-emerging nations?

It is possible to take either of two overall views with respect to the economies of the United States and the USSR. We might assume that these two economic systems contain more similarities than differences, that as industrialized or industrializing economies they face similar problems and can be expected to handle them in substantially the same manner. As a corollary we might also assume that as the level of Soviet industrialization approaches our own, her economic development and institutions should be very similar to ours. In other words, not only will there be a convergence of the total products; there will also be a convergence of the respective economic institutions.

Perhaps the best summation of this viewpoint, which ordinarily treats both systems as forms of "state capitalism" or "state managerialism," was given by Norman Thomas at his 75th birthday dinner in New York in November, 1959. Mr. Thomas placed himself in the "school of those who believe that if we can avoid catastrophe and if we should continue our present directions of economic evolution in both the U.S.A. and USSR, our two *economic* systems in the coming decade will be so nearly similar as to abolish acute ideological conflict." This viewpoint is also apparently held by Arnold Toynbee who recently described the Communist regime in Russia as "bent on raising its subjects' material standard of living to the American level, and, when this has been achieved, as it surely will be one day, there will be little to choose between America and Russia as a domicile from the poor man's point of view."[1]

On the other hand, we might take the general viewpoint that there are significant structural differences between the two economic systems and, furthermore, that these diversities will tend to be magnified as time goes by. It is this latter position which I wish to assume as a working hypothesis underlying the comparisons and contrasts comprising this study. This growing diversity is not necessarily believed to be a source of conflict; on the contrary, when we come to the study of the role of foreign trade in the two economies we shall see that the two systems would seem to be more complementary than competing with the result that sources of *economic* conflict between the two systems may be largely illusory.

By taking this position, I would not deny that in some respects the two economic systems may begin to resemble each other superficially. Already it may be pointed out that the competitive pressures on the United States to match the Soviet rate of growth have brought forth some suggestions which, if followed, would give our economy certain Soviet-type trimmings. When the Soviet Union began to trade seriously with the West in the fifties, the cry almost immediately arose that we could engage in "economic warfare" more effectively by establishing a monopoly to carry on

[1] Arnold J. Toynbee, "Spiritual Freedom Is the Great Difference," *New York Times Magazine,* January 15, 1961, p. 30. There are many other proponents of this theory of "convergence," although most of their interpretations are broader in scope than mere economics. See Jan Tinbergen, "Do Communist and Free Economies Show a Converging Pattern?", *Soviet Studies,* April, 1961, pp. 333–341; Erich Fromm, *May Man Prevail?,* Doubleday, Garden City, New York, 1961, p. 81; Oskar Morgenstern, *The Question of National Defense,* Vintage Books, New York, 1961, p. 324; Pitirim Sorokin's views as reported in the *New York Times,* October 15, 1961, p. 7; and Robert L. Heilbroner, *The Making of Economic Society,* Prentice-Hall, Englewood Cliffs, N.J., 1962, pp. 230–231.

our foreign trade, just as the Russians do.[2] At other times, certain roving Americans, on their return from the Soviet Union, have suggested that we establish various central planning units in Washington to enable us to meet the Soviet challenge.[3] It is also true that historical forces operating in our system seem to be pushing us in the direction of greater centralization of our own decision-making. But this growing application of federal economic powers would have probably come about eventually via the dissemination and acceptance of Keynesian principles even if there were no Russian challenge. We might also note the growing trend towards planning in the military sector of our economy where it can euphemistically be referred to as "logistics." Under our Secretary of Defense McNamara, a budgeting technique of five-year program packaging now requires the various armed services to estimate not only the initial cost of a weapons system but also the maintenance costs over the ensuing five years.

On the other side of the world, on the other hand, forces are seemingly operating to bring about changes designed to reduce the need for quite so much centralized decision-making. Partly this "regionalization" may be developing from the necessity to cope with the growing complexity of the decision-making process in these economies. In addition, the Russians and Czechs must certainly be familiar with the experience of our large United States corporations, such as General Motors or General Electric, which have for some time pursued a policy of decentralization in the interests of greater efficiency.[4] At any rate, it is probably too early to assess the significance of this movement towards regional decision-making in some of the areas within the Soviet

[2] For an answer to those who see a need for this device see Lynn Turgeon, "The Significance of Soviet Trade Policies," *Illinois Business Review,* July, 1961, pp. 6–8.

[3] For example, Senator Hubert Humphrey has proposed that the United States meet the growing Soviet challenge with a "grand design for peace —a seven-year plan of our own." See *New York Times,* May 10, 1959, p. 2. Earlier William Randolph Hearst, Jr., pleaded for a permanent "National Planning Board" to implement successful competitive coexistence. *New York Journal-American,* March 1, 1955.

[4] In this connection, see Peter F. Drucker, *Concept of the Corporation,* Beacon Press, Boston, 1960, pp. 41 *et seq.*

bloc, particularly in view of the "localism" which has sprung up in its wake.[5]

It is sometimes contended that Soviet planners under Khrushchev have recently been forced to institute "capitalist" incentives to make their economy function more efficiently. This seems to me to be a misreading of the facts. The need for substantial worker and managerial incentives was recognized very soon after the introduction of effective central planning in the late twenties and their growing use was defended at the time on the basis of the then underdeveloped nature of the Soviet economic system. As a consequence, extreme incentives for both labor and management have characterized the Soviet economy since 1931. As the Soviet economy has become more developed, however, there seems to have been a slight reduction in the use of the more extreme personal incentives, at least as far as the industrial sector is concerned.

There may be some truth in the above argument with respect to the growing use of "carrots" to the extent that greater incentives are now being employed in the agricultural sector. For most of what we might call the pre-Khrushchev period, the Russian collective farmers had little incentive to produce more food since even the most energetic farmer working on the most fertile agriculture lands was very inadequately rewarded for his efforts. Only recently has the whole level of payments to agricultural workers been raised substantially, resulting in some closing of the gap between urban and rural levels of living. Thus even this move towards greater overall incentives in the agricultural sector may be interpreted broadly as a feeble step in the direction of lesser income differentiation for the economy as a whole.

It is also true that for all practical purposes collectivization of

[5] "Localism" refers to the practice of nonfulfillment of obligations to deliver specified parts, goods, and products to other regions that depended upon them. Already there is some evidence that the Russians may be back-tracking on their initial regionalization, at least with respect to the RSFSR. A new agency, the All-Russian Economic Council, with extensive powers over regional economic councils has been created in Moscow to coordinate industrial management in the Russian Republic. See *New York Times,* June 21, 1960, p. 3.

agriculture has been abandoned for at least the time being in Poland and Yugoslavia, both of which must be regarded as non-capitalist-oriented economies. Furthermore, Soviet officials have praised Polish agricultural developments and have conceded that farm collectivization is not necessarily an essential step in the building of socialism.[6] Nevertheless, other members of the Soviet and neutralist bloc seem to be relentlessly pushing their agricultural collectivization. On balance, the move away from the small family farm seems in the long run to be irreversible in the non-capitalist-oriented economies.

Soviet planners today also seem to be more solicitous about the welfare of consumers now that some of the dividends from rapid economic growth are being passed along to Soviet workers and employees. However, it should be noted in connection with the distribution of these benefits that while advertising is not entirely absent in the Soviet Union, it bears little resemblance—either with respect to quantity or quality—to the output of our Madison Avenue. Instalment credit has also been introduced on a tentative basis in a number of noncapitalist-oriented economies, but, as we shall see in Chapter VI, the motivation behind this institutional change seems to be somewhat different from what it is in capitalist-oriented economies.

If it is true, as this writer holds, that unique economic institutions will eventually characterize capitalist and noncapitalist-oriented economies, or that superficially similar institutions will have different rationales for their existence as well as for their development or lack of development, what is the explanation for this existing and growing diversity? The principal factor tending to explain existing institutions and institutional change in the two economies is held to be what might be called their respective "basic problems."

The basic problem of the Soviet economy has been and is one of "over-commitment" while that of our United States economy today is frequently, if not exclusively, one of "under-commitment"

[6] See "Russian Praises Polish Farming," *New York Times,* February 4, 1962, p. 15.

of our resource utilization. At the very least, it must be admitted that the United States economy has fluctuated in the past between over-commitment (expansion) and under-commitment (contraction).

Since 1928 Soviet planners have consistently tried to do more with their available economic resources than was physically possible. The targets of the plans have in all cases been maximal and the goals have frequently been under-fulfilled, although perhaps somewhat less so in recent years. The Russians have attempted to invest more of their resources than has been warranted by their available manpower and capital, at least given the imperfections and unforeseen bottlenecks which developed after the planning stage.

Although it seems evident that over-commitment has been endemic in the Soviet economy, the rationale behind this phenomenon is not clear. Perhaps it is only due to poor planning by the central authorities. Conceivably, the plans may have been correctly drawn up, but there has been insufficient slack in the system. That is to say, perhaps pipe lines have been inadequately filled and inventories have been too skimpy to keep individual nonfulfillment from spreading more generally throughout the system. But, whatever the rationale behind this bias towards over-commitment, the result is crystal clear. A perpetual seller's market for goods, services, and labor power has been created.

In the United States economy today, on the other hand, we ordinarily have just the reverse basic problem. There is apparently a chronic tendency on the part of those who make our investment decisions to under-commit our resources. That is, under conditions of relatively full employment of labor and/or capital, the amount of resources that income recipients would voluntarily release for potential investment—in other words, income they would not consume—is frequently, if not chronically, incompletely utilized by private and government investment decision-makers. For the economy as a whole, the resulting failure to absorb fully what we might label "full employment voluntary nonconsumption" produces a condition which can be described as relative high-level stagnation with growing under-employment of both our capital stock and labor force, especially the former.

It is true that in periods of war, intensified cold war, or recovery from past wars this basic problem is either eliminated or reduced substantially, and its place is taken by a problem similar to the one the Russians have. But I dare say that we can at least hope that these periods of war and near-war will be fewer and farther between in the years ahead. If so, what effect will the possible continued existence of this underlying basic problem have on our developing institutions?

The basic problems of the two economies may be summarized as follows: The Soviets and other noncapitalist-oriented economies tend to generate problems and institutions reflecting inadequate supplies in relation to the effective demand for both producers' and consumers' goods. We in the United States, on the other hand, tend to be preoccupied with problems related to an inadequate effective demand in relation to our growing production capabilities. To put it another way, we operate under conditions which may be best described as a growing buyer's market with considerable underemployment of our resources; they have a perpetual seller's market with over-full employment. If this is the case, what are the possibilities that either or both systems will be be able to solve, or at least mitigate, their respective basic problems? And what effect will solving or failing to solve these respective problems have on the economic development of the two systems under conditions of competitive coexistence?

II ⁓ *Labels for Comparative Economic Systems*

ACCORDING TO THE "CONVENTIONAL WISDOM" currently being dispensed in college courses dealing with comparative economic systems, at least four labels can be meaningfully employed: capitalism, fascism, socialism, and communism. The respective examples of the above economic systems, each of which is usually discussed in comparative isolation and at some length, are the economies of the United States, Nazi Germany, Great Britain or perhaps Sweden, and the Soviet Union.

A case can undoubtedly be made for an independent study of the economic ideologies associated with each of these four labels, especially if one pursues an historical approach to the subject. However, in looking at the economies of the world today, as well as the direction in which they are developing, one wonders how much significance should be attached to any detailed, independent study of either fascism or socialism as defined under the conventional classification.

Such fascist economies as have existed certainly bore a very close resemblance to capitalist ones by virtue of the fact that private, unequal ownership of the means of production generally remained as a salient feature of the fascist economic system. There was perhaps more of an obligation on the part of the private owners of capital to utilize the means of production than there ordinarily has been under peacetime capitalism. There might have been some expansion of state ownership of capital plant and equipment as exemplified by the Volkswagen enterprise projected in Fascist Germany; likewise, a considerable range of social welfare measures also developed in prewar Germany. But both of these latter developments can also be found to varying degrees in contemporary capitalist-oriented welfare states.

Socialism, according to the conventional classification, implies a gradual transfer of the means of production from private to social ownership. It is sometimes referred to as "evolutionary socialism" to distinguish it from communism or "revolutionary socialism." Historically, this system of ideas has been quite important, despite the fact that evolutionary socialist economic systems as going concerns for lengthy periods of time are not easily identifiable. In practice, if the experience of Great Britain or Sweden is any criterion, the gradual transition has usually stopped well before the major share of the means of production has been transferred from private to social ownership.

One of the political difficulties involved in any evolutionary transition to socialism lies in the fact that the implementation of further socialization may result in a short-run decline in levels of living as owners of capital scheduled to be socialized refrain from undertaking necessary repairs or new investment. The mere announcement of a program of further socialization by a non-capitalist-oriented government might be sufficient to cause a short-run decline in investment, employment, national income, and levels of consumption. Since evolutionary socialist governments must frequently stand for election, the transition problem undoubtedly appears formidable to practical socialist politicians.

Another factor which has probably stymied the process of evolutionary socialism in the Western world has been the existence of the USSR as a living example of a completely socialized economy. The association of socialization in the Western public mind with the repression, hardship, and lack of personal freedom which have accompanied the development of socialism in the USSR undoubtedly explains a certain amount of understandable hesitancy towards movement in this direction.

After World War II, the British economy under a Labor government seemed for a time to be evolving slowly towards socialism and appeared to be a suitable subject for independent study.

But since the assumption of power by British Conservatives, further socialization has not only ceased, but in some areas such as steel, there has been de-socialization. It is true that even British Conservatives frequently display a sound grasp of Keynesian fiscal policies, but this must be interpreted as a recognition by the Conservatives of the fact that the late Lord Keynes was more interested in extending the life expectancy of capitalism than he was in promoting socialism.

At one time it was also fashionable to consider the Scandinavian economies—especially that of Sweden—as constituting a "middle-way." Although the welfare state activities are well developed in these countries, about 90 per cent of all capital is still operated for private profit and there is little indication that this percentage is being reduced. In fiscal policy, the Swedes have recently begun to rely more heavily on indirect or sales taxation rather than on direct or income taxation, which had formerly been highly regarded by evolutionary socialists as a tool to bring about egalitarian socialism.[1] The growth of the Common Market—which is dominated by a capitalist-oriented ideology—should allow for the continued polarization of Western European economies, and lead them still further along what is essentially a capitalist path of development.

As a consequence of the virtual demise of fascist and evolutionary socialist economies as living organisms, I have simplified matters somewhat by reducing my labels to two: noncapitalist-oriented and capitalist-oriented economic systems. The former label covers all economies which are consciously progressing with the socialization of industry and/or the collectivization of agriculture. The latter label would cover both any possible emerging fascist economies and existing welfare states with substantial but relatively frozen sectors of public ownership. Each label represents a broad net and undoubtedly conceals a considerable amount of diversity. It is to this heterogeneity that I now wish to turn briefly.

[1] See Werner Wiskari, "Swedes Receive Tax Rise Calmly," *New York Times,* January 28, 1962, p. 7.

NONCAPITALIST-ORIENTED
ECONOMIES

Communism is only the ultimate goal of the now fully social-ized economy of the USSR. Though the Communist Party of the Soviet Union unquestionably occupies the "commanding heights," the economy of the USSR operates at present on so-cialist principles, attempting to obtain services "from each ac-cording to his ability" and to distribute products "to each accord-ing to his contribution." This principle of distribution is to be distinguished from the ultimate method of distribution under full communism when commodities and services will be distrib-uted "according to need." [2] (This distinction between the two stages of socialism originated in Marx's *Critique of the Gotha Programme* written in 1875.)

Countries outside the USSR but within the Soviet bloc are said to be only "on the road to socialism," or "within the socialist camp." While the USSR is politically a federation of socialist republics, the governments of Eastern Europe (excluding the German Democratic Republic), Mongolia, and China are labeled "People's Democracies" or "People's Republics." The East Ger-man government is a "Democratic Republic" as is the govern-ment of North Viet Nam, while North Korea is the only "Peo-ple's Democratic Republic." [3]

These different political labels might conceivably have been applied to virtually identical economic systems. While it is true that all economies in the Soviet bloc maintain essentially the same ideological base, it would be dangerous to exaggerate the mono-

[2] Distribution according to "need" does not necessarily imply complete equality since differences such as tastes and physical requirements would undoubtedly remain under communism.

[3] The dissimilar labels attached to the East German, North Korean and North Vietnamese regimes may stem from the fact that the Soviet bloc does not wish to recognize officially the bisection of the original countries as being a permanent state of affairs.

lithic nature of the noncapitalist-oriented economies, even those within the Soviet bloc. Just as democracy is practiced in various forms by capitalist-oriented governments (for example, there are democratic monarchies or democratic republics; democracies with strong or weak executive branches; and democracies endorsing eventual socialism or capitalism), so too is the "building of socialism" taking diverse forms, especially in the Khrushchev era. At present we might distinguish at least seven roads to socialism —and ultimately presumably also to communism—in the world:

1. The USSR has been unique in that it not only considers itself to have achieved socialism as early as 1936, but also that it is steadily approaching communism.[4] According to the Soviet definition, socialism is an economic system in which it is no longer possible for man to "exploit" his fellow man: in other words, it is no longer possible for a Soviet citizen to "employ labor power for the purpose of extracting surplus value." [5] Unlike the situation in other noncapitalist-oriented economies, with the exception of Czechoslovakia, both industry and agriculture are entirely socialized or collectivized in the USSR.

[4] At the Twenty-first Party Congress, Premier Khrushchev predicted that, in contrast to the evolution towards socialism, all economies within the Soviet bloc would eventually achieve communism at about the same time, implying Soviet and Czechoslovakian economic assistance for the less developed members of the socialist camp. See *Pravda,* January 28, 1959, or *The Current Digest of the Soviet Press,* March 11, 1959, p. 13. A Polish writer in the economic journal *Zycie Gosepodarcze* picked up Premier Krushchev's blank check and inquired whether Poland might not qualify for special assistance from the Soviet Union and Czechoslovakia. See *East Europe,* June, 1959, pp. 36–37. However, the theoretical conclusion about the simultaneous transformation apparently allows for a transition within one historical epoch. See Sh. Sanakoyev, "The Socialist Community and Mankind's Progress," *International Affairs,* No. 3, 1962, p. 10. According to this Soviet author, "it would be strange, to say the least, if the Soviet Union, having completed the building of socialism ahead of other countries were to wait for the leveling up of the general economic development of the Socialist countries before starting on the construction of Communism."

[5] Surplus value is a Marxist term encompassing what under capitalism is paid out in the form of rent, interest, profits, or dividends.

2. In the Chinese case, we have a predominantly agrarian economy, saddled with what appears to be a population surplus, whose leaders are seeking to industrialize the country at an unprecedented pace. Unlike the Soviet Union, Chinese agriculture has apparently not only been collectivized but even "commune-ized." It is perhaps too early to evaluate this peculiarly Chinese development, but it seems likely that the Chinese, like the Russians before them, have been forced to backtrack and develop a system of incentives similar to those which have evolved in the USSR.[6] For the time being, xenophobia, as reflected in incidents such as those in and around the Formosan Straits or along the Tibetan border with India, may serve to unify the Chinese populace behind the regime and to generate worker enthusiasm, but wage and salary inequalities will probably prove to be more reliable as well as less dangerous in the long run. Another peculiarity of the Chinese road to socialism consisted of the fact that capitalist enclaves persisted in the industrial sector after they were eliminated in rural areas.

3. In many respects, Eastern European countries, other than Poland and Yugoslavia, seem to be following the Soviet example. However, there are vast differences in the degree of industrialization found in these countries and these differences are reflected in their somewhat different economic developments. In Czechoslovakia, where the communists took over a comparatively industrialized economy, the level of living is higher than it is in the Soviet Union. Consequently, as we shall see, such things as capital exports, administrative regionalization, local responsibility for consumers' goods and construction industries, uniform agricultural prices, and the elimination of capital-pooling by the Machine Tractor Stations are all apparently practicable here as well as in the Soviet Union.[7] Recently the Czechs have decided

---

[6] The commune was one of the early experimental Soviet agricultural organizations. For further information on the commune see Maurice Dobb, *Soviet Economic Development Since 1917,* Routledge and Kegan Paul, London, 1948, p. 223.

[7] For some interesting differences between Czech and Soviet developments, see Paul Underwood, "Czechs Skeptical of Soviet Plans," *New*

that their economic development was sufficiently far advanced to enable them to be labeled the second socialist country, and to assume the title, Czechoslovak Soviet Socialist Republic.

On the other hand, in a country like Albania, where industry was virtually nonexistent at the time the communists took over, the level of living is very low and so-called Stalinist or draconic economic measures—to an increasing extent resembling the Chinese model—are still very much the vogue. Collectivization of agriculture is proceeding in all of these countries, albeit at a relatively slow pace in comparison with that which took place in the USSR at the end of the twenties. Industry, however, is almost completely socialized in most instances.

4. In Poland since 1956, it has been admitted that the attempted collectivization of agriculture was a failure, and voluntary organizations called "agricultural circles" are now encouraged. However, the collectivization of agriculture remains as a theoretic goal of the ruling Communist Party. Some private enterprise at the distribution level is now encouraged. There are apparently more internal liberties, and experimentation seems to be the keynote in Polish economic development. Polish economists, for example, study the writings of Keynes with considerable objectivity, engage in non-Marxist controversies on the possible merits of so-called "marginal cost pricing," and in general are permitted to be more critical of their regime than is the case in other countries in the Soviet bloc.

5. Since 1948 Yugoslavia has been pursuing her own little path to socialism. As in Poland, collectivization of agriculture failed. At present the Yugoslavs are attempting to raise agricultural productivity by relying on an old Balkan institution, the *zadruga*. The zadruga is similar to a Western producers' cooperative in its operations. Ownership of land remains private, the total acreage per family being limited to 25 acres by Yugoslav law. The zadruga provides credit for seed, may or may not provide for the

---

York Times, May 6, 1959. Cf. also M. S. Handler, "Czechs Announce 11 per cent Rise in Output," *New York Times,* November 20, 1959, p. 15.

mechanical cultivation and harvesting of the crops, markets the harvest, and sells supplies to the peasants.[8] In the sixties, the Yugoslav government began using higher guaranteed farm prices and lower taxes to encourage membership in the cooperatives and to discourage the independent peasants.[9]

In the industrial sector, the Yugoslavs have been experimenting with "workers' councils," the operations of which bear some resemblance to the ideas of our own economic syndicalists. Some decentralization of the administrative and planning functions occurred in Yugoslavia long before it did in the Soviet Union, and there has apparently been some autonomous price-setting guided by market forces on the part of industries and/or plants.[10] Private enterprise is restricted to small-scale production where—in addition to the owner's family—up to five workers may be employed.[11] Finally, in the field of international finance, the Yugoslavs are beginning to participate in capitalist-oriented monetary and trading institutions.[12] The Yugoslav Constitution of 1962 has changed the country's formal name to the Federal Socialist Republic of Yugoslavia. Since 90 per cent of the farm land is still privately owned, the Yugoslav's use of the term "so-

---

[8] See Paul Underwood, "Co-ops Improving Yugoslav Farms," *New York Times,* March 15, 1959, p. 26.

[9] Paul Underwood, "Yugoslavs Press Farming Reform," *New York Times,* August 22, 1962, p. 8.

[10] According to John Kenneth Galbraith, *Journey to Poland and Yugoslavia,* Harvard University Press, Cambridge, 1958, p. 98, about 70 per cent of all prices are determined by the individual enterprises. Commodities, the prices of which are fixed, include such things as utilities, steel, and fertilizer.

[11] In 1961, increased limitations on these enterprises engaged in production have been decreed. Private taxicabs and trucking are also being restricted. See Paul Underwood, "Yugoslavia Widens Curbs on Private Businesses," *New York Times,* July 26, 1962, p. 2.

[12] Paul Underwood, "Dillon Assures Aid for the Yugoslavs on Fiscal Changes," *New York Times,* July 21, 1960, p. 3. According to this article, Yugoslav participation in the International Monetary Fund, the General Agreement on Tariffs and Trade, and the Western Free Market Trading Community is imminent. There also seems to be the possibility that the Yugoslavs may permit foreign investment in hotels in an effort to stimulate tourism.

cialist" to describe their government constitutes a still further deviation from the accepted practice in the Soviet bloc.[13]

6. Indian socialism, in some respects at least, resembles British evolutionary socialism as envisaged in the *plans* of the British Labor Party. While the Soviets have conceded at times that the Indians are engaged in building socialism, these concessions may stem from political motivations rather than from substantive economic bases. In India, private enterprise, including capital imports from capitalist-oriented economies, is encouraged side by side with the development of socialist enterprise, part of which is built and equipped by the USSR. Some sort of guide lines are provided by five-year plans and agricultural cooperatives are being organized in rural areas.

7. The most recent claimant to a revolutionary socialist path is Castro's Cuba. Beginning as a nationalist, anti-imperialist movement, the Cuban revolutionary regime has in a relatively short space of time instituted programs of land reform and expropriation of both foreign and domestic capital which, if followed by a substantive planned investment program, would undoubtedly carry the Cuban economy well along the road to socialism. A Ministry of Industry headed by Major Ernesto Guevara now directs all Cuban industry and is responsible for carrying out a four-year industrialization plan.[14]

It is probably too early to say whether or not a number of newly emerging nations should also be included in this seventh category. But at least the following countries would seem to be potential entrants: Egypt, Guinea, Ghana, British Guiana, Indonesia, and Ceylon.

In some sense then, what we find within the Soviet or neutralist areas are various approaches or roads to socialism and perhaps eventually to communism. We shall be examining primarily

[13] See Paul Underwood, "Belgrade Offers Draft of Charter," *New York Times,* October 20, 1962, p. 8.

[14] See R. Hart Phillips, "Cuba Reshuffles Economic Offices," *New York Times,* February 25, 1961, p. 2.

the Russian model in some detail and be referring to the economic system of the Soviet Union as "Soviet socialism" to distinguish it from its first cousins, Polish and Yugoslav socialism, and its more distant relatives, Indian and Cuban socialism. But in some connections we may also care to note interesting independent developments outside the USSR.

CAPITALIST-ORIENTED ECONOMIES

Capitalism is an economic system characterized by the private, unequal ownership of the means of production or tools with which man produces his livelihood. Under such an arrangement, title to the means of production is transferable; in other words, there is a well-developed market for land and capital goods. It might be added that there is no obligation on the part of the owner of land or capital to utilize fully his means of production or to engage in new investment activities at all times. The basic force propelling economic activity under capitalism is the search for at least a "normal" or "favorable" rate of return.

Although there is no formal ideology associated with capitalism, there is an informal set of ideas upon which the majority either agree or else do not hold radically differing ideas. Recently some of the more outspoken believers in capitalism have become conscious of this lack of a formal ideology and have attempted to soften the alleged unpleasant connotations associated with the capitalist system by developing the thesis that our economy has changed sufficiently to warrant the label, "people's capitalism." Books such as the *Capitalist Manifesto* by Louis Kelso and Mortimer Adler might also be considered as efforts to match the Russians by filling this ideological void.

Attempts by our late Secretary of State John Foster Dulles, Norman Thomas, and *Fortune* magazine to classify the economic system of the Soviet Union as "state capitalism" also seem to reflect the unattractive connotations associated with the old-fashioned capitalist label.[15] According to their definition, capitalism is simply any system under which capital is accumulated with no consideration taken of the various underlying productive relationships.

Even if we were to accept this definition of capitalism, we would still have to admit that the Soviet economy is a more effective accumulator of capital than any capitalist system to date. Roughly 25 to 30 per cent of Soviet income is invested year after year. Not only is the percentage of national income invested lower under capitalist-oriented economies, but the rate of accumulation also fluctuates considerably from one year to the next. Furthermore, as we shall see in Chapter XII (see p. 338), from a theoretical standpoint the Soviet system may eventually be better able to "taper off" the capital accumulation process or adjust from an economy with relatively high investment to one with relatively little net investment.

Although capital accumulation takes place under both capitalist-oriented and noncapitalist-oriented economic systems, the moving force behind this accumulation is radically different. Under capitalist-oriented economies, there must be what investors regard as a satisfactory rate of return before accumulation or what economists call "investment" can take place. It is true that capitalist-oriented governments have frequently stepped in with subsidies to private investors, or have even undertaken very large capital accumulation projects themselves in recent years. But in all capitalist-oriented economies operating in a peacetime situation, private investment guided by the profit motive is ordinarily responsible for the bulk of investment or accumulation taking place.[16]

[15] This label has also been applied to the economy of Fascist Germany and its application to the Soviet economy undoubtedly tends to blur the differences between the two principal types of economies.

[16] The French economy in the early sixties may represent an exception to this generalization. The French government finances about 25 per cent of total investment directly. An additional 25 per cent represents investment by local government and nationalized industries, and by private industries resorting to state-controlled sources of finance. See Edwin L. Dale,

There is probably about as much diversity among the capitalist-oriented economies as there is among the noncapitalist-oriented ones. As indicated above, there are varying degrees to which the capitalist-oriented welfare state has evolved. Social security is an accepted institution in all well-developed capitalist-oriented economies, the benefits to some extent varying in proportion to the degree of affluence that has been achieved. Free or subsidized medical care, especially for the aged, is also rapidly becoming a necessity for even the most capitalistic of the capitalist-oriented economies.[17]

In most capitalist-oriented economies there is great reliance on indirect measures of control, particularly monetary and fiscal measures. In the United States and West German economies, especially, balanced budgets and monetary measures such as changes in interest or rediscount rates command the greatest respect of the authorities.[18] Fiscal steps such as changes in tax and spending rates are resorted to only in grave emergencies. Great Britain, Australia and France, on the other hand, tend to lean to a greater extent on fiscal planning, that is, on tax reductions or increased government spending to eliminate or reduce unemployment, even if this means budgeting for a greater government deficit.

In the international field, there is great confidence placed in the pursuance of "sound" or "orthodox" monetary policies, largely utilizing the services of the International Monetary Fund and the World Bank to carry through such policies. Inflation must be controlled even at the cost of growing domestic unemployment since a "favorable" balance of trade is the hallmark of success. Even Yugoslavia, although basically a member of the noncapitalist-

---

"State Planning and Financing Called Key to France's Growth," *New York Times,* September 15, 1962, p. 9.

[17] For a summary of the extent to which West European countries have national health services or insurance systems that provide their citizens with medical care, see *New York Times,* May 27, 1962, p. 52.

[18] The chief advocate of budget-balancing, even if it means cutting proposed defense expenditures, in Western Germany appears to be Dr. Ludwig Erhard. See Sydney Gruson, "Bonn Embroiled in Budget Crises," *New York Times,* September 13, 1962, p. 7.

oriented club, has apparently become convinced that the advantages of membership in the International Monetary Fund are sufficient to offset any difficulties created for their domestic planning as a result of the linking of their currency into the framework of the capitalist-oriented international money markets.

At the present time, most of the underdeveloped countries not mentioned in the previous section should probably be classified as "capitalist-oriented," although their commitment to a capitalist path of development hinges to a great extent on the receipt of substantial capital assistance from the well-developed capitalist-oriented economies, including part of the United States agricultural surpluses. It seems likely that these countries will also be inclined to accept Soviet capital assistance provided there are no political strings attached. Clearly many of the nonaligned countries are not really committed to either the capitalist or the noncapitalist path of development at the present time.

The economic problems of the capitalist-oriented underdeveloped countries are in some respects similar to those faced by presently well-developed capitalist-oriented economies a hundred years ago or the problems facing Soviet planners in the twenties. The possibility of importing capital from both power blocs would seem to be a factor working in their favor. In many cases, however, their developmental problems are accentuated by the existence of what appears to be a surplus undernourished and uneducated populace. At any rate, it seems clear that neither the developmental solutions arrived at by Western countries in the nineteenth century nor the more recent experience of the USSR in the period of centrally planned growth is completely applicable to the problems faced by the noncommitted countries.

III ∾ Comparative Economic Statistics

GREAT CAUTION MUST BE EXERCISED in interpreting comparative economic statistics of capitalist and noncapitalist-oriented economies. By a process of careful selection and/or appropriate weighting, it becomes possible to "prove" either that the Soviet economy is hopelessly outclassed in its competition with the United States or else that the Russians are on the verge of overtaking us. Since most of the analyses and judgments presented in subsequent chapters are based to a considerable extent on statistical materials released by Moscow and Washington, it seems worthwhile to devote some time at the outset to an examination of the nature of the economic data emanating from the two opposing camps, as well as to their manipulation.

AVAILABILITY AND RELIABILITY OF DATA

Soviet economic statistics for the twenties are both relatively detailed and reliable, particularly when one considers the comparatively disorganized and underdeveloped state of the Soviet economy at the time. Part of this early emphasis on the collection and publication of economic statistics—which seems unusual for a relatively frugal economy—was undoubtedly a carry-over from the pre-revolutionary regime. In contrast to our own historical statistics, Czarist data on production and distribution were relatively detailed and reliable, even as far back as the nineteenth century. One of the earliest works on national income accounting was published in Russia in 1906 by Sergei Prokopovicz, who was eventually deported from the Soviet Union. Shortly after the revolution, the Russians were also pioneers in the development of input-output analysis, which is only practicable if a country's economic statistics have reached a fairly well-developed state.

Beginning around 1930—midway in Plan I—a drastic policy change affected the publication of Soviet economic data. Among other things, such basic economic tools as the consumers' price index disappeared as soon as retail prices began to soar and it became evident that the disinflationary price policy envisaged in the initial Five-Year Plan could not be carried out. Data on the production and consumption of consumers' goods, as well as a great deal of information on agricultural output, acreage and livestock, were particularly hard hit by the decline of statistical information. Following the purge trials of 1937, the ringing down of a statistical "iron curtain" was virtually complete. The best statistical source during the 15-year period between the end of the trials and the death of Stalin in 1953 was the "classified" 1941 Annual Plan captured by the Germans when they occupied the Ukraine.

This growing paucity of published Soviet statistics occurred at a time when there was a marked improvement in the quantity and quality of United States statistics. New Deal measures such as the provisions of the Social Security Act establishing unemployment insurance permitted us for the first time to make fairly reliable estimates of the number of unemployed in this country. The annual reports required by the Securities and Exchange Commission, as well as the intensive studies of our economy by the Temporary National Economic Committee, also added important new knowledge about our own economy. The Keynesian emphasis on macroeconomic concepts undoubtedly also served to stimulate the study of national income and the corresponding refinement of our national income accounting practices.

Since 1956 there has been a veritable outpouring of Soviet statistical handbooks, most of which also throw some light on the state of the Soviet economy in 1940, which is frequently the base year for the recently released data.[1] Although some of the information published is remarkably detailed, there are still important lacunae which have not been filled, particularly with respect to labor force and wage statistics. In addition, virtually all information dealing with the production of nonferrous and rare metals is still classified information. As we shall see in Chapter X (see pp. 252–257), official information on Soviet defense expenditures is especially obscure.[2]

Although Soviet statistical practices differ considerably from our own, on the whole it would be difficult to prove that the statistical data with which their planners actually work are less complete than ours. Since the success of central planning depends in large measure on the existence of reliable, detailed statistical information, it does not seem likely that the Russians have economized on the collection of economic statistics, even though the results have frequently been withheld from the general public. In addition, there is no evidence which would indicate that the detailed data used by the inner planning circles differ significantly from selected data disseminated for propaganda purposes.[3]

In some respects, Soviet statistical data are certainly superior to our own. It is about as easy for ordinary economists to obtain information on production costs in capitalist-oriented economies as it is for an outsider to obtain access to the Kremlin's most

[1] For a listing of the most important of these handbooks, see the recommended readings at the end of this chapter.

[2] In contrast to the obscurity of the Soviet budget report, our own budget frequently divulges information which has been previously given "in guarded executive hearings." For the complaint of Senator Howard W. Cannon in this regard, see the *New York Times*, February 13, 1962, p. 26.

[3] For a comparison of the confidential data in the 1941 Annual Plan with the official handouts at the time, see Lynn Turgeon, "On the Reliability of Soviet Statistics," *The Review of Economics and Statistics,* February, 1952, pp. 75–76. These general conclusions with respect to Soviet statistics also seem to apply to the development of Chinese statistics after 1949. In this connection, see Alexander Eckstein, "Economics and the Study of Mainland China's Development," *The American Economist,* Volume V, November, 1961, p. 2.

guarded military secret.[4] The Russians, on the other hand, make a determined effort to learn and publicize the relative cost levels in different plants, as well as detailed structures of production cost, since these data can be employed as levers to exhort the laggards to catch up with the more progressive economic accounting and producing units.

In general, the operational requirements of the two economies are such that greater statistical detail, standardization, and accuracy is probably required in the Soviet Union, although it would be difficult to prove that any greater accuracy has in fact been attained. In a capitalist-oriented economy, where inventories are ample, if not excessive, and where market forces are allowed comparative freedom to operate, statistics are largely collected *ex post* or for the record, and comparatively few critical decisions are based necessarily on the statistics themselves. Under such conditions, heavy reliance can be placed on estimates obtained by indirect procedures, and cost economies can be attained through the process of sampling.[5]

On the other hand, in a noncapitalist-oriented economy operating with chronically unreliable inventories and attempting to guide or control market forces in a perpetual seller's market, the reliability of statistics should take on added importance. A great many crucial *ex ante* decisions in a centrally planned economy would seem to be based on the assumption that the statistical margins of error are relatively small. In many respects, it would seem that the successful operation of our United States economy during World War II also required more complete and up-to-date knowledge of our production and consumption statistics by

---

[4] The attempt of Senator Kefauver's Subcommittee on Antitrust and Monopoly to obtain cost data from the steel companies is an example of the difficulties involved in the United States. For the steel industry's defense of cost secrecy, see Kenneth S. Smith, "Steel Men Defend Secrecy on Costs," *New York Times,* September 8, 1962, Section III, p. 1.

[5] With the exception of budget studies, there seems to have been a bias against the use of sampling techniques in Soviet statistics. In this connection, see Vsevolod Holubnychy, "Organization of Statistical Observations in the USSR," *The American Statistician,* June, 1958, p. 17.

such agencies as the War Production Board for reasons similar to those prevailing in the Soviet economy at all times.

In general, United States statistical information is probably more comprehensive for the consumers' goods sector where many of our nongovernmental resources are involved in an attempt to predict and motivate the future pattern of consumption, at least partly on the basis of past trends and experiences. In the Soviet economy, however, relatively few resources have been utilized on such things as consumer budget studies or attempts to satisfy consumers' tastes, in contrast to the large numbers of bookkeepers and economists involved in collecting and interpreting Soviet production statistics. This relatively greater emphasis on the collection and analysis of consumption data in the United States and production statistics in the Soviet Union seems quite natural in view of the respective stages of development and the contemporary basic problems of the two economies.

PROBLEMS OF INTERPRETATION

Difficulties encountered in the interpretation and comparison of economic statistics might be considered under the following headings: (1) definitional differences in the yardsticks employed by capitalist and noncapitalist-oriented economies; (2) valuation difficulties, including index number problems; (3) calculated distortions for propaganda purposes; and (4) difficulties arising simply from a lack of sophistication.

1. *Differing yardsticks.* One of the most important definitional differences between capitalist and noncapitalist-oriented economies is found in connection with the concept of national income. In calculating a measure of overall annual product or "pie," the Russians adopted from the very beginning a measure which is less inclusive than our own. In line with Marxist ideology, commodities constitute the principal ingredient in their pie since pay-

ments for services not intimately associated with material production are excluded.[6] Inasmuch as the Russians' service sector—with the exception of the education and public health components—is fairly underdeveloped, at least in relation to our own, comparative measures of national income show that the Russians lag least when the yardstick used is defined in Soviet or Marxist terms. In other words, by some coincidence, each country has adopted a concept of national income which presents its economic system in the most favorable light.

Another important measure of growth peculiar to most non-capitalist-oriented economies is the so-called index of "gross industrial production," (GIP). This measure of production omits agricultural activity, which has tended to grow more slowly in the past, and is therefore one of their fastest growing series. No attempt is made to eliminate double-counting of materials transferred between reporting units. The nearest United States equivalent to this Soviet industrial production index is our Federal Reserve Board index of industrial production which covers something over one-third of all goods and services produced. Although commodities are selected from all stages of the production process (for example, iron ore, coke, pig iron, and steel), the weighting system used by the "Fed"—in contrast to the Soviet calculation—represents the value added to each commodity in the process of manufacturing. If there were no tendency for the amount of double-counting to change over time, there would be no serious objection to this Soviet measure of GIP. In other words, we may be just as interested in the rate of industrial growth as we are in the absolute magnitudes involved.

However, there is some evidence that the amount of double-counting has increased over time in the calculation of the Soviet index of GIP. Professor Strumilin has recently studied the relationship between the growth rates of his index of net industrial production and the official Soviet index of gross industrial pro-

[6] It is interesting to note that one of our pioneer economists, Professor George Tucker, made estimates of our annual income in the mid-nineteenth century, in which he limited his calculations to material production.

duction, his findings indicating that the latter series has grown much faster than the former in the postwar period. Apparently the general shortage of materials in the thirties induced managers of enterprises to produce their own materials and parts rather than to rely on outside sources of supply, so that material transfers were minimized. In the postwar period, the general amelioration of the critical supply problem has allowed managers to divest themselves of certain production functions resulting in greater internal specialization and overall division of labor.[7] As a consequence, the importance of material transfers between independent reporting units has increased. According to Strumilin, in 1956 net industrial production apparently grew by less than 9 per cent, in contrast to the 11 per cent increase claimed for gross industrial production in that year.[8]

On the other hand, the improvement of supplies since World War II and a growing emphasis on so-called "qualitative indices" such as the targets for increasing labor productivity and reducing production costs—in contrast to the earlier priority assigned to "quantitative" goals—may have reduced incentives for falsification of output reports by enterprise reporting units. It has been contended that the worst statistical distortions have tended to disappear in recent years despite the fact that some distortion still remains.[9] If this is so, the recorded official rates of industrial growth in recent years may have some downward bias reflecting the gradual elimination of statistical falsification and manipulation.

[7] However, the July, 1960 Plenum of the Communist Party of the Soviet Union stressed the urgency for even greater specialization and reliance on outside sources of supply. Some success in increasing the percentage of purchased materials has apparently been achieved in the production of locomotives. See N. S. Maslova *et al., Zarabotnaia plata i sebestoimost' produktsii v promyshlennosti SSSR* (Wages and Production Cost in Industry of the USSR), Ekonomizdat, Moscow, 1960, p. 41.

[8] See S. G. Strumilin, *Ocherki sotsialisticheskoi ekonomiki SSSR 1929–59 gg.* (Essays on the Socialist Economy of the U.S.S.R., 1929–59), Gospolitizdat, Moscow, 1959, p. 236. See also Elizabeth Marbury, "A Note on Some Soviet Statistics," *East Europe,* November, 1960, p. 17.

[9] In this connection, see Naum Jasny, "How 'Phoney' are Soviet Statistics?" *The Statist,* February 2, 1962, p. 330.

2. *Weighting problems.* As all economists are well aware, the end result of statistical computations may vary greatly depending on the weighting system employed. In such cases, politics may rear its ugly head and dictate the use of weighting sytems producing the most favorable results. For example, the long usage by the Russians of an outmoded weighting system for their gross industrial production index resulted in a substantial upward bias in their claimed rates of growth, at least until 1950. During these early years, all industrial products were valued in terms of so-called 1926–27 "constant ruble prices."

The relative price structure in 1926–27 was such that commodities which tended to grow fastest in the subsequent process of rapid Soviet industrialization (machinery and producers' goods) were produced in small quantities and sold for relatively high prices in that early period. On the other hand, commodities that were already produced in relatively large quantities in 1926–27 and which grew more slowly during the planning period (for example, consumers' goods) had relatively low prices. In other words, there was a negative correlation between relative prices and relative physical quantities produced in 1926–27, but a positive correlation between these relative price or value weights and the relative rates of growth for the different output series during the industrialization drive. This same phenomenon can be observed in the development of our own economy and the use of an earlier, outdated weighting system tends to magnify greatly our overall rate of growth.[10]

To complicate matters further, new products introduced after 1926–27 were assigned their own artificial 1926–27 "constant ruble prices," which in many cases may have reflected the cost inflation

[10] See the calculations of United States machinery output using 1899 and 1909 prices in Alexander Gerschenkron (assisted by Alexander Erlich), *A Dollar Index of Soviet Machinery Output, 1927–28 to 1937,* Rand R-197, Rand Corporation, Santa Monica, California, April 6, 1951, p. 52. The studies of Richard Moorsteen indicate that the distortion caused by early year weights is largely confined to the early stages of industrialization. See his *Prices and Production of Machinery in the Soviet Union, 1928–1958,* Rand R-370-PR, Rand Corporation, Santa Monica, June, 1962, pp. 130 *et seq.*

that occurred in the thirties and forties, or the artificially inflated initial costs of production.[11] Since these new products constituted in most cases the fastest growing series, the assignment of artificially high price or value weights to these fast-growing commodities may have created results which greatly exaggerated the actual overall rate of industrial development.

While such results undoubtedly pleased the Soviet propaganda experts, both inside and outside the USSR, the index was subject to scholarly criticism, even within Soviet academic circles.[12] In the fifties, when the political position of the Soviet regime had become less tenuous, Soviet statisticians were permitted to revise their weighting system—though not their earlier series of results between 1928 and 1950—with the result that any upward bias caused by the price or value weights has apparently been fairly minimal since 1950.[13]

Valuation difficulties also arise in making comparisons of national income or GNP in capitalist and noncapitalist-oriented economies. Assuming that both calculations are made in accordance with either the Soviet or Western definition of national income, there still remains the problem of converting the resulting aggregates into a common currency such as dollars or rubles. If the two economies are at a similar stage of development and have similar pricing practices and institutions, the problem might be simply solved by using a realistic foreign exchange rate between the two currencies. But even among Western

[11] This contention is specifically denied by V. Starovsky, *"O metodike sopostavleniia ekonomicheskikh pokazatelei SSSR i SSHA"* (About the Methods of Comparing Economic Indexes of the USSR and USA *Voprosy Ekonomiki,* No. 4, 1960, p. 111. To the extent that subsidies out of the government budget kept the prices of raw materials at artificially low levels, and gains in machine-building productivity were substantial, this new product bias may have been exaggerated by Western students of the Soviet economy. In this connection, see Abram Bergson, *The Real National Income of Soviet Russia Since 1928,* Harvard University Press, Cambridge, 1961, pp. 185–186.

[12] See, for example, D. V. Savinsky, *Kurs promyshlennoi statistiki* (Course of Industrial Statistics), Third edition, Gosplanizdat, Moscow, 1949, pp. 86, *et seq.*

[13] See Norman M. Kaplan and Richard H. Moorsteen, "An Index of Soviet Industrial Output," *American Economic Review,* June, 1960, p. 304.

economies, there are great differences in the relative internal purchasing power of currencies in different markets.[14] Difficulties of this type are especially great in making comparisons between the United States and the Soviet Union. Generally speaking, the ruble commands relatively greater purchasing power internally in the producers' goods area, while the dollar has relatively greater purchasing power in our consumers' goods markets.

This conversion problem can be tackled by estimating separate ruble-dollar conversion rates for the different sectors of national income, such as consumption, investment, defense, and government administration. To some extent, even these separate conversion rates will also vary depending on whether the individual ruble-dollar ratios *within* these broad sectors are weighted according to the Soviet or United States product-mix. As a consequence, the resulting comparison of the two total products produces vastly dissimilar results depending on whether the valuation is made in terms of rubles or dollars. According to one well-known calculation of this type, Soviet gross national product was about one-fourth the United States level in 1955 when calculated in ruble prices compared with about one-half the United States level when valuations were made in terms of dollars.[15] The total Soviet product (as well as most of its components) is smaller relative to ours when the components of both total products are valued in rubles as compared with the results when dollar valuations are used as weights.

The explanation of this phenomenon lies in the fact that there is generally a negative correlation between relative costs or prices

---

[14] See Milton Gilbert and Irving B. Kravis, *An International Comparison of National Products and the Purchasing Power of Currencies,* Organization for European Economic Cooperation, Paris, 1954, pp. 14–17; and Milton Gilbert and Associates, *Comparative National Products and Price Levels,* O.E.E.C., Paris, 1958, pp. 29–33.

[15] Morris Bornstein, "A Comparison of Soviet and United States National Product," in *Comparisons of the United States and Soviet Economies,* Part II, p. 388. For a Soviet interpretation and criticism of these results, see V. Kudrov, "Anti-Scientific Methods Employed by Bourgeois Economists to Compare the National Incomes of the USSR and the U.S.," *Problems of Economics,* August, 1961, p. 41.

and the relative physical quantities produced in the two countries similar to the correlation noted above in connection with the Soviet 1926–27 ruble prices. Consumers' goods and services, which are relatively *less* important in the Soviet economy, receive *more* weight when a ruble valuation system is used; producers' goods, which are relatively *less* important in the United States economy, tend to receive *more* weight when a dollar valuation system of weights is employed.

This effect of the relative cost structures in the two countries (which will be discussed again in connection with international trade in Chapter XI) is further accentuated by the fact that there is a different impact of taxes on the two sectors in the Soviet Union, and profits in the two sectors in the United States.[16] Both taxes and profits represent the margin between production costs and prices. In the Soviet Union, huge turnover taxes are levied primarily on consumers' goods, thus tending to emphasize still further the relative importance of consumers' goods in a ruble weighting system. On the other hand, profit margins in the United States are probably on average higher in the producers' goods sector than they are in the production of consumers' goods, thereby enhancing still further the relative value of producers' goods in the dollar weighting system.

Since our economy shines in the relative quantities of consumers' goods we produce, its superior position vis-à-vis the Soviet economy is emphasized by using the ruble weighting system. On the other hand, since the Soviets tend to make a relatively better showing in their producers' goods sector, a dollar weighting system minimizes the gap between the two total products. Thus, each system tends to achieve a more favorable picture of its own national income vis-à-vis the other country by valuing both total products in the currency of its competitor.

Another weighting problem arises in connection with the computation of a so-called cost-of-living index such as our Consumers' Price Index. As we shall see in Chapter VI (see p. 96), an

---

[16] The differential impact of taxes on the two sectors in the United States and profits in the two sectors in the USSR seems comparatively negligible.

early year weighting system tends to produce results indicating a greater overall price increase than is the case when a current or more recent year weighting system is employed. As a result, the particular weighting system used in any cost-of-living index will have an important bearing on the resulting measure of real wage changes. If a country is worried about inflation and/or is anxious to emphasize the gains in real wages, one of the things statisticians can do is to keep the weighting system as up-to-date as possible.[17]

3. *Calculated distortions.* Calculated selection or distortion of economic statistics has been developed into a fine art in the Soviet Union. In interpreting statistical data, Soviet statisticians have long been made aware of the necessity of accentuating the positive and eliminating the negative. From the earliest days after the revolution, "bourgeois objectivity" has been frowned upon and statistics were considered to be a weapon in the class war. In the event there was not a great deal to boast about, as was especially true during and for some time after World War II, a policy of silence seemed most appropriate. For a long time, the annual Soviet economic results of plan fulfillment contained only series which showed production gains over the previous year. But recently there has been a tendency for the Russians to divulge series which show output declines for one reason or another. It might be assumed that the current failure to publish series for nonferrous and rare metals was designed to cover-up areas of weakness, but in view of recent Soviet exports of aluminum, tin, and chrome, this assumption does not seem to be warranted.

As the Russians tend to close the economic gap between the two systems, it would not be too surprising to find our government or business statisticians employing statistical procedures

---

[17] For some recent recommendations along these lines, see Richard E. Mooney, "Economists Urge Price-Index Shift," *New York Times,* May 2, 1961, p. 24. In the United States, before this policy could be adopted, the understandable objections of unionized workers covered by escalator clauses would have to be overcome.

which will postpone the eclipse for as long as possible. Already we may note some attempts either to beef up our recorded rate of growth or to obscure areas of weakness.

Recently the steel industry has begun to feel defensive about its operating rate, that is, steel production measured as a percentage of capacity as reported by the American Iron and Steel Institute. As a result, spokesmen for the industry began to "de-emphasize" this measure in 1961, just as they did in the 1957–58 recession.

The Federal Reserve Board, whose "tight money" policy under the Eisenhower Administration has been criticized as a factor retarding our rate of growth in the late fifties, overhauled its statistical machinery used to chart our industrial growth at the end of 1959. By including additional, fast growing series which had been previously ignored—the output of electric and gas utility output, for example—and updating the weighting system from 1947 to 1957 so as to give greater weight to automobiles, machinery and steel, the Fed was able to show an increase in our industrial production which was 8 per cent higher than the increase indicated for the decade by the previous series.[18]

There is also a tendency for pressures to mount on economic statisticians engaged in measuring two of our currently most important economic problems: unemployment and balance of payments deficits. With respect to the former problem, Professor Paul Samuelson has proposed the adoption of a so-called "residual method" of reporting the percentage of the labor force that is unemployed, a technique which would be a more sensitive indicator of improvements in the unemployment picture.[19] With regard to recording our balance of payments deficit, Secretary of the Treasury Dillon has criticized a European method of

[18] "Revised Industrial Production Index," *Federal Reserve Bulletin,* December, 1959. It should be noted, however, that the new weights produce a lower rate of growth for the period after 1953 as compared with the former weights. For a criticism of the revised index of industrial production, see Victor Perlo, "The Revised Index of Industrial Production," *American Economic Review,* June, 1962, pp. 496–513, and reply by Clayton Gehman.

[19] See his letter to the Editor of the *New York Times,* November 12, 1961, p. 8E and also Leon Keyserling's reply the following week.

calculating our "basic balance" which omits the flow of short-term money and thereby minimizes the overall deficit.[20]

The pressure to manipulate statistics is particularly strong before elections in the United States. In November, 1962, Secretary of Labor, W. Willard Wirtz, issued a statement claiming that the Kennedy Administration had succeeded in reducing unemployment significantly. By failing to make seasonal adjustments in his unemployment data, Secretary Wirtz exaggerated the achievements of the Administration in creating employment by 1,216,000 jobs.[20a]

Although we already include more services in our computations of national income as compared with the Russians, we might conceivably further expand our coverage and obtain considerable propaganda advantage. A rather large amount of our total economic activity in the United States is not as yet fully reported for national income accounting purposes. Housing construction, which is estimated on the basis of building permits, is especially poorly reported in small communities. According to a study reported in the *Wall Street Journal*, as much as $10 billion in construction activity may go unreported yearly. There is also no way to check on the output of our increasingly expanding "do-it-yourself" sector. The value of such goods has been estimated at between $17 and $20 billion annually.[21] Many hours of home gardening and private transportation service

[20] See Richard E. Mooney, "Dillon Criticizes Payments Report," *New York Times*, June 26, 1961, p. 35. It may seem strange to find Secretary Dillon attempting to *emphasize* rather than deemphasize these difficulties. Perhaps it illustrates a certain dilemma on the part of our Administration. Emphasis on a difficulty is necessary to obtain legislative action; minimizing the difficulty tranquilizes both the electorate and the legislative body. Shortly after the Kennedy Administration assumed office, two well-known economists were given the task of reexamining the statistical aspects of our balance of payments problem. See Richard E. Mooney, "Payments Study Sifts Statistics," *New York Times*, March 13, 1961, p. 43. According to the *New York Times*, March 13, 1961, p. 43, the present method of calculating the country's balance of payments is under review.

[20a] See James McCartney, "Wirtz Admits 'Invalid' Data," *The Washington Post*, December 13, 1962, p. 18.

[21] See Herbert Koshetz, "The Merchants View," *Wall Street Journal*, November 8, 1959.

also remain uncounted each year in the United States, and the growth of suburban living would tend to increase the relative importance of these activities as time goes by.

A number of important services are excluded from our national income accounts because of the difficulties involved in estimating and valuing their magnitude. Housewives' services are probably the most important omission from our measure of the total goods and services produced annually. According to one estimate, all unpaid-for services of housewives may add as much as $3,000 per annum to each family's income.[22] Although these services may be on the decline, they are being replaced by our large and growing stock of durable consumers' goods, the services of which are also excluded by our income accountants. Although we include the services of our housing stock as measured by rental income, no account is taken of the yearly services of our prodigous stocks of automobiles, washers, dryers, vacuum cleaners, home freezers, and other conveniences except for those rented by concerns such as Hertz. Since the services of both housewives and durable consumers' goods are relatively underdeveloped in the Soviet Union, their inclusion in comparisons of overall output would undoubtedly magnify the statistical gap that currently exists between the total products of the two economies.[23]

4. *Unsophisticated comparisons.* Finally, we might list a few problems of interpretation arising as a result of comparing isolated indicators out of context or merely from a lack of sophistication. From the fact that the Russians are mining more tons of coal yearly than we are we might be inclined to assume that this is one sign that the Russians are on the verge of overtaking us.

[22] See "Housework: What It's Worth," *The Kiplinger Magazine,* March, 1961, p. 21.

[23] A whole range of illegal activities might also be considered for inclusion in our comparisons of total product. The United States economy probably has an edge in the output of such services as gambling, prostitution, and the distribution of narcotics. Moonshining, bribery, and counterfeiting activities are probably about on a par in the two economies, while the Russians would seem to have surpassed us in black market activities.

To make a meaningful comparison, however, we would first have to deflate their impressive total tonnages to take account of the fact that a considerable percentage of their total consists of low calorie lignite. It is also possible that Soviet tonnages are measured before beneficiation. A better measure of the relative economic strength would be to compare total fuel requirements, including oil, gas, wood, peat, and coal. The United States economy obtains both absolutely and relatively much more energy from petroleum at the present time, although the Russians are currently making considerable progress in substituting oil for coal in satisfying their fuel requirements.

Today one frequently runs into a calculation indicating that the absolute increases in output in the West exceed those of the entire Soviet bloc.[24] A few years ago it was also fashionable to claim that the absolute gap between the economy of the United States and the USSR was increasing. While this is still true for such fast growing series as electric power, for the economy as a whole the absolute overall increases in the two economies are currently of roughly the same magnitude, at least during periods of our economic growth. The important thing to be remembered in this connection is that as long as economies in the Soviet bloc grow by twice the percentages obtained in the Western bloc, even our presently greater absolute increases in the West will disappear ultimately.

The crude death rate for the United States is approximately 9.3 per 1,000 population, while that of the Soviet Union is 7.2 per 1,000, making it probably one of the lowest in the world. However, this extremely low death rate can be explained—at least in part—by the youthfulness of the Soviet population due to an abnormally high casualty rate among elderly persons as a result of the hardships of World War II. If we were to apply United States age-specific death rates to a population structure similar to that of the Russians, we would find that our crude death rate would then be only 6.2 per 1,000, instead of the 9.3 per 1,000 it was in 1961. This explains why the average life ex-

[24] For example, see "Non-Red Nations Gain in '60 Output," *New York Times,* March 5, 1961, p. 3.

pectancy at birth in the Soviet Union is still only 69 (64 years for men and 72 for women), while ours is over 70 (66 for men and 73 for women).

In 1959 engineers with diplomas in the Soviet Union numbered 987,000 compared with 505,000 in the United States. Additions of young engineering graduates to the labor force in that year amounted to 108,600 and 38,000 in the two respective countries. While the Soviet Union has undoubtedly been turning out a relatively large supply of engineers, as compared with the United States, it should be remembered that engineers more frequently perform managerial and planning functions in the Soviet Union since courses in business administration and management or marketing are non-existent.[25] As a consequence, isolated comparisons of total engineers in the two countries give an exaggerated picture of the level of technology in the Soviet Union. The percentage of engineer-technicians in the Soviet industrial labor force—which would seem to be one indicator of the level of technology—seems to have held fairly stable at nine per cent during the past five years. The growth in the absolute numbers of Soviet engineers would also seem to reflect to some extent the rapid expansion of Soviet technical assistance programs for developing economies, either within the bloc or in the noncommitted areas.

CONCLUSIONS

It is hoped that the evidence presented above on the difficulties involved in comparing capitalist and noncapitalist-oriented economic statistics has impressed the reader with the many pitfalls which must be avoided if meaningful statistical comparisons are to be made. About the only thing we can be reasonably sure of is the fact that Soviet statistics will no doubt show that their economy has overtaken the United States capitalist model long

---

[25] For example, even the new head of the principal planning agency, has an engineering background.

before the actual event occurs. By the same token, our economic statisticians should certainly be able to conceal the fact for some time thereafter.

Recommended Readings

ABRAHAM S. BECKER, "Comparisons of United States and USSR National Output, Some Rules of the Game," *World Politics*, October, 1960, pp. 99–111.

*ABRAM BERGSON, "Reliability and Usability of Soviet Statistics: A Summary Appraisal," *The American Statistician*, June–July, 1953, pp. 19–23.

***MORRIS BORNSTEIN, "Comparisons of Soviet and United States National Product," in *Comparisons of the United States and Soviet Economies*, Joint Economic Committee, Congress of the United States, Part II, U.S. Government Printing Office, Washington, 1959, pp. 377–395. (Hereafter cited as *Comparisons of the United States and Soviet Economies.*)

*ROBERT CAMPBELL, "Problems of United States-Soviet Economic Comparisons," in *Comparisons of the United States and Soviet Economies*, Part I, pp. 13–30.

GREGORY GROSSMAN, *Soviet Statistics of Physical Output of Industrial Commodities, Their Compilation and Quality*, Princeton University Press, Princeton, 1960, especially Chapter 5.

NORMAN M. KAPLAN and RICHARD H. MOORSTEEN, "An Index of Soviet Industrial Output," *American Economic Review*, June, 1960, pp. 295–318.

ELIZABETH MARBURY, "A Note on Some Soviet Statistics," *East Europe*, November, 1960, pp. 16–19.

*ALEC NOVE, "1926–27 and All That," *Soviet Studies*, October, 1957, pp. 117–130.

* indicates that reading is included in: Franklyn D. Holzman, *Readings on the Soviet Economy*, Rand McNally and Company, Chicago, 1961.

** indicates that reading is included in: Morris Bornstein and Daniel R. Fusfeld, *The Soviet Economy, A Book of Readings*, Richard D. Irwin, Homewood, Illinois, 1962.

*** indicates that reading is included in both of above sources.

STEPHAN E. SCHATTMAN, "Dogma vs. Science in Soviet Statistics," *Problems of Communism,* January–February, 1956, pp. 30–45.

V. STAROVSKY, "On the Methodology of Comparing Economic Indices of the USSR and USA," *Voprosy Ekonomiki,* No. 4, 1960, pp. 103–117 (reprint of International Arts and Sciences Press).

Russian Statistical Handbooks

Tsentral'noe statisticheskoe upravlenie pri sovete ministrov SSSR, *Narodnoe khoziaistvo SSSR,* statisticheskii sbornik (National Economy of the USSR, Statistical Handbook), Gosstatizdat, Moscow, 1956. (Hereafter cited as *Narodnoe khoziaistvo 1955*)

Tsentral'noe statisticheskoe upravlenie pri sovete ministrov SSSR, *Narodnoe khoziaistvo SSSR v 1956 godu, statisticheskii ezhegodnik* (National Economy of the USSR in 1956, Statistical Yearbook), Gosstatizdat, Moscow, 1957. (Hereafter cited as *Narodnoe khoziaistvo 1956*). Yearbooks with the same title cover the years 1958, 1959 and 1960 and are referred to as: *Narodnoe khoziaistvo 1958, Narodnoe khoziaistvo 1959,* and *Narodnoe khoziaistvo 1960.*

IV ⚬ Consumption and Investment Decision-Making

INDIVIDUALS AND COUNTRIES both theoretically face a similar major economic decision at any given time: to consume or not to consume. The rational purpose of nonconsumption is to permit a diversion of resources to more roundabout and efficient ways of doing things. The resulting activities—which are referred to by economists as "investment" or "capital accumulation"—are more productive than existing direct methods of production and therefore promise greater overall consumption in the long run. Thus, while investment activity may require a cut in present consumption, future consumption possibilities are enlarged by an amount greater than any loss in current consumption.

A struggling student working his way through college is obviously limiting his present consumption possibilities in the expectation that his investment in higher education will pay off in greater lifetime consumption. Similarly, developing countries devote a portion of their labor and material resources to the construction of time-consuming projects—steel complexes, electric power installations, railroads—which may result in no immediate increase in personal consumption but rather benefit their citizens generally only after the lapse of some gestation period.

The more prosperous the individual or country, the less is the relative burden of any given investment program in terms of the required nonconsumption. Wealthy families may have to do without a second or third car in order to finance a higher education for their offspring; poorer families may literally have to take in their belts to achieve the same goal. By the same token, near-affluent capitalist-oriented societies may have chronic underutilization of their labor and capital resources so that any additional accumulation becomes relatively costless in terms of any consumption foregone. To the extent that there is considerable disguised unemployment in developing countries, it may also be possible for them to accumulate capital simply as a result of the more effective employment of their underutilized resources. But, in general, any substantive investment program in these developing areas must take place as a result of some nonconsumption or at least certain limitations on current increases in consumption.

The impact of investment on consumption is especially clear whenever accumulation takes place at a rapid rate over a relatively short period of time, as was the case in the Soviet Union in the thirties or in Eastern Europe after World War II. In a sense, Soviet consumers are today benefiting from the nonconsumption of an earlier generation just as it is undoubtedly also true that the high American level of living today is partly the result of our ancestors' nonconsumption in the last century. There would thus seem to be a common denominator between our age of the "Robber Barons" and their "Stalinist Era"; and there is a certain irony in the fact that our historians are rewriting history to emphasize the progressive role played by the Robber Barons, while Russian historians presently are at least in the process of desanctifying Stalin, if not also his policy of forced industrialization.

AGGREGATE CONSUMPTION AND INVESTMENT

Perhaps the single most important comparative advantage of the noncapitalist-oriented economies is their ability to restrict increases in aggregate consumption for extended time periods, and thereby to utilize a relatively higher percentage of their inner resources in capital accumulating projects. The proportion of income devoted to investment (that is, income not personally or communally consumed) has probably been averaging between 25 and 30 per cent year after year in most economies within the Soviet bloc. Since aggregate investment decision-making in the noncapitalist-oriented economies is almost completely divorced from the personal decisions of consumers to nonconsume, the central planners are effectively restrained from investing only to the extent that labor incentives and productivity must not be impaired by the restricted consumption that is provided.

In most capitalist-oriented economies, only between 15 and 20 per cent of all income is invested even in times of prosperity, while in periods of recession or depression, net capital accumulation may dwindle or virtually disappear.[1] In our earlier economic development, capital accumulation tended to be concentrated in the upswing of the business cycle and to fall off sharply in times of recession or depression. Also in wartime—even when the destruction has been confined to enemy real estate—there has also been a tendency for the rate of gross capital accumulation to decelerate as repairs and replacement of existing capital were postponed.

As a result of this postponed capital replacement and destruction of previously accumulated capital during wars, postwar recovery years have frequently been characterized by fairly sus-

---

[1] Gross investment accounted for 16 per cent of the nation's output in 1929 but only two per cent of a much lower total product in 1932. Net investment in the latter year was negative, indicating a situation in which replacement investment fell short of actual wear and tear. In the fifties, gross investment has fluctuated between 13 and 16 per cent of GNP except for 1950–51 and 1956 when it was somewhat above 16 per cent. See Joint Economic Committee, "Variability of Private Investment in Plant and Equipment," U.S. Government Printing Office, Washington, 1962, p. 12. These percentages are obtained when calculations are made in so-called "current" prices. When calculated in "constant" 1929 prices, the percentage for gross investment falls substantially between 1929 and 1959. See R. A. Gordon, "Differential Changes in the Prices of Consumers' and Capital Goods," *American Economic Review,* December, 1961, p. 951.

tained periods of capital accumulation as compared with more normal times. Wartime destruction of capital undoubtedly explains to some extent the sustained capital accumulation in both Western Germany and Japan after World War II. This high rate of investment, coupled with the relative absence of defense expenditures in these two economies—at least in comparison with those in the Soviet Union—would seem to account for their very rapid overall growth rates which up to now have more or less matched the rates being achieved in noncapitalist-oriented economies.

The erratic course pursued by capital investment in capitalist-oriented economies reflects the fact that aggregate investment is the end product of a myriad of investment decisions. Each of these investment decisions is made rather independently on the basis of the expected rates of return, which in turn are affected by changes in technology and consumer tastes. It is therefore not too surprising to find that exact correspondence is infrequently achieved between aggregate planned investment and the resources voluntarily released by consumers via their nonconsumption at any given time.

Instead, there seems to have been an alternating over-commitment and under-commitment of investment resources relative to voluntary nonconsumption, a factor which has been responsible for our business fluctuations. At some time during the upswing of the cycle, aggregate investment plans tended to exceed near-full employment voluntary nonconsumption. At this stage or even earlier due to bottlenecks, prices began to rise, but with wages tending to lag behind other prices so that a part of investment activity tended to come out of resources released by "forced" rather than voluntary nonconsumption. Near the upper turning point, wages became less "sticky" and tended to rise as fast as or faster than other prices in conditions of over-full employment, thereby cutting into profit rates, expected rates of return, and eventually into the aggregate private investment forthcoming.

In the downswing of the cycle, consumers were releasing resources through their nonconsumption, but aggregate investment was inadequate to absorb the released resources, resulting in growing unemployment of both labor and capital. Eventually at some lower level of national income with the accompanying unemployment, voluntary nonconsumption out of the lower incomes was reduced to a point where the resources released could be absorbed by the aggregate investment forthcoming.[2] Thus, consumers' sovereignty—the principle that consumers through their consumption or nonconsumption vote for the goods that are to be produced as well as when they will be consumed—with respect to the overall consumption-investment decision has apparently been ephemeral at best.[3]

In the years since World War II, the above-described nature of our earlier business fluctuations seems to have undergone some change. A commitment to full or near-full employment— partly as a result of the 1946 Employment Act, but also as a consequence of the economic competition from the challenging Soviet bloc—has improved the stronger bargaining position of labor inherited from the New Deal. This commitment, supplemented by the fairly common escalator clause, has meant that wages have tended to keep up with, if not ahead of, price increases in the upswings of economic activity. As a consequence, the high rates of return, overinvestment, and forced nonconsumption characterizing earlier upswings has been generally minimized. Similarly on the downswings, stable or stepped-up government expenditures—especially in the defense sector—have tended to compensate for the sluggish private investment at these times, thereby acting as a brake on any precipitous fall in national income. As a result, old-fashioned business cycles seem to have been largely replaced by more frequent "ripples" in inventory investment and disinvestment activity along the crest of a high plateau of total product.

---

[2] At the lower turning point, a stimulus to the rate of return was no doubt eventually provided by the reduction of the rate of capital accumulation during the downswing of the cycle and the continued growth of the potential labor force, resulting in a generally lower capital-labor ratio in the economy and justifying higher real rates of return for capital.

[3] For a contrary and more conventional view, see Robert W. Campbell, *Soviet Economic Power,* Houghton Mifflin Company, Boston, 1960, p. 146.

Since our labor force, capital resources, and technology are all still expanding, we are faced with a growing unrealized potential that certainly bears little resemblance to the wishes of supposedly sovereign consumers. At a minimum, this unrealized potential was responsible for an annual loss of $50 billion in early 1961 when the Kennedy Administration and Chairman Heller of the Council of Economic Advisers took office.[4] Generally speaking, it would seem that, more often than not, it is investors' sovereignty that is the factor determining the overall consumption-investment decision and the resulting rate of growth in capitalist-oriented economies.

In most noncapitalist-oriented economies, on the other hand, no pretense is ordinarily made regarding consumers' sovereignty with respect to the overall consumption-investment decision.[5] In contrast to capitalist economies, investment by the government, which for all practical purposes is the sole or at least the principal investor, has always absorbed resources in excess of those voluntarily released by fully employed consumers through their nonconsumption. In some real sense, present consumers have had to be "exploited" for the supposed benefit of future generations. An exception to this policy is apparently claimed by Yugoslavian socialists. The Yugoslavs at least wish to convey the impression that their goal is to have actual consumption determined by consumers' preferences.[6]

Forced nonconsumption via the prewar and wartime infla-

---

[4] By the middle of 1962, Chairman of the CEA Heller, claimed that this unrealized potential had been reduced to $30 billion, but another former member of the CEA, Leon Keyserling, claimed that instead it now amounted to $73 billion. See "State of the Economy and Policies for Full Employment," *Hearings Before the Joint Economic Committee, Congress of the United States, 87th Congress, Second Session, August 7–22, 1962,* U.S. Government Printing Office, Washington, 1962, pp. 108, 247.

[5] It might be noted that freedom of choice, which is sometimes confused with consumers' sovereignty, seems to be the prevailing method for distributing most commodities and services in both the United States and the USSR, except during wartime or similar emergencies. In the Soviet Union, rationing was resorted to in the "unusual" periods from 1930 to 1935 and from 1941 to 1947.

[6] See Janez Stanovnik, "Planning Through the Market," *Foreign Affairs,* January, 1962, p. 254.

tionary process and continuing large margins between price and cost levels since the war, supplemented by compulsory bond purchases until 1958 and a mildly progressive income tax until 1965 at least, have been the predominant sources of the resources devoted to Soviet capital accumulation. As a result of this steady plowing back of resources into new investment, the Soviet total product—and especially industrial production—has been in a state of perpetual upswing or "secular exhilaration." While there may have been some fluctuations in the rates of increase—due to such unplanned events as agricultural crises, uprisings within the bloc, or growing neutralism and honored requests for capital assistance from developing areas—the average annual increase in Soviet industrial production has consistently averaged a little less than 10 per cent in recent years.[7] In other noncapitalist-oriented economies, the rate of industrial development has been somewhat less smooth, particularly in countries where agriculture continues to occupy a large percentage of total economic activity and political loyalties to the regime are weaker.

The fact that consumers' sovereignty with respect to the overall consumption-investment decision in the USSR is still being violated might at first sight appear to be inconsistent with the price disinflation that has characterized the Soviet economy since 1947. But as we shall see when we come to Chapter VIII (see p. 190), there were two principal factors responsible for Soviet inflation before 1947: (1) continued and at times increasing violation of consumers' sovereignty with respect to the consumption-investment decision insured that the effective demand for consumers' goods would chronically exceed their limited supply at prevailing prices; and (2) increases in labor productivity were generally less than increases in average money wages causing unit labor costs—which in the last analysis are the principal determinants of production costs in the Soviet Union—for most products to

[7] According to independent calculations by our Central Intelligence Agency, from 1952 to 1958 the average annual rate of increase in Soviet industry was 9.5 per cent. See *New York Times,* April 9, 1959, p. 8. The official Soviet claim is that the annual increase in industrial production was 11.6 per cent during the fifties.

rise. Although the former condition has undoubtedly continued to some extent, the latter relationship has now been reversed and production costs—albeit with a few exceptions—have been generally falling. The recent overall disinflation might therefore be explained by the fact that the increases in supply are outweighing increases in effective demand or purchasing power, and, at the same time, overall production costs are falling faster than retail prices.[8] In other words, the impact of inflationary forces reflecting the violation of consumers' sovereignty with respect to the consumption-investment decision may still be evidenced by a growing margin between the level of retail prices and production costs generally, or at least a price-cost margin that is not as yet being reduced substantially.

STRUCTURE OF PERSONAL
CONSUMPTION AND NONCONSUMPTION

Within the aggregate personal consumption allowed by Soviet central planners, some account may be taken of individual consumers' goods shortages in selecting the channels into which the planned limited investment in consumers' goods industries

---

[8] Once the greater price inflation in consumers' goods relative to producers' goods had created a substantial margin between prices of consumers' goods and costs of production generally, as was evident by 1949, it was the change in the extent of the violation of consumers' sovereignty, in relation to any changes in consumers' saving habits, rather than the violation *per se* which controlled the overall price movements. It should also be mentioned that increases in savings banks deposits by comparatively large amounts annually in recent years are perhaps indicative of the fact that voluntary nonconsumption is becoming more important and that the violation of consumers' sovereignty with respect to the consumption-investment decision is less pronounced than formerly. The violation still shows up, however, in the fact that the prices of consumers' goods are still high in relation to their production costs, as compared with the price-cost margins under capitalist-oriented economies. But as we shall see in Chapter VI, the higher percentage of communal or collective consumption and the low and declining percentage of direct taxation are also responsible for the large and perhaps growing gap.

is directed. This would seem to be only possible, however, if there are no conflicting demands for the resources from heavy industry, which has had—and continues to have—the highest priority. But in general, this limited consumers' sovereignty within the consumption-mix pales into insignificance when compared with the structure of consumers' goods produced in capitalist-oriented economies. The range of different commodities, the varied choice within commodities, and the general quality and sales appeal of our consumers' goods (all of which will be considered further in Chapter VI) attest to the fact that our consumers are quite literally "kings," certainly in relation to the position of Soviet consumers.

Both capitalist and noncapitalist-oriented economies violate consumers' sovereignty in the case of individual commodities deemed injurious to health and morals. For example, we both discriminate against consumers of hard liquor by imposing relatively higher taxes on these products. In the case of the Soviet Union, the objective of their stiff tax on vodka is to cut down on hangovers and to step-up labor productivity, while religious scruples apparently still underlie our own taxes on alcoholic beverages.[9]

The resources released as a result of personal nonconsumption —whether they be obtained "voluntarily" as in the United States today or to a great extent by "force" as in the USSR—can be utilized or absorbed by both economies in five principal ways: (1) replacement of existing capital as a result of wear and tear, new technological advances, tax incentives, etc.; (2) investment representing net additions to capital stock; (3) inventory investment; (4) positive balances on current account in connection with foreign trade; and (5) defense and other communal consumption.[10] Let us now examine these absorbers in an effort to determine certain underlying principles of growthmanship.

---

[9] The effect of higher vodka prices after January 1, 1958, in the Soviet Union is reflected in the seven per cent drop in the sales of alcoholic beverages generally in that year. See *Narodnoe Khoziaistvo 1959*, p. 634.

[10] Communal consumption refers to the practice of providing or distributing certain goods and services, particularly the latter, without prices.

1. Replacement of existing capital is less significant as a component of gross investment in noncapitalist-oriented economies. Until fairly recently, replacement due to obsolescence was condemned by Soviet economists as a nonsocialist practice. But increasingly in the fifties, theoretical discussions as to the possible merits of capital replacement began to appear in Soviet economic journals.[11] As we shall see in the following chapter (see p. 81), there may have been little sense in replacing antiquated capital as long as extensive rural overpopulation existed. In any event, it seems clear that a great deal of capital investment in noncapitalist-oriented economies still represents net additions to the total stock of capital rather than replacement of existing stock. Because of this fact, gross investment—including both net additions to and replacement of capital stock—is more high-powered in its effect on Soviet economic growth than it is in the United States where there is a considerable and possibly growing dichotomy between gross and net investment.[12] As the Soviet economy matures, we should expect to find a greater share of gross investment to represent capital replacement rather than net additions to capital stock, in which case, this development would con-

[11] Beginning in 1955—and especially at the Twentieth Party Congress in 1956—the previously held idea that obsolescence was peculiar to capitalist-oriented economies was revised. See editorial, *"Za dal'neishee razvitie ekonomicheskoi nauke"* (For a Continuous Development of the Science of Economics), *Voprosy Ekonomiki,* No. 12, 1955, p. 8; and N. Nekrasov, *"Technicheskii progress i ekonomika proizvodstva"* (Technical Progress and the Economics of Production), *Voprosy Ekonomiki,* No. 6, 1955, pp. 12–13. Because of this lack of replacement, it seems doubtful, as both Oxenfeldt and Villard maintain, that the "Soviet Union's equipment is as new as that of any nation in the world—on the average." See Alfred R. Oxenfeldt, *Economic Systems in Action,* Revised edition, Rinehart, New York, 1957, p. 93; Henry H. Villard, *Economic Development,* Rinehart, New York, 1957, p. 173. A survey of machine tools in Soviet factories located in the four most important industrial areas recently disclosed that tools over 20 years old constituted more than 25 per cent of the total stock. See Harry Schwartz, "Soviet Machinery to be Cut in Price," *New York Times,* August 8, 1960, p. 29.

[12] According to Samuelson, depreciation, or the difference between gross and net investment, is running around one-twelfth of our gross national product. See Paul Samuelson, *Economics,* Fifth edition, McGraw-Hill, New York, 1958, p. 222.

stitute a factor tending to slow down their overall rate of growth.

In the United States, replacement of existing capital is looked upon with much favor generally, especially during periods of recession or underemployment of resources. Accelerated depreciation laws or tax credits for new investment are advocated to stimulate artificially the replacement of existing capital since in effect these practices permit temporary interest-free use of government tax revenue for such investment purposes. Recently the National Machine Tool Builders Association, an industry association representing our many relatively small and inefficient producers of machine tools, has appealed for legislative and administrative changes in our depreciation laws to arrest the precipitous downward trend in total machine tool orders.[13]

2. Investment representing net additions to capital stock constitutes the bulk of Soviet industrial investment since their economic development is still at a comparatively early stage. In contrast to the development of capitalist-oriented economies— where such things as cotton textiles rank high among the early types of investment activity—this investment is directed almost exclusively into Soviet heavy industry. From the beginning of the planning era, light and food processing industries have absorbed only between five and 10 per cent of all nonagricultural investment in the economy. According to some recent data presented in Table IV-A, there is also little indication in the current Seven-Year Plan that resources are scheduled to be directed towards the light and food processing industries in significantly increasing amounts. However, it should be mentioned that capital investment in the light and food processing industries grew by 15 per cent compared with the overall increase in capital investment of 11.5 per cent in 1960; in 1961, capital investment in light industry alone grew by 18 per cent compared with an overall increase in capital investment of nine per cent over the previous year.

[13] See "Machine Tool Orders Plummet," *New York Times,* March 28, 1961, p. 47. At other times, this same industry has put pressure on Washington to stockpile machine tools in the interest of national defense and, incidentally, greater sales in the industry.

TABLE IV-A

Capital Investment in Different Branches of Industry, Construction, Transportation, and Communication, USSR, Selected Periods and Years[1]

Branch or sector (1)	Achieved Investment 1952–1958 (billion "heavy" ru.) (2)	As % of Total in listed categories (3)	Planned Investment 1959–1965 (billion "heavy" ru.) (4)	As % of Total in listed categories (5)	Investment in Col. (4) as % of Col. (2) (6)	Investment in 1960 as % of 1959[2] (7)	Investment in 1961 as % of 1960[3] (8)
1. Iron and steel	4.08	7.2	10.0	8.5	245	112	108
2. Chemicals	1.99	3.5	10.0–10.5	8.9	502–528	133	n.a.
3. Oil and gas	7.22	12.7	17.0–17.3	14.7	235–240	110	108
4. Coal	6.12	10.8	7.5–7.8	6.6	122–127	n.a.	n.a.
5. Electric power	7.51	13.2	12.5–12.9	11.0	166–172	104 (109)[4]	107
6. Machine building	6.55	11.5	11.8	10.0	180	123	114
7. Lumber, paper, and woodworking	2.55	4.4	5.8–6.0	5.1	229–237	106	n.a.
8. Light industry and food processing	4.0	7.0	8.0–8.5	7.2	200–212	115	118[5]
9. Construction and construction materials	6.15	10.8	11.0–11.2	9.5	179–182	116	101
10. Transportation and communications	10.74	18.9	20.9–21.4	18.2	195–199	112	104
a. Rail transportation only	5.93	10.4	11.0–11.5	9.6	185–194	n.a.	n.a.
Total in above categories:	56.89	100.0	117.4	100.0	206	111.5[6]	109[6]

[1] Unless otherwise noted, all data and calculations are from *Narodnoe Khoziaistvo 1958*, p. 84. Original data have been converted into new "heavy" rubles effective on January 1, 1961.

[2] *SSSR v tsifrakh v 1960 godu* (The USSR in Figures in 1960), p. 18.

[3] *Pravda*, January 23, 1962, p. 2.

[4] Figure in brackets refers to heat and power stations.

[5] Refers to increased investment for light industry only.

[6] Increases refer to all investment except for collective farms.

56

This tendency for noncapitalist-oriented economies to channel investment into net additions to plant and equipment for investment goods industries produces a high-powered effect on overall industrial growth. It is true that investment in consumers' goods industries has an effect on the annual output of consumers' goods and hence on industrial production as soon as these factories have been completed and equipped with machinery. However, investments in factories producing investment goods not only augment the output of capital goods and industrial production as soon as they are completed; they also increase the potential for raising production and consumption levels in future years. In other words, while the *products* of consumers' goods and service industries (for example, TV sets and advertising) are consumed rather rapidly and do not add anything directly to future rates of growth, the *products* of investment goods industries (for example, machinery generally) exercise a continuing impact in subsequent years until they are worn out or scrapped. It seems clear that should there be a relative rise in the share of investment in consumers' goods and service industries in the Soviet Union, this would also be a factor making for lower overall Soviet economic growth.

There is another important difference between the two economies with respect to investment in plant and equipment. In capitalist-oriented economies, this type of investment has been intimately geared to changes in consumption. This relationship between some types of investment and changes in consumption is referred to as the "acceleration principle," and it has been generally recognized as a powerful factor making for our economic instability, especially at the upper turning point of the cycle. According to this principle, a mere slowing down of the rate at which aggregate consumption is increasing results in an actual decline in aggregate investment and quite possibly in total income and product. The operation of the accelerator is weak when there is considerable excess capacity as there is at present in the United States, since increases in consumption can be satisfied simply by increased utilization of existing capacity rather than by increasing net investment in plant and equipment.

In such a situation, however, the accelerator may still be expected to stimulate the inventory investment and disinvestment which seems to underlie the ripples in our economic activity in the post-Korean years. As mentioned above, the national defense establishment—which is completely independent of changes in consumption and represents a relatively atypical seller's market within our economy—serves as a huge built-in stabilizer braking any serious fall in economic activity. Since there is no necessary or direct relationship between the consumption and investment goods sectors in noncapitalist-oriented economies, the acceleration principle need not create any special difficulties with respect to economic fluctuations for Soviet central planners, any more than it did for our own economy during World War II.[14]

In addition to net investment in industry, there is also the possibility of investment in agriculture, housing, educational plant and equipment, transportation, and communications. In recent years, the Russians seem to be devoting relatively more of their investment outlays to industry and agriculture where a given investment results in a more substantial increase in output, rather than to housing, education, transportation, or communications, where there is a relatively smaller immediate payoff in terms of the increase in output.[15] In their economic development to date, the USSR has sought to limit investment in housing and transportation, in particular, with the result that overcrowded housing and intensively-used transportation have been

[14] At least one American economist has claimed that the acceleration principle is universally applicable to all economies. See William Loucks, *Comparative Economic Systems,* Sixth edition, Harper, New York, 1961, p. 9.

[15] Robert W. Campbell, *op. cit.,* pp. 156–157, gives a clear summary of Soviet and United States investment patterns. See also, Harry Schwartz, "U.S. Reports Rise in Soviet Capital," *New York Times,* April 16, 1961. According to a comprehensive study of investment in the United States and the Soviet Union, it appears that the Soviets are currently investing absolutely more capital than we are in industry and agriculture. In 1959, it was 70 per cent higher in industry and more than twice as high in agriculture. In housing and in transportation and communications, our investment was almost twice as great as the Soviet counterpart. Total capital investment in the two economies seems to be about on a par in the early sixties.

characteristic features of Soviet socialism. In the future, should there be a shift in investment in the direction of more housing construction—as would be required by the development of *agrogorods* (agricultural cities)—or transportation (especially in privately owned autos), this would also tend to slow down their overall growth.

3. Inventory investment plays a comparatively important role in the Soviet economy at present, possibly as a carryover from the earlier incentives to hoard materials in the thirties. The serious shortages of raw materials and the uncertainties of the transportation and supply system at that time probably tended to encourage the hoarding of material inventories. In the postwar years, although the supply situation seems to have improved and limitations on working capital available to enterprises are better enforced, Soviet managers have been slow to change their ways and still tie up considerable working capital in the form of inventories.[16] The low interest rate charged to enterprises on their loans for working capital has also probably contributed to a lack of economy with respect to plant inventories. Since prices are fixed for long periods of time, and such price changes as do occur are generally downward, speculative investment in inventories in the expectation of windfall gains should be less prevalent in the Soviet economy than it is in the capitalist-oriented economies.

Enterprises in capitalist-oriented economies have apparently tended to maintain smaller inventories than their noncapitalist-oriented counterparts, at least in the industrial and trade sectors. But there seems to be a tendency for inventories to accumulate in our economy under the auspices of the Federal Government.[17]

[16] See R. W. Campbell, "Soviet and American Inventory-Output Ratios," *American Economic Review,* September, 1958, pp. 549–565. For some confirmation of this phenomenon as applied to Czechoslovakia, see Boris P. Pesek, "Soviet and American Inventory-Output Ratios Once Again," *American Economic Review,* December, 1959, pp. 1030–1033. It should be pointed out that these findings contradict Soviet claims on this score.

[17] In this connection, see Joint Economic Committee, "Subsidy and Subsidylike Programs of the U.S. Government," U.S. Government Printing Office, Washington, 1960, pp. 66–67. Also Richard E. Mooney, "Nation's

Since World War II, our government has become a significant investor in inventories of "surplus" agricultural products, "strategic and critical materials," machine tools, etc.—at least partly in an effort to stimulate employment and profits.[18] By early 1962 the total stocks of our government exceeded $7.7 billion and seemed likely to continue to grow.[19] With prices slowly drifting upward, as they were in the fifties, there would seem to be smaller risk involved in this type of investment than was the case when prices occasionally fell sharply. If present conditions of relative price stability persist for any length of time, we might expect larger inventories eventually to characterize capitalist-oriented economies. If so, there would also have to be net investment in our storage facilities as well.

4. Any positive balance on current account in the balance of payments is also considered to be a component of our net investment. This type of investment results whenever our exports of

Materials Stockpiles Run From Agar to Zirconium," *New York Times,* February 1, 1962, p. 11.

[18] The lead and zinc stockpile program in 1954 was carried out by establishing stockpile objectives which were not related to military needs, but rather were designed to maintain or raise market prices in these depressed areas. See Richard C. Coburn's letter to *New York Times,* July 19, 1962, p. 26. As a result of these government purchases, the supply of lead exceeded the military target objective by 466 per cent; the supply of zinc by 887 per cent. Senator Stuart Symington, in commenting on the late Senator Henry C. Dworshak's testimony before the special subcommittee investigating the stockpiles, is quoted as saying, "I'm glad you came in because you cleared up once and for all that this stockpiling thing was used as a method for alleviating unemployment." See "Eisenhower Role in Surplus Cited," *New York Times,* July 19, 1962, p. 1. Profits of 1,000 per cent or more on the stockpiling of low-grade chromite ore were apparently the result of the stockpiling of this metal. See "Inquiry Hears of 1,000% Profit on a Low-Grade Ore Stockpile," *New York Times,* August 2, 1962, p. 11. In answering these charges, the President of the Hanna Mining Company claimed that their stockpiling profits of 38 per cent in nickel were "not a great deal larger" than their earnings on commercial sales. See *New York Times,* October 16, 1962, p. 26.

[19] See Joe Western, "Kennedy Faces Trouble Trying to Trim Size, Costs of U.S. Hoard," *Wall Street Journal,* February 2, 1962, p. 1. Any disposal program would tend to depress prices and profit margins with the result that little reduction in excess inventories can apparently be expected.

goods and services generally exceed our imports. This positive balance reflects our investments abroad which should theoretically result in our greater future consumption if and when repayment can ever be made. However, since repayment must in the last analysis be made in commodities, services, or gold, relatively limited domestic markets may make any eventual repayment, in other than gold, extremely difficult.

The Soviet Union also seems to be moving towards a positive balance on their current account as a result of their capital advances to developing areas, including those countries within the Soviet bloc. However, in Soviet trade relations with advanced capitalist-oriented economies, they have a negative balance as reflected by the annual outflow of $200 to $250 million worth of gold from the USSR to the Western gold markets in London and Switzerland and the growing extension of short-term credits by Western European bankers to the Soviet bloc. As an alternative to investment in producers' or consumers' goods industries within the Soviet Union, investment abroad would seem to slow down their overall growth, in contrast to our own economy where such developments tend to create new jobs and have a stimulating effect on our overall growth. Only if the alternative is unemployment of these resources, do capital exports tend to stimulate growth. Since the internal market in the USSR is virtually unlimited, eventual repayment of present Soviet loans is more likely than it is for the United States.[20] In this event, any future repayments by developing areas would tend to accelerate the Soviet rate of growth.

5. Defense establishments today constitute some of the most important users of resources released as a result of personal nonconsumption. It seems obvious that these military expenditures,

[20] This virtually unlimited internal market has not always been recognized by the Russians themselves. According to the late J. V. Stalin, writing in his last months, "it will soon come to pass that these (socialist) countries will not only be in no need of imports from capitalist countries, but will themselves feel the necessity of finding an outside market for their surplus products." See his *Economic Problems of Socialism in the USSR,* International Publishers, New York, 1952, p. 27.

insofar as they are the alternative to investment in heavy industry, tend to act as a drain on the potential growth rate of noncapitalist-oriented economies. Investment in the capacity to produce military weapons is in some respects similar to investment in consumers' goods industries in that the product of such expenditures is frequently "consumed" either by rapid obsolescence of the "hardware" or by the firing of the end product into outer space.

With respect to the growth of capitalist-oriented economies, the role of defense expenditures is mixed. In Great Britain in the postwar period, it seems clear that the relatively high percentage of national income devoted to defense expenditures has probably tended to hold down their overall growth, since the alternative use of the resources was no doubt one of capital replacement and/or additions of new plant and equipment at a faster rate.[21] In the United States, on the other hand, it is not at all clear that defense expenditures have been cutting into our growth rate. As a matter of fact, our years of greatest economic growth since World War II have been during the Korean conflict when defense and military expenditures were at their postwar zenith until the Kennedy Administration. In addition, the results of the research and development carried out in the name of defense undoubtedly spill over and stimulate capital replacement and net investment in the nondefense sectors of our economy.[22]

Other types of communal consumption, such as expenditures for health, education, and government administration, are also financed out of the resources released by personal nonconsumption. In general, these expenditures probably tend to slow down overall growth in noncapitalist-oriented economies in the short run. However, the impact of resources allocated to education and

[21] During the fifties, the British gross national product rose at an average annual rate of only 2.6 per cent, the lowest rate of increase among the advanced capitalist-oriented economies.

[22] According to Emile Benoit, "it is precisely the threat to this dynamic element in our life . . . that may constitute the chief economic hazard of disarmament." See his "Affording Disarmament: An Analysis, A Model, Some Proposals," *Columbia University Forum,* Winter, 1962, p. 5.

medicine is difficult to measure since worker longevity and productivity is enhanced in the long run as a result of these investments in human resources. To the extent that a population is in poor health and illiterate, expenditures for public health and education should ultimately have a significantly favorable impact on the growth rate. On the other hand, additional expenditures for government administration would seem to have little positive effect on the overall rate of growth under any circumstances.

While there has been some relative expansion of education and health services in the Soviet Union in recent years, there may have been a relative contraction in expenditures for their administrative apparatus.[23] In the United States—as the Galbraithians have been quick to point out—there has been a tendency for our decision-making apparatus to neglect both education and public health. At the same time, the operation of "Parkinson's Law" has insured a steady growth in our comparatively "unproductive" administrative and regulatory complex.

ALLOCATING RESOURCES RELEASED BY NONCONSUMPTION

According to conventional economic theory, the interest rates in capitalist-oriented economies ration the resources released by nonconsumption among competing uses. Investment projects promising a rate of return in excess of going interest rates are undertaken; those which promise expected rates of return below the going interest rates remain "on the shelf," possibly to be utilized if interest rates fall or if technical inventions in the field improve cost and profit expectations.

[23] According to David Granick, "Parkinson's law of self-generation of administrative and office personnel does not seem to have applied to Soviet industry of the postwar years." See his "Soviet-American Management Comparisons" in: Joint Economic Committee, *Comparisons of the United States and Soviet Economies,* Part I, p. 146. See also material presented below in Chapter X (see p. 257), on Soviet budget allocations for administration.

Increasingly there has been pressure for capitalist-oriented central governments to enter the investment decision-making markets via subsidies for areas subject to rates of return on investment which are below those which private investors consider to be "normal." The areas which have been most frequently subject to artificial investment stimuli outside the normal market process—either by direct or indirect subsidies—are the following: agriculture, transportation, education, housing, foreign investment, and national defense. In addition, a growing amount of our investment is being financed internally out of undistributed profits and depreciation allowances, to some extent with little resort to the tests of the capital market.

In noncapitalist-oriented economies, interest rates have played little or no role in allocating investment-type activities. However, in the intellectual ferment that has characterized the Khrushchev era, there has been increased talk about the need to use interest rates or interest-type calculations in order to achieve greater rationality in the investment decision-making process. In the very early days of planning, the range of investment choice open to the central planners was probably fairly limited so that there was probably less need for determining the most economical type of production process. In the course of time, as the Soviet economy has developed into the second ranking world economic power, the range of alternative investments has widened to the point where the calculation of comparative costs and returns has assumed increased importance. Actually the chaotic state of the Soviet internal price structure—which is only in the process of being rectified in 1963—also reduced the meaningfulness of most calculations of alternative cost. Finally, some of the investment decisions, particularly with respect to the location of industry, were affected more by political or military considerations, with the result that economists took a back seat in the decision-making process.

REFLECTION OF BASIC PROBLEMS IN CONSUMPTION-INVESTMENT DECISION-MAKING

The basic problems of the two principal world economies with respect to overall consumption and utilization of resources released by personal nonconsumption are pretty much the reverse of one another. In the United States, personal consumption tends to be weak, despite the efforts of our most diligent waste makers to stimulate effective demand, and the resources that would be released by full employment nonconsumption are generally more than ample to accommodate the five principal uses discussed above. Thus, when Keynesian solutions, in addition to measures to stimulate consumers' demand, are suggested for our lagging growth or high level stagnation, they usually involve, among other things, a stepping up of government intervention in one of the following forms: (1) accelerated depreciation allowances to stimulate capital replacement and growing scrap supplies; (2) inventory stockpiling of "surplus" materials; (3) increased government-financed foreign aid or government insured private investment in developing areas; (4) increased defense and other communal consumption allocations. While increasing expenditures in all four of these areas contribute to the stabilization of our overall economic activity at a relatively high level, and do perhaps result in greater growth than might be expected in their absence, they are not especially conducive to the more rapid growth we formerly obtained when our fifth use of resources released by personal nonconsumption—investment in additions to plant and equipment—was having its heyday.[24]

In advanced capitalist-oriented economies other than the United States and Canada, there is relatively greater investment

[24] For a recognition of this fact, see Joseph R. Slevin, "The Reluctant Consumer-Culprit in Slowdown," *New York Herald Tribune,* February 26, 1962, p. 25.

demand for net additions to their plant and equipment, in part stimulated by the capital destruction which took place during World War II, but also by the growing Common Market in Western Europe and the resulting need for net investment in larger scaled and more specialized operations. In addition, increasing trade with the Soviet bloc, including short-term loans to make this possible, has been helpful in maintaining demand for capital goods, as we shall see in Chapter XI (see p. 292). As a result, there has been less need for West European countries to stimulate their economies by encouraging the other four absorbers of full employment voluntary nonconsumption.

In the developing capitalist-oriented economies, investment in social capital by the central government—supplemented by private investment—creates conditions of excess purchasing power, and demand-pull inflation is frequently rampant. However, this extreme inflationary pressure should not be interpreted as a reflection of the fact that these economies, like those of Western Europe, are operating at or near their production-possibilities curves, since undoubtedly a great deal of disguised unemployment still exists.

In noncapitalist-oriented economies, personal consumption is also pressing chronically against the five principal absorbers of resources released via personal nonconsumption. These governments therefore tend to take a diametrically opposite view of the four government measures advocated by our Keynesians. Since all of these measures stimulate activities which compete with the still much needed net additions to capital plant and equipment in these economies, any relative expansion of these essentially "make-work" or employment creating activities tends to slow down their overall growth.

The economic reasoning behind Professor Seymour Melman's *Peace Race* now becomes clear.[25] By challenging the Soviets to a competition in the supply of foreign capital assistance to the developing areas, we press even harder on the other absorbers, as well as improvements in consumption, and present Soviet

[25] See Seymour Melman, *The Peace Race,* Ballantine, New York, 1961, p. 317.

strategists with somewhat of a dilemma. Whether the Soviet Union would in effect "sue for peace," as Professor Melman seems to assume, or would merely allow their growth rate to slacken, is conjectural however.[26] In any event, it seems clear that our underutilized potential gives us much greater flexibility in an era of competitive coexistence.

Recommended Readings

ROBERT W. CAMPBELL, *Soviet Economic Power,* Houghton Mifflin, Boston, 1960, Chapter 7, "Control Over Resources."

MAURICE DOBB, "Rates of Growth Under the Five-Year Plans," *Soviet Studies,* April, 1953, pp. 374–375, especially. Also reprinted in his *Economic Theory and Socialism,* International Publishers, New York, 1955.

*GREGORY GROSSMAN, "Scarce Capital and Soviet Doctrine," *The Quarterly Journal of Economics,* Vol. LXVII, No. 3, August, 1953, pp. 311–343.

NORMAN KAPLAN, "Capital Formation and Allocation," in Abram Bergson, editor, *Soviet Economic Growth,* Row Peterson, New York, 1953.

*"Recommendations of the All-Union Scientific-Technical Conference on Problems of Determining the Economic Effectiveness of Capital Investments and New Techniques in the USSR National Economy," *Problems of Economics,* I, No. 9 (January, 1959), pp. 86–90.

*BENJAMIN WARD, "Kantorovich on Economic Calculation," *The Journal of Political Economy,* Vol. LXVIII, No. 6, December, 1960, pp. 545–556.

[26] A similar economic reasoning underlies the suggestion in 1958 of William C. Foster, now director of the U.S. Arms Control and Disarmament Agency, that we should boost our military budget by 10 to 20 per cent. Writing in the September, 1958, issue of the *General Electric Defense Quarterly,* Foster argued that such an increase would force the Russians to follow suit and "would take away from their people the already sparse good things of life they have."

V ⁓ Extracting
Agricultural Produce

THE AGRICULTURAL SECTOR represents an important source of resources available for nonconsumption activities and it is usually a basis of early or so-called "primitive" capital accumulation. In addition, food and fibre products are the mainstay of the entire consumption sector in the early stages of economic development. Increasing agricultural productivity releases a potential industrial labor force, and this increased productivity, supplemented by rural nonconsumption, provides in large measure the means for the subsistence of those new workers released to engage in roundabout ways of doing things in the nonagricultural sector. As economies develop industrially, the nonconsumption of the urban population and increasing industrial labor productivity represent added sources of resources required for capital accumulation projects. Furthermore, as levels of living rise, the industrial sector begins to assume the burden for a larger share of the total consumption requirements of both the rural and urban population, a phenomenon which will be examined in the following chapter.

AGRICULTURAL DEVELOPMENT IN NONCAPITALIST-ORIENTED ECONOMIES

With the exception of Czechoslovakia, which had already made considerable industrial progress before World War II, all noncapitalist-oriented economies have begun their planned industrialization with substantial rural overpopulation, a seemingly inexhaustible source of a potential industrial labor supply. As a result of this rural overpopulation or disguised unemployment—which was especially evident at times other than during planting or harvesting months—total agricultural output could undoubtedly have been at least maintained using considerably fewer full-time agricultural workers in the process. But the problem these developing economies faced was not quite that simple. It was necessary not only to maintain but to increase substantially total agricultural production, utilizing fewer farmhands in the process. In order to produce effectively in the mines, factories, construction projects, and transportation facilities of the growing nonagricultural sector of the economy, the labor force released by the agricultural sector suddenly developed larger calorie requirements. The explanation for these increased food requirements lies in the fact that industrial workers eat like harvest hands throughout the year, rather than just seasonally. Furthermore, the production of any additional agricultural surplus could be used to accelerate the rate of industrialization if it were exchanged abroad for the machinery and technical knowledge of the advanced capitalist-oriented economies.

The problem of extracting the agricultural surplus from developing economies within the Soviet sphere of influence since World War II can be illustrated to some extent by looking at the Soviet experience in the twenties, although in most cases the problems of the newer noncapitalist-oriented countries have probably been of lesser magnitude. This is due not only to their profiting from some of the lessons learned from the earlier Soviet experience, but also to Soviet capital assistance and technology, especially after the 1956 uprisings in Eastern Europe and the elimination of war reparation payments which had been largely extracted through the joint stock companies. According to an estimate of our Central Intelligence Agency, various economic concessions probably have cost the USSR as much as $3 billion over a period of years.[1] In the case of Poland and Yugo-

[1] Joint Economic Committee print, *Comparisons of the United States and Soviet Economies,* Supplemental Statement on Costs and Benefits to

slavia, the use of United States agricultural surpluses in recent years has also been helpful.

Shortly after the October Revolution, the Bolsheviks fulfilled their campaign promises by nationalizing such industry, transportation, and banking as they had inherited from the previous regime. Since Russia was essentially a relatively underdeveloped country with roughly 80 per cent of the entire labor force still engaged in agricultural pursuits, it was not politically feasible to ignore the peasants' demand for individual landholding.[2] Consequently the former large estates were divided initially among the relatively large numbers of land-hungry peasants. It soon became evident that total agricultural output was being jeopardized by this land reform since some of the former efficiency resulting from large-scale cultivation was being lost as a result of the parcelization of the estates.

To complicate matters further, a so-called "scissors" crisis had developed in the Soviet Union by 1923 and continued through the mid-twenties. This crisis refers to the opening of the internal "price scissors"—the relation between industrial prices (the upper blade) and agricultural prices (the lower blade). Economists today would probably say under similar circumstances that the terms of trade had moved drastically against the farmers and in favor of the industrial sector.

Market forces, which had been allowed to develop more freely

---

the Soviet Union of Its Bloc and Pact System: Comparisons with the Western Alliance System, U.S. Government Printing Office, Washington, 1960, pp. 2, 10. According to official communist claims, the Soviet Union had to extend more than $300 million in credits to Hungary alone in the single year, 1957, and the credits since then are said to have been very high. See *New York Times,* April 9, 1961, p. 11.

[2] Of all the noncapitalist-oriented economies, only Cuba seems to have been able to circumvent successfully the desires of the peasants for individual landholding immediately after the revolution. Even the Cuban cooperatives—which were established for the production of major crops such as sugar and coffee, and specialized activities like cattle-raising, fishing and charcoal manufacturing—are scheduled to be converted into state farms. See "Castro Taking Over Farms of Peasants," *New York Times,* August 20, 1962, p. 1. However, in mainland China the interim private ownership of farms by peasants was relatively short-lived.

after the introduction of the New Economic Policy in 1921, tended to drive farm prices down to lower levels as supplies improved following a relatively rapid agricultural recovery. At the same time, the socialized industrial sector was very slowly regaining its prewar level of efficiency, labor productivity was low, and costs of industrial products were correspondingly high. There is also some evidence that the industrial enterprises, which perhaps significantly were organized into cartel-like "syndicates" and "trusts," were establishing high, inflexible prices for their products, reflecting not only their relatively high costs of production but also substantial rates of profit.[3] It soon became clear to Soviet farmers that their terms of trade were none too favorable if and when industrial products were even obtainable from the cities. As a result, the rural population increased their personal food consumption, and, on their own initiative, also invested some of their cheap grain in private livestock holdings.

This stepped-up personal consumption and investment of grain and other agricultural crops by Soviet farmers reduced the exportable surplus which, in the case of grain, had accounted for over one-third of all Russia's exports before the Revolution. Since no long-term credits were forthcoming from abroad, some agricultural commodities had to be exported to pay for essential imports of machinery and technical assistance. The generally greater decline in the prices of farm products relative to the prices of machinery on international markets further complicated this problem by requiring ever greater physical quantities of exported products, as we shall see when we come to Chapter XI.

The vanishing marketable agricultural surplus also threatened to create a bottleneck holding up the urban supplies of food and fibre required for any great expansion of the industrial labor force. In addition to the problem of feeding and clothing the urban workers, there were also difficulties involved in enticing the surplus farmers into the cities—and into the industrial labor force—in view of the comparative prosperity in rural areas.

[3] In this connection, see Maurice Dobb, *Soviet Economic Development Since 1917*, Routledge and Kegan Paul, Ltd., London, 1948, p. 171.

Shortly after the introduction of the First Five-Year Plan (Plan I), the necessity for the state to recapture what had formerly been an agricultural surplus gave rise to the collective farm system that has since characterized the Soviet Union as well as most noncapitalist-oriented economic systems.[4]

Prior to the launching of Plan I, a most interesting ideological controversy raged within Soviet planning circles. Economists like Preobrazhensky argued that, in order to industrialize, the agricultural surplus was required as a source of primitive socialist accumulation. In this connection, these economists felt that an open price scissors might be most useful in extracting the surplus. The opposition, however, took the view that any continued existence of the wide gap between the levels of industrial and agricultural prices would threaten the so-called *smychka* or coalition originally forged by Lenin between the peasantry and the proletariat. Although a number of economists who advocated the maintenance of the differential price levels were liquidated, the eventual collectivization of agriculture represented some posthumous vindication of their position. For the development of collective farming, in effect, institutionalized the open scissors via relatively low agricultural procurement prices, which were maintained for most compulsory deliveries by the collectives to the state from 1929 to 1953. As Stalin admitted in one of his more candid moments, the Russian peasant was temporarily required to overpay for his industrial products,

---

[4] As mentioned in Chapter II, both Poland and Yugoslavia seem to have at least temporarily deviated from this Soviet pattern of development. The differences with respect to the organization of Chinese and Cuban agriculture appear to be less substantive. In this connection, it is interesting to note that the peasants in Yugoslavia and Poland have apparently been the chief beneficiaries of the results of the postwar industrialization. The failure of these governments to capture enough of the agricultural surplus may also explain some of the economic difficulties (for example, inflation) which seem to persist here, especially in Yugoslavia. See John Kenneth Galbraith, *Journey to Poland and Yugoslavia,* Harvard University Press, Cambridge, 1958, pp. 40, 95. According to a recent report, Polish farmers increased their incomes three times as fast as did city dwellers in 1961. See "Russian Praises Polish Farming," *New York Times,* February 4, 1962, p. 15.

and in turn, he was to be underpaid for his agricultural crops.[5]

In retrospect, it seems clear from the Soviet experience that in the early stages of a rapid industrialization, and in the absence of large capital loans or agricultural surpluses from abroad, the agricultural sector must be a primary source of the nonconsumption and increased productivity which serve as bases of capital accumulation. A rough monetary measure of the surplus extracted from the Soviet agricultural sector might be obtained by comparing the low compulsory procurement prices at which agricultural products were commandeered from collective farms by the Soviet state and the high retail prices charged for these products in government retail outlets. The difference, which corresponds roughly to the profits and turnover taxes comprising the margin between the state's low procurement cost and the retail selling price for agricultural products processed by the state, was a major source of the investment funds plowed back into new plant and equipment.

Until after Stalin's death, agriculture also tended to receive a comparatively small share of the total investment outlays from the government budget.[6] As a result of the relatively low priority assigned to this sector, agricultural targets were chronically underfulfilled by substantial margins. This was especially the case in the early thirties when the *kulaks'* resistance to collectivization coincided with a severe drought, resulting in an overall decline in the total agricultural output and the famine conditions which ensued. According to one estimate, output in 1932 was

[5] This "tribute" or super-tax on the Soviet farmer is referred to in Stalin's *Sochineniia* (Collected Works), Vols. XI, p. 159 and XII, pp. 49–51. English edition, Vol. XII, pp. 52 *et seq.* Although this tribute was originally supposed to disappear within a few years, it continued in effect until the Khrushchev era.

[6] Despite the fact that total Soviet agricultural investment apparently overtook that of the United States as early as 1955 and is now more than twice as great as our total investment in agriculture, investment in industry apparently was still three times greater than it was in agriculture in 1959. See United States Central Intelligence Agency, "A Comparison of Capital Investment in the United States and the USSR, 1950–59," February, 1961. For a digest of these results, see Harry Schwartz, "U.S. Reports Rise in Soviet Capital," *New York Times,* April 16, 1961.

about a fifth below the total agricultural product in 1928.[7] In general, although rural levels of living rose somewhat in the mid-thirties and again after World War II, country life in 1953 was probably not substantially different from the conditions of life prevailing there before the Revolution.[8] Since the transfer of population from rural to urban areas was one of the government's key objectives in carrying out the industrialization program, this continuing rural poverty undoubtedly facilitated the semi-voluntary movement of new workers to the cities.[9]

The extraction of the agricultural surplus has been carried out by two types of agricultural organizations: the collective farm or *kolkhoz* and the state farm or *sovkhoz*. The collective farm, nominally a self-governing cooperative, is administered by a chairman and governing board. This form of agricultural organization has accounted for the bulk of total agricultural production and was organized in such a manner that the risk of poor harvests was borne by the collective farmers themselves rather than by the state. At the end of the harvest year, the income of the collective farm (both in money and in kind) is divided among members in proportion to their "labor day" contributions.[10] In addition to working on the collective farm,

[7] See D. Gale Johnson and Arcadius Kahan, "Soviet Agriculture: Structure and Growth," in *Comparisons of the United States and Soviet Economies,* Part I, p. 205.

[8] The one notable exception to this generalization would seem to be the relative economic position of members of cotton-growing collective farms in Central Asia. The procurement price for cotton has always been relatively high and country life in Central Asia had undoubtedly improved in comparison with pre-revolutionary conditions.

[9] Labor Reserve Schools recruited both volunteers and draftees from the countryside for training as industrial and transportation workers between 1940 and 1955. Compulsory drafting was finally eliminated by a decree of March 18, 1955. See United States Department of Labor, Bureau of Labor Statistics, *Principal Current Soviet Labor Legislation,* BLS Report No. 210, January, 1962, p. 58.

[10] "Labor days" did not necessarily correspond to calendar days, since more than one labor day credit could be obtained for a calendar day's work at a job requiring special skills or efforts. Collective farmers were required to perform a minimum number of labor days for the kolkhoz. After performing this minimum number of labor days, the farmers could devote any of their remaining time to their personal plots of land.

members are also allowed to maintain a small piece of property—about an acre, the exact amount varying with the fertility and availability of the land—around their houses. These private plots, which constituted a concession to the desires for landholding on the part of the former peasants, have been cultivated rather intensively in most cases, and the farmers could also keep a cow, some poultry, etc.[11]

The surplus fruit, vegetables, milk, and meat produced on the individual plots—as well as some of the produce from the kolkhoz—could be sold in collective farm markets established in the towns and cities. In 1940, about one-fifth of all food sales occurred in these markets. The retail prices on these markets are established by the free play of market forces resulting in ever-fluctuating prices, usually at a level somewhat above that set by the government for similar products sold in the official retail outlets. In the winter time, the collective farm market prices have been considerably higher than those prevailing in the state stores, while at times during the summer they have been lower. Towards the end of the day, prices also tended to drop for the still unsold items. In recent years, the average price of all goods sold on the collective farm market has been about 35 per cent above the price level for the same food products sold in the state retail network. In addition to these two price levels, there is the price level of commodities sold by the farmers to the consumers' cooperatives acting as middlemen. This so-called "commission trade," which was introduced in 1953, is carried out at prices which were about 10 per cent above the official state store prices.[12]

The state farms, on the other hand, were organized in much the same manner as the industrial enterprises and, for this reason, they were considered to be a more advanced form of socialist

[11] In recent years, collective farmers have been encouraged to sell their privately held cows to the kolkhoz. For an interesting account of some of the difficulties encountered, see Max Frankel, "Too Many Cows Cause Problems for Soviet Collective Farms," *New York Times,* March 6, 1959, p. 4.

[12] See *Narodnoe Khoziaistvo 1960,* p. 719. For a discussion of the importance of commission trade, see Marshall I. Goldman, "Commission Trade and the Kolkhoz Market," *Soviet Studies,* October, 1958.

organization. Since workers on state farms received a fixed wage or salary, plus piece-work incentive payments, the risk of poorer harvests has tended to be borne more by the state than was the case for the collective farms. State farmers were covered by the state social security system and were also permitted to cultivate private plots of land which they rented from the state farms. In addition, they could buy milk, meat, and vegetables from the sovkhoz at cost. At the management levels of the state farm, bonuses similar to those in effect for industrial managers, were paid for overfulfillment of targets. Much of the experimental work in Soviet agriculture was carried out on the state farms and, despite their generally greater productivity vis-à-vis the kolkhozy, these organizations frequently operated at a financial loss to the state until 1956.[13]

Shortly after the collectivization of agriculture, Machine Tractor Stations were established to facilitate the pooling of existing agricultural machinery. As a result of this pooling of relatively scarce capital, agricultural machinery was undoubtedly utilized more intensively than was the case in our own agricultural sector. In 1930, for example, the Russians claimed that their tractors were being worked on the average about four times as many hours as our own. The collective farmers rented the services of the agricultural machinery manned by salaried personnel of the Machine Tractor Stations, for which the collective farm paid both in kind and in money. It is generally believed that the Machine Tractor Stations were also useful politically in keeping the government apprised of any grass-roots dissension.

After 1953, Premiers Malenkov and Khrushchev, especially the latter, have proven themselves to be true friends of Soviet farmers. Agricultural procurement prices were raised very sharply for deliveries by the collective farms, and the blades of the price scissors have been closed to a great extent.[14] As a result of these

[13] For some comparative data on labor productivity on sovkhozy and kolkhozy see N. S. Khrushchev, *Report on the Program of the Communist Party of the Soviet Union,* Vol. II, Crosscurrents Press, New York, 1961, p. 79.

[14] According to one calculation, the procurement prices received by collective farms on average increased by four-fold between 1950 and 1958. See Nancy Nimitz, "Soviet Agricultural Prices and Costs," in *Comparisons*

higher procurement prices, cash payments to collective farms and individuals for farm products acquired by the government, including payments of government controlled cooperatives, rose from 3.13 to 14.49 billion "heavy" rubles between 1952 and 1959.[15] Now that the blades of the price scissors have been closed to some extent, it has become more feasible politically to compute and publish information on the production costs of various agricultural products. As a result, there has been a campaign to organize cost accounting on the farms in order to get at least some idea of the following relationships: the existing relative production costs for different products; the costs of the same commodities produced in different geographical areas; and the relative costs of agricultural products coming from the kolkhozy and sovkhozy.[16]

There have also been some postwar amalgamations of existing collective farms. These "share-the-wealth" mergers frequently involved the uniting of the more efficient and prosperous farms with some of their less prosperous counterparts, and a greater sharing of the differential rent which had previously been earned on the more fertile land. From a total of 250,000 collective farms in 1949, the number had been reduced to 44,000 by 1960.

At the same time that the total number of collective farms was decreasing due to amalgamations, the number of state farms was increasing. Most of the "virgin lands" opened up in Kazakhstan and Siberia during the fifties have been organized as state farms since no collective farm could be expected to bear the great risks involved in tilling these marginal areas. In addition, the Soviet government has encouraged existing collective farms to pay their members in advance of the harvest on a regular salaried basis and, in some cases, collective farms have been formally reorganized as state farms. As a result of these developments, the total

---

of the United States and Soviet Economies, Part I, p. 271. At these higher prices, the deliveries eventually shifted from a compulsory to a voluntary basis.

[15] See *Narodnoe Khoziaistvo 1959,* p. 325.

[16] For some of the difficulties involved in comparing costs of production on sovkhozy and kolkhozy, see Alec Nove, *The Soviet Economy,* Praeger, New York, 1961, pp. 183, *et seq.*

number of state farms rose from 4,858 in 1953 to 7,400 by January 1, 1961. At present the average acreage for state farms runs around 58,000 acres compared to less than 6,000 acres for the average collective farm. Despite the growing importance of the state farms, collective farms still cultivate about two-thirds of all plowland.

In 1958 a decision was made to break up the Machine Tractor Stations and the pooled agricultural equipment was sold to the individual collective farms. In a relatively short space of time, almost 8,000 of these enterprises were disbanded and replaced by 3,500 technical-repair stations designed primarily to service the machinery now owned and held by the collective farms. By 1960 there were only 34 Machine Tractor Stations still in existence.

The demise of the Machine Tractor Stations undoubtedly reflected the more plentiful supply of capital available to the agricultural sector as well as greater confidence in the political reliability of the farmers. In the early thirties, when these institutions were organized, the supply of capital in the agricultural sector was short and the farmers were of doubtful political inclination. As the supply of capital improved, the practice of pooling scarce capital was no longer as necessary and the institution has tended to disappear in the Soviet Union. In Czechoslovakia, which is also fairly well advanced industrially, the Machine Tractor Stations have been quietly dissolved.[17] But in Bulgaria and Rumania, which are comparatively underdeveloped noncapitalist-oriented economies, the stations were retained, possibly as a reflection of both the shortage of capital and the somewhat doubtful political reliability of the farmers. However, reports indicate that Bulgarian collective farms will soon begin to buy the farm equipment of certain Machine Tractor Stations.[18]

Because the agricultural machinery of the Machine Tractor Stations was sold to the collective farms—either for cash or on credit, if the farm was too poor—some of the added income resulting from the new higher agricultural procurement prices

[17] Paul Underwood, "Czechs Skeptical of Soviet Plans," *New York Times*, May 6, 1959, p. 13.

[18] See *East Europe*, April, 1962, pp. 38–39.

was undoubtedly taken back by the government. In addition, new agricultural machinery is now being sold rather than given to the collective farms. This is in contrast to the existing practice with respect to investment in machinery for industrial enterprises which comes out of the government budget with no charge to the enterprise.[19] On balance, however, it seems clear that there has been a sharp increase in capital investment in agriculture. From 1956 to 1960, agricultural investment amounted to 27.2 billion rubles compared with 13.9 billion in the previous five years.[20] This added capital, coupled with the greater personal incentives to persons employed in the agricultural sector, has produced some improvement in the total agricultural picture. According to the official Soviet claims, total agricultural output in 1960 was 61 per cent higher than it averaged in the period 1949 to 1953.[21]

Despite these recent advances made by Soviet agriculture, it seems clear that labor productivity in the Soviet agricultural sector is still very much lower than it is on the farms in the United States. The Soviets only claim that labor productivity in their agricultural sector is 20 to 30 per cent of ours, and it is quite possible that their productivity is as low as one-sixth of ours.[22] Furthermore, although labor productivity in Soviet agriculture has apparently been rising by over five per cent per an-

[19] Poland seems to be an exception in this regard since Galbraith claims that the Poles are using an accounting rate of interest of between seven and 10 per cent. See his *Journey to Poland and Yugoslavia,* Harvard University Press, Cambridge, 1958, p. 41.

[20] N. S. Khrushchev, *Documents of the Twenty-second Congress of the CPSU,* Vol. I, Crosscurrents Press, New York, 1961, p. 89.

[21] *SSSR v tsifrakh v 1960 godu* (The USSR in Figures in 1960), Gosstatizdat, Moscow, 1961, p. 173.

[22] For Russian claims, see A. Aganbegian, *"Dognat' i peregnat' SShA po urovniu proizvoditel'nosti truda"* (To Reach and Surpass the Level of Labor Productivity of the United States), *Sotsialisticheskii Trud,* No. 4, 1959, p. 11. For our estimate, see *Soviet Economic Growth: A Comparison with the U.S.,* U.S. Government Printing Office, Washington, 1957, p. 73. According to Ia. Ioffe, *"Uroven' proizvoditel'nosti truda v SSSR i v SSHA"* (The Level of Labor Productivity in the U.S.S.R. and in the U.S.A.), *Planovoe Khoziaistvo,* No. 3, 1960, p. 53, output per worker in Soviet agriculture was one third of the U.S. level of productivity in 1958.

num, our own agricultural labor productivity has also been growing by roughly this same percentage so that the relative inefficiency and backwardness of Soviet agriculture persists.[23]

The very low productivity of labor in Soviet agriculture is certainly a reflection of the fact that not only is the capital available per farmer low, but also that a sizeable rural overpopulation or disguised unemployment still persists on Soviet farms. It is also one explanation for the fact that so much apparently obsolete capital (at least by our standards) still remains in operation in Soviet industry and why so little capital replacement has as yet taken place there. Despite the antiquated nature of much Soviet industrial plant and equipment, workers employed in these backward sectors and using these outdated machines are undoubtedly contributing more to the total product of the Soviet economy than they would contribute were they working in what is currently their most likely alternative employment back in the agricultural sector. It might also be added that this relatively obsolete capital equipment in the factories also serves as a comparatively inexpensive training ground for raw recruits fresh from the countryside.

There are a number of other reasons for the relative lag in Soviet agriculture with respect to productivity, not the least of which is the fact that the natural agricultural resources of the USSR are not particularly well suited for the best results. Much of Soviet wheat production takes place in areas where the growing season is short, and soil and climatic conditions are similar to those found in the Dakotas, Montana, and in Western Canada. In the newly cultivated "virgin lands," where over 90 million

---

[23] According to V. Mashenkov and P. Minakov, *"Rezervy rosta proizvoditel'nosti truda v sel'skom khoziaistve"* (Reserves for the Growth of Labor Productivity in Agriculture), *Planovoe Khoziaistvo,* No. 1, 1959, p. 91, recent and planned changes in Soviet agricultural labor productivity are as follows:

Annual Increases in Labor Productivity

Type of Organization	1951–53	1954–58	1959–65 (Plan)
Collective farms	5.1%	6.4%	10.4%
State farms	5.1%	6.2%	6.5% to 6.9%

acres were opened up over a five-year period in the fifties, rainfall is unreliable and satisfactory crops can probably be expected in only about two or three of every five years.[24]

The poverty of Russian agricultural resources, incidentally, may have been partly responsible for its noncapitalistic operation even before the Revolution. In Czarist times, a rural cooperative organization called the *mir* or commune undertook a periodic reallotment of land as well as a redistribution of tax liabilities among the peasant families in rural settlements. In the West, particularly in the poorer regions of the United States and Canada, agricultural cooperatives also developed more frequently than they did in our more fertile farming areas in an attempt to spread the risks of dry farming in these areas. Likewise, in Bulgaria, Poland, and Yugoslavia, there was a prerevolutionary tradition of buyers' and sellers' cooperatives which may also reflect the poor quality of their soil for agricultural purposes.[25] A fairly convincing case can be made for the hypothesis that the uncertain nature of farming operations in some agricultural areas of the world has been more conducive to cooperative or collective farm organizations as compared with regions with fertile soil and plentiful rainfall. At any rate, there was something of a prerevolutionary precedent for both the collective farms that have dominated Soviet and Bulgarian agriculture, and for the looser cooperative organizations currently being utilized by the noncapitalist-oriented regimes in Poland and Yugoslavia.

Except for postrevolutionary Chinese—and perhaps Cuban—developments, agriculture seems to be the last sector to be fully collectivized in noncapitalist-oriented economies. The difficulties associated with socializing agriculture may be due to the fact that Marx did not sing his siren song for the benefit of the peasants. After all, it was somewhat more difficult to convince

[24] During the first five years, the virgin lands have produced three good crops and one fair one. However, the crop has declined steadily between 1958 and 1961. See Harry Schwartz, "Harvest Worry Rising in Soviet," *New York Times,* September 20, 1962, p. 9.

[25] In this connection, see M. S. Handler, "Bulgarians Add to Irrigated Land," *New York Times,* February 22, 1959, p. 33.

farmers that they were divorced from their means of production since, in a good many cases, they owned them even if they were relatively small plots of land and primitive farm implements. Marx predicted that the revolution would occur first in the most industrially advanced countries and thus did very little theorizing about the eventual socialization of agriculture, not to mention the extraction of the agricultural surplus. As a matter of fact, he left the Russians with virtually no roadmap for socializing industry either.

Despite the lack of Marxist guide lines, it is fairly clear that the Russians know where they are going in agriculture. The recent conversions of some collective farms into state farms would seem to indicate that the days of the collective farm may be rather limited. The collective farmers are faced with increasing restrictions on their ability to sell the produce grown on their private plots in the neighboring collective farm markets.[26] In some cases, the farmers are being urged to give up their private plots altogether so that they may devote all of their time to the collective. The recent attempts to revive the *agrogorod* or small agricultural settlement of apartment-type dwellings surrounded by some of the urban cultural amenities seem to point in the same direction.[27]

The Soviet farmer of the distant future will no doubt live in an agricultural settlement where conditions will be virtually indistinguishable from those of his urban counterpart. Until communism or their affluent society is achieved, the farmer will receive a fixed salary plus bonuses related to productivity from the agricultural collective, and he will be covered by the state

[26] A decree of February 26, 1961, limited the direct sales of surplus produce from the individual plots to the collective farm markets and required that sales be made to consumers' cooperatives instead. See *Pravda,* February 26, 1961, p. 2 or *The Current Digest of the Soviet Press,* March 22, 1961, p. 9. This decree was undoubtedly aimed at reducing the time wasted by the peasant haggling with customers in the collective farm markets.

[27] See *New York Times,* May 14, 1959, p. 5 and May 17, 1959, p. 2 for Premier Khrushchev's suggestions for expanding apartment houses and public utilities for rural villages. A more recent article appeared in the *New York Times,* February 19, 1961, p. 108.

social security system. While he may engage in gardening as a hobby, it seems doubtful that the collective farm market will continue as an outlet for his surplus produce. In most noncapitalist-oriented economies, there will undoubtedly be different paths to this same objective, and the rate of change may be determined by local conditions, but the ultimate objective would seem to be quite similar.

AGRICULTURAL DEVELOPMENTS IN CAPITALIST-ORIENTED ECONOMIES

In comparison with the Soviet Union, agriculture in the United States has been developing under somewhat different conditions. Our agricultural development has taken place, in large part, on more richly endowed farmlands and, furthermore, it has been unencumbered by any serious rural overpopulation. In addition wars seem to have done comparatively little damage to our agricultural investments and resources, in sharp contrast to the effects of recent wars on Soviet territory.

Despite these important differences, a basic similarity exists between the agricultural sectors of the two countries: industrialization has been financed to some extent in both countries by the extraction of an agricultural surplus. Except for periods of war and its immediate aftermath, our farmers have also tended to be exploited, subtly of course, as a consequence of the farmers' position on the lower blade of the internal price scissors. This was particularly true in the latter part of the nineteenth century when the terms of trade seemed to move chronically against the American farmer, partly as a consequence of monopolistic price-fixing on the part of our rapidly growing industrial trusts. Again in the decade after World War I, our agricultural sector failed to share in the general prosperity of the country. Although our economy as a whole suffered in the thirties, the difficulties of our farmers in the midwestern dust bowls seemed to have surpassed the plight of urban dwellers during the Great Depression.

The economic position of the American farmer improved enormously as a result of the increased food consumption during both World Wars, and farm income has remained fairly high since World War II as a result of the full or near-full employment conditions which have continued during the late forties and fifties throughout the Western world. Nevertheless, as farm families entered the sixties, they could look back on a period of declining incomes since the Korean conflict, with the result that their average incomes were lower relative to nonfarm incomes than at any time since the thirties. In addition, the production of more types of agricultural products seem to be coming under the restrictive output arrangements organized by the Department of Agriculture under the Agriculture Marketing Agreement Act of 1937.

Despite this decline in farm incomes, increases in man-hour productivity during the past twenty years have been about three times greater for agricultural workers than they have been for their nonfarm counterparts. Farm output per man-hour has increased three-fold in the past twenty years, and it has almost doubled in the last ten years. As a result of increased applications of capital and technology, it has been possible for the progressive sectors of agriculture to maintain fairly profitable operations to a great extent as a result of falling costs, rather than via rising prices. Where productivity gains have been on the low side and where prices have been especially weak—and political lobbies correspondingly strong—government price supports have also tended to keep some farm incomes from falling too drastically. But in general, agricultural supports have as yet been confined to a fairly small number of select crops so that the overall terms of trade are still largely operating against the agricultural sector of our own economy.

As in the case of the Soviet Union, higher urban levels of living have resulted from the operation of the internal price scissors and have stimulated the emigration of our rural population to the industrial areas. However, in periods of serious industrial unemployment, this rural exodus has slowed down or even been reversed, as was the case in the thirties. In some of our more fertile agricultural areas, particularly those that have also benefited from government price supports, levels of living in rural areas may be approaching those in the cities. But generally speaking, some of our worst pockets of poverty remain in the agricultural sector. In 1958, for example, over a million farm families had incomes of less than $2,000.

The family unit is still the basis of our agricultural organization, despite the fact that corporate commercial farming has made some headway in recent years. Large corporate farms still account for no more than one per cent of the total farm acreage, although the large commercial operators account for a quarter of total farm output and agricultural experts predict that corporate farming will expand, partly in response to ever greater capital requirements for profitable agricultural operations. A typical contemporary corporate farm in the United States might be responsible for the cultivation of 5,000 acres of rich Iowa farm land or almost the size of an average collective farm in the Soviet Union.

There has been a sharp increase in the average size of farms in the United States, partly as a result of this growing trend towards corporate farming. In the past twenty years, the average farm size has risen almost 75 per cent or from about 174 acres in 1940 to 302 acres in 1959. The growing mechanization of agricultural operations has also permitted larger family-operated commercial farms, which account for over one-half of all farm output, to continue their profitable existence alongside the corporate commercial farms.[28]

Greater mechanization also underlies the decline in the employment of hired hands, as evidenced by the fact that there were on the average only 1.9 million persons so classified in 1960 as compared with about 3.3 million between 1910 and 1930. In some areas, great reliance is still placed on the use of migrant

[28] Nevertheless, concern for the future of the family farm is strong enough to justify the creation of a 25-member national Agricultural Advisory Commission to propose national policies for saving this traditional agricultural unit. See "A Board Surveys the Family Farm," *New York Times,* July 22, 1962, p. 41.

workers and their families who follow the crops eking out a pitiful existence.[29] But even here farm mechanization, stimulated by the growing threat of the extension of minimum wage legislation to farm workers and union attempts to organize these workers, will probably cut into our future migrant labor requirements. For example, experimental mechanized tomato pickers costing $12,000 each have recently been tested and reportedly can be operated at a labor cost of $2 per ton compared with a cost of around $7.50 per ton for hand labor.[30]

Latest census reports show that 80 per cent of our farms now use tractors compared with 63 per cent a decade earlier. Our tractor supply now totals over five million units compared with a little less than two million units in the Soviet Union in 1960.[31] Similarly, there have been substantial increases in our stock of trucks, grain combines, other harvesters, mechanical hay balers, and milking machines.

In addition to new types and increasing supplies of farm machinery, other ingenious applications of capital and scientific research are now being employed in our agricultural sector. Air-conditioning, for example, now permits our hens to lay more eggs and our contented cows to give more milk during the warm summer months. Broiler chickens, hogs, and cattle also fatten more quickly when they enjoy controlled temperatures. Our Agriculture Extension Services also encourage farmers to take advantage of improved production practices, better seeds, more and better fertilizer, irrigation via sprinkler systems, and pesticides. Among the more startling scientific developments has been the recent experimentation with "multi-eared corn" by our agricultural scientists. According to some early tests, yields as high

[29] The 100,000 children of migrant laborers, whose average family earnings are less than $1,000 per annum, now receive on the average the equivalent of less than a fourth grade education, the minimum standard for literacy in the United States.

[30] *New York Times,* September 4, 1960, p. 70.

[31] On July 1, 1960, there were 1,921,000 units (in terms of 15 horsepower units) according to *SSSR v tsifrakh v 1960 godu* (The USSR in Figures in 1960), p. 172. The annual rate of increase in the Soviet Union is running around 250,000 units.

as 163 bushels per acre have been obtained, compared with the current average yield of slightly over 60 bushels per acre, which itself represents a 37 per cent increase in productivity per acre during the past decade.[32]

The future development of United States farming seems to lie in the direction of a continued reduction of our labor force engaged in agriculture and an increase in the scale of operations. According to official estimates, by 1970 total farm employment may be down to four million persons or less, compared with a total employment of slightly over seven million in 1960, which itself represented a 25 per cent reduction in the past decade. The chief factor which could conceivably hold up the relentless rural exodus would quite possibly be the growing industrial unemployment. The greater capital requirements for efficient farm operations should also accelerate the growth in the scale of operations and the need for incorporation. In some cases, shares of common stock are being offered to the public to finance operations approaching the $1 million mark.[33] It is estimated that in Iowa—which is considered to be typical of other farm states—172,000 present day farms will be consolidated into 95,000 units by 1975. In view of the tax and limited liability advantages now associated with incorporation, it can be presumed that at least some of the contemporary differences between agricultural and industrial organization will tend to disappear in the United States, just as they are being eliminated in the Soviet Union.[34]

It seems quite certain that our rapidly growing total agricultural output will continue to exceed our slowly increasing domestic requirements in the future. Thus, we are faced with

[32] See Roger A. Simpson, "Scientists Lift Corn Yields While Kennedy Strives to Cut Glut," *Wall Street Journal,* January 31, 1962, p. 1.

[33] For an account of the prospectus for a large automated production of hogs raised on concrete from "farrowing to market," see William M. Blair, "Two Iowans Seeking to Finance Automated Production of Hogs," *New York Times,* April 20, 1960, p. 31.

[34] In 1959 a change in the Internal Revenue Code made it possible for a closely held farm to incorporate and reap the advantages of incorporation—such as limited liability—while being taxed like a partnership instead of at high corporate rates. See Donald Janson, "Large Iowa Farm Typifies a Trend," *New York Times,* April 2, 1961, p. 53.

growing farm surpluses, lower relative farm incomes, and greater internal pressure to continue and expand the feeding and clothing of the unfortunates in the developing areas of the world at a nominal charge to the recipients.

As the service sector of our economy continues to grow at its phenomenal pace, we may expect agricultural income and product to continue their relative decline as components of total income and product. At the present time, agriculture accounts for only about five per cent of our total income and product. Likewise, agricultural labor should also continue to decline in relative importance from its present position, where it accounts for roughly eight per cent of our total labor requirements.

REFLECTION OF BASIC PROBLEMS IN AGRICULTURAL DEVELOPMENTS

The basic complementary problems of the two economies are most clearly reflected in the agricultural policies, practices, and institutions of the two societies. Our government's agricultural policy is by and large directed towards attempting to keep down our internally marketable agricultural product via soil banks, quotas, crop destruction, political gifts abroad such as "Food for Peace," subsidized sales abroad under Title I of Public Law 480, etc.[35] In addition, internal food consumption is artificially stimulated by free school lunches, free distribution of surplus foods, or the use of food stamp plans, not to mention public relations campaigns designed to encourage people to drink more milk.

The Russians, on the other hand, are straining every muscle to increase their productivity and agricultural supplies. They are expanding their area of cultivation into marginally productive

[35] Government agricultural research and dissemination of information on the improvement of farming methods—which were largely initiated before World War I when we still suffered from scarcity problems rather than abundance—are of course inconsistent with the major share of our present day agricultural policy, which is inspired by our persistent problems of oversupply.

areas; we have been spending millions of dollars to take our poorer land out of cultivation. While low agricultural productivity is their principal problem, ours is one of too great productivity in relation to our effective demand for most products. Rural overpopulation is still plaguing the Russians, while we are experiencing too rapid a release of surplus farmhands in relation to our industrial labor requirements. Whereas we are dumping our surplus agricultural products abroad at prices which are well below those charged internally, they are paying premium prices for imported agricultural produce from the developing areas. While they are investing billions of rubles to insure the fact that their per capita agricultural output will surpass ours, we are also spending billions to curb our output and thereby guarantee the same end result. Under these diametrically opposed operating conditions, crop failures resulting from "acts of God" are commonly regarded as a blessing in disguise in the United States, while they still cause grave concern and distress in noncapitalist-oriented economies generally, as has been demonstrated in mainland China in the early sixties.

In underdeveloped capitalist-oriented economies, crop failures are also of some concern, although United States agricultural surpluses can usually be relied upon in such emergencies. If the crop failure affects an export crop, such as sugar or coffee, it may simply reduce the unexportable surplus above the export quota allocated by some international commodity agreement. Or it may result in higher world market prices for the smaller amount exportable, so that total foreign sales revenue and foreign exchange may remain virtually unchanged as a result of such calamities.

Recommended Readings

MAURICE DOBB, *Soviet Economic Development Since 1917,* Routledge and Kegan Paul, London, 1948, Chapters 7 through 9. (Includes material on so-called "scissors crisis.")

ALEXANDER ERLICH, "Preobrajenski and the Economics of Soviet Industrialization," *Quarterly Journal of Economics,* February, 1950, pp. 57–88.

*———, "Stalin's Views on Economic Development," from Ernest Simmons, editor, *Continuity and Change in Russian and Soviet Thought,* Harvard University Press, Cambridge, 1955, pp. 81–99.

NAUM JASNY, "The Soviet Statistical Yearbooks, 1955–1960," *Slavic Review,* March, 1962, especially pp. 141–148.

*D. GALE JOHNSON and ARCADIUS KAHAN, "Soviet Agriculture: Structure and Growth," *Comparisons of the United States and Soviet Economies,* Part I, pp. 201–237.

NANCY NIMITZ, "Soviet Agricultural Prices and Costs," in *Comparisons of the United States and Soviet Economies,* Part I, pp. 239–284.

ALEC NOVE, "Was Stalin Really Necessary?" *Encounter,* April, 1962, pp. 86–92.

*LAZAR VOLIN, "Agricultural Policy of the Soviet Union," in *Comparisons of the United States and Soviet Economies,* Part I, pp. 285–318.

*———, "The Peasant Household Under the Mir and Kolkhoz in Modern Russian History," from Caroline Ware, editor, *The Cultural Approach to History,* Columbia University Press, New York, 1940, pp. 125–139.

WALTER W. WILCOX and WILLARD W. COCHRANE, *Economics of American Agriculture,* Second edition, Prentice-Hall, Inc., Englewood Cliffs, New Jersey, 1960, especially Chapter 17, "Agriculture in a Dynamic, Developed Economy."

WALTER W. WILCOX, "Agriculture's Income and Adjustment Problem," in *Economic Policies for Agriculture in the 1960's,* Joint Economic Committee, United States Government Printing Office, Washington, 1960.

VI ⚮ Levels of Living

NOWHERE IS THE CONTRAST between capitalist and noncapitalist-oriented economies more obvious to the casual observer than it is in the area of distribution. The buyer's market which typifies advanced capitalist-oriented economies in peacetime results in the following features: a large number of shops filled with attractively displayed consumers' goods; polite sales personnel making absolutely certain that the "customer is always right"; an almost infinite variety of products from which to choose; and clever promotional gimmicks designed to entice consumers into parting with their money. In contrast, the chronic seller's market found in all noncapitalist-oriented economies is frequently characterized by too few retail outlets; stores which are poorly stocked with comparatively shoddy merchandise; a relative lack of consumers' choice as to color or model; erratic supplies and either occasional or frequent queues.

There are also major institutional differences with respect to the principles of distributing goods and services in the two types of economies. In general, there is a much broader range of free or partially subsidized services provided by the state in noncapitalist-oriented economies. As a result of this large sector of communal consumption, the distribution of medical and dental services, education, public transportation, and housing tends to be more or less egalitarian in the noncapitalist-oriented economies. However, as we shall see in Chapter VII (p. 133), wage incomes in these economies are highly differentiated with the result that there is considerable inequality in the distribution of those goods and services which are priced at levels designed to ration their inadequate supply.

93

The growing relative importance of this communal consumption sector in the noncapitalist-oriented economies complicates the problem of measuring improvements in the levels of living within these societies over time. In addition, since the relative growth of the so-called public sector—with the exception of the defense establishment—is as yet not being duplicated in the United States, it is becoming increasingly difficult to make comparisons between levels of living in the two major examples of contemporary economic systems at any given time.

CHANGES IN LEVELS OF LIVING WITHIN NONCAPITALIST-ORIENTED ECONOMIES

The transition from a capitalist to a noncapitalist orientation has usually resulted in some initial deterioration or stagnation in levels of living. An initial phase of inflation, rationing, and austerity has usually been experienced as a result of any or all of the following factors: internal opposition from elements inherited from the previous regime; hostile activities originating outside the country; inexperience in planning and managing the economy; and a sharp increase in investment or defense activities, which do not contribute to present consumer welfare.

The experiences of the Soviet economy after the introduction of the First Five-Year Plan in 1928 are perhaps also to some extent illustrative of what has occurred in Eastern Europe after World War II and of what is currently taking place in mainland China and Cuba. By 1928 Soviet consumption had more or less returned to prerevolutionary levels, following the sharp decline in living conditions resulting from the disruptive effects of World War I and its aftermath.[1] A certain amount of growing unemployment existed, and per capita urban housing space, although inadequate by our standards, was fairly satisfactory, at least in comparison with the subsequent housing situation. Although

[1] See Abram Bergson, *The Real National Income of Soviet Russia Since 1928*, Harvard University Press, Cambridge, 1961, p. 8.

Russian women had always been relatively important as a component of the labor force, generally speaking they still maintained their more traditional role as homemakers at the start of the planning era.

As the government investment projects of Plan I began to take shape, the unemployed labor was absorbed into the active labor force, overfull employment conditions developed, and it became practicable to eliminate unemployment insurance as an institution. The rapid collectivization of agriculture resulted in serious disruptions within the agricultural sector, including the wholesale slaughtering of livestock by recalcitrant peasants who had been investing their grain surpluses in livestock since the scissors crisis. Job openings and comparatively higher levels of living in the cities attracted large numbers of displaced peasants into the urban areas where they entered the nonagricultural labor force.[2] Since the state investment plans gave priority to heavy industry over consumers' goods industries, including housing construction, there was a marked deterioration in both the availability of consumers' goods and the amount of urban housing space per capita. Although money wages rose rapidly, the consumers' price level—especially for agricultural products sold on the free market—increased at a still faster rate and real wages declined sharply.[3] In order to prevent unnecessary hardship and starvation among those earning subsistence wages, an extensive system of rationing was introduced in 1929–30 and continued in effect until 1935.

As a result of the urban labor shortage created by the demands of the government's huge investment program and the concomitant decline in real wages—or what the chief breadwinner could

[2] According to the calculations of Oleg Hoeffding, real per capita income of urban households was about 1.7 times as large as real per capita income of rural households. See his *Soviet National Income and Product in 1928,* Rand R-255, Rand Corporation, Santa Monica, California, 1954, p. 68.

[3] Real wage changes are calculated by deflating or dividing the change in money wages by the change in a so-called cost-of-living index. If there is a decline in the consumers' price level, as there was in the Soviet Union between 1947 and 1954, the change in money wages must of course be inflated to obtain the change in real wages.

buy with his take-home pay—there was a large influx of former housewives into the labor force as Soviet families attempted to maintain previously attained levels of living. Some improvement was registered in the consumption sector during Plan II (1933–37), but it seems clear from Dr. Chapman's extensive studies that real wages in 1937 were still well below their level in 1928, and that per capita consumption generally, including communal services, was only slightly above the preplan level.

During this initial period of austerity, there were violent shifts in the structure of consumers' purchases. In particular, meat and fats tended to drop out of many consumer budgets and, in their place, calorific requirements were increasingly obtained from potatoes and sugar. Because of this drastic change in the consumption-mix, the calculation of price indexes for this early period is significantly affected by the choice of a weighting system. If a 1928 weighting system is employed—rather than one of a later year such as 1937—any increase in Soviet real wages tends to be minimized (or any decrease maximized).

As was mentioned in Chapter III, this phenomenon is due to the fact that consumers tend to "beat" the cost-of-living index to the extent that up-to-date weights are not employed. All prices of consumers' goods do not rise or fall in the same proportion. On the average, consumers tend to increase their relative consumption of items with lower-than-average price increases (or greater-than-average price declines) and reduce their relative consumption of products or services with greater-than-average price increases (or lower-than-average price declines). Since the cost-of-living index is a weighted average of the individual price relatives for all items consumed, the more recent or up-to-date the weighting system, the greater the weight that will be assigned to the lower price relatives. As a consequence, there will be a lower cost-of-living index as compared with the results obtained with an earlier year weighting system. Thus, when a 1928 weighting system is used to calculate a Soviet cost-of-living index, the rise in the consumers' price level is emphasized and the decline in real wages during the first two Five-Year Plans is considerably greater than it is when a 1937 weighting system is employed. According to Dr. Chapman's calculations, the decline in real wages, including health and education benefits, between 1928 and 1937 is 37 per cent when a 1928 weighting system is employed and only 12 per cent when a 1937 weighting system is used.[4]

After 1937 there was a brief period when levels of living may still have been rising but increased defense expenditures prior to World War II—including military operations in the Finnish War during the winter of 1939-40—began to cut into consumption by 1940 and rationing was reinstituted in that year. Living conditions declined sharply following the Nazi attack and the ensuing scorched earth policy, with the result that per capita consumption was probably still at least one-third below the 1937 level by the end of the war. Rationing was abolished by the end of 1947, and the prewar levels of consumption were again attained by 1950. During the fifties, the rate of increase in Soviet consumption was pretty much on a par with that of gross national product generally. As a result of this doubling of consumption in the fifties, per capita consumption—including communal consumption—is today more than double what it was before the planned industrialization drive. Nevertheless, real wages in the early sixties were only slightly higher than they were in 1928.

Two principal factors underlie this interesting dichotomy between the magnitude and direction of the changes in real wages

[4] Dr. Chapman's original calculations were presented in "Real Wages in the Soviet Union, 1928–52," *Review of Economics and Statistics,* May, 1954, p. 150. It can of course be argued that some consumer satisfaction or utility is lost in the process of substituting starches and carbohydrates for proteins, as was the case in the Soviet Union between 1928 and 1937. But in the case of less drastic substitutions, such as the widespread replacement of butter by margarine in the United States pattern of consumption since the thirties, it would be difficult to prove that consumers' health or satisfaction has been significantly affected. In general, consumers at lower and middle income levels in capitalist-oriented economies tend to go shopping with their eyes on prices and "specials" for the week so that the actual consumption-mix for any given week is comparatively flexible depending upon what retailers are featuring. Whether this flexibility with respect to substitution between products on the part of consumers results in less satisfaction is certainly questionable.

and per capita consumption in the Soviet Union. Overall consumption rose primarily because of greater labor participation rates—principally working wives and senior citizens—and also because of the rural exodus which enabled a steadily growing share of the total population to enjoy the relatively higher levels of living provided outside agriculture.

With the improvement in Soviet levels of living there have been gradual changes in the consumption-mix away from rye bread and potatoes and towards more fruit, milk and dairy products, and meat. In other words, the changes in the structure of consumption between 1928 and 1937 are being reversed as levels of living rise. In addition, except at very low income levels, there has been a tendency for food to account for a decreasing share of the budgetary expenditures, and for clothing and durable consumers' goods to assume an increased relative importance. According to recent Soviet budget studies, the greatest income elasticity of demand—or responsiveness of consumers to higher incomes—is to be found in the case of cultural and educational goods and services, and for manufactured goods generally.[5] Only at lower income levels is the increase in income being taken in the form of significantly greater food consumption. The average Russian consumer today certainly does not suffer from lack of calories, although he may suffer from a certain monotony in his diet, especially in the winter months when fresh foods are in scarce supply. His greatest sources of complaint with respect to living conditions, however, are no doubt still to be found in the lack of attractively designed clothing and durable consumers' goods, delays in repairing the durable consumers' goods he obtains, and, especially, the lack of housing space. On a per capita basis, housing is still only slightly above the preplan level, despite considerably greater investment priorities for housing construction since 1957.

One of the most difficult but important things to take into account in measuring changes in levels of living is the increase in collective or communal consumption in the Soviet Union.

[5] For a report of some recent Soviet budget studies, see *Problems of Economics,* Vol. IV, No. 4, August, 1961, pp. 1–22.

Professor Bergson's calculations of real outlays for health care and education indicate that there was more than a seven-fold increase in these communal services between 1928 and 1955.[6] The increase in Soviet education expenditures shows up primarily in school enrollment between grades five through the university, where the increase was six-fold between 1928 and 1958. The number of doctors and hospital beds per capita have increased over four-fold; if quality improvement could be taken into account, the overall gain would have been even more impressive. Already there are more Soviet doctors per ten thousand inhabitants than there are in Western countries.[7] Although some provision had already been made by 1928 for temporary compensation (due to illness, accident, pregnancy, and childbirth), for permanent disability insurance, and for insurance protecting dependent survivors of deceased insured workers, old-age insurance for all wage earners and salaried employees was only more slowly adopted during the thirties. The increasing number of workers covered by social insurance and the widespread grants and pensions of various sorts provided under the social assistance program have meant that pensions and allowances tended generally to increase as a percentage of household income after 1928. Pensions and allowances were only 3.2 per cent of household outlays for consumption in 1928, but were 10.4 per cent of these outlays in 1958 after the improvements provided by the new pension law of 1956.[8]

There is considerable variation in the provision of these communal services in the various noncapitalist-oriented economies, depending on their stages of development. If we take social and cultural expenditures provided out of the government budget as a percentage of total budgetary expenditures in 1960, we find

[6] Abram Bergson, *op. cit.,* pp. 64, 66.

[7] In 1960 there were 18.6 doctors per 10,000 population in the USSR compared with 13.3 in the United States in 1959. It should be pointed out that roughly three-fourths of the Soviet doctors are women and the average quality of Soviet doctors is below that in the United States.

[8] Figures are based on Abram Bergson, *op. cit.,* and preliminary figures from forthcoming study by Nancy Nimitz on Soviet national income in 1956–58.

that they accounted for anywhere from 12.3 per cent in the Chinese People's Republic to 39 per cent in Czechoslovakia.[9] In the USSR, the percentage allocated to education, health, and social security has risen steadily from 23.5 per cent of all budgetary expenditures in 1940 to 34.1 per cent in 1960. The Russians claim—and Western studies tend to bear out the fact—that about one-fourth of all consumers' income is currently being distributed without charge. By 1980 it is planned to expand this communal consumption to one-half of the total income by adding rent, utilities, noon meals, and transportation to the sphere of un-priced goods and services.

Most of the work that has been done on Soviet levels of living refers to the urban areas where only about one-half of all Soviet inhabitants live. It seems clear, however, that levels of living in rural areas are still well below those in the cities, despite the relatively greater improvements in the farmer's lot in the Khru-shchev era, and perhaps even over the entire period of planning. Per capita consumption of grain products and potatoes is known to be much higher on the farms; social security coverage is spotty at best; and durable consumers' goods are even less available in rural areas than they are in the cities. Only with respect to living space, where conditions are perhaps less cramped, does the Soviet farmer seem to be somewhat better off than his city counterpart.

CHANGES IN LEVELS OF LIVING IN CAPITALIST-ORIENTED ECONOMIES

In the United States, real per capita consumption increased by 55 per cent between 1929 and 1959—compared with the doubling which has taken place in the USSR during the same period—and it has taken us nearly the past fifty years to double our real per

---

[9] For a breakdown showing the importance of various sectors of the budget within the Soviet bloc, see A. G. Zverev, *Natsional'nyi dokhod i finansy SSSR* (National Income and Finances of the USSR), Gosfinizdat, Moscow, 1961, p. 186.

capita consumption.[10] However, our real per capita consumption approximately doubled between 1869 and 1895, so that the overall Soviet rate of growth in per capita consumption since 1928 is certainly not without precedent in capitalist-oriented economies. The most unusual aspect of this development of consumption in the Soviet Union—in comparison with improvements in levels of living in capitalist-oriented economies—is the relative withholding from consumers of the gains in total output for the first two decades, and the subsequent sharp increases in consumption which took place during the third decade.

The increases in per capita consumption in the United States during the period since 1929 have also been somewhat irregular, though less so than was the case in the Soviet Union. The percentage increases in the United States for the three decades were as follows: thirties, four per cent; forties, 30 per cent; and fifties, 15 per cent. The most significant difference between changes in consumption in the two economies during the past thirty years has been the opposite impact of World War II on levels of living. The war produced directly or indirectly—largely through the rapid deficit-financed expansion of effective demand and employment—the sharpest recent growth in our consumption, at the same time that it depressed levels of consumption in the Soviet Union. The same relatively different impact of the war is also to be found in West European capitalist-oriented economies which suffered in all respects as a consequence of World War II, but which have made very rapid progress in raising levels of living in the fifties.[11]

The relationship between gains in real wages and in real per capita consumption in our early economic history to some extent

---

[10] Data refer to personal consumption expenditures per capita in constant (1954) dollars. See *Statistical Abstract of the United States, 1961*, p. 301.

[11] The role of adequate effective demand in West European expansion in the fifties and a contrasting lack of effective demand which has retarded United States economic development in the fifties, is recognized by analysts of the twenty-nation Organization for Economic Co-operation and Development. See Edwin L. Dale, Jr., "United States Growth Lag is Tied to Demand," *New York Times*, April 11, 1962, p. 15.

resembles the above-mentioned corresponding Soviet developments. Between 1870 and 1929, real per capita consumption in the United States increased by over four times while real annual wages in manufacturing increased by only 2.6 times. The explanation for this dichotomy is also in part similar to that advanced above in connection with Soviet developments, namely, the rapid exodus of population from agriculture to industry— from an area of low productivity and consumption to one of higher productivity and consumption.

On the other hand, since 1929 there has been a reversal of the previous relationship between changes in our real wages and in our real per capita consumption. This new tendency for real wages to increase at a faster rate than per capita consumption was especially evident in both the thirties and fifties, whereas in the forties both series grew by about the same percentage. In the fifties, for example, real wages and salaries per employee man-hour grew by 33 per cent, while per capita personal consumption expenditures rose by 15 per cent.[12] It seems likely that the growing underutilization of our potential labor force is the principal factor underlying this changed relationship between the two series, although the slowdown in the rural exodus, greater saving by income recipients, and the tendency for agricultural incomes to fall relative to nonagricultural incomes are undoubtedly also contributing factors.

As in the Soviet Union, the operations of "Engel's Laws," describing as they do consumers' qualitative patterns of behavior, are quite evident in the United States.[13] At the turn of the century, the average United States worker spent most of his income on three basic requirements—food, shelter, and clothing. Since social security benefits were unknown, he also probably made some feeble attempts to "save for a rainy day." In the

[12] See *Statistical Abstract of the United States, 1961*, pp. 217, 301.

[13] The following information on changes in workers' and consumers' patterns of expenditures in the twentieth century is based, to a great extent, on the excellent summary of the U.S. Departmnt of Labor, *How American Buying Habits Change*, U.S. Government Printing Office, Washington, 1959.

representative family, 43 per cent of the total income went for food in 1901 compared to the 28.5 per cent weight assigned to the food component in the Bureau of Labor Statistics' Consumer Price Index in December, 1960. Transportation, which accounted for less than 2 per cent of total consumer expenditures in 1901, now absorbs almost 14 per cent of the worker's budget. Medical services accounted for 2.7 per cent of all expenditures at the turn of the century and now absorb 5.7 per cent of the total; recreation, education, and reading now account for 5.4 per cent compared with 2.7 per cent of the total in 1900. Rent, including fuel and light, has been comparatively stable as a component of total expenditures, accounting for between 20 and 25 per cent of the total in both periods, while clothing has declined relatively from 13.0 to 8.8 per cent of all expenditures in workers' and consumers' budgets.

Within these broad categories of expenditures there have been important changes in the consumption-mix. With respect to foods generally, the most significant relative change has been the decline in cereals and bakery products and their replacement by fresh or frozen fruits and vegetables (other than potatoes). The introduction of mass refrigeration and frozen foods generally has also minimized seasonal fluctuations in our consumption of the latter. A higher degree of food processing and a greater amount of dining out has also released the modern housewife from many formerly time-consuming jobs in the kitchen. The spread of information on diet and nutrition, coupled with the statistical evidence on the effects of overweight on life expectancy, has increased the diet-consciousness of many United States consumers. As a consequence, the average calorific intake in the United States fell slightly from 3,270 to 3,230 calories per day between 1935 and 1955. For those individuals with comparatively little will power, an important new service industry has also developed around the "science" of weight-reduction.

In the field of transportation, the advent of the automobile has literally revolutionized our mode of living. As recently as 1917–19, transit cost outlays represented only 1.8 per cent of average annual expenditures for current consumption. The subsequent development of the privately-owned automobile as a prestige symbol, and the ease with which it may be bought on instalment credit, has made it essential as well as possible for every family to possess one or more modern chariots. Accompanying the mass purchase of automobiles has been the concomitant development of character-less suburbia, each with their inevitable local shopping centers, resulting in both the decline of the former central business districts and the erosion of efficient public transportation.

The growth in the medical component of total expenditures reflects, among other things, the widespread adoption of health insurance, which at the same time has tended to reduce the former need to save in an unorganized manner for medical emergencies. The reduction of the work week by about 30 per cent since the turn of the century—coupled with longer paid vacations, more time spent in school, and earlier retirement— has created more voluntary leisure time and stimulated consumer demand for more education and recreation services, especially for travel. A system of unemployment insurance has reduced the impact of compulsory leisure and further lessened the need for consumer saving based on so-called "precautionary" motives. The elimination of some of the economic hazards to life has been at least partly responsible for the phenomenal growth of consumers' credit. Total consumer credit outstanding now accounts for about 16 per cent of total disposable personal income compared with 8 per cent in 1929.[14]

INTERNATIONAL COMPARISONS OF LEVELS OF LIVING AND PRICES

As a rough estimate, Soviet real per capita consumer income, including communal consumption, was about 35 per cent of the United States level in 1960. While this broad aggregative comparison is interesting, it nevertheless conceals certain wide vari-

[14] *Statistical Abstract of the United States, 1961*, pp. 306, 456.

ations in the relative importance of the various components of consumption in the two countries. As a result, we might look at some of the individual physical series connected with the consumption sector, as a reflection of the priorities which different societies may assign to the various factors commonly associated with levels of living in the process of development.

Our previous discussion of the relative stagnation in Soviet agriculture, as well as the constant references in current periodicals to the crisis affecting Soviet farming, might lead one to assume that Soviet consumers are rather poorly fed. On the contrary, the average calorific intake of Soviet consumers is probably higher than it is in the United States, and necessarily so, in view of the generally colder climate in the Soviet Union.[15] Whatever crisis there may be in Soviet agriculture shows up primarily in the pattern of food consumption and in the relatively large amount of resources tied up in the agricultural sector. The average Russian still consumes about three times as much flour and potatoes as his American counterpart, despite the fact that the per capita consumption of these two products seems to be declining. The typical Russian also consumes somewhat more fish than we do, and, while they may consume more butter than we do, we have an edge with respect to margarine, so that our overall fat intake is higher in the United States. Our consumption of milk and sugar is still somewhat superior to that of the Russians, but here the gap seems to be closing rapidly due to Premier Khrushchev's determined campaign to overtake us in milk consumption and the large-scaled imports of Cuban sugar since the American embargo. On the other hand, we consume over two or three times as much meat or eggs as the Russians.

Clothing and shelter are probably next to food in order of

[15] At the higher income levels the average food intake of Soviet citizens contains in excess of 3,500 calories daily. In contrast to the positive correlation between caloric intake and income in the Soviet Union, we find that in the United States, a study of obesity in New York showed that there is a negative correlation between overweight and income levels. Obesity was seven times more frequent among women of the lowest socioeconomic levels than it was among those from the highest level of income. See *New York Times,* September 14, 1962, p. 18.

priority for consumers, at least in areas subject to extremely low temperatures. Only in wool fabrics, however, do the Russians seem to have surpassed our per capita consumption, and this is undoubtedly explained by the relatively severe Russian climatic conditions. For most clothing items, our consumption is still nearly double that of the Russians; if quality is taken into account, the gap is still greater.

On the average we have four times as much living space per person as do the Russians. In the cities, their percentage of housing with electricity is almost as high as ours, but in the rural areas, electrification is less than half as prevalent as compared with the United States. The existing gap with respect to central heating, indoor plumbing, and telephones can only be described as enormous.

Once societies have solved their three basic requirements, they usually turn to durable consumers' goods, which are to a great extent produced exclusively in the nonagricultural sector. Only in such items as sewing machines, motorcycles, or bicycles does Soviet consumption compare favorably with our own. For most durable consumers' goods, the gap is on the order of 10 to 1, despite the fact that the Soviets are currently making their greatest progress in this sphere. In capitalist-oriented economies, this sector is subject to wide year-to-year fluctuations in consumers' demand and is considered to be a destabilizing factor with respect to the economy as a whole.

As consumer desires for durable consumers' goods become relatively satiated, the next stage seems to be the development of the service sector, and it is here that the Soviet consumers suffer most in comparison with the United States. Not only in the United States, but also in Great Britain and Sweden, more people are now employed in the service and distributive industries than in manufacturing.[16] Ordinary repair services, which most capitalist-oriented economies develop at an early stage, are comparatively underdeveloped in the Soviet Union.

[16] For an interesting account of the stabilizing effect of this development on advanced capitalist-oriented economies, see Nicholas A. H. Stacey, "A Commercial Revolution," *The Listener,* August 25, 1960.

In the stage of near-affluence, more and more people may opt for leisure in capitalist-oriented economies. In this respect, the Russian worker is already pretty much on a par with his American counterpart with respect to the compulsory work week—particularly if we consider his paid vacations—although he is expected to use his newly-acquired leisure for self-improvement activities, which the state hopes will increase his productivity per man-hour. The East European countries are lagging behind the Soviet Union in this respect, just as the West European countries are lagging behind the United States. In both parts of divided Europe, the 46 to 48-hour work week seems to be the norm.

Last but not least, emotional security with respect to ill health, old age, and unemployment, also becomes a possibility if not a necessity in advanced industrialized economies. It is here that the noncapitalist-oriented economies have made the greatest strides forward. Although the West European capitalist-oriented economies have also made progress in reducing these hazards, the United States seems to be lagging unnecessarily in this regard.

An expression of the number of minutes or hours it takes a worker to earn a given food or durable consumers' good item in two economies is an indicator of relative consumer welfare which superficially would seem to be a physical measurement of well-being. It is an index of relative welfare that is used frequently to cite the superiority of the workers' lot in capitalist-oriented economies. Western travelers in noncapitalist-oriented economies are frequently asked how many hours or days of labor is required to earn a given item (camera, auto, etc.), and the local inhabitants are duly impressed by the answers. According to a recent calculation by our Bureau of Labor Statistics, the average Moscow worker has to work much longer than the New York City worker to buy certain basic consumers' goods. For potatoes, he has to work about three times as long; for beef and milk, four times; for eggs, eight times; for butter, nine times; and for sugar, 21 times.[17]

[17] See Edmund Nash, "Purchasing Power of Workers in the USSR," *Monthly Labor Review,* April, 1960, p. 363.

Actually, the basis for such calculations is a money relationship rather than a real or physical one. In these United States government studies, ruble and dollar prices for various consumers' goods in the United States and the USSR are divided by the corresponding average wage in dollars or rubles to obtain the required working time in the two countries. As a hypothetical example, we might assume that the average hourly wage is two dollars in the United States, and 50 kopecks or half a ruble, in the USSR. With bread selling in the domestic markets for 20 cents and 5 kopecks, respectively, the working time required to buy a loaf of bread would be six minutes in each country.

Since such calculations simply measure the relationship between wage and price levels in the two countries, they are really not terribly meaningful, and, furthermore, they are becoming less so over time. We might easily imagine two countries with essentially comparable levels of living, but with vastly different relationships between their wage and price levels, depending on the importance of communal or partially-subsidized consumption and whether or not taxes are deducted from wages or included in the prices of consumers' goods. Since the USSR is gradually increasing the share of communal consumption over time, and is also apparently in the process of eliminating the income tax, it seems clear that such calculations as those of our Bureau of Labor Statistics are rapidly losing any validity they might once have had. In our capitalist-oriented economy, we tend to minimize communal consumption on the dual assumptions that production for profit promotes more efficient production methods, and that the practice of attaching prices to consumers' goods and services encourages their more economical use. We have also tended to prefer direct taxes, such as the income tax, in the twentieth century, since its so-called "progressiveness" is believed to be useful in redistributing incomes and thereby in serving to stimulate consumption and discourage saving for the economy as a whole. As a result of these institutional differences, as well as the high rate of expenditure for investment and defense, there is a huge "gap" between the production costs of Soviet consumers' goods (which are basically a reflection of the wage level) and the retail prices of the same products.

The meaningfulness of prices for food, clothing, and durable consumers' goods would seem to depend chiefly on the disposable income available for these purposes. It can probably be assumed that the average Russian family still has about 85 per cent of its gross pay intact after paying (or not paying) for such relatively inflexible requirements as shelter and household operations, medical and dental services, education, transportation, direct taxes, insurance, gifts, dues, and contributions. On the other hand, the average United States family has probably already disposed of close to 60 per cent of its gross income on these comparatively "fixed" expenditures. The reasons for this differential are that the Russians still rely primarily on public transportation; pay only about 5 per cent of their income for rent; [18] are in the process of eliminating the income tax; and pay little or nothing for medical and educational services. In Eastern Europe, these same institutional differences prevail, and even in Western Europe, a higher percentage of indirect taxation, partially subsidized housing and public transportation, and free medical services are all to be found, although not to the same extent as in the Soviet Union.

Assuming that the median family income in the United States is approximately $6,000 yearly and that a comparably representative Russian family might earn as much as 2,000 rubles per year, the disposable income available for food, clothing, durable consumers' goods, personal care, and recreation would amount to roughly $2,400 and 1,700 rubles, respectively.[19] In other words,

[18] For the relatively few Soviet citizens owning their own home, taxes, insurance, and miscellaneous expenditures bring up this percentage somewhat.

[19] In 1960, the median income of all United States families was about $5,600 according to United States Department of Commerce, *Current Population Reports—Consumer Income,* January 17, 1962, Series P-60, No. 37, p. 1. This figure is adjusted upward to exclude agricultural families and to make it more nearly comparable with the income of the representative Soviet family. Soviet family income is estimated on the basis

the representative United States family has about $1.40 for each ruble the Russian family has available for relatively "free spending" on these uses. To put it another way, the Soviet family has 70 per cent as many rubles as the American family has dollars for these out-of-pocket expenditures.

There are a number of ways in which we might use this rough calculation in order to get a clearer picture of the meaning of Soviet prices for food, clothing, durable consumers' goods, personal care, and recreation. If we multiply current Soviet price quotations by 1.4, we can obtain a fairly realistic idea of what the absolute and relative prices would look like to average American families with their present dollar disposable income for out-of-pocket expenses, that is, the dollar-equivalents of Soviet prices.[20] Or, conversely, we might imagine what it would be like to have 70 per cent of our present disposable income available for food, clothing and durable consumers' goods, and have to go shopping in markets with goods and services priced with current Soviet price-tags. Finally we might say that existing ruble prices would have to be on average about 70 per cent of our current dollar prices in order to have an equivalent purchasing power of the two currencies with respect to these day-to-day expenditures. A comparison of our current prices with the Soviet price quotations after January 1, 1961, presented in the accompanying Table VI-A

---

of the fact that the average income per member at the margin between relatively low-income and relatively middle-income families was 40 rubles per month in a recent budget analysis. Assuming a four-member family, the average monthly family income would be 160 rubles. On a yearly basis, this would amount to 1,920 rubles which is adjusted upward to take into account the fact that this was only the lower limit of the relatively middle-income family. See A. Aleshina and Ia. Kabachnik, "Some Results of an Experimental Survey of Worker Family Budgets," *Problems of Economics,* Vol. IV, No. 4, August, 1961, p. 4.

[20] Since the current official rate of exchange, which is unilaterally set by the Russians, values the ruble at $1.11, it would seem that the dollar is undervalued relative to the ruble at the official rate of exchange. On the other hand, if the prices of most producers' goods are converted at the official exchange rate, the dollar either appears to be overvalued, or else the exchange rate is much more realistic.

would show that most of these goods and services are more expensive for Russians than they are for Americans. Rye bread at 7 kopecks per pound would be equivalent to 9¢, or cheaper than it is in the United States. On the other hand, hamburger at 80 kopecks equals $1.12 per pound, while butter at 1.50 rubles is converted to a price of $2.10 per pound. It will be observed that bread, potatoes, salt fish, and cabbage are the best buys among the foodstuffs, and must comprise a good share of the diet at lower income levels. The prices of milk, fish, beef, liquors, and cigarettes are pretty much on a par with prices in our markets. At the other extreme, the prices for pork, butter, sugar, fresh fruits and vegetables, and all imported products (coffee, tea, and citrus fruit) are outlandish by our standards. Luckily, most Soviet workers and students are able to eat a rather substantial three-course noon meal at their school, institution, or factory cafeteria or restaurant for 50 to 60 kopecks, or the equivalent of 70 to 85¢ daily.

In comparison with the United States price structure, clothing is relatively much more expensive than food. Consumers' durables are not as expensive as we might have imagined. Since the prices of these items (except for automobiles) are more or less designed to ration their inadequate supply, it seems clear that not too much disposable income remains after the family's more pressing expenditures for food and clothing. The prices which are charged for renting the services of various durable consumers' goods are quite reasonable and, in view of the shortage of storage space in Soviet living quarters, such renting practices would seem to represent a sensible approach to the problem of obtaining the maximum use out of their limited consumers' capital. Likewise, the prices for recreation goods and services seem to be quite reasonable.

TABLE VI-A

Retail Prices for Food, Clothing, Consumer Durables, Personal Care
and Recreation, USSR, 1962

Food	Price (rubles per lb. or indicated unit)		Price (rubles per lb. or indicated unit)
Rye bread (pumpernickel)	.07	Squash (each)	.10 *
White bread	.13	Potatoes	.05–.14 *
Butter	1.50–1.64	Onions	.04–.09 *
Eggs (dozen)	1.20–1.56	Cucumbers	.23 *–1.00
Milk (quart)	.20	Beets (each)	.03 *
Sugar	.41	Radishes	.30
Margarine	.64	Carrots	.16
Fat (beef or pork)	1.14 *	Currants	.32
Cheese	1.27–1.55	Gooseberries	.36
Macaroni	.21	Crab apples	.18 *
Pot cheese	.55	Cherries	.23 *
Pork or ham	.86–1.09	Raspberries	.82 *
Lamb (first quality)	.86	Pears	.16 *
Lamb (second quality)	.68	Oranges	.64
Beef (first quality)	.91	Dates	.64
Beef (second quality)	.72	White raisins	.98
Duck	.86	Pistachios	.82
Turkey	1.25	Dried prunes	.75
Chicken	.75–1.20	Dried apricots	1.36 *
Pheasant (2–3 lbs.)	2.08	Strawberries	.75
Beef kidneys	.64	Lemons (each)	.35
Steak	1.35	Prune pie	.35
Pork sausage	1.20	Chocolate cake	.59
Hamburger	.77–.80	*Piroshki* (knishes)	.05
Beef (stewing)	.55	Coffee	1.82
Mutton	.59	Tea	3.18
Fish (average)	.50	Cocoa	4.09
Fish (coarse salt)	.18	Soft drinks (2¢ plain)	.02
Sturgeon	2.77	Champagne (liter)	2.97
Salami	1.59	Vodka (liter)	5.74–6.14
Bacon	1.23	Benedictine wine	8.28
Canned stuffed cabbage (3)	.68	Beer (small bottle)	.16
Frozen ravioli	.68	Ice cream cone	.15–.19
Cabbage	.05–.30 *	Chocolate candy	1.64
Tomatoes	.30 *–.41	Cigarettes (box of 25)	.22
Cauliflower	.16	Cigars (10)	1.32–2.72
Scallions	.12	Milk shakes (10 oz. glass)	.18
Garlic (bunch)	.10 *	Noon meal at work	.55

	Price (rubles)		Price (rubles)

CLOTHING			
		Woman's rayon dress	15.00–36.44
		Woman's wool dress	30.00–80.00
Man's wool suit	82.00–180.00	Woman's wool suit	55.00–120.00
Man's summer sport		Woman's wool skirt	20.00–30.00
jacket	25.00–37.00	Woman's coat	110.00–140.00
Man's fall coat	151.00–181.00	Woman's cotton	
Surburban coat (fur		tweed skirt	7.45–10.00
collar)	54.00	Woman's spring coat	49.90–162.00
Trench coat	155.00–196.00	Woman's cotton	
Man's summer suit	12.80–80.00	weave suit	41.40
Man's overcoat	104.00–235.00	Sheath dress (rayon	
Man's spring coat	120.00	crepe)	37.90
Gabardine slacks	31.00–42.00	Colored plastic rain-	
Rayon slacks	13.00–21.00	coat	6.80
Man's shirt	6.50	Nylon stockings	1.38–3.20
Man's sport shirt	9.60	Woman's silk blouse	8.35–15.00
Chinos	5.50–6.00	Woman's cotton blouse	6.45
Corduroy slacks	10.00	Knit underwear	10.00–20.00
Polo shirts	9.00–13.00	Cotton panties	1.35–1.99
Suspenders	.95–1.95	Underslip	12.00–18.00
Ties	.72–2.99	Negligee	11.00–25.00
Wool scarves	2.00–7.57	Nylon gloves	4.50
Undershirt	1.60	Ladies' handbags	2.67–12.30
Net T-shirts	1.90	Shoes (high heeled)	23.00–56.00
Shorts (cotton)	1.50–1.90	Rubber boots (high	
Belts	.90–2.00	heeled)	5.05–9.50
Sweat shirts	9.50	Open heel and toe	
Man's shoes	9.00–32.50	shoes	3.36–6.70
Man's crepe-sole		Silver fox fur piece	169.00
shoe	43.00	Bikini	1.84
Man's canvas shoes	3.56–6.75	Teenager's synthetic	
Man's rubbers	2.63	fur coat	130.00
Man's galoshes	5.85	Umbrellas	3.42–7.00
Man's bedroom		Persian lamb coat	177.00
slippers	3.75	Silver fox fur coat	248.50
Man's fur hat	6.30	Sun glasses	.60–2.64
Man's straw hat	4.00		
Man's felt hat	15.00	CHILDREN'S CLOTHING AND TOYS	
Man's felt boots	14.00		
Man's wool sox	1.10–1.73	Corduroy jackets	8.40
Man's cotton sox	.38–.50	Suits (50% wool)	20.80
Woman's cotton		Sailor suits	14.30
housedress	6.00–18.00	Overalls	7.60

TABLE VI-A (*Continued*)

Boy's slacks	8.15	Pen (Chinese	
Boy's cap	2.50	"Parker 51")	7.50
Boy's fur cap	4.52–10.40	Pen and pencil set	3.50
Boy's shirt	2.12	Fountain pen	
Underwear	2.80	(gold pt.)	6.00
Sandals	1.48–7.25	Slide rule (7-scale)	2.02
High shoes	4.45	Miniature chess set	.80
Booties	.84	Ink (bottle)	.17
Summer suits	6.00–9.00	Colored pencils (set	
Girl's dress	7.00–10.00	of 8)	.80
Fall coat	18.00–44.00	Pen knife	7.55
Snow suits	23.50	Top	1.10
Girl's slip	7.50	Woodworking tool kit	7.60
Bathing suit	2.30	Consumer Durables	
Girl's school uniform	19.72		
Mittens	.65–.80	Automobile,	
Boy's pajamas	6.80	"Volga"	4200.00 (wait)
Boy's sneakers	2.40	Automobile,	
Boy's stockings	.40–2.00	"Moskvich"	2500.00 (wait)
Girl's velvet bonnet	2.30	Automobile,	
Child's blanket		"Zaporozhets"	1800.00
(½ wool)	7.80–41.00	TV sets (12-inch)	194.00
Cotton handkerchiefs	1.10–2.00	TV sets (15-inch)	250.00–324.00
Toy airplane for		Vacuum cleaners	40.00–90.00
riding	28.00–35.00	Washing machines	75.00–225.00
Pull toys	1.16	Refrigerators	85.00–310.00
Puppets	2.00–3.80	Radio receiver	40.00
Child's books	.12–.17	Record player	16.50–30.00
Rubber balls	.40–.60	Sewing machines	75.00–170.00
Erector sets	8.00	3-way combo (TV,	
Globe (18-inch)	1.48	radio-phono)	384.00
Mechanical toys	2.60	Projector (8 mm.)	80.00
Model boats	1.15	Floor polisher	28.00
Radio construction		Electric iron	5.02
kit	10.00–30.00	Electric coffee	
Large telescope	6.50	percolator	8.30
Child's guitar	6.50	Electric samovar	16.50–20.00
Doll (20-inch)	11.00–17.00	Electric tea pot	6.00–7.00
Doll (rubber)	4.00	Electric hair clippers	35.00
Brief cases (imitation		Electric mixer	80.00
leather)	4.00–8.00	Broiler oven	25.00
Pen (ball point)	2.40	Electric fan (8-inch)	8.00

Price (rubles)		Price (rubles)	
Electric hot plate	3.50	Permanent wave	2.00
Typewriter (portable German)	150.00	Dye job	2.00
		Manicure	.30
Typewriter (Soviet)	110.00	Eyelash curler	1.50
Typewriter ribbon	.38	Face cream	.40
Cameras	11.00–50.00	Shoeshine	.10
Alarm clock	3.00–5.00	Hair curlers (set of 5)	.30
Travel clock (large)	15.00	Toothpaste	.13–.30
Wrist watches	22.00–50.00	Shaving brush	.54
Bicycles	45.00–60.00	Electric razor	15.00
Motorbikes	154.00		
Motorcycles	420.00	RECREATION	
Aluminum frying pan	.75	Bass drums	71.00
Kettles	2.90–4.95	Clarinet	91.60
Stainless steel setting for 3	11.64	Violins	15.00–27.50
		Balalaikas	4.25–8.50
Mirrors (2-feet diameter)	10.50	Accordions	108.00–407.00
		Harmonicas	2.00–3.50
Light bulbs (60 watts)	.18	Recordings	.45–.57
		Football	3.50
Family divan	130.00	Film (roll)	.35
Pillows	3.50	Newspaper	.02
Desk lamp	4.00–7.50	Movie admission	.30–.50
Floor lamp	21.00	Theater seats	.50–2.50
Movie cameras	35.00–95.00	Gasoline (gallon)	.24–.30
PERSONAL CARE		RENTALS (PER DAY)	
Shoe brush	.94	Vacuum cleaner	.40
Toilet soap	.18–.22	Sewing machine	.20
Toilet paper	.24	Camera	.50
Hair cut (crew)	.25	Rubber boat	.80
Lipstick	.30	Tent for camping	1.20
Perfume (3-oz.)	2.20–7.50	Tennis racket	.20
Shampoo	.20	Phonograph	.30
Hair set	.40	Washing machine	.50

Price information was collected or checked by Mr. Arnold Miller on his visit to the Soviet Union in the summer of 1962. Quotations followed by asterisks were collected in Kiev collective farm market at 3 p.m., July 26, 1962.

REFLECTION OF BASIC PROBLEMS IN INSTITUTIONS CATERING TO CONSUMERS

As most intelligent readers are well aware, the Russians make at least some use of advertising, model or product changes, and instalment credit. Since it may seem strange to find these institutions in economies characterized by chronic seller's markets, we might profitably spend some time examining these developments in noncapitalist-oriented economies, and their relationship to their United States counterparts.

1. *Advertising.* In the Soviet Union, advertising is limited primarily to the dissemination of information on new products or services, particularly ones which might make for improved workers' health or productivity. Such things as the poster advertisements advising Soviet citizens to "drink champagne" may fall into this category. As a substitute for vodka or illegal liquor obtained from "moonshining" activities, champagne might produce fewer morning-afters interfering with worker productivity. A considerable amount of Soviet advertising is of a negative character, designed to warn consumers of the deleterious effects of vodka, tobacco, or illegal abortions. Actually advertising is only one of many levers designed to discourage "unsocialist" activities in the area of consumption, since differential taxes and stiff prison or even death sentences for speculators and bootleggers are also employed.[21] Advertising is also used extensively to implement the fiscal requirements of the government by encouraging citizens to refrain from spending and to put their excess rubles into savings accounts, government bonds, lottery tickets, or insurance. Radio and billboard advertising is also employed to recruit skilled workers. Display advertising is poorly developed in the Soviet Union, although a number of the newer noncapitalist-oriented economies have somehow managed to res-

---

[21] For an account of the 1961 home-brewing laws, see "Home-Brew Surge Worrying Soviet," *New York Times,* April 8, 1962, p. 19.

urrect a few imaginative window trimmers. Advertising in news-papers, magazines, and on TV or radio is comparatively inof-fensive (and also unimaginative), being largely of an informative character. What little advertising there is might be accurately described as the embodiment of the "soft sell." For example, a Moscow newspaper advertised Caspian herring using this in-triguing line: "The quality of this herring is in no way inferior to other brands of herring." Pictorial illustrations are rare and advertisements are almost never designed to whet the sexual appetites (conscious or subconscious) of their readers. One of the most interesting recent experiments in Soviet advertising occurred in conjunction with the government's decision to im-port Brazilian coffee in exchange for Soviet oil, about which more is said in Chapter XI. A foreign organization, the Brazilian Coffee Institute, was given permission to try directly to influence the tastes of the traditionally tea-drinking Russians.

In the United States, advertising is of course well-developed and is certainly one of our "growth" industries at the present time. In 1960 advertising expenditures were estimated to have amounted to between 11 and 12 billion dollars or about two per cent of our total product. Advertising accounts for 1.4 per cent of the sales dollar by manufacturing and retail trade industries. Our heaviest spenders for advertising are the tobacco companies where such expenditures account for 5.2¢ per sales dollar, fol-lowed closely by beverages and chemicals with 4.9¢ and 3.6¢ per sales dollar, respectively. Newspapers continue to be the most important advertising media, accounting for about one-third of all expenditures, followed by direct mail and TV—both of which account for about 15 per cent of the total.

Although advertising expenditures have increased at only about the same rate as gross national product since 1935, during the fifties they increased at a rate which was 13 per cent in excess of that for our total product. As might have been expected, advertising expenditures in the United States declined absolutely in 1942 and declined relative to gross national product for the remaining war years when our own seller's market prevailed. There is some evidence in the postwar years that advertising is becoming less effective as a stimulator of sales. According to a recent study by Dr. Bernard Shull of the Federal Reserve Bank of Philadelphia, as reported in a speech before the Association of National Advertisers, the volume of sales per each dollar of advertising expenditure has declined "precipitously" from $116 in 1947 to $90 in 1960.[22]

Madison Avenue, which has slowly replaced Wall Street as a favorite target for attack by social critics, no doubt syphons off some of our most creative minds for which it pays accordingly very well indeed.[23] Arnold Toynbee, following the general lines advanced earlier by Vance Packard, even goes so far as to argue that an economy "that depends for its survival on the artificial stimulation of material wants seems unlikely to survive for very long."[24]

It is true that the bulk of these expenditures would seem to be redundant from the social standpoint, at least to the extent that they are in effect substitutes for price competition. The development of trading stamps and special "give-aways" with major purchases are also designed to avoid lowering prices and "ruining the market." Trading stamps, as a substitute for lower prices, reduce what would otherwise show up as freely disposable income. Thus, instead of allowing consumers to choose freely among all goods and services, or even to nonconsume, trading stamps force consumers to "buy" from a somewhat restricted group of rather mediocre products. In 1961, nearly $600 million worth of goods were disposed of in this manner and total employment in the trading stamp industry, either in distribution or redemption of the stamps, was estimated to be 100,000 persons.[25] As such, these forms of non-price competition are de-

---

[22] See *New York Times*, May 22, 1962, p. 47. To some extent, this decline may be due to the shift from a seller's to a buyer's market between these years.

[23] Anyone doubting the concentration of talent in our advertising sector need but compare the quality of TV advertising with the accompanying programs.

[24] For an account of Toynbee's pamphlet and the answer of the advertising industry, see *New York Times*, September 15, 1961, p. 44.

[25] "Trading Stamps Find Their Way From Grocers to Corporations," *New York Times*, July 13, 1962, p. 29.

signed primarily to counteract competitors' advertising or other "hard sell" activities, rather than to give significant new information or satisfaction to consumers.

Along with the growth of advertising and salesmanship, there has developed an interest in packaging as a device to stimulate consumption in capitalist-oriented economies. The package has become much more than a functional container; it has become the product's salesman in the self-service supermarket. In the early sixties, this rapidly growing industry was accounting for over $20 billion in economic activity.[26] Data contained in the 1954 Census of Manufacturers indicate that the cost of packaging averaged about 20 per cent of the value of goods shipped; in some industries, packaging costs rose to 40 per cent of the total value of the commodities sold. In sharp contrast to our experience in stimulating the output of paper, the Soviets have recently been forced to limit the circulation of newspapers and books because of serious deficiencies in their cellulose and paper industry.[27] In addition, *Pravda* or *Izvestiia* frequently serve a dual purpose as wrapping paper.

2. *Proliferation of models and products.* In noncapitalist-oriented economies there are only occasional model changes. The main problem facing Soviet planners in their dealings with managers of enterprises would in fact appear to be the opposite: how to stimulate the conversion of production from older, poorly designed models to newer, better engineered products. Although the Russians certainly deserve no credit for their automobile styling, which essentially apes our own or German design to a great extent, at least they do not feel compelled to differentiate each year's product with a slightly different grill or rear end. Nor are they planning to introduce semi-annual model changes such as are at present being contemplated by Detroit's auto manufacturers. Want creation—engineered by motivation research experts—is a highly developed art in our advertising community, while such a policy would seem to be the height

[26] William M. Freeman, "Packages Assume Role of Salesmen for Retail Outlets," *New York Times,* October 7, 1962, Section III, p. F 1.

[27] "Soviet Suffering Paper Shortage," *New York Times,* January 29, 1961, p. 27.

of folly in a noncapitalist-oriented economy with its chronic seller's market and perpetual shortages of consumers' goods.[28]

The proliferation of products currently being experimented with by our enterprising producers and salesmen would seem at times to be calculated to appeal to the all-too-prevalent irrationality of man, providing relatively little utility at a comparatively high cost. These somewhat dubious uses of resources are especially questionable when one considers the coexisting pockets of poverty in our own country and the chasm of destitution existing in the growth-starved areas of the world. Among the recently advertised innovations designed to titillate American consumers we might note the following: an Italian-made bird cage of clear and translucent glass trimmed with "brass-plated gold" selling for $750; a beautifully crafted hot dog cart to "make *al fresco* entertaining a positive pleasure," selling for $695; the famous Universal Coffeematic, rendered in 14-carat gold with 250 diamonds and 150 rubies selling for a mere $50,000; sunglasses for man's best friend at a nominal cost of $25; an electronic golf computer so you "no longer need wait for warm and dry days to practice driving for distance and accuracy" selling for $1,595; a gold golf putter for that "special occasion" priced at $1,475; a gold-plated toothbrush for only $5; a 14-carat gold key ring decorated with a coral hand (sporting a tiny diamond ring) which holds a tassel tipped with ruby beads selling for $225; or a 5-foot pepper mill for $75.

3. *Instalment credit.* One of the most recent developments in noncapitalist-oriented economies is the advent of instalment credit. In early 1959, experiments with instalment credit were reported in several Ukrainian towns following some earlier experience with consumers' credit in Eastern Europe. By October, 1959, the practice was extended to the entire USSR, and by 1960 total sales on credit amounted to 63 million "heavy" rubles, or less than one per cent of total retail turnover in state and coopera-

[28] In this connection, see the work of that pioneer deflator of conventional wisdom, J. K. Galbraith, *The Affluent Society,* Houghton Mifflin, Boston, 1958, pp. 158–160.

tive outlets.[29] Of the total sales on credit, more than half represented clothing sales. Other products which are subject to instalment buying include radios, cameras, bicycles, motorcycles, sewing machines, and watches. The charges are very nominal since they amount to a one to two per cent service charge; the down payment is high and the period for repayment is short by our standards.

In the noncapitalist-oriented economies of East Europe, instalment credit practices vary from country to country. In Poland, for example, although the loans are "interest free," there is a five per cent service charge; a 15 per cent down payment and 18 months to pay. In a number of the East European countries, instalment credit is limited to special groups of persons: newlyweds, large families, or those especially productive workers recommended by their trade unions.[30] Thus, the motivating factor behind instalment credit in these instances would seem to be the encouragement of productivity rather than the stimulation of consumption. Since most consumers in these countries have ample liquid funds at their disposal, it would seem that this institution is designed primarily to serve the needs of those in the lower income groups.

Czechoslovakia has instituted a practice which would appear to be particularly well suited to the needs of these relatively frugal economies. A Czech citizen can buy an automobile at the present time for the equivalent of $5,880 (conversion at the official exchange rate). However, if he is willing to wait two or three years and can afford to put down $2,800, he can get the car at the end of 2 or 3 years for a total price of only $3,920. In other words, by "paying now and driving later," the Czech can earn a rather substantial rate of interest. As of January 1, 1959, about 50,000 Czechs had subscribed to this instalment plan-in-reverse.[31]

---

[29] *Narodnoe Khoziaistvo 1960*, Gosstatizdat, Moscow, 1961, p. 686.

[30] See Kathleen McLaughlin, "Satellite Lands Go Into the 'Red,'" *New York Times*, March 1, 1959, Section III, p. 1.

[31] See Paul Underwood, "Czechs Shunning Political Unrest," *New York Times*, February 15, 1959, p. 21. There are some indications that a similar practice exists in the Soviet Union for the purchase of housing in advance

In capitalist-oriented economies, instalment credit has proven its popularity with both consumers and businessmen. In the fifties, there was almost a three-fold increase in total instalment credit compared with less than a 1.8-fold increase in gross national product. Since the rates of interest on such credit are very substantial, this institution tends to increase the actual prices paid by United States consumers using credit by a rather significant amount. West European capitalist-oriented economies are also expanding "hire purchase" at a rapid rate, despite the fact that the movement is viewed with a great deal of suspicion by governments and consumers alike.[32] Even Japan is making great strides in adopting this institution, and at present about 80 per cent of all automobiles sold in Japan are on credit.[33] An even greater variety of commodities and services are now being bought on the "never-never," in an attempt to stimulate greater sales. One of the more recent innovations has occurred in Canada where funerals on credit are being encouraged in an attempt to sell more elaborate and costlier services.[34]

There would seem to be little doubt that instalment credit is providing an important supplement to our effective demand at the present time.[35] Unfortunately, however, in periods of recession there is a tendency for additions to outstanding credit to shrink or disappear, thereby adding to the problem of maintaining aggregate demand at a time when it has also been most needed. There has also been a tendency for consumers' instal-

---

of construction. See Andrew Shonfield, "A Russian and Money," *New York Herald Tribune,* July 4, 1959, p. 6.

[32] For an account of some of the troubles facing European finance houses, in their search for "solid profits," see Edwin L. Dale, "Instalment Credit Advances in Europe Despite Roadblocks," *New York Times,* June 12, 1961, p. 42.

[33] In the United States, the purchases of automobiles on credit have fallen from 66 per cent of the total sales in 1955 to about 60 per cent of the total in 1962. See Edward T. O'Toole, "Consumer Credit Gains Momentum," *New York Times,* April 22, 1962, Section III, p. 10.

[34] See *New York Times,* August 20, 1961, p. 86.

[35] In 1962 the net increase in instalment credit is expected to approximate $4 billion. See Edward T. O'Toole, "Consumer Credit Gains Momentum," *New York Times,* April 22, 1962, Section III, p. 1.

ment credit to rise more slowly in the 1961–62 recovery as compared with the earlier 1954–55 and 1958–59 recoveries.[36] Apparently there is a reluctance on the part of consumers to go into debt beyond what some economists call "the 13 per cent ratio." Historically, the consumer has not extended his borrowing beyond the point where it would take more than 13 per cent of his income after taxes to meet his debt payments.

PASSING ON CONSUMPTION GAINS TO CONSUMERS

There are a number of ways by which gains may be passed on to consumers as productivity grows and the potential for increasing consumption rises. In the Soviet Union, the potential annual increase in consumption seems to be averaging about five per cent on a per capita basis, while in the United States, currently it is between one and two per cent. In general, we may distinguish six general ways in which these gains can or could be distributed to consumers:

1. One of the simplest ways would be to let wages and salaries rise by a sufficient amount to absorb the increased supply of consumers' goods and services.

2. Another method to effect the required distribution of the additional goods and services would be to lower prices by an amount sufficiently great so as to dispose of the added supplies, or clear the market.

3. A country might consider lowering direct taxes by an amount sufficient to create the necessary purchasing power to absorb the additional goods.

4. The government might wish to increase the amount of communal consumption and thereby release additional effective demand that was formerly being absorbed by these priced goods and services.

5. The system might opt for better packaging, more advertising, and a proliferation of rather esoteric products.

6. It may borrow demand from the future by lending additional sums to present-day consumers via the institution of instalment credit.

[36] *Ibid.*

Actually all economic systems combine various aspects of these six alternatives. In the Soviet Union between 1947 and 1954, the second method was favored although there were also small concomitant increases in money wages. Since 1954, price reductions have been minimal and wage increases have been more substantial. But there has also been a tendency to use methods 3 (lower direct taxes) and 4 (additional communal consumption), especially in recent years. In noncapitalist-oriented economies, the fifth and sixth methods are still barely tapped and should in all probability never have to be emphasized to any significant extent.

In the United States, while the first method—rising wages—is used extensively, it has seldom been possible to employ the second method, that is, falling price levels. Although wage increases are more common as a means of distributing the fruits of industrialization, they have usually created demand in excess of that required to absorb the increases in goods and services. As a consequence, the price level has ordinarily risen, although by a smaller amount than wages, so that on balance, there has been a fairly steady rise in our consumption. There have been occasional feeble efforts to employ method 3 but in general tax decreases are rare in capitalist-oriented systems. We have also used method 4 recently, at least to the extent that we have increased our defense appropriations. In general, however, our system tends to opt for methods 5 and 6 at all times, except during periods of war, when the use of both advertising and installment credit is restricted.

Recommended Readings

CAMPBELL, COLIN D. and ROSEMARY G., "Soviet Price Reductions for Consumer Goods, 1948–54," *American Economic Review,* September, 1955, pp. 609–625.

CHAPMAN, JANET, "Real Wages in the Soviet Union, 1928–52," *Review of Economics and Statistics,* May, 1954, pp. 134–156.

GOLDMAN, MARSHALL I., "Product Differentiation and Advertising—Some Lessons from Soviet Experience," *Journal of Political Economy,* August, 1960, pp. 346–357.

————, "The Cost and Efficiency of Distribution in the Soviet Union," *The Quarterly Journal of Economics,* August, 1962, pp. 437–453.

KAPLAN, NORMAN and WAINSTEIN, ELEANOR, "A Comparison of Soviet and American Retail Prices in 1950," *Journal of Political Economy,* December, 1956, pp. 470–491; and note in December, 1957 issue, p. 543.

MADGE, CHARLES, "The Standard of Living in Moscow, 1952," *Soviet Studies,* January, 1953, pp. 229–236.

MILLER, JACOB, "The Standard of Living in Moscow, 1937," *Soviet Studies,* January, 1953, pp. 237–242.

*NASH, EDMUND, "Purchasing Power of Workers in the USSR," *Monthly Labor Review,* April, 1960, pp. 359–364.

***NOVE, ALEC, "Toward a 'Communist Welfare State?'," *Problems of Communism,* January–February, 1960, Vol. IX, No. 1, pp. 1–10, and comments by Schwarz, Wolfe, de Jourenel, Wiles, Lowenthal and Mehta.

***TURGEON, LYNN, "Levels of Living, Wages and Prices in the Soviet and United States Economies," in *Comparisons of the Soviet and United States Economies,* Part I, pp. 319–340.

United States Department of Labor, *How American Buying Habits Change,* U.S. Government Printing Office, Washington, 1959.

VII ∾ Labor Under Contrasting Economic Systems

LABOR AS A FACTOR OF PRODUCTION and wages, the price of this factor, would seem to play a similarly important role in all economic systems operating with contemporary technology under conditions of scarcity rather than absolute abundance. Monetary payments in the form of wages or salaries are ordinarily used as incentives to induce greater effort on the part of the existing labor force, as well as guideposts to the younger generation in their personal investments in training and education. Presumably there will have to be some relationship in any economic system between relative wage and salary payments and some or all of the following factors: the skill or effort required, including time invested in the education necessary for the job; the disutility or danger involved to the individual; the relative output per worker; the presently available supply of particular skills; and the general prestige associated with the occupation.

In addition to their function as incentives for workers and employees, wages and salaries constitute a factor cost to the employer or manager, and the price which the enterprise has to pay in the form of wages or salaries will influence its production costs and profits. In other words, these prices paid for labor power will presumably play some role in the resource allocation and types of investment decisions made in the different systems, regardless of whether these decisions are made by central planners or businessmen.

Looking at wages from still another standpoint, they are also ordinarily a major source of the effective demand required to purchase the commodities and services turned out by the economic system, and their general level should more or less allow a clearing of the market. At the same time, the structure of wages and salaries will also have an important bearing on the distribution of the material benefits of an economic system. On the other hand, wages and salaries are usually only a comparatively minor source of the voluntary savings which can be mobilized for nonconsumption or investment purposes.

As we have already pointed out in the previous chapter, increases in money wages and salaries in excess of rises in the cost-of-living are the principal means by which workers and employees in capitalist-oriented economies have been able to raise their levels of living.[1] In contrast, the noncapitalist-oriented economies have more frequently been able to distribute some of the real gains to consumers in the form of falling retail price levels.[2] In addition, in comparison with capitalist-oriented systems, they also seem to be offering a wider range of goods and services outside the price system so that workers' levels of living might still be rising even though there were no substantial change in either wage or price levels. An attempt is generally made to distribute this communal consumption more on the basis of need rather than in accordance with the purchasing power available to the workers or employees.

There is another major difference in the relative importance

---

[1] An exception to this feature of capitalist-oriented economies is the growth in recent years of so-called "fringe benefits," such as pensions, insurance, paid vacations, and medical care—at least partially financed at the expense of the employer.

[2] In addition to the Soviet experience discussed in the following chapter, workers in Czechoslovakia and Rumania have received substantial benefits from falling price levels in recent years. See E. Konovavov, *"Pod'ëm zhiznennogo urovnia narodov stran sotsializma"* (The Rise in the Level of Living of People in the Socialist Countries), *Voprosy Ekonomiki,* No. 1, 1962, p. 96.

of wages and salaries in the two principal economic systems. Whereas current productive effort by labor is virtually the sole source of money income in noncapitalist-oriented economies, wages and salaries are only the most important form of income in capitalist-oriented economic systems. In economies of the latter type, monetary payments are also made to individuals for the use of their land and the buildings constructed thereon; in the form of dividends on common stock; in substantial interest payments on bonds and savings accounts held by individuals; and in the form of personal profit, resulting either from investment initiative or from windfall or capital gains due to the fluctuation of prices. This is not to say that some interest payments do not arise on savings accounts or from the holding of government bonds in noncapitalist-oriented economies, or that speculation never results in windfall gains to some individuals in these societies, but rather that interest, dividends, rent, and profits are comparatively insignificant sources of personal income in these countries.

Thus, while wages and salaries are less important as a means of obtaining all the goods and services produced in noncapitalist-oriented economies (due to their larger share of communal consumption), they do comprise a higher percentage of the total labor and nonlabor money incomes of citizens in these economies as compared with the wages and salaries of their capitalist-oriented counterparts. Because wages and salaries at the same time play both a less-inclusive and a more-inclusive role in distributing all goods and services produced in noncapitalist-oriented economies, it becomes somewhat difficult to interpret the wage stratification existing in the two types of economies as an indication of relative equality or inequality resulting from the entire distributive process. However, since the greater communal consumption existing in noncapitalist-oriented economies tends to be equally distributed—and the greater nonlabor incomes in capitalist-oriented economies tend to be unequally distributed—we should not be blind to the fact that considerably greater stratification in the wage structure of the noncapitalist-oriented economies is not necessarily inconsistent with their possibly greater overall equality with respect to the entire income distribution.[3]

At the outset, it seems clear that somewhat different wage structures and policies might better satisfy the developmental requirements of economies at the various stages in their economic growth. According to two respected Western labor experts, there is the "tendency for substantial wage differentials to arise with the growth of modern industry, and the subsequent tendency for differentials to shrink gradually as industrialism matures."[4]

In the early stages of economic development, when skilled labor is scarce and the savings of society are low, greater inequality in the wage structure would appear to be particularly auspicious from at least three standpoints: (1) wider stratification serves as a greater stimulus for unskilled workers to develop their skills; (2) unequal earnings with relatively low starting salaries encourage employers to hire comparatively larger numbers of unskilled workers who had formerly constituted part of the disguised rural unemployment; and (3) unequal earnings create the potentialities for a somewhat greater amount of voluntary savings and a slightly lower aggregate consumption by the labor force.

Since piece-rates serve to bring out the best efforts of particularly talented individuals, they tend to accentuate wage inequalities and might therefore tend to be encouraged in such a developing economy. On the other hand, a more mature economy —one which is already blessed with a highly skilled nonagricultural labor force, but which is being handicapped in its later

---

[3] The more or less egalitarian distribution of a large sphere of communal consumption in noncapitalist-oriented economies would seem to provide something of a floor below which levels of living would not be permitted to sink. With the establishment of such a floor, a certain amount of labor incentive may be lost in the process. As a result, greater inequality in the payments for the remaining share of total consumption may be required in order to maintain incentives which are comparable to those prevailing in economies not providing such a floor.

[4] See Lloyd G. Reynolds and Cynthia H. Taft, *The Evolution of Wage Structures*, Yale University Press, New Haven, 1956, p. 373.

development by a tendency towards insufficient effective demand in relationship to its productive capabilities—might logically wish to move away from piece-rate payments and develop a wage structure featuring greater equality for precisely opposite reasons.

WAGE POLICY IN NONCAPITALIST-ORIENTED ECONOMIES

As provided by Article 118 of the Soviet Constitution, the principle underlying Soviet wage policy is payment by results; that is, wages must correspond to the quantity and quality of goods produced. There is supposedly equal pay for equal work regardless of sex, age, race, or nationality. In practice, although this principle may be used to determine relative wages within smaller economic units such as individual plants, the wage structure as a whole has deviated from this principle in a number of respects.[5] To an important extent, the planners appear to have added their own values as a factor in relative wage determination. As Soviet theoreticians express it euphemistically, under socialism the "law of value" loses its role as an automatic regulator of the distribution of labor among the different branches and regions.[6]

[5] Among the possible exceptions to this principle, we might mention the following: progressive piece rates, geographical differentials, some relatively unproductive workers covered by minimum wage legislation, overtime and holiday pay.

[6] The "law of value" is a Marxist expression used to describe the functioning of an economy in which commodities tend to be exchanged in proportion to their labor content. Supposedly the operation of free market forces under capitalist-oriented economies produces this tendency. In the noncapitalist-oriented economies, on the other hand, consumers' goods prices considerably exceed their average labor costs, including both live and "stored-up" labor. If the law of value were allowed to regulate investment and the proportion of labor distributed among the different branches, Soviet light industries, which are the most "profitable" would be developed at the expense of heavy industry and would also tend to

In a very general sort of way, wage movements in the USSR and the other noncapitalist-oriented economies seem to be exhibiting the above-mentioned expected tendencies in the course of their economic development. Wage inequality has been magnified during the period when rapid industrialization took place, and it has been reduced as the Soviet economy matured. It is true that immediately after the revolution—particularly during the period of so-called "War Communism" from 1918–21—there was a great deal of extreme wage equality. But as soon as the counterrevolutionaries and interventionists had been repulsed, prewar wage inequalities were restored during the period of the New Economic Policy in an effort to bring the economy back to prerevolutionary production levels. After the economy had more or less recovered its wartime and postwar losses, M. P. Tomsky, Chairman of the Central Council of Trade Unions, began pursuing a deliberate policy of wage equalization, in part as a consequence of pressures from abroad.[7]

The leadership of the relatively independent trade unions of that early period, as well as many visiting friendly foreign socialist delegations, somehow imagined that wages should be more equal under socialism than they had been under the Czar or under the contemporary capitalist-oriented countries of Europe. This brief period during which greater wage equalization was a policy objective of the trade unions was brought to a rude end in 1931 when Stalin decided that "wage-leveling" was an unmitigated evil holding up the rapid industrialization process; thereafter, inequality of wages became a virtue of Soviet socialism.[8]

Under the new basic wage rates introduced by the state plan-

pay relatively higher wages. In this connection, see Josph Stalin, *Economic Problems of Socialism in the USSR,* International Publishers, New York, 1952, p. 21.

[7] In this connection, see Abram Bergson, *The Structure of Soviet Wages,* Harvard University Press, Cambridge, 1946, p. 187.

[8] The significant turning point was Stalin's address on June 23, 1931, before a conference of economic managers. See J. V. Stalin, *Sochineniia* (Works), Vol. 13, Moscow, 1952–54, p. 57.

ners after 1931, the highest paid industrial workers might have a base pay which was four times higher than that of the least skilled worker.[9] In addition to the increasing dispersion in the basic rates, bonuses based on exceeded norms and over-fulfilled production targets contributed to still greater wage inequality.

Proportional (or straight) piece rates, which were fairly common in Russia before the revolution, had already achieved a certain amount of general acceptance in the twenties, despite the existence of the relatively independent trade unions. By 1926–27, the proportion of man-hours paid by piece-rate was, on the average, 61.2 per cent of all-man-hours worked in industry.[10] During the thirties, however, there was an even further relative expansion of piece-work so that by 1938, 75 per cent of all Soviet industrial workers were being paid on this basis. Furthermore, progressive piece-rates, which had formerly been opposed by the trade unions, were introduced in the early thirties. Under this form of payment, output in excess of the worker's norm was paid for at vastly higher piece-rates which increased progressively as the excess output rose.

The Stakhanovite movement, which encouraged workers to rack up new individual production records regardless of cost, was another well-publicized development contributing to this growing trend towards inequality in wage and salary payments

[9] There has been a rather arbitrary classification of all jobs below foreman into roughly seven to 12 grades with ratios of the highest to the lowest basic rate ranging from 2.0:1 to 4.0:1, depending on the industry and the period. Assignment to a specific grade depends on the competence and qualifications of the worker, the complexity and difficulty of the work, and its importance to the national economy. The actual grade classification of jobs and individuals is a function of management personnel. Sometimes a special commission, but most often the foreman, determines these assignments in accordance with job descriptions and detailed instructions found in special handbooks (*tarifno-kvalifikatsionnye spravochniki*), formerly published by the ministries of the various industries.

[10] See M. Romanov, *"Proizvoditel'nost' truda, zarabotnaia plata i izderzhki na trud v gosudarstvennoi promyshlennosti SSSR"* (Labor Productivity, Wages, and Labor Expenditures in State Industry of the USSR), *Ekonomicheskoe Obozrenie,* No. 3, 1929, p. 117.

after 1935. During this early period, engineer-technicians as a group received average salaries which were over two and one-half times higher than the level of average wages of production workers, a phenomenon which undoubtedly reflected the general shortage of these skills in the country at that time. White-collar workers during the early thirties received average earnings which were 50 per cent higher than those of production workers.

In addition to the above-mentioned changes in the wage and salary structures within each industry, there was a fundamental reform in the inter-industry wage structure. On the eve of Plan I, the inter-industry wage structure probably reflected to a great extent the free play of labor market forces which had been permitted to develop in the twenties, and was as yet relatively unaffected by the government's principal action modifying the operation of the "law of value"—the violation of consumers' sovereignty with respect to the consumption-investment decision. The operation of labor market forces during the preceding period of the New Economic Policy was reflected in the fact that wages had increased at a faster rate in the light industries than they did in heavy industry.[11] As a consequence, by 1928 workers engaged in printing, shoe manufacturing, leather and furs, and the needlecraft trades were among the most highly paid. On the other hand, coal and iron ore miners, loggers, oil drillers, and iron and steel workers were less well paid. Of the branches of industry which were destined to have a higher priority in the government's industrialization plans, only workers in machine-building, electric power stations, and chemicals were among the more highly paid personnel.[12]

[11] V. Maier, and V. Markov, "Voprosy mezhotraslevogo regulirovaniia zarabotnoi platy v SSSR" (Problems of the Inter-Branch Regulation of Wages in the U.S.S.R.), Sotsialisticheskii Trud, No. 2, 1958, p. 51.

[12] The higher wages in machine-building and electric power stations may reflect a decision of the Plenum of the Central Committee of the Communist Party in August, 1924, according to ibid., p. 52. Higher wages for workers in electric power stations may also be due to the priority given to electric power development as a result of the GOELRO in 1920. Higher wages in machine building may be the result of an initially higher skill composition in this sector, as well as of the relative shortage of the required skills.

After Stalin's momentous dictum of 1931, a significant change occurred in the relative wages paid in a number of heavy industrial branches. The basic wage scales were revised upward for coal miners; for workers in ferrous metallurgy, including the iron ore, manganese, and coke sectors; for employees in heavy chemicals; and for those employed in machine-building.[13] The higher government priority attached to goal fulfillment in heavy industries generally during the early thirties also meant that managers in these sectors had to rely more heavily on bonuses, overtime, and progressive piece-rates in fulfilling output targets in these key sectors. As a result, by 1935 the top-paying branches were, in descending order: oil drilling, electric power stations, machine-building, coal (which has remained the top-paying branch since sometime before World War II), iron and steel, iron ore mining, and chemicals.

In the years since Stalin's death, there have been a number of changes in the wage structure which might conceivably be referred to as constituting a second "income revolution."[14] Following the Twentieth Party Congress, the basic wage rates have been gradually revised during the latter half of the fifties and early sixties under the supervision of the State Committee on Labor and Wages, and the differentials between skilled and unskilled occupations have been narrowed. The ratios of extreme rates in the wage scales issued in 1960 and 1961 were generally in the neighborhood of two to one or 1.8 to one, compared with the earlier ratios of between four to one and 2.8 to one.[15]

Minimum wages, which in 1962 amounted to 40 or 45 rubles per month, are being raised at a much faster rate than average wages generally, and are expected to continue their relatively

[13] See A. E. Pasherstnik, *Pravovye voprosy voznagrazhdeniia za trud rabochikh i sluzhashchikh* (Legal Problems in the Compensation of Wage Earners and Salaried Employees), Moscow, 1949, pp. 220, 221.

[14] One of the first Sovietologists to recognize this movement towards greater equality was Isaac Deutscher. See his *Russia in Transition*, Coward-McCann, New York, 1957, pp. 11 *et seq.*

[15] Before the recent revisions, there may have been only a few workers actually in the lower wage categories so that the effective spread might have been considerably less than that indicated by the ratios of the extreme rates.

faster growth until 1970 at least. In the current Seven-Year Plan, minimum wages were scheduled to rise from 27 or 35 rubles to 50 or 60 rubles monthly, or by between 70 and 80 per cent. At the same time, average wages for all workers were supposed to increase by only 26 per cent. During the current decade, according to the new Twenty-Year Plan, real incomes of lower paid workers and employees are scheduled to triple at the same time that real incomes of all personnel will be almost doubled.

Piece-rates are being gradually replaced by time rates, and the institution of the progressive piece-rate has apparently been virtually discarded. In comparison with 1936, the percentage of total workers paid according to proportional piece-rates had fallen from 79.2 per cent to 51.9 per cent in ferrous metallurgy; from 80.8 per cent to between 48 and 51 per cent in coal mining; and from 68.3 to 45 per cent in the chemical industry.[16]

Since 1952, references to Stakhanovites have largely, if not completely, disappeared from the Soviet press. There has also been a steady decline in the gap between the average earnings of engineering-technical personnel and those for production workers, although this development was evident even before Stalin's death. At present these highly trained employees receive only about 50 per cent higher average wages than production workers generally—or about the same differential that applied to the salaries of white-collar workers generally and their relationship to average workers' wages in the thirties. In the meantime, white-collar personnel have steadily lost relative ground, with the result that they are now paid average salaries which are below the average wage for production workers. This wage discrimination against white-collar workers is undoubtedly a factor implementing government pressures for the relative reduction in the numbers of nonproductive personnel within the Soviet economy. There have been some reductions in the salaries earned at the very highest income levels, and there is also

[16] See E. Kapustin, *"Proizvoditel'nost' truda i zarabotnaia plata"* (Labor Productivity and Wages), *Sotsialisticheskii Trud*, No. 4, 1962, p. 20.

some evidence that inter-branch wage differentials have been reduced in the fifties. As a result of all these measures aimed at greater equalization since 1956, upper-to-lower income ratios today are probably no higher than they were thirty years ago, before Stalin's momentous policy decision.[17]

Despite the planned drift towards greater equality in the Soviet wage and salary structure, there are evidently certain limits beyond which this "leveling" will not be permitted to go. The use of collective payments systems, in which wages are distributed evenly among workers of production teams, has recently been carried too far. According to the Chairman of the State Committee on Labor and Wages, A. P. Volkhov, only team operations in mining, building, assembly line work, and team servicing of large equipment and machines in the steel and chemical industries are considered suitable for such collective payment systems.[18]

These changes in Soviet wage policy since 1956 have been mirrored only slightly in Eastern Europe. As might be expected, in view of their more advanced stage of development, the Czechs have apparently carried out a revision of their wage scales similar to that of the Soviet Union. But in less-developed Poland, where there have been complaints by economists that the existing wage differentials are too low to provide sufficient incentives, the machine-building sector has just completed a wage revision designed to bring about greater inequality.[19]

---

[17] Professor Murray Yanowitch interprets this change in terms of the increased supplies of skilled technicians and engineers, and a reduction in the pool of unskilled workers as a result of heavy educational expenditures.

[18] See Theodore Shabad, "Moscow Official Attacks Trend Toward Leveling Workers' Pay," *New York Times,* April 5, 1962, p. 8.

[19] See E. Farberova, *"Ob uporiadochenii oplaty truda rabochikh na mashinostroitel'nykh predpriiatiiakh pol'skoi narodnoi respubliki"* (About the Revision of Workers' Wages in Machine-Building Enterprises in the Polish People's Republic), *Trud i zarabotnaia plata,* No. 4, 1962, p. 58. For the complaints of Polish economists, see John Kenneth Galbraith, *Journey to Poland and Yugoslavia,* Harvard University Press, Cambridge, pp. 38, 42.

LABOR POLICY PROBLEMS IN
NONCAPITALIST-ORIENTED ECONOMIES

1. *Labor mobility*. As a result of the seller's market for labor power and the over-full employment conditions which developed soon after the introduction of Plan I, there has been a chronic tendency for excessive labor mobility to plague Soviet planners. In 1960, despite the fact that the number of workers who left industrial enterprises under the economic councils declined by nearly five per cent as compared with 1957, roughly four out of every 10 workers in the USSR apparently quit their jobs at some time during the year.[20] According to one authority, this rate of mobility is about 10 times higher than that normally experienced in the United States. Labor mobility is unusually high in Siberia where living conditions are especially austere. Despite relatively higher monetary payments for equivalent work, experience has shown that wage increases that are not accompanied by opportunities for spending such income have created an unstable labor force.[21]

Between the years 1940 to 1956, however, Soviet workers were not legally permitted great freedom of movement, and labor pass books helped enforce this relative immobility. Decrees

[20] See I. Kaplan, *"Anketnoe obsledovanie prichin tekuchesti kadrov v promyshlennosti sovnarkhozov"* (A Questionnaire Study of the Causes of Labor Turnover in Industry under the Economic Councils), *Trud i zarabotnaia plata,* No. 3, 1961 (translated in *Problems of Economics,* Vol. IV, No. 8, 1961), and Arcadius Kahan, "Labor Turnover in the Soviet Union," *Monthly Labor Review,* No. 1, January, 1962, pp. 17–19. See also the exchange of views between Kaplan and Kahan in *Monthly Labor Review,* August, 1962, pp. 900–902. This decline in mobility between 1957 and 1960 may reflect the fact that labor mobility in 1957 was unusually high due to the rescinding of the wartime legislation the previous year.

[21] See "Workers' Exodus Hampers Siberia," *New York Times,* July 1, 1962, p. 10; also Theodore Shabad, "Thousands Quit Work in Siberia Over Low Wages and Bungling," *New York Times,* November 12, 1962, p. 1.

adopted in October, 1940, forbade all employees of state enterprises and institutions (with a few exceptions) to leave their work without official permission. Despite these legal restrictions on mobility, higher wages were decreed by the Soviets immediately after the war for workers performing industrial jobs in the eastern areas of the USSR, presumably in an effort to attract additional workers into these areas. There is also considerable evidence that labor mobility was a problem in the early fifties even though the restrictive wartime legislation was still on the books.[22]

This experience in legally freezing workers to their jobs and compulsory work assignments seems to be an exception to the basic Soviet wage policy brought about by the stresses and strains of wartime and postwar reconstruction conditions. Generally speaking, the Soviet government relies on market forces and relatively higher wages to attract labor into the geographical areas and types of employment which are desired by the planners but which may entail workers' disutility. The only exception to this basic policy of relying on market forces seems to be found in the case of Soviet students who, after they have completed their higher education at government expense, are generally required to serve three or four years at a job designated by the authorities.[23] The severe housing shortage in recent years and the fact that a great deal of housing is built and controlled by the factories has meant that critical housing space is frequently tied up with a worker's employment. The housing shortage therefore acts as something of a stabilizing factor on potentially even greater mobility of labor under these over-full employment con-

[22] N. A. Bulganin reported that in 1954 Union and Republican Ministries (excluding logging) took on 2,923,000 workers, but at the same time, 2,802,000 workers left these enterprises, not counting those transferred to other work in an "organized way." See N. A. Bulganin, *Tasks of the Further Development of Industry, Technical Progress and Better Organization of Production,* Foreign Languages Publishing House, Moscow, 1955, p. 46.

[23] Actually, graduates may have a number of possible assignments from which to choose, and, in practice, this requirement is more of a moral obligation, administered with considerable leniency.

ditions. In addition, some of the social insurance benefits have not become fully effective until after a lapse of time at a worker's new employment.[24]

The mobility of agricultural labor into the urban areas following collectivization created what would superficially seem to be a problem with respect to the qualitative indices in the industrial sector. In the Soviet Union, many uneducated labor recruits released by the agricultural sector in the early thirties streamed into the industrial labor force where they received what amounted to on-the-job training. In effect, what had been disguised rural underemployment was superseded by disguised industrial underemployment in the short run. The immediate result of this influx of unskilled labor into the factories was a marked deterioration in the indexes of labor productivity and a corresponding rise in production costs, as relatively unproductive workers and employees were added to the factory payrolls.

On mainland China today, a similar phenomenon has been reported by visitors. A good many raw recruits are apparently standing around watching skilled and semi-skilled workers perform their complicated tasks. When the factories now being constructed are finished, the new recruits will presumably be better prepared to man them. Thus, there may be what economists call "external economies" involved in this initial over-manning of factories, that is, there are gains to the entire system which cannot be measured in terms of the single factory's economic accounts. The heavy influx of untrained personnel into the Yugoslav labor force has also resulted in only token increases in industrial labor productivity in some years and high or rising production costs.[25]

[24] Individuals changing jobs of their own volition lost their sick pay eligibility for six months under social insurance rules until January 1, 1960. For the decree ending this penalty, see United States Department of Labor, Bureau of Labor Statistics, *Principal Current Soviet Labor Legislation,* Bureau of Labor Statistics Report No. 210, January, 1962, p. 120. There is still some loss of pension payments connected with labor mobility however.

[25] In 1958, for example, labor productivity rose by only one per cent over the previous year. See Paul Underwood, "Yugoslavs Show Rise in Economy," *New York Times,* March 20, 1959, p. 5.

Since the Yugoslavs have been attempting to cooperate with the Western international monetary institutions, this on-the-job training, despite the considerable external economies involved, may be contributing to their inflation and resulting balance of payments difficulties. In Hungary, too, there has been a tendency for increases in labor productivity to be disappointing. Since 1950, labor productivity has increased by only about 41 per cent in contrast to the doubling of output per worker in the Soviet Union over this same period.[26]

2. *Labor productivity.* One of the most important measures of economic progress is the index of increasing labor productivity. The central planners in the noncapitalist-oriented economies make extensive use of productivity measurement in their operation and management controls. This measure when combined with information on the change in the labor force also provides economists with a rough measure of increased production or output, though not necessarily increased consumption. Since problems connected with increasing labor productivity will be discussed at some length at this point, we should first make certain that we understand exactly what is meant by this frequently misunderstood concept.

Labor productivity is a qualitative index measuring efficiency in the utilization of labor, given the worker's skill and capital equipment at his disposal. It is a measure of output per unit of input, inputs being expressed in terms of the single factor of production, labor. Outputs in cases of simple, homogeneous commodities can be measured in physical units. But if the final product is heterogeneous, as is the case with most machinery, it is necessary to value the units of output with some set of prices. For the economy as a whole, valuation of the individual components of total output is also necessary. Depending on the set of prices chosen (that is, early or later year), considerable variation can be obtained in the calculated overall change in output, as has already been pointed out in Chapter III (See page 32).

---

[26] See M. S. Handler, "Productivity Lag Cited in Hungary," *New York Times,* July 29, 1962, p. 5.

Since the Soviet measures of output were valued in 1926–27 "constant" rubles until 1950, the official Soviet series ostensibly reflecting changes in overall industrial labor productivity has a distinct upward bias, until at least that date.[27]

The labor inputs can also be measured in a number of ways. Sometimes only the inputs of production workers are employed; at other times, we may wish to take into account the entire labor input including, in addition to production workers, the inputs of engineer-technicians and white-collar employees. For other purposes we may wish to include capital inputs along with the labor inputs of our denominator, but this is really another story.

One thing should be made clear at the outset. In no sense is any increase in labor productivity attributable to greater labor intensity. To the extent that labor productivity has risen in any modern economy, this is due primarily to the fact that workers have greater technical skills and larger quantities of machinery at their disposal.

It is also evident that changes in the structure of the labor force will have some impact on the results obtained when labor inputs are measured by either of our two basic methods. As industrialization takes place, it is a well-known fact that there will be a growing share of the total labor force accounted for by engineering and technical personnel. In the Soviet Union, for example, 25 per cent of all workers and employees in machine-tool manufacturing are now engineer-technicians, while in some of our United States industries such as petroleum refining, over one-third of all workers and employees are now classified as engineers or technicians.

As our economy has matured, there has also been a tendency for white-collar workers to increase in relative importance, so that ordinary production workers are becoming less important as time goes by. If output per worker is calculated solely in terms

---

[27] It is possible that there may be new elements working in the same direction after 1950. In this connection, see Francis Seton, "The Tempo of Soviet Industrial Production," *Bulletin of the Oxford University Institute of Statistics,* February, 1958, pp. 6–7.

of the inputs of production workers, as is sometimes the case in our United States calculations, the increases in labor productivity shown may simply reflect this substitution of engineers and white-collar workers for production workers.

In the Soviet labor force, the percentage of engineers and technicians used in the productive process has also increased, but it is still probably on average below that prevailing in our economy. However, in contrast to the growing importance of white-collar workers in the United States, and also in the Soviet Union in the early thirties, there has apparently been a recent reduction in their share of the total Soviet labor force. In other words, the relative increase in engineer-technicians tends to be offset by the relative decline in white-collar workers. Thus, for the Soviet economy, it does not seem to make too much difference in the results obtained whether one takes into account only production workers or includes engineers and white-collar workers in the labor inputs used to calculate changes in Soviet labor productivity.[28]

Ordinarily the number of unemployed workers is excluded from our calculations of labor productivity in the United States. When comparisons are made between output per worker in the United States and the Soviet Union, and the unemployed are excluded from the former's labor inputs but do not exist in the latter, there is probably some bias in our favor. In the postwar period, this bias was probably insignificant, but it would probably grow in the sixties in the event that our unemployment were allowed to mount.

One of the most important problems confronting central planners in noncapitalist-oriented economies is a decision concerning the share of the increased productivity that is to be passed along to consumers generally. It seems clear from Soviet experience that there need be no direct correlation between gains in labor productivity and increased consumption. As we have

[28] Between 1956 and 1960, for example, the increased output per worker was the same regardless of the method of calculating the labor input. See *Narodnoe Khoziaistvo 1960*, p. 161.

noted in the preceding chapter, per capita consumption in the Soviet Union was stagnating during the thirties. At the same time rather substantial gains were being made in output per worker particularly during Plan II (1933–37). For the most part, these gains in labor productivity were being achieved in sectors of the economy which did not directly affect the consumer. In the last analysis, then, changes in per capita consumption depend primarily on labor productivity changes in consumers' goods industries, together with changes in the labor force employed in these sectors.[29] Increases in output per worker or employment in heavy industry or defense may increase the potentiality for higher consumption in the long run, but these gains need never come into fruition, especially if the gains in productivity are achieved in the defense sector.

In Yugoslavia the relationship between gains in labor productivity and per capita consumption in recent years have been the reverse of the one prevailing in the USSR in the thirties. Although output per worker has been relatively sluggish, there has undoubtedly been a considerable improvement in per capita consumption in Yugoslavia. A partial explanation for this phenomenon, in addition to assistance from abroad, is undoubtedly the fact that the Yugoslav labor force employed in the consumers' goods sector has expanded fairly rapidly as a result of the rapid rural exodus. In Czechoslovakia and the Soviet Union, on the other hand, the principle has been laid down that the rate of increase in labor productivity must exceed the rate of increase in real wages.[30] Presumably this policy may reflect the decision

[29] It is sometimes mistakenly assumed that per capita consumption depends on either the proportion of the total population working and the average output per worker—or that productivity is the basis for determining the living standards of a nation. Compare, for example, G. R. Barker, *Incentives and Labor Productivity in Soviet Industry,* Basil Blackwell, Oxford, p. 2; and William Ebenstein, *Today's Isms,* Second edition, Prentice-Hall, Englewood Cliffs, N.J., 1957, p. 56. Net imports (or exports) of consumers' goods or depletion (or additions to) of government stockpiles may also contribute to rising (or falling) per capita consumption in the short run.

[30] See Leon Greenberg, "International Conference on Labor Productivity," *Monthly Labor Review,* January, 1962, p. 20. This relationship

of the Czechs and Soviets to export capital, as well as the decision to increase communal consumption, which is ordinarily not accounted for in real wage calculations. In other words, part of the increased productivity of the Czech and Soviet economies is being used to assist other less developed members of the bloc or the neutralist countries.

During the postwar years in the Soviet Union, despite the official policy to the contrary, there has been a tendency for the gains in consumption to be pretty much on a par with the increased output per worker. Both series have been increasing by at least five per cent per annum during the fifties. The new Twenty-Year Plan provides for a continuation of this recent trend through the sixties, but in the seventies labor productivity is scheduled to rise at a faster rate than consumption. An explanation for this phenomenon may be the fact that labor participation rates are to fall in the seventies as larger numbers of students, wives, and senior citizens take advantage of greater educational and leisure opportunities. Or conceivably the Russians may anticipate greater capital exports, particularly in the form of engineer-technicians providing technical assistance to the developing countries.

In addition to the problem of deciding how much, if any, of the gain in productivity is to be passed along to workers generally in the form of higher consumption, there is the question of whether or not all workers are to share equally in any consumption gains. The fact that the gains in productivity were being achieved unevenly throughout Soviet industry in the thirties created special problems for the planners. For example, the unevenness of the impact of productivity change, when accompanied by a high percentage of fully employed workers on piece-rates, inevitably led to a cost-push inflation of the type that plagued Soviet producers' goods industries until 1949.

In the Soviet economy, the relationship between changes in money wages and labor productivity is the principal factor de-

---

between increases in labor productivity and real wages is considered to be an essential principle in Soviet planning, according to N. A. Bulganin, *op. cit.*, p. 39.

termining movements in unit labor costs and, in the long run, the costs and prices of producers' goods.[31] If money wages are allowed to rise faster than labor productivity, unit labor costs and eventually prices will also rise; conversely, if the reverse relationship persists for any length of time, unit labor costs and prices should eventually fall.

It is believed that gains in labor productivity within some of the leading sectors of heavy industry were of roughly the same order of magnitude as the increases in money wages during the thirties. For example, this may have been true in the sector of non-ferrous metallurgy producing aluminum; the sector of the chemical industry manufacturing sulphuric acid; the Kuznetsk and Magnitogorsk Metallurgical Combines; and for machine-building and metalworking as a whole. The infrequent or inadequate changes in the work norms in these sectors undoubtedly meant that there was a rather close correspondence between gains in labor productivity and the increases in money wages. In other sectors and industries, where substantial gains in labor productivity were not being achieved for one reason or another, increases in money wages far exceeded the increases in output per worker, resulting in rising unit labor costs and, eventually, in higher prices. In other words, the planning authorities appear to have been forced to pursue an inflationary wage policy in these sectors which have lagged with respect to productivity gains. In order to attract workers to important branches, as well as to keep workers in nonprogressive plants and industries relatively satisfied with their lot, the authorities were frequently forced to sanction "wages increases" which far exceeded their capacity to increase output per worker.

Over the entire planning era, but particularly before 1947, the increases in labor productivity in coal mining and logging were well below the average gains for basic industries as a whole. It seems clear then that the relative generosity with respect to

---

[31] For a further discussion of this long-run relationship between costs and prices in the producers' goods sector, see Lynn Turgeon, "Cost-Price Relationships in Basic Industries during the Soviet Planning Era," *Soviet Studies,* October, 1957.

wage increases in these industries must have been dictated by considerations other than labor productivity gains. Perhaps the wage increases were necessary to reduce frequent bottlenecks in the supplies of fuel and construction materials. In addition, under conditions of over-full employment, larger increases in money wages in these sectors might have been necessary to overcome the greater worker disutility associated with laboring in the mines and forests.[32]

In the extractive industries generally, depletion appears to have been a factor at times in keeping gains in labor productivity at a minimum or, in some instances at least, in actually causing the national average level of labor productivity to fall in certain periods. This depletion seems most apparent in the case of iron ore mining since 1937, underground coal mining after 1940 (postwar increases in labor productivity have been largely the result of a relatively greater expansion of open pit coal mines), crude oil extraction around 1940, and timber cutting throughout the period studied. The relatively above-average wages and wage increases granted to workers and employees in most of these industries may perhaps be interpreted as a recognition by Soviet authorities of the fact that depletion is a social cost, the burden of which certainly should not be borne by any particular group of workers or employees.

During the thirties and forties cost inflation was disguised for extended periods as a result of the fact that subsidies were being paid to key raw material producing industries. As a consequence of this policy of subsidizing these nonprogressive sectors, the rising cost of materials and fuel did not immediately show up in the official price data upon which managers made their decisions. Thus, there was an artificial incentive for Soviet managers to economize on their inputs of labor, which was the principal factor of production with rising money costs. Paradoxically, although capital tended to be the factor in short supply

[32] Possibly employment for working wives may have been more difficult to find in coal mining or logging areas with the result that higher dependency ratios prevail in these sectors. High wages for principal breadwinners would therefore be required to make ends meet.

relative to labor for the economy as a whole, it may in some cases have been used rather wastefully, or else in places where it was economically unjustified, since it was obtained by managers out of the government budget without capital charges. Since there was a chronic wage inflation during these early years—sometimes amounting to as much as a 20 per cent increase in a single year—and the prices paid by managers for materials, fuel, and machinery were generally unchanged for long periods, there was something of an artificial incentive for factory management to economize on labor inputs in their operating decisions.

Actually, during these early years, quantitative targets tended to receive priority over the qualitative goals of increasing labor productivity and lowering production costs, so that in its effect, the government subsidization of fuel and materials had less impact on managerial incentives to reduce labor inputs than might be supposed. Nevertheless, the fact remains that significant increases in labor productivity were being achieved during the middle thirties, especially in such sectors of heavy industry as machine-building, aluminum, and electric power. This surprising Soviet success in raising labor productivity in the thirties—at a time when there was a relatively abundant supply of unskilled labor and a general withholding of consumption gains as incentives for labor—would seem to be partially a result of the rapidly rising money wage costs coupled with the policy of subsidizing the output of fuel and raw materials out of the government budget. A further and perhaps even more important explanation for these successes was the rapid increase in capital-labor ratios as a result of the investment priorities assigned to heavy industry.

By the fifties, the relative supplies of capital and labor in the Soviet economy had become pretty much the reverse of those existing in the previous decades. The sharp decline in the birth rate during World War II meant that the relatively abundant labor supply existing during the thirties had dwindled and been replaced by a severe labor shortage that will only be alleviated after 1964 when the more normal postwar birth rate begins to have a favorable effect on the net additions to the Soviet labor force. At the same time, the supplies of capital equipment have continued to grow and the government's subsidization of fuel and raw materials has been minimized, even though it still persists in a few industries such as logging and coal mining. Thus, while the gains in industrial labor productivity during the fifties have certainly been both more steady and more pervasive as compared with the thirties, the impetus behind these gains has changed. The real shortages of labor and the growing overall priority assigned to the qualitative indices, rather than any wage inflation have guided managerial decision-making in this regard. Since 1948, the average increase in money wages has fluctuated between only two and four per cent per year.

According to official Soviet claims, industrial output per worker approximately doubled during the fifties. Allowing for a certain amount of upward bias in Soviet calculations, it seems fair to say that the Soviets are at present increasing annual output per worker in industry by five or six per cent on the average, or by roughly the same rate of increase as in the thirties after the initial influx of peasants into the labor force had taken place. In the thirties, the propelling factor would seem to have been the monetary incentives—wage inflation and the subsidization of fuel and materials. In the fifties, the impetus to economize on labor inputs came from real labor shortages which were not accompanied by wage inflation due to the government's success either in lowering or stabilizing the retail price level.

In addition to the above-mentioned great variations in the rates of change in labor productivity in different industries, there is considerable variation in the current relative efficiency of different Soviet industries and sectors with respect to labor productivity when compared with the output per worker in the corresponding United States industry or sector.

For Soviet industry as a whole, it has been estimated by our Western specialist, Professor Walter Galenson, that industrial labor productivity in the mid-fifties was on the average about 40 per cent of our own. In their own independent calculations, the Russians later found that industrial output per worker averaged closer to 50 per cent of that in the United States. In construction, the Russians claim that output per worker is 60 per cent of our construction workers' productivity which probably reflects, as much as anything else, the relative backwardness of our own construction industry when it comes to the application of pre-fabrication techniques. In transportation, the Russians claim that labor productivity is one-third of ours, while, as we have already mentioned in Chapter V, output per worker in Soviet agriculture is certainly less than one-third of that prevailing on our own farms.

Within Soviet industry, the most favorable comparison with respect to Soviet labor productivity is found in machine-building, metallurgy, and in the food processing and light industries where output per worker is about one-half or something more than half of ours.[33] In the production of metal-cutting machine tools, especially those which the Russians produce on an assembly line basis, the Russians may have actually achieved levels of labor productivity which are as high or higher than our own. Likewise, some of their newer iron and steel plants and perhaps their defense plants (although little concrete information is available on this latter score) may have achieved levels of labor productivity which are pretty much on a par with our own. On the other hand, in their coal mines output per worker is only a quarter of our productivity level.

These great variations in relative labor productivity in the Soviet economy as compared with our own reflect to some extent the relative natural resource endowments of the two countries. The limitations of Soviet natural resources are especially striking in some of the extractive industries where, as we have already noted, depletion acts as an important factor limiting gains in output per worker. In particular, the Soviet coal miners seem to have been struggling against serious natural resource

[33] For Soviet studies of labor productivity in the Soviet Union vis-à-vis the United States, compare A. Aganbegian, *"Dognat' i peregnat' SShA po urovniu proizvoditel'nosti truda"* (To Reach and Surpass the Level of Labor Productivity of the United States), *Sotsialisticheskii Trud*, No. 4, 1959, p. 11, and D. Karpukhin, *"Elektrifikatsiia narodnogo khoziaistva i rost proizvoditel'nosti obshchestvennogo truda"* (Electrification of the National Economy and the Growth in the Productivity of Social Labor), *Voprosy Ekonomiki*, No. 4, 1959, p. 40.

deficiencies, especially in the Donets Basin. As a result, despite great investments in coal mining, the increases in their labor productivity have been modest, even by our standards. But the most influential factor explaining relative labor productivity in sectors of the Soviet economy is undoubtedly the past investment policy of the planners. Where investment priorities have been high, the latest capital equipment was forthcoming in relatively large amounts, resulting in a more rapidly growing output per worker. On the other hand, where investment priorities have been low, increases in labor productivity, and eventually levels of relative productivity, have been correspondingly less impressive. Thus, to the extent that the planners' investment preferences have resulted in greater increases in output per worker in certain sectors, they may also have influenced the relative sharing of the gains in consumption among piece workers employed in the different sectors.

WAGE MOVEMENTS IN CAPITALIST-ORIENTED ECONOMIES

From our earliest days in the United States, labor has been a comparatively scarce factor, at least in relation to the factor proportions existing in Europe. Rural overpopulation has been of negligible importance throughout our economic history so that additional supplies of industrial labor were frequently obtained in periods of rapid economic growth via the immigration of European and Asian labor. Since in many cases these immigrants consisted of young and vigorous men, they represented an economic windfall to our economy. They were raised in poorer economies during their unproductive years and came to the United States to work during their most productive period. If they decided to retire in their native land, so much the better from the standpoint of our developing economy.

According to some economic historians, our relatively free land policy in the nineteenth century apparently acted as a "safety valve" preventing occasional periods of industrial unemployment from having serious depressing effects on money wages. Our generally high and secularly rising industrial wages resulting from this chronic scarcity of industrial labor seemingly encouraged United States entrepreneurs to economize on labor through the introduction of labor-saving devices.

As our frontier disappeared, labor became less scarce during periods of recession, but our restrictive immigration laws introduced in the early twenties helped to slow down any possible growing relative abundance of labor. By the time of the Great Depression, labor superficially appeared to be a relatively abundant factor in view of our serious unemployment problem. However, considering the even greater underutilization of capital at that time, labor would still seem to have been the scarcer of the two factors for the economy as a whole. The reduction of the average work week as a result of the Fair Labor Standards Act in 1938 may also have contributed to a continuation of the relatively short effective labor supply. In addition, minimum wage legislation also resulted in the exclusion from the labor force of those few unfortunates who could not produce enough to compensate any employers who were compelled to pay the legal minimum wage.

Partly as a result of the New Deal labor legislation, stronger labor unions were also restricting the supply of labor in key industries and attempting to take over the role of pressing for relatively high and constantly increasing money wages. In the war and postwar years, full and near-full employment has insured that the money wage increases obtained by these strong unions would spill over into the nonunionized sectors.

Due to the continuing shortage of labor in the United States, either because of natural conditions or man-made institutional developments, money wage levels have risen fairly steadily throughout our economic history. But since price levels generally have also risen in a secular fashion, these higher money wages have not always been translated into equivalent increases in real wages. Nevertheless, as we have noted in the previous chapter, substantial increases in real wages have accompanied our general economic development.

The increases in our real wages have been so obvious that even the Russians have finally conceded that Marx may have been wrong when he claimed that "the general tendency of capitalist production leads not to the raising of the average wage level, but to its lowering." [34] At present it is only claimed that there has been a *relative* worsening of the conditions of the working class under capitalism. According to Soviet theorists, our general economic progress has brought about rising workers' requirements which are more difficult for present workers to attain as compared with our grandfathers' ability to satisfy their lower requirements of that period.[35]

While all workers have increased their real income over time, some individuals have been more successful than others. In the Soviet Union, we have already noted that it was largely the planners' preferences utilizing market forces which determined the relative gains made by different groups of workers. In capitalist-oriented economies, the factors determining the relative wage levels in different occupations and industries at any time—and the changes in relative wages over time—are less clear.

Economists, as usual, seem to be split in their answers to this question. Economic theorists tend to answer in terms of the demand and supply curves for labor in different occupations or industries. The marginal value product—or the value that the added worker contributes to the employer's revenue—underlies the demand curve, while the marginal disutility of labor—or what it takes to overcome the worker's inherent distaste for labor—is the basis for the supply curve. On the other hand, the labor economist is inclined to think of relative wages as being determined by the degree of market imperfection—whether this imperfection origi-

[34] The first inkling of the revision of the Marxist tenet that real wages would fall under capitalism seems to have appeared in a discussion of the third edition of the Russians' textbook on *Political Economy*. See *Voprosy Ekonomiki,* No. 11, 1957, pp. 103, *et seq.*

[35] In this connection, see Harry Schwartz, "Moscow Revises Economic Theory," *New York Times,* March 4, 1962, p. 14. For an authoritative discussion of the so-called law of absolute and relative impoverishment of labor, see Earl Browder, *Marx and America,* Duell, Sloan and Pearce, New York, 1958, pp. 83–94.

nates as a result of union organization, monopolistic-oligopolistic competition, or both.

Over the long haul, most economists tend to agree that our labor unions have had comparatively little success with respect to increasing the share of income payments going to labor or in reducing the portion going to profit earners.[36] It is still possible to argue, however, that without unionization, the share of the total product going to labor would have fallen, as Marx had predicted, but there is no way of proving this. It is true that there is usually a rather sharp initial increase in money wages accompanying the unionization of an occupation or industry. But after this initial spurt, wages in the unionized activity may actually lag behind the increases in the nonunionized sectors, particularly in periods of full or near-full employment.

Most economists would also agree that unionization has had some impact when it comes to improving working conditions or in reducing social tensions. Our trade unions undoubtedly exercise some disciplinary control over their individual members' actions, and it is this function of our unions which has helped bring about their greater acceptance by our management personnel. The unions are also in the vanguard when it comes to pressing for more leisure via a lower compulsory work week or for greater fringe benefits.

In recent years, as the capitalist-oriented economy of the United States has matured, wage movements seem to be exhibiting tendencies suitable for our historical requirements, in that the wage spread between skilled and unskilled labor has tended to be reduced.[37] In many industries, across-the-board settlements

[36] Although there is some evidence that there has been a "profit squeeze" in recent years, the share of interest payments has risen, partly due to the fact that our tax laws have created a bias favoring the raising of capital by selling bonds rather than stock. There may also be a tendency for some profits to be concealed in liberally reported depreciation which was allowed after 1954.

[37] Despite the tendency for wages to move in the direction of greater equality, there is little indication that wealth or income is being more equally distributed, at least in recent years. For a questioning of the movement towards greater equality on the basis of the history of differentials in payments by the McCormick Works of the International Harvester

in postwar wage negotiations have resulted in wage increases of about the same magnitude so that the percentage increases for the wages of unskilled workers have been generally greater than the percentage gains for skilled workers, at least since 1933. Our labor unions have generally tended to resist the use of piece-rates and, as more industries have become unionized, this resistance has been intensified. In addition, our secular inflation of the forties and fifties has apparently been a factor resulting in somewhat greater wage equality.[38]

One statistical method of measuring the decreasing differential between the wages of skilled and unskilled workers would be to calculate the ratio of the third to the first quartile of a wage distribution. One study—covering about 40 per cent of the non-farm wage earners in the United States—found that between 1939 and 1956, this ratio declined from 1.64 to 1.37. Although there are serious questions concerning the comparability of the data, according to some unpublished work of Professor Yanowitch, this ratio in the Soviet Union has been in excess of 1.8 during the period between 1929 and 1959.[39]

LABOR PROBLEMS IN CAPITALIST-ORIENTED ECONOMIES

1. *Labor mobility*. Since the United States economy today normally operates with a considerable backlog of unemployed labor,

---

Company, see Robert Ozanne, "A Century of Occupational Differentials in Manufacturing," *The Review of Economics and Statistics,* August, 1962, pp. 292–299.

[38] However, according to one writer, this movement towards greater equality has slowed down and may be reversed in the future, as inflationary forces are brought under control and as automation creates a greater demand for highly skilled labor. See Richard Perlman, "Forces Widening Occupational Wage Differentials," *The Review of Economics and Statistics,* No. 2, 1958, pp. 107–115.

[39] United States data from Bureau of Labor Statistics as cited by P. Homan, A. G. Hart, and A. W. Sametz, *The Economic Order,* Harcourt, Brace, New York, 1958, p. 285.

labor mobility is ordinarily much less of a problem here than it is in the noncapitalist-oriented economies generally. Labor mobility was a serious problem, however, under our over-full employment conditions existing during World War II. As a result of this mobility, and in the interest of winning the war, some of the more crucial members of our civilian labor force were temporarily frozen in their jobs in somewhat the same manner as most Soviet workers were after October, 1940.

2. *Creating employment opportunities.* A major task facing the United States economy—and those who propose to guide its development—will be the creation of job opportunities for the increasing number of job applicants expected in the present decade. Our labor force has been growing by an average of 825,000 annually for the last decade. By 1970, it should be growing by twice that figure because the babies born in the postwar baby boom will be attempting to enter the labor market. Already in 1963, we are having difficulties creating sufficient new job opportunities to absorb our teenagers as they reach working age. But the impact of the postwar baby boom will not really hit our economy until 1964 and thereafter. It would seem that 1964 is a crucial year with respect to both the United States and Soviet economies. Their recent problems related to the war-induced labor shortage will begin to be alleviated in this year, while our employment problems created by the postwar bulge in births will just be starting.

3. *Wage-price policy.* There has been considerable talk about the need for developing a wage policy consistent with price stability in capitalist-oriented economies. In our case, one of the most common suggestions involves a limiting of annual wage increases in any sector to the gain in productivity for the economy as a whole. If the historical rate of increase in labor productivity is two per cent per annum, then wages could rise by no more than this percentage in any year. For industries or sectors where increases in productivity are less than two per cent, some increases in prices would be justified; for those sectors where labor productivity increases exceed two per cent, price reductions would be in order. This latter part of the prescription

is obviously the most difficult aspect of the policy, in view of the reluctance of firms in monopolistically competitive industries to reduce prices except under rare circumstances. At any rate, it should be noted that such a policy is designed only to maintain labor's share of the total pie and it is just conceivable that the share going to labor should increase in the process of economic maturation.[40]

During the fifties in the United States, there was a subtle change in the forces responsible for our price rises. Excess demand, or what is sometimes referred to as "gap" inflation, in part generated by the mobilization of resources during the Korean conflict, was the principal factor responsible for the inflationary movement in prices during the early fifties. Later, when there was obviously little or no excess demand, but rather a growing percentage of idle capacity in both producers' goods and consumers' goods industries, prices still rose gently—in large part because of rising unit overhead costs, especially sales expenditures and interest payments. By the end of the decade, stability seemed to characterize our price movements, albeit with growing underutilization of our labor and capital resources. To the extent that prices (including wages) did not fall when ex·cess capacity and unemployed labor power developed, "adminis·tered" price policy, either from the side of monopolistic enter prise or unions, could be judged the culprit.

If price stability has been achieved in the United States, as seems likely, it still remains as something of a problem in Western Europe with their full or near-full employment economies at the present time.[41] In Great Britain, the demand for a wage policy to control inflation and rectify balance of payments deficits

[40] In this connection, see Martin Bronfenbrenner, "Some Neglected Implications of Secular Inflation," in Kenneth K. Kurihara, *Post-Keynesian Economics,* Rutgers University Press, New Brunswick, N.J., 1954, especially pp. 53 *et seq.*

[41] Between 1958 and 1962, average wages rose by the following percentages in Western Europe: West Germany—34%; France—34%; Sweden—31%; Italy—18%; and Great Britain—17%. The increases in the cost of living in these countries ranged from 8 to 21 per cent during these years. See *United States News and World Report,* June 18, 1962, pp. 77–78.

has been answered by "wage pauses," which are made necessary by the rather small increases in labor productivity being achieved. In Western Germany, on the other hand, there have been unsuccessful attempts to devise a wage policy which will prevent the runaway inflation for which the Germans have a special phobia. Chancellor Adenauer ordered the preparation of a memorandum in 1959 dealing with the expected changes in labor productivity and prices, upon which both employers and unions tacitly agreed to negotiate their contracts.[42] However, by the first quarter of 1962, wages and salaries were increasing at an annual rate of 13 per cent despite the fact that productivity was rising by only 5.5 per cent.[43]

REFLECTION OF BASIC PROBLEMS IN LABOR INSTITUTIONS AND ATTITUDES

1. *Role of trade unions.* Most Russian workers, as well as the managers of enterprises, belong to trade unions organized along industrial lines. In 1959 about 53 million Russian workers belonged to some 23 industrial trade unions.[43a] Functionally these organizations in the Soviet Union bear little resemblance to their Western counterparts, despite their similar labels. The principal objective of the Russian trade union, at least since the demise of Comrade Tomsky, would appear to be one of stimulating production and labor productivity. The trade union attempts to accomplish this objective by supplying such "carrots" as better housing or paid vacations in trade union rest homes to the most productive members of the labor force. Unlike Western trade unions, these Soviet organizations have comparatively

[42] See Arthur J. Olsen, "Bonn Avoids Risk of Labor Strife," *New York Times,* February 14, 1960, p. 21.

[43] *New York Times,* June 7, 1962, p. 2.

[43a] Following the reorganization of Soviet administration in 1963, the various trade unions were combined under two trade union councils, one concerned with industry and the other with agriculture.

little to say about money wage determination, although they do check on the observance of labor legislation and administer certain "fringe benefits." They are expected to improve labor discipline (reduce absenteeism, labor mobility, etc.); encourage "socialist competition" between different plants; and represent worker and employee interests with respect to working and living conditions (safety, lighting, and housing). In addition, the unions administer social insurance covering temporary disability, sickness, and maternity benefits; funeral allowances; pensions to the permanently disabled and those past retirement age who continue working; children's aid; the provision of rest homes and sanitoriums; travel assistance; and welfare payments to indigent families. In short, their trade unions are an important instrument in administering "cradle-to-the-grave" security.

An objective of Western trade union activity is ostensibly that of increasing the workers' share of the total pie. However, as was mentioned above, our unions in practice have been able to negotiate improvements in money wages, and to a lesser extent, in real earnings, but in the long run they seem to have had little success in changing the share of total income going to labor. As in the Soviet Union, our trade unions undoubtedly exercise some disciplinary control over individual members' actions and thereby minimize social tensions.

Unlike the Soviet trade unions, our labor organizations are not expected to spur their members on to greater productivity heights, although one of the bases upon which unions negotiate money wage increases is the improvement of labor productivity or the so-called "improvement factor." In periods of full employment, our unions can be more enthusiastic about raising output per worker. But, generally speaking, raising labor productivity is considered to be a function of management in capitalist-oriented economies. Occasionally a progressive management will make an agreement with a union tying in higher wages with cost reductions.[44] There seems to be a general feeling among trade union

---

[44] See David R. Jones, "Steel Union and Kaiser Agree in Principle on Revolutionary Pact," *Wall Street Journal,* August 22, 1962, p. 1. Under this agreement, one-third of the cost savings will be passed along to workers in the form of higher wages.

leaders (not without reason in view of past experience) that too rapid an increase in labor productivity may possibly confront them with an even more serious unemployment problem. Thus, such productivity-spurring devices as piece-rates are regarded as leading to "speed-ups" and are ordinarily vigorously opposed.[45] When unemployment becomes a chronic problem, as it seems to be in the sixties, our trade unions are frequently in the vanguard when it comes to pressing for a shorter work week with the same take-home pay. Our trade unions also frequently oppose the extension of freer trade or more lenient immigration laws in the belief that our highly paid workers are unable to compete with "cheap foreign labor." Recently our trade unions have allocated some of their own resources to assist in the development of independent trade unions and higher wages in capitalist-oriented countries abroad.

2. *Worker innovations.* In the United States, the factory suggestion box is frequently used by management in an attempt to discover better ways of doing things. Furthermore, rather substantial rewards are sometimes made to workers for their suggestions. But this practice does not appear to be nearly so effective as a stimulant to labor productivity as it is in the USSR, where it operates on a nationwide basis under state auspices. There are two major types of rewards for inventions in the Soviet Union. In both instances, cost economies or savings are the basis for the determination of incentive payments.

According to current Soviet legislation, which revises an original decree issued in 1931, workers who are responsible for inventions receive "author's certificates" entitling them to receive compensation plus such privileges as partial exemption from taxes and better housing.[46] The compensation is based on the

[45] In the United States, only 27 per cent of all workers in manufacturing are covered by piecework or bonus-type payments. See L. Earl Lewis, "Extent of Incentive Pay in Manufacturing," *Monthly Labor Review,* Vol. LXXXIII, May, 1960, pp. 460–462.

[46] For an up-to-date account of workers' rewards for innovation, see P. J. Federico, "Soviet Law on Inventions and Patents," *Journal of the Patent Office Society,* January, 1961.

highest cost economies achieved in any of the first five years following the innovation. If the economies are over 10,000 rubles, the incentive payment amounts to two per cent of the saving plus 210 rubles, but in no case does the total payment exceed 2,000 rubles. For other workers, incentive payments are made for lesser inventions or "rationalizations"—cheaper ways of accomplishing a given task. For these less important improvements, only .5 per cent of the total cost saving plus 86 rubles is paid for economies exceeding 10,000 rubles, with a 500 ruble ceiling. According to one report, the total return for an invention is seldom in excess of 600 rubles.[47] Nevertheless, a fairly large number of people obtain additional income from this source. From 1956 to 1958, nearly 100 million rubles were paid out to rationalizers and inventors for their contributions.[48] In 1959, two million persons submitted 3.5 million suggestions, of which 2.16 million were accepted; by 1961, the number of accepted suggestions reached 2.5 million.[49] There are also rewards for those who aid in bringing about the utilization of inventions, and the returns from the author's certificates are inheritable by the inventor's descendants.

In addition, there is a patent system of lesser importance than the author's certificates. It differs from our system in that the inventor has no right to restrict the use of his patent. According to the Russians, patents which hold an invention out of use are considered to be a vestige of capitalism. Generally speaking, there would seem to be more significant "grass roots" sources of increased output per worker in the Soviet system, although when we come to the section on management in Chapter IX, we shall see that the noncapitalist-oriented systems are not completely free from forces tending to retard innovation.

[47] See Irving R. Levine, *Main Street, U.S.S.R.*, Doubleday, New York, 1959, p. 93.

[48] G. Anisimov, *"O povyshenii material'noi zainteresovannosti rabotnikov predpriiatii vo vnedrenii novoi tekhniki"* (About Increasing the Material Interest of Workers of Enterprises in the Introduction of New Techniques), *Voprosy Ekonomiki*, No. 6, 1959, p. 32.

[49] Editorial, *"Piat' let raboty v novykh usloviiakh"* (Five Years of Work Under the New Conditions), *Planovoe Khoziaistvo*, No. 5, 1962, p. 7.

3. *Automation*. Attitudes towards automation also differ considerably in capitalist and noncapitalist-oriented economies. In the United States, only the more "progressive" trade unions in periods of full employment attempt to convince their members that there is little to fear from labor-displacing devices. In the Soviet Union, on the other hand, since there has been no unemployment of any consequence for over thirty years, trade unions are much more successful in selling the advantages of automation to their members. The end result of this lack of opposition to automation is the fact that the automatic controls employed in Soviet power and steel industries are apparently the equal of those in the United States, despite the superiority of the United States automatic control industry generally.[50] Soviet scientists are reportedly more advanced than United States engineers in the theoretical development of non-linear controls of a type that can make fast and sensitive corrections when a disturbance materializes in the machinery they are governing. The Russians are planning to build automated steel and power plants with capacities far larger than those of existing enterprises. During the next twenty years, they expect to witness the use of complex automation of steel production on a massive scale with gradual introduction of fully automated shops and plants. In these plants, all "hot" processes, such as the smelting of pig iron and the manufacturing of steel, would be handled by automation.[51] One of the most impressive examples of modern industrial engineering is the First State Ball Bearing Plant in Moscow, where one separate factory of the establishment, almost fully

[50] These are the opinions of Professor Rufus Oldenburger, chairman of the United States delegation attending the first congress of the International Federation of Automatic Control. See Seymour Topping, "Automation Held Lagging in Soviet," *New York Times,* July 1, 1960, p. 4.

[51] See "Automated Steel Planned in Soviet," *New York Times,* August 20, 1961, p. 11. For a generally favorable evaluation of contemporary Soviet steel technology, see M. Gardner Clark, *Economics and Technology: The Case of Soviet Steel,* Reprint series No. 109 of New York State School of Industrial and Labor Relations, p. 27. This article appeared originally in Nicholas Spulber, editor, *Study of the Soviet Economy: Direction and Impact of Soviet Growth, Teaching and Research in Soviet Economies,* Vol. XXV, Russian and East European Series, Indiana University Publications, Bloomington, 1961.

automatic, produces two million ball bearings yearly with 12 production workers and 18 maintenance engineers.[52] In Czechoslovakia, where the agricultural labor reserves have apparently been largely exhausted, great stress is also being placed on intensive automation.[53] As a first measure to meet the growing manpower shortage, the Czech government has begun to introduce electronic computers on a fairly big scale. About 1,500 sets of computers produced in Czechoslovakia are said to be in operation, solving management and production problems.

In contrast to the enthusiastic acceptance of automation in the noncapitalist-oriented economies, we find the widespread opinion in the United States that computers and automation are threatening to create vast unemployment and social unrest for this nation.[54] It is predicted that cybernation will eliminate entire job categories ranging from factory and farm workers to bank tellers and middle-management executives. According to the rather sensational study cited above, the government would have to support part of the released population through public works, the ultimate effects of which would certainly "not be conducive to maintaining the spirit of a capitalistic economy."

4. *Unemployment.* Officially no unemployment exists in the Soviet Union, although undoubtedly both frictional and seasonal unemployment can be detected.[55] Consequently there has also

---

[52] See Walter H. Waggoner, "Briton Bids West Speed Production," *New York Times,* December 13, 1959, p. 18.

[53] See "Czech Industries Spur Automation," *New York Times,* February 11, 1962, p. 24.

[54] Donald N. Michael, "Cybernation: The Silent Conquest," Center for the Study of Democratic Institutions, 1962. For an account of this study, see *New York Times,* January 29, 1962, p. 1.

[55] Seasonal unemployment is of considerable importance in both logging and peat extraction. According to one estimate, the average duration of unemployment per worker was between 28 and 31 days. See Arcadius Kahan, *loc. cit.,* p. 18. For an account of the importance of frictional unemployment in the USSR, see N. Kokosov, *"Uluchshut' ispol'zovanie trudovykh resursov sibiri i dal'nego vostoka."* (To Improve the Utilization of Labor Resources in Siberia and the Far East), *Sotsialisticheskii Trud,* No. 2, 1961. In the Krasnoyarsk territory, people who leave their jobs spend an average of thirty days between the time of their discharge until they are admitted to a new job.

been no system of unemployment insurance since October, 1930. Some economists feel that the low level of labor productivity in Soviet industry or agriculture reflects disguised unemployment.[56] If this is so, this means that unemployment has been socialized along with most everything else since some wage earners must be paid wages which exceed their marginal value product. My own feeling is that the Russians suffer from over-full employment chronically and that their labor market resembles our own situation during World War II. One might say that we had disguised unemployment at that time because some employers hoarded skilled workers in excess of their immediate requirements or that some Southern tenant farmers could have been more profitably re-located into urban factories. One can also make similar observations about the Soviet economy, particularly during the thirties when skilled labor was very scarce and sometimes hoarded, or with respect to their agricultural sector where disguised unemployment still exists despite thirty years of intensive industrialization. But, on the whole, this is not a very important phenomenon, and it is becoming less so as the years pass.

Along with the lack of unemployment insurance, there is also a comparative absence of what we might call an organized labor exchange bringing buyers and sellers of labor power together. It is this lack of an organized labor market that the Russians cite whenever they deny the existence of a market for labor.

---

[56] In this connection, see A. R. Oxenfeldt and E. Von den Haag, "Unemployment in Planned and Capitalist Economies," *Quarterly Journal of Economics,* February, 1954, pp. 43–60. See also Warren W. Eason, "Labor Force Materials for the Study of Unemployment in the Soviet Union" in National Bureau of Economic Research, *The Measurement and Behavior of Unemployment,* Princeton University Press, Princeton, 1957. The latter source points out that unemployment reached a peak of 1.7 million persons or two per cent of the labor force in 1929. Since that time, the labor force has grown at a rate of less than two per cent per annum while national income has been growing at between five and 10 per cent. According to Eason, "the expansion of output, together with the relatively high rate of investment, would seem to have been adequate for the full employment of the labor force." Actually, however, if the labor productivity claims of the Russians were accepted at face value, some unemployment might still be possible.

Information on job openings and hirings is apparently passed by word of mouth, as well as by radio and billboard advertising. One United States economist has suggested that the establishment of an organized office of employment in the USSR might serve a useful purpose.[57] On the other hand, if information on job opportunities were more readily available to workers, it might also tend to stimulate the already high degree of labor mobility.

Some concern has recently been expressed with regard to the possible development of technological unemployment in the USSR.[58] But, in general, technological displacement, and the resulting need for retraining workers, does not seem to worry Soviet planners, operating as they do in a chronic over-full employment situation where jobs are constantly seeking workers.

In contrast to the lack of worry about unemployment in the Soviet Union, there is at present considerable worry about unemployment in the United States. The principal question in the fifties seems to have been whether or not a certain percentage of our labor force—say seven per cent—must be unemployed in order to insure price stability. Those economists who are worried about inflation are inclined to take a rather cavalier attitude towards unemployment since a large percentage of unemployed resources is a pretty sure guarantee of little inflationary pressure. Professor Galbraith in his *The Affluent Society,* for example, sees the solution largely as one of increasing the size of unemployment compensation payments.[59] For Galbraith, a rising GNP *per se* is relatively immaterial and the size of the unemployed labor force of only marginal significance in the whole picture. Apparently

[57] Emily Clark Brown, "The Soviet Labor Market," *Industrial and Labor Relations Review,* Vol. X, No. 2, January, 1957, p. 199.

[58] See Emily Clark Brown, "A Note on Employment and Unemployment," *Soviet Studies,* Vol. XII, January, 1961, No. 3, pp. 231–239.

[59] More recently Galbraith has taken the position that direct price and wage controls may be required in the sector where "administered prices" prevail. See Edwin L. Dale, "Controls Urged to Curb Inflation," *New York Times,* March 12, 1959. The problem posed by this latest solution is one of drawing the line between industries subject to direct controls and those allowed to remain outside the price control apparatus.

a large unemployed "reserve army" receiving adequate unemployment compensation is a symptom of affluence.

5. *Labor participation*. Institutions and attitudes with respect to labor participation are the opposite of each other in capitalist and noncapitalist-oriented countries. In the Soviet Union, where a great many incentives are used to obtain greater participation, the percentage of the population employed rose from 46.2 to 47.5 per cent between the 1939 and 1959 censuses. For females, the increase in labor participation was still more significant, rising from 38.4 to 41.5 per cent.[60] The percentages for the United States are consistently below the corresponding figures for the Soviet Union, and they are also essentially stable.[61] Although there is a steadily rising percentage of females in the United States labor force, there is an offsetting decline in the percentages of very old and young men.

Attitudes towards retirement and old age pensions are also considerably different in the Soviet Union as compared with the United States. In the United States, persons over 65 receiving Federal old age pensions have been practically excluded from full time employment due to the fact that their additional earnings have in the past been limited to $1,200 per year. In the USSR, on the other hand, until 1956 workers could continue working at full pay and still receive their admittedly inadequate pensions. After 1956, only 50 per cent of the minimum pension, or 15 rubles per month, has been paid to working persons earning less than 100 rubles per month; no pension whatsoever is paid to employed persons earning in excess of 100 rubles monthly, which is above the average wage. Eligibility for retirement begins for most Soviet men at 60 and for most women at 55.[62] Until recently the size of the Russian old age pensions was such that retirement was out

---

[60] E. Kapustin, *"Proizvoditel'nost' truda i zarabotnaia plata"* (Labor Productivity and Wages), *Sotsialisticheskii Trud*, No. 4, 1962, pp. 13–14.

[61] See C. D. Long, *The Labor Force Under Changing Income and Employment*, Princeton University Press, Princeton, 1958.

[62] Coal miners and workers in other difficult occupations are eligible for pensions five years earlier. Mothers of five or more children are also deservedly eligible at this earlier age.

of the question, but as a result of the marked improvement in the benefits since 1957 Soviet citizens are now retiring for the first time.[63]

The Russians now claim that the average pension amounts to 60 per cent of the average wage the pensioner earned prior to the time he was eligible to receive a pension. The comparable percentage for the Czechs is 50 per cent, while in the United States, it is 20 per cent, according to a Soviet source.[63]

Retirement is a comparatively recent institutional development in our economy also. At the turn of the century, voluntary retirement was virtually non-existent. More than two-thirds of all men 65 and over in 1890 considered themselves as part of the labor force, but by 1960 less than one-third felt that they were part of the labor force. More than one-half of the retired persons surveyed in a recent study had been forced into retirement by the employer's policy with respect to age.

In addition to a much larger percentage of elderly people who work either by choice or necessity in the Soviet Union, there are some other minor sources of additional labor which are comparatively unutilized in the United States. The armed forces in the Soviet Union are frequently made available for more "productive" labor. A few years ago, when coal output was lagging in the Donbas, Soviet troops were sent down to help overcome the bottleneck. Occasionally United States armed forces are used to help out in disaster areas, but they are believed to be less important sources of productive labor in our economy as com-

---

[63] E. Konovavov, *"Pod"em zhiznennogo urovnia narodov stran sotsializma"* (The Rise in Levels of Living of the People in Countries of Socialism), *Voprosy Ekonomiki,* No. 1, 1962, p. 9. No all-Union information has been divulged on the proportion of pensioners who continue working, but apparently those individuals earning more than 100 rubles per month when they become eligible for retirement are deferring their retirement. In addition, there are undoubtedly strong social and psychological pressures to continue working as long as possible. It has been estimated that about 20 per cent of all persons receiving pensions may continue working in the Soviet Union. See United States Department of Health, Education and Welfare Social Security Administration, *A Report on Social Security Programs in the Soviet Union,* U.S. Government Printing Office, Washington, 1960, p. 45.

pared with the USSR. In mainland China, the use of the army as an important component of the labor force has been acknowledged by the authorities.[64] Officers and men of the army contributed 40 million man-days to industry and agriculture in 1959, or the equivalent of 16 days per soldier. The Chinese army helped build water conservation and irrigation projects and factories, tended gardens and raised hogs in their "leisure hours."

The same comparison would also apply to prison or unfree labor. Such work in our prisons is encouraged primarily for therapeutic reasons. In the Soviet Union, prison labor is utilized not only for therapeutic reasons, but it has frequently been a fairly important source of productive labor in the building of various public works such as canals. Like everyone else in history, however, the Russians have found unfree labor to be less productive as compared with free labor, and seemingly there has been a tendency towards less reliance on so-called slave labor since 1953. Professor Harold Berman of Harvard was told by the Deputy Prosecutor General of the USSR, P. I. Kudriavtsev, that in 1957 the number of prisoners in the Soviet Union was less than 30 per cent of the total detained prior to Stalin's death. At that time, Kudriavtsev apparently "wanted to convey the impression" that about three million persons had been under detention in March, 1953, while in 1957 less than one million were still detained.[65]

During the next few years, students will be relied upon for more labor in the USSR as well as in Eastern Europe.[66] Many

[64] See "Red China Using Army for Labor," *New York Times,* February 3, 1960, p. 2.

[65] See H. J. Berman, "Soviet Law Reform—Dateline Moscow 1957," *The Yale Law Journal,* July, 1957, pp. 1192, 1194 and 1195. Earlier, Naum Jasny, utilizing data contained in the confidential 1941 Plan, estimated that camp inmates amounted to 3.5 million persons at the end of 1940. See his "Labor and Output in Soviet Concentration Camps," *Journal of Political Economy,* October, 1951, p. 416.

[66] Apparently some difficulties have arisen in connection with the hiring of young people. See Anthony Maxwell, "Juvenile Unemployment in the USSR," *Soviet Survey,* October–December, 1958, p. 63. In May, 1956, a law was passed to the effect that workers between the ages of 16 and 18 were to be paid for a full 8-hour day although they could only work 6

young people will be compelled to take up industrial jobs after 8 or 9 years of schooling and, as a consequence, they will be forced to continue their higher education at night. Even full-time day students will be expected to contribute a certain amount of time weekly to physical pursuits. Student labor is also of some importance in our economy, particularly during the summer months. But because more years are being spent in school, only one-third of all young men between 14 and 19 years of age were either job-seekers or job-holders in 1960, compared with over half of all young people classified in this manner in 1890.[67] Child labor continues to be employed extensively in the agricultural sectors of both economies, but there has been some recent pressure to extend existing restrictions on the use of child labor to the agricultural areas of the United States.[68]

A higher percentage of women in the labor force seems to be one characteristic of highly industrialized countries generally. Women accounted for 18 per cent of the labor force in the United States in 1900, but by 1956, this had risen to 31 per cent of the total and it is still increasing.[69] Among the noncapitalist-oriented economies, the USSR is highest with women now comprising 45 per cent of the industrial labor force compared with 28 per cent in 1929. In part, this heavy reliance on women workers reflects the wartime manpower losses. Despite this high percentage of women in their labor force, a Soviet manpower expert has called for a more energetic effort to bring housewives and other relatively inactive women in the 50 to 55 age bracket into the labor force. According to this Soviet writer, these women

---

hours. Young people between the ages of 14 and 16, could work only 4 hours daily. As a result, some Soviet factories became reluctant to hire these young people who were less productive with respect to their wages, as compared with adults.

[67] See Will Lissner, "A Third of Women Join Labor Force," *New York Times,* September 23, 1962, p. 43.

[68] See Bess Furman, "Farm Child Labor Abuse Scored; Law Urged to Help All Under 14," *New York Times,* February 7, 1959, p. 22.

[69] According to Will Lissner, *loc. cit.,* more than one-third of all women of working age are actually seeking employment in the United States today compared with less than one-fifth in this position in 1890.

could be used in white-collar posts and thereby release younger, able-bodied persons for direct production work.[70] The opening up of boarding schools recently was also designed to encourage younger women to enter the labor force and turn over the task of child-rearing to the state. During the current Seven-Year Plan, it is hoped to release between five and six million Soviet women from kitchen and child-rearing chores to full-time employment.

The German Democratic Republic with about 39 per cent of their labor force composed of women is next highest with respect to the participation of women in the labor force, while Czecho-slovakia maintains an industrial labor force with women con-stituting over 37 per cent of the total.[71] Polish and Hungarian women comprise about one-third of their respective labor forces. Even in little Albania, 28 per cent of the labor force is female. On the other hand, in mainland China only 13 per cent of the labor force were women as late as 1957.

In periods of unemployment in the West, there is ordinarily considerable pressure for women to give up their places in indus-try. One of the expected "benefits" from the growth of English unemployment in 1958 was the anticipated retirement of some women workers from the labor force. Another effect of serious unemployment on the labor force in the West is the greater dis-crimination against non-whites, senior citizens, and youthful, in-experienced job applicants which occurs in such periods. The great-est progress that has been made by our non-whites in their search for job equality, for example, seems to have been made in periods of full or near-full employment such as we had during World War II.

6. *Strikes*. The right to strike constitutes another institutional difference between the United States and the USSR. Although

---

[70] See *Trud,* January 22, 1959, as cited by Leon M. Herman, "The Seven-Year Haul," *Problems of Communism,* March–April, 1959, p. 12.

[71] See Nauchno-issledovatel'skii institut truda, *Statisticheskii sbornik po voprosam truda i zarabotnoi platy v evropeiskikh sotsialisticheskikh stranakh* (Statistical Handbook on Problems of Labor and Wages in European Socialist Countries), Gosplanizdat, Moscow, 1959, pp. 35, 67, 89, 117 and 162.

brief work stoppages have been reported in the Soviet Union in connection with such things as norm revision, the right to strike is not included in the Soviet constitution.[72] In our economy, strikes are of some importance in restricting our output and overall economic welfare. If possible, they are usually avoided by both labor and management. At times, however, when demand is weak and inventories are plentiful, resistance to the strike may be weakened as was apparently the case in a number of our recent steel strikes.

A sit-down strike such as occurred in the late fifties in Bloomfield, New Jersey, when General Electric closed its industrial air conditioning plant, would not take place in the Soviet Union since there has never been any occasion when Soviet factories have been forced to close—except during the Nazi invasion. All Soviet plant and equipment, no matter how outdated it is by our standards, generally remains in operation since workers in these plants are still more productive than they would be were they occupied in their present alternative use back on the farms. Eventually as rural unemployment is reduced, some older plants may be planned to cease operations but this should not cause too much trouble in view of the likelihood that the Soviet seller's market and over-full employment will continue.

It seems clear that the labor practices and institutions of the United States and the USSR reflect their respective buyer's and

[72] Strikes were of some importance in the Soviet Union in the twenties when the trade unions pursued more traditional objectives. In connection with the recent norm revisions, some sit-down strikes or work stoppages are rumored to have taken place as in the Kaganovich Ball Bearing Plant in Moscow. Kazakhstan mechanics and drivers reportedly have struck as a result of the farms' failure to provide partial payment in kind for their labor. Strikes over living conditions around the new iron and steel complex at Temir-Tau in Kazakhstan have also been reported. In addition, Odessa dockers have stopped work in protest against the shipping of butter to Cuba. In Eastern Europe, work stoppages have been reported at the Poznan railroad shop. See *New York Times,* December 2, 1956, p. 1; September 30, 1960, p. 2; May 15, 1960, p. 33; June 25, 1961, p. 54; and March 6, 1960, p. 4. In effect, the high degree of labor mobility may be considered a reflection of strikes on an individual rather than a collective basis.

seller's markets. Soviet labor institutions and practices might be described as "expansionist." Every effort is made to increase labor participation rates by obtaining the services of under-utilized manpower whether it be among the very young, the very old, or among women. More productive ways of doing things tend to be eagerly sought and promptly introduced. On the other hand, most of our own labor institutions and practices can be termed "restrictionist." [73] We attempt to reduce the applicants for employment by encouraging our young people to remain in school for as long as possible and by forceably retiring older people while they are still potentially productive. In addition, while management is generally ever seeking more productive ways of doing things, labor organizations at best are only luke-warm to the new technology, if not actually acting as a brake on our economic progress. In a very real sense, labor in the Soviet Union has been harnessed with a powerful set of incentives while our labor force is generally fettered with various institutional restrictions.

SIGNIFICANCE OF RELATIVE GAINS IN LABOR PRODUCTIVITY IN CONTRASTING SYSTEMS

The comparatively successful harnessing of Soviet labor with an elaborate set of material incentives shows up in the fact that industrial labor productivity in the Soviet Union is probably increasing at between two and three times the rate at which it is growing in the United States. Not only is output per worker

[73] One of the few "expansionist" activities on the part of our trade unions occurred when the International Ladies' Garment Workers Union decided to allocate union funds for industry-wide advertising of the product of their labor. Institutional advertising in the form of pleas to look for the union label is also widespread. The use of union funds to finance housing construction might also be considered as "expansionist." The United Hat, Cap and Millinery Workers Union has conducted a campaign encouraging their members to join with management in an attempt to slow down the trend towards hatlessness.

growing at a faster rate in the Soviet Union, but the increases are being achieved at a more even pace than is the case in the United States.[74] Our labor productivity actually declines in periods of recession and increases at a very rapid rate during recovery. Since the total number of industrial workers in the Soviet labor force is only somewhat greater than the numbers in our industrial sector, the lag in Soviet labor productivity relative to our own reflects roughly the lag of Soviet industrial production relative to ours. It follows that the closing of the gap in relative output per worker will also narrow the gap between the total industrial outputs of the two countries.

Professor Galenson has made some assumptions concerning the speed with which this gap will be closed. These alternatives in the rate of growth in industrial labor productivity are reproduced in Table VII-A. The third alternative is very possibly the most realistic, but the fourth is at least possible. Although there are great fluctuations in the rate of increase in labor productivity in the United States, our historical rate of increase seems to be about two per cent per annum. The projected estimates of relative labor productivity in Table VII-A are based on the initial assumption that industrial labor productivity in the Soviet Union was 40 per cent of the United States level in 1953. Since this figure has been quoted approvingly by the Russians, presumably it may have a slight upward bias. Nevertheless, if the most realistic rates of growth prevail, by 1970 Soviet labor productivity should be roughly 70 per cent of our own. To the extent that their industrial labor force surpasses ours by then, total Soviet industrial production will exceed 70 per cent of ours. On a per capita basis, Soviet industrial production would be considerably less than 70 per cent of ours by 1970. If the fourth but less likely alternative should prove correct, however, Soviet industrial production by 1970 should be very nearly the same as our own.

---

[74] In 1961, the annual increase in output per worker of four per cent in the Soviet Union was slightly lower than has been the case in recent years, no doubt reflecting the fact that all industrial workers were required to cut back their work week to 41 hours regardless of any deleterious effect on output.

TABLE VII-A

ALTERNATIVE RATES BY WHICH GAP IN LABOR PRODUCTIVITY
WILL BE CLOSED

Alternative Annual Percentage Rates of Increase in Output per Worker (Compounded)	Soviet Productivity as % of United States Productivity	
	By 1960	By 1970
1. United States—2%; USSR—3%	44	49
2. United States—2%; USSR—4%	49	59
3. United States—2%; USSR—5%	53	71
4. United States—2%; USSR—6%	59	86

Source of data: Walter Galenson, *Labor Productivity in Soviet and Amer-ican Industry,* Rand R-257, Rand Corporation, Santa Mon-ica, California, January, 1954, p. 263.

Recommended Readings

BARKER, G. R., "Soviet Labor," University of Birmingham, *Bulletins on Soviet Economic Development,* June, 1951.

***BROWN, EMILY CLARK, "The Soviet Labor Market," *Industrial and Labor Relations Review,* Vol. 10, No. 2, January, 1957, pp. 179–200.

———, "A Note on Employment and Unemployment in the Soviet Union in the Light of Technical Progress," *Soviet Studies,* Vol. XII, No. 3, January, 1961, pp. 231–239.

EASON, WARREN W., "Labor Force Materials for the Study of Un-employment in the Soviet Union," in National Bureau of Eco-nomic Research, *The Measurement and Behavior of Unemploy-ment,* Princeton University Press, Princeton, 1957.

*———, "Problems of Manpower and Industrialization in the USSR," in *Population Trends in Eastern Europe, The USSR and Mainland China,* Proceedings of the Thirty-sixth Annual Confer-ence of the Millbank Memorial Fund, 1960.

GALENSON, WALTER, "The Soviet Wage Reform," in *Proceedings* of 13th Annual Meeting of International Relations Research Asso-ciation, 1960, pp. 250–265.

———, *Labor Productivity in Soviet and American Industry,* Co-lumbia University Press, New York, 1955, especially Chapter I.

GLIKSMAN, JERZY, "Soviet Labor and the Question of Productivity," *Monthly Labor Review,* June, 1957, pp. 702–706.

————, "The Control of Industrial Labor in the Soviet Union," Rand RM-2494, Rand Corporation, Santa Monica, February 15, 1960.

GREENBERG, LEON, "International Conference on Labor Productivity," *Monthly Labor Review,* January, 1962, pp. 20–23.

KAHAN, ARCADIUS, "Labor Turnover in the Soviet Union," *Monthly Labor Review,* January, 1962, pp. 17–19.

*KANTNER, JOHN F., "The Population of the Soviet Union," in *Comparison of the United States and Soviet Economies,* 1959, Part I, pp. 31–71.

NOVE, ALEC, "The State and the Wage-Earner," *Soviet Survey,* Vol. 6, October–December, 1958, pp. 28–34.

OXENFELDT, A. R. and VON DEN HAAG, E., "Unemployment in Planned and Capitalist Economies," *Quarterly Journal of Economics,* February, 1954, pp. 43–60.

YANOWITCH, MURRAY, "Changes in the Soviet Money Wage Level Since 1940," *American Slavic and East European Review,* April, 1955, pp. 195–223.

————, "Trends in Differentials Between Salaried Personnel and Wage Earners in Soviet Industry," *Soviet Studies,* January, 1960, pp. 229–252.

**————, "Trends in Soviet Occupational Wage Differentials," *Industrial and Labor Relations Review,* January, 1960, pp. 166–191.

U.S. Department of Labor, Bureau of Labor Statistics, "Principal Current Soviet Labor Legislation," BLS Report No. 210, January, 1962.

VIII ~ Overall Price Movements and Price Policies

IN THE PRECEDING THREE CHAPTERS, we have discussed in some detail the nature of the procurement prices paid by the non-agricultural sector for farm products; the retail prices paid by consumers for goods and services entering into their household budgets; and the factor prices paid by managers for the services of labor in the contrasting systems. It would now seem appropriate to consider price policies and overall price movements in the two economic systems, whether they are determined consciously by the central planners through their shaping of the underlying market forces as they are in the noncapitalist-oriented economies, or whether they are determined primarily by market forces and indirectly modified by government action, as is frequently the case in capitalist-oriented economies.

PRICE POLICY AND PRICE MOVEMENTS IN NONCAPITALIST-ORIENTED ECONOMIES

Soviet economists in their writings have expressed altogether uniform ideas with regard to appropriate overall price policy. In their collective opinion, inflation is closely related to original sin, something which must be obscured as much as possible in their own system but, at the same time, something which is considered to be inherent in the operation of contemporary capitalist-oriented economies. In theory since 1927, Soviet planners and economists have accepted as a guiding principle the following classic quotation of the late J. V. Stalin: [1]

The basic line along which our industry must proceed, the basic line which must determine all of our further steps—this is the line of the systematic lowering of the cost of production of industrial products, the line of the systematic lowering of the selling prices on industrial goods.

But in practice until fairly recently, there has been little concrete evidence in the period of the five-year plans, that the amount of inflation was any less under Soviet planning than it has been under contemporary capitalist-oriented economies. As a matter of fact, the prewar hyper-inflation in the Soviet economy contrasted sharply with the sagging price levels in most capitalist-oriented economies at the same time.

World War II exercised a strong inflationary pressure on the price levels throughout the world, and especially within the USSR. In varying degrees, the overall movements of nonagricultural prices in the postwar years have also been upward in most capitalist-oriented markets of the world. In the Soviet Union, on the other hand, a new and significant development has occurred. Since 1948, the general level of consumers' goods prices has either been falling or else remained comparatively stable and, beginning in 1950, the prices of producers' goods likewise finally began to reflect the disinflationary dogma which had been mouthed ever since Stalin's speech in 1927.[2] On the other hand,

---

[1] J. V. Stalin, *Sochineniia* (Works), Vol. IX, Moscow, 1948, pp. 193–194. There is some question whether, in fact, the quotation cited may not have been applicable to a specific problem of the time—the scissors crisis—rather than to long-run price policy. Nevertheless, the quotation has usually been interpreted along the latter lines. For information on the scissors crisis in the mid-twenties, see Maurice Dobb, *Soviet Economic Development since 1917,* Routledge and Kegan Paul, London, 1948, p. 215.

[2] The term "disinflation" is more precise than the more commonly used "deflation." Economists ordinarily make a valid distinction between gen-

the state procurement prices for agricultural products to be processed by the government's food processing and light industries
have been rising rapidly during the Khrushchev era.

The extent of the price inflation in the Soviet Union during
the period of the five-year plans prior to the more recent period
of disinflation has now been fairly well established, despite the
general lack of published official Soviet price indexes between
1930 and 1940. United States economists, working with official
Soviet price quotations contained in numerous price handbooks
available in this country, have recently published their findings,
some of which are summarized in Table VIII-A.[3] The series may
be grouped into the prices of five major categories of products
or services: consumers' goods, agricultural products, producers'
goods other than machinery, machinery, and money wages.

It seems obvious from the data assembled in Table VIII-A
that inflation in the Soviet Union has scarcely been of the "creeping" variety. It is also clear that the impact of Soviet inflation was
very unevenly distributed throughout the economy. If we examine the price changes from 1928 to 1955, a period for which
most comparisons can be made, we find that the greatest inflation was felt in foods generally where prices rose about 12-fold
during the entire period.[4] The increase in the agricultural pro-

---

erally falling prices which are accompanied by relatively full employment
and rising national income—disinflation—and falling prices which are
accompanied by increasing unemployment and falling national income—
deflation.

[3] All of the Soviet price idexes are computed using weights which refer
either to the year 1937 or to the given year. If the weights used were
those of an earlier year (say 1928), undoubtedly the inflation shown
would have been somewhat greater. The consumers' goods prices refer
to Moscow, which is considered to be representative of the USSR generally.

[4] Since the official government prices—except for agricultural procurement prices—have generally remained stable since 1955, the following
observations would also apply to consumers' goods and producers' goods
up to 1960. Liquor and automobile prices rose in 1958, but these have
been counterbalanced by some rather minor price reductions. In 1961—
as will be discussed presently—the government "wiped out" the bulk of
this price inflation in the Soviet nonagricultural sector by simply moving
all decimal points one digit to the left.

curement prices for foods was of approximately the same magnitude, while the increase in procurement prices for all agricultural products was even greater. At the other extreme, the price increases in the machinery producing sector were comparatively well-controlled, amounting to less than 2.2 times the 1928 level. Rent, utilities, transportation and entertainment also experienced relatively little inflation (at least by Soviet standards)—the prices of these services rising by less than five times. The increase in the prices of producers' goods, other than machinery, was also about five-fold, while all nonfood consumers' goods prices rose approximately eight-fold. Gross money wages increased about 12 times during the same period; after deductions for taxes and compulsory bond sales, the increase in annual net money wages was probably about 11-fold. It may be worthwhile to look behind these overall average price increases and examine the relative price gains of some of the individual commodities comprising the indexes.

TABLE VIII-A

SUMMARY OF PRICE INDEXES FOR SELECTED ECONOMIC SERIES, USSR,
AND THE UNITED STATES

$(1947-49 = 100)$

Series			Year			
						1960 as % of
	1928	1937	1940	1955	1960	1928 *
(1)	(2)	(3)	(4)	(5)	(6)	(7)
USSR						
1. All foods	4	29	38	48	50	1250
2. All consumers' nonfoods	8	33	43	64	62	780
3. All consumers' goods and services	6	32	41	56	56	930
4. Collective farm market prices	—	29	58	66	63	220
5. Agricultural procurement prices	23	95	100	473	782	3400
6. Rent, utilities, transportation, and entertainment	23	49	n.a.	106	106	460
7. Machinery	54	77	82	118	115	210
8. Basic industrial goods	35	78	94	178	178	510
9. Workers' money wages	10	35	54	124	145	1380

Series	Year					1960 as % of 1928 *
(1)	1928 (2)	1937 (3)	1940 (4)	1955 (5)	1960 (6)	(7)

UNITED STATES
1. All foods	65	52	48	111	120	185
2. Rent	120	84	87	130	142	118
3. Consumers' price index	73	61	60	115	126	173
4. Farm products	59	48	38	90	89	151
5. Wholesale prices, excluding farm products and food	66	61	59	117	128	194
6. Metals and metal products	65	66	63	137	154	237
7. Machinery and motive products	n.a.	n.a.	66	128	153	232
8. Textile products and apparel	68	54	52	95	96	141
9. Hourly earnings in manufacturing	41	46	49	139	167	404

* Soviet percentages are rounded. Collective farm market percentage is based on 1937. United States index for machinery and motive products is based on 1940.

n.a. = not available.

Notes to Table VIII-A

USSR:

1. Through 3.: All foods, consumers' nonfoods, and all consumers' goods and services: Janet G. Chapman, "Retail Prices and Real Wages in the Soviet Union Since 1928," Columbia Ph.D. Dissertation, Table VII. Extrapolations to 1960 are based on official Soviet price indexes in *Narodnoe Khoziaistvo 1960,* p. 716.

4. Collective farm market prices: Janet G. Chapman, *op. cit.,* p. 224.

5. Agricultural procurement prices: Nancy Nimitz, "Soviet Agricultural Prices and Costs," in *Comparisons of the United States and Soviet Economies,* Part I, pp. 252, 271, supplemented by calculations by Professor Karcz in Abram Bergson, *The Real National Income of Soviet Russia Since 1928,* Harvard University Press, Cambridge, 1961, p. 416.

6. Rent, utilities, transportation and entertainment: Chapman index numbers from earlier study. Figure for 1955 actually refers to 1952.

7. Machinery: Moorsteen indexes, variable weights of given year as presented in Abram Bergson, *loc. cit.*

8. Basic industrial goods: Bergson, Bernaut, and Turgeon index (1937 weights) given in *ibid.*

9. Workers' money wages: author's own calculations of gross money wages from various official Soviet sources.

UNITED STATES:

1. Through 3. All foods, rent, and consumers' price index: United States Department of Commerce, *Historical Statistics of the United States,*

Colonial Times to 1957, pp. 125–128, supplemented by data in *Survey of Current Business,* February, 1962, pp. S-7, 8, 15.

4. Through 8. Farm products, wholesale prices, excluding farm products and food, metals and metal products, machinery and motive products, and textile products: Department of Commerce, *op. cit.,* p. 117.

9. Hourly earnings in manufacturing: Department of Commerce, *op. cit.,* p. 92.

1. *Consumers' goods*. Looking at consumers' goods prices first, we find some evidence of the relative priorities assigned to the different consumption items by the government planners. Products which have experienced greater-than-average price increases are presumably those which had smaller increases in supply caused by a relatively low investment priority—goods on which the government deliberately wished consumers to cut their increases in consumption, if not also their original consumption level.

Among food items which experienced especially sharp price increases from 1928 to 1955 are the following: sunflower oil—34.2 times; buckwheat grits—27.6 times; pork—22.4 times; vodka—21.9 times; rye flour—19.0 times; herring—17.8 times; and eggs—17.4 times.[5] These price increases are all substantially greater than the roughly 12-fold average price increase for foods generally.

A number of these greater-than-average price increases probably reflect specific, as opposed to general, government interference with consumers' sovereignty. The higher price increase for rye flour undoubtedly was intended to dissuade Russian homemakers from the time-consuming task of baking bread. Similarly the higher-than-average price increase for vodka may have been designed to control drunkenness which is somewhat of a problem in the USSR.[6]

[5] These and other data on consumers' goods prices were obtained from the pioneer works of Janet Chapman, especially her Ph.D. dissertation, "Retail Prices and Real Wages in the Soviet Union Since 1928," Columbia University.

[6] However, it should be noted that, according to official claims, per capita consumption of vodka has declined from 8.5 liters to about 6.9

At the other extreme, consumers' goods with higher investment priority, those with weak or declining demands, or foods emanating primarily from the private plots might be expected to experience relatively smaller price increases. In this category, we find that the lowest price gains among food products were as follows: salt—4.4 times; wheat bread—7.1 times; fresh cabbage—8.9 times; and potatoes—6.6 times. We would expect Russian consumers on the average to substitute the consumption of these latter items for products included in the earlier category. This is pretty much what took place, at least during the thirties, as we have already noted in Chapter VI. In more recent years, as levels of living have risen, consumers have tended to shift their purchases to foods with higher protein content with the result that relatively lower prices for these commodities have still rationed more or less effectively the available supplies.

We can also examine the relative price increases for different nonfood consumers' goods, which experienced an average price increase of eight-fold from 1928 to 1955. The greatest price gains are found in the following products: pure woolens—27.1 times; sateen—20.2 times; cotton sheeting—17.7 times; calico—16.3 times; and soap—12.4 times. On the other hand, smaller-thanaverage price increases are recorded for most books and newspapers, the prices of which ordinarily multiplied less than five times. The prices of economic journals and Lenin's collected works increased by only 50 per cent, surely a bargain for anyone so inclined. Other relatively small price increases between 1928 and 1955 occurred for the following commodities: tobacco prod-

---

liters yearly. In 1955, the Soviets claimed a per capita liquor consumption of only 3.5 liters (in terms of absolute alcohol) compared with 4.5 liters in the United States and 12.8 liters in France. See V. P. Zotov, *Pishchevaia promyshlennost' sovetskogo soiuza* (The Food Industry of the Soviet Union), Pishchepromizdat, Moscow, 1958, p. 114. Alcoholism is believed to be more of a problem in the East European noncapitalist-oriented economies. In economies where consumers' goods tend to be in inadequate supply relative to effective demand, considerable quantities of alcohol can be purchased with excess purchasing power even at relatively high prices. In a sense, it may be said that vodka has replaced religion as the opiate of the people in such a situation.

ucts, 33 times and matches, 4.5 times. Thus, it is interesting to note that the government apparently has made no effort to discriminate against smokers via the relative price structure as it seemingly has done with regard to the drinking of hard liquor.

In addition, the prices of a large variety of consumers' durables which were either not produced in 1928, or else were supplied in small quantities at that time, rose relatively less than the average price increase for consumers' nonfoods. These latter products include: sewing machines, phonographs, cameras, and TV sets. The relatively small price increase for TV sets may help to explain why Western visitors are frequently puzzled by the fact that, although the Russians appear to be poorly clothed by our standards, TV antennae sprout from many dilapidated rooftops.

2. *Producers' goods*. We might now briefly examine the relative price increases among the different producers' goods in an effort to learn planners' priorities here. Again we might suppose that products experiencing relatively little inflation had higher investment priorities than those experiencing greater-than-average price increases. Compared with the overall increase in producers' goods prices of about five-fold, the prices of electric power, chemicals, and machinery generally, only doubled or tripled their original price level. It so happens that the expansion of the output from these industries has also been faster than the growth attained in most other sectors of heavy industry. In other words, there was a negative correlation between the growth in the physical output of producers' goods and their relative price increases.

At the other extreme, producers' goods experiencing relatively greater inflation include most of the extractive industries—coal and wood products, in particular. The average price for coal rose 9.7-fold, while timber product prices rose 5.4 times between 1928 and 1955, and still more if we consider the 1957 price hike for timber products. Despite the relatively large investments in some of these branches, many of these sectors have been subject to depletion, or the exhaustion of easily accessible resources. As a result, the growth in their physical output in a number of cases has probably been only average or even below average.[7]

3. *Agricultural procurement prices.* Agricultural procurement prices—while also subject to inflation—have behaved in an entirely different manner in comparison with other prices in the Soviet Union. Between 1928 and 1948, the average price increase for these commodities amounted to only about 4.3 times. But since then, particularly after 1953, there has been a sharp rise in the relative prices paid to Soviet farmers for their output. In theory at least, the new prices being paid to the agricultural sector since 1958 are supposed to cover not only their costs of production, but also to provide the internal resources out of which a great deal of agricultural investment comes.[8] The actual costs of producing agricultural crops have only come to light since 1955 when the decision was made to calculate the costs of producing agricultural products on a basis which is roughly comparable with that used for industrial products.[9]

There were also internal differences in the procurement price increases within the agricultural sector. Between 1928 and 1950, procurement prices for food products rose by 2.7-fold, while the procurement prices of raw materials on the average increased by 12.2 times; after 1950, the relative price increases were reversed; food product prices rose by almost seven-fold, while raw

[7] It seems clear that the use of early year weighting systems will attach greater importance to these inflation-prone series and a lesser importance to the series with relatively small price increases. As a result, early year weights tend to show greater overall inflation in producers' goods in much the same manner as they do for consumers' goods.

[8] In practice, the procurement prices for meat products have been considerably below their costs of production. The 35 per cent increase in the procurement prices for meat effective June 1, 1962, will undoubtedly go a long way towards wiping out this former subsidy to meat consumers. See data on costs of production and procurement prices in *Izvestiia*, June 1, 1962.

[9] Before the late fities, the cost of production of agricultural commodities was calculated on a complicated labor-day basis from which it was virtually impossible to learn the actual production costs of agricultural products. This ambiguity with respect to costs of production on the collective farms was apparently useful in disguising the magnitude of the surplus being extracted.

material prices increased by only 70 per cent. For the entire period, food prices rose by almost 18 times, while raw material prices increased by almost 21-fold.

4. *Wages and salaries.* Average wage increases in the different producers' goods industries were also subject to widely varying degrees of inflation. During the period 1928 to 1955, money wages in producers' goods rose about 12-fold. But among the different producers' goods industries, the wage increases ranged all the way from roughly nine to 11-fold in machine-building, electric power stations, and cement to approximately 18 or 19-fold in logging and coal mining.[10] The average wage increases for most consumers' goods branches were less than those for the lowest of the producers' goods industries. For example the average wage increases were around seven-fold for workers in printing, boot and shoe manufacturing, and in sewn goods.

FORCES UNDERLYING OVERALL INFLATION AND DISINFLATION IN NONCAPITALIST-ORIENTED ECONOMIES

It is obvious that there is considerable variation in the extent to which inflationary forces have been reflected in different sectors of the Soviet economy. In explaining these differences, we must distinguish at the outset between inflation in consumers' goods on the one hand, and producers' goods on the other. The considerably greater increase in most consumers' goods prices

[10] The large percentage increases in loggers' and coal miners' wages were due in part to the extremely low level of wages in these industries in 1928. On the other hand, the comparatively modest increase in the wages of workers and employees in machine-building and electric power was in part due to their relatively high wage level in 1928. The skill composition was high in machine-building in 1928 but relatively low in logging and coal mining so that increasing skill composition in the latter two industries may have significantly affected average wages. Finally, the geographic shift of coal mining and logging operations to eastern areas where wages are higher was probably more significant than it was for machine-building.

as compared with the prices of producers' goods is facilitated by the fact that the Russians have for all practical purposes severed direct connections between the underlying market forces in the two principal sectors. It thus becomes possible to have entirely different principles of price formation, as well as considerably different results, for each branch.

1. *Consumers' goods*. The inflation in the consumers' goods branches has originated chiefly from the demand side of the market. Soviet authorities endeavor, although not always with success, to establish consumers' goods prices which will more or less clear the market, that is, prices which will just distribute what has been produced for sale. These prices which ration the supply of consumers' goods are only vaguely related to their unit production costs since it is not only the increase in labor productivity in these sectors, but also the increase in the number of workers employed here which affects the overall supply of consumers' goods. In some cases, the central planners may decide to distribute certain consumers' goods or services at prices which do not cover their production costs, either on a temporary or a permanent basis, much in the same manner as we in the United States handle our postal services. In other words, consumers' goods prices may either be well above their production cost or below the cost of production, depending on the government's price policy.

To say that inflation in consumers' goods branches is not affected by changes in production costs is not to imply that the production costs of consumers' goods have not risen, for in fact, they may actually have risen at a somewhat faster pace than the production costs of producers' goods. This is due to the fact that capital investments have been relatively less in light industry and have generally resulted in smaller gains in output per worker.[11] Thus, there is undoubtedly a relationship between the

[11] According to one Soviet writer, between 1928 and 1953, labor productivity in heavy industry grew almost two times faster than it did in light industry. See I. Malyshev, *"Nekotorye voprosy tsenoobrazovaniia v sotsialisticheskom khoziaistve"* (Questions of Price Formation in a Socialist Economy), *Voprosy Ekonomiki*, No. 3, 1957, p. 99.

relatively greater inflation in consumers' goods branches and the government's investment priorities to the extent that less investment here resulted in smaller increases in the available consumers' goods supplies than might otherwise have occurred if the investment priorities for consumers' goods industries had been higher. On the other hand, depletion is relatively inconsequential in its effect on the production costs of consumers' goods so that the natural handicaps with respect to raising productivity and lowering production costs are less here than they are in the extractive industries. The net effect of these two factors working in opposite directions on the final production costs of consumers' goods relative to those of producers' goods is unknown, but it is believed that real costs may have fallen more rapidly (or risen more slowly) in the producers' goods sector, at least in recent years.[12]

Roughly speaking, the fixed prices on food products sold in the state and cooperative retail stores are set somewhat below the freely-determined prices for the same products distributed through the collective farm markets, whenever such commodities are sold in both establishments. In the collective farm market, which now accounts for less than 10 per cent of the total food sales in the Soviet Union, the forces of supply and demand establish ever-fluctuating market prices in noncapitalist-oriented economies, in much the same manner as they do in farmers' markets in capitalist-oriented economies. In the absence of government price controls in the state and cooperative retail stores, the equilibrium prices for foods for the entire economy would no doubt settle somewhere between the present collective farm market

[12] Between 1948 and 1959, the various wholesale price indexes, according to official Soviet calculations, fell as follows: heavy industry—4%; light industry—26% and food industry—48%. See A. Bachurin, *"Peresmotr optovykh tsen i nekotorye voprosy teorii"* (The Wholesale Price Revision and Some Theoretical Questions), *Planovoe Khoziaistvo*, No. 1, 1962, p. 15. However heavy industrial prices were raised by 56 per cent in 1949 in order to eliminate subsidies, so that the real cost and price reductions were apparently greater in the heavy industrial sector. See G. Kosiachenko, *op. cit.*, p. 16.

price level and the lower official state and cooperative store prices.[13]

However, not all consumers' goods are sold on the collective farm markets and here the government may rather arbitrarily set prices, sometimes even below costs. On the other hand, even for most of these nonfoods, the government usually attempts to establish prices which ration the relatively small supply of goods among all those consumers with effective purchasing power. The existence of queues merely attests to the fact that the planners do not always succeed in these objectives.

The difference between the fixed prices established in the state and cooperative stores and the production costs of consumers' goods is largely absorbed by profits and turnover taxes, the rates of the latter fluctuating as necessary to mop up the large margin or gap between the production cost and the price levels required to ration existing supplies.

To the extent that the central planners wish to exercise discretionary price policy, that is, set prices considerably below the equilibrium price level, as has been the case with automobiles in the past, they must reconcile themselves to informal rationing, queues, waiting lists, and the accompanying problems of speculation and black marketing operations.[14] On the other hand, if the government sets a price which is too far above the equilibrium price level for products not sold on the collective farm market— as is the case with liquor—it is possible that illegal operations or moonshining activities will spring up to create an unofficial, cheaper supply of the product.

What determines the level of prices on the collective farm market or the price set by the government to ration the distribution

---

[13] The analogy in the United States would be rent control as still retained in New York City. If price controls on controlled housing were lifted, the new equilibrium price level for housing space would certainly be somewhere between the artificially high price level for noncontrolled housing and the artificially low price level for controlled housing.

[14] For an account of some recent gray-marketing activities, see Theodore Shabad, "Soviet to Expose Gray-Marketers," *New York Times,* July 2, 1962, p. 5.

of food and nonfood consumers' goods not sold on the free market? As in capitalist-oriented economies, the basic determinants are aggregate supply and aggregate demand. Ultimately the supply of different food products sold on the collective farm market will be determined by government incentives for farmers and investments in the different agricultural products and consumers' goods branches, as well as by the varying meteorological conditions and the government's stockpiling and import-export policy in the short run.[15] The aggregate demand for these products is determined by the money incomes, primarily wages and salaries, paid out by state enterprises, whether they be in the industrial sector, in the government's new construction activities, in its communal consumption services, or in the agricultural sector.

By devoting a very high proportion of its manpower and investment resources to industries and sectors which are not at present turning out priced consumers' goods and services, the government must pay out a large amount of potential purchasing power which will have no corresponding consumers' goods to absorb it, providing voluntary savings and direct taxation do not neutralize this excess purchasing power. The impact of the chronic excess purchasing power on the relatively slowly increasing output of priced consumers' goods and services could only have resulted in a tremendous demand-pull inflation in the consumers' goods sector. The continuation of this division of resources between consumption on the one hand, and investment and communal consumption activities on the other, results in the maintenance of a high consumers' goods price level in relation to the money wage level.

2. *Producers' goods.* In contrast to the price formation for consumers' goods, demand is seldom a factor in the determination of producers' goods prices since most heavy industrial goods have been "funded," meaning that they were allocated or rationed physically by the central planners, rather than by the price sys-

[15] In 1957 imports amounted to more than 10 per cent of domestic sales of consumers' goods.

tem.[16] Thus, there is no legal possibility for the demand of factory managers to bid up the official prices of these commodities. As we shall see in the following chapter, however, some extralegal devices may be employed to circumvent the planners' wishes in this respect. In exceptional cases, such as for tin and lead, there have been sudden sharp increases in the prices of producers' goods which have been unrelated to changes in their production costs; but these exercises in discriminatory price setting within producers' goods, which are designed to discourage the consumption of producers' goods in especially critical supply, have been comparatively rare.

In the producers' goods industries then, it is primarily the relationship between the changes in money wages and labor productivity which explains the change in their cost and price levels. Since Soviet production costs ultimately reflect expenditures for the single productive factor, labor, the level of production costs is also determined by these variables. Generally speaking, the relationship between the growth of money wages and labor productivity was roughly as follows between 1928 and 1960. From 1928 to 1930, there was a brief interlude when gains in labor productivity in producers' goods industries generally exceeded increases in money wages, and both production costs and prices for producers' goods fell, as called for by Stalin's early dictum underlying the overall price policy of Plan I. But beginning in 1930, the reverse relationship was allowed to develop, that is, money wage increases were permitted to exceed gains in labor productivity, resulting in a rather all-pervasive cost-push inflation. This state of affairs continued in varying degrees until 1947, after which time, Soviet wage and price policy

[16] The classification of certain commodities as "funded" was dropped after 1959, but the principle remains that commodities in seriously short supply will be rationed by *Gosplan*. At present, estimates of the number of products to be distributed by the planners vary from 800 to 1500. At the time of Stalin's death, there were 1600 "funded" commodities, and by 1958, the number had been pared to 760. See Herbert S. Levine, "The Centralized Planning of Supply in Soviet Industry," in *Comparisons of the United States and Soviet Economies,* Part I, p. 166.

has once again followed along the lines anticipated, and to some extent achieved, at the beginning of the industrialization drive.[17] As a result, disinflation has occurred in most, but not all, producers' goods branches for the past decade.[18]

Among the different producers' goods industries, branches in which wage increases have been above average and where gains in productivity have been below average (for example, coal) have shown the greatest cost and price inflation. On the other hand, in the branches where wage increases have been on the low side and gains in labor productivity have been above average, such as in electric power stations, there has been comparatively little cost and price inflation. It seems clear that, with respect to producers' goods, there has been little or no positive correlation between the growth in labor productivity in the different branches and the corresponding increases in money wages —although there was undoubtedly some positive correlation *within* the different branches and *within* individual factories. The two industries where money wages increased the most, coal mining and logging, were considerably below average in achiev-

---

[17] Although real costs were falling after 1947, the virtual elimination of government subsidies to heavy industry in 1949 resulted in a significant average price increase on January 1, 1949. Thereafter both costs and prices generally were either falling or stable.

[18] The logging industry appears to be the principal exception to this generalization, and timber prices were raised substantially in 1957. The coal industry has also run into cost-push troubles since 1955. Between 1955 and 1959, average coal miners' wages have risen by 33 per cent despite the fact that productivity has risen by only nine per cent. See Harry Schwartz, "Russian Maps Price Rise for Oil," *New York Times,* February 20, 1962, p. 45, for digest of article by G. Kosiachenko, *"Sovershenstvovanie optovykh tsen na produktsiiu tiazheloi promyshlennosti i tarifov na gruzovye perevozki"* (The Improvement of Wholesale Prices on Products of Heavy Industry and Transportation Charges), *Finansy SSSR,* No. 12, 1961, pp. 17–21. However, in 1961 the average production cost of coal was reduced by 1.25 per cent according to A. A. Boiko, *"Itogi raboty ugol'noi promyshlennosti v 1961 g. i zadachi na 1962 g."* (Results of the Work of the Coal Industry in 1961 and the Tasks for 1962), *Ugol',* No. 1, 1962, p. 4. Despite this improvement, the average price for coal was still 19 per cent below its production cost according to P. Ivanov, *"K peresmotru optovykh tsen i tarifov,"* (Towards a Revision of Wholesale Prices and Rates), *Kommunist* No. 7, 1962, p. 54.

ing increases in labor productivity. Over the entire period, output per worker rose only about two and one-half times in coal mining, while logging labor productivity was only a trifle higher in 1955 than it was in 1928. If we take the recent period from 1940 to 1955, this dichotomy between the two rates of increase is still striking. Labor productivity in logging and coal mining increased by only nine and 24 per cent between these years, respectively (or well below the average for all industrial workers), while average wages in both of these branches increased by considerably more than the average wage increase of about 2.3-fold for all industrial workers combined.[19] It is the lack of positive correlation between wage and productivity changes that is primarily responsible for the widely different impact of cost-push inflationary forces among the Soviet producers' goods branches.

Of secondary importance in explaining the inflation in different producers' goods branches are the prices of materials purchased by the different industries. Industries consuming relatively large amounts of coal, the price of which has increased considerably more than the average, would be expected to reflect greater inflation than industries which consumed relatively more electric power, the price of which has scarcely risen.

Thus, in both the consumers' goods and producers' goods industries, the key factor in explaining inflation or disinflation would seem to be wages and salaries, either per worker or in the aggregate. In the producers' goods sector, it is the relationship between the change in the average wage rate and the rate of change in labor productivity; in consumers' goods, it is the relationship between the change in the total wage bill or fund and the change in the output of goods and services available for distribution— the consumers' commodity fund.[20]

It seems clear from the above analysis that, theoretically at

---

[19] V. Maier and V. Markov, *"Voprosy mezhotraslevogo regulirovaniia zarabotnoi platy v SSSR"* (Problems of the Inter-Branch Regulation of Wages in the USSR), *Sotsialisticheskii Trud*, No. 2, 1958, pp. 51–52.

[20] Changes in pensions, taxes, and savings are also minor factors affecting consumers' disposable income.

least, the Soviet government could pursue comparatively independent overall price policies in the sectors of the economy producing producers' and consumers' goods. Increases in labor productivity could be greater than increases in money wages in the producers' goods industries generally, resulting in an overall lowering of costs and prices here. At the same time, increasingly more resources might be devoted to expanding producers' goods and defense or other communal consumption relative to priced consumers' goods with the result that new excess purchasing power would tend to bid up immediately the prices on the collective farm market and eventually the official prices reflecting what is required to more or less ration both food and nonfood items. These higher equilibrium prices for consumers' goods would eventually be reflected in higher turnover tax rates to absorb the growing margin between the level of production costs and the new required higher price level. On the other hand, we could just as easily imagine conditions in the future which might result in rising costs and prices for producers' goods accompanied by falling consumers' goods price levels.

A study of the period since 1950 clearly indicates that a disinflationary price policy has been successfully pursued in the producers' goods sector as a whole, although there are exceptional industries as we have noted. With respect to consumers' goods, however, a paradoxical development occurred shortly after Stalin's death. Despite ostensibly greater relative investments in consumers' goods industries and agriculture, food prices began to rise on the collective farm market until by 1955, they were 16 per cent above the 1950 level. In addition, the annual price reductions in commodities sold in state stores virtually ceased after 1954.[21]

[21] In 1957 there were price reductions on medicines, watches, canned fish, fruits and vegetables, food concentrates, fat, pork, poultry, and smoked goods. Gains to consumers resulting from these reductions were said to be 500 million rubles. On July 1, 1959, reductions of about 15 to 20 per cent affected the prices of watches, bicycles, radios, cameras, nylons, wines, and children's toys. Total gains to consumers were said to be 600 million rubles. On March 1, 1960, price reductions affecting fox furs, electric sewing machines, silverware, cameras, radios, sporting goods, marma-

This phenomenon would seem to be best explained by the fact that the planners simply increased excess purchasing power much too fast relative to the steadily improving supply of consumers' goods. Very large increases in the money incomes of the collective farmers resulting from higher government procurement prices meant that the farmers may have been more inclined to increase their food consumption rather than to sell as much of their home-grown produce on the collective farm market. By 1956, however, the government planners seemingly had again brought excess purchasing power more or less under control. As a result, the collective farm market price level has dropped by five to 10 per cent since 1955, although in 1960 it was still slightly above the 1950 price level.

What are the prospects for a continuation of the price stabilization or disinflationary price policy in the two sectors? In the producers' goods sector, the revision of the wage structures and the shortening of the official work week from 46 to 41 hours in recent years has undoubtedly put the disinflationary price policy to a severe test. It seems unlikely that the wage structures could have been revised without at the same time entailing either a rather substantial increase in money wages, or else a rising dissatisfaction on the part of those workers adversely affected by the revision. During the past few years when the wage revisions have been taking place, the annual increases in money wages have therefore been running around four per cent, compared with a two per cent increase in the early years of the disinflationary price policy after 1947.

Similarly, the gradual shortening of the official work week may have adversely affected the increases in output per man-year, especially in transition years such as 1961. At that time, all non-progressive sectors were forced to cut their working time even though their total output in 41 hours was expected to be less than that formerly produced in the longer work week.[22] To the extent

---

lade, cocoa, coffee, and evaporated milk meant savings to consumers of 250 million rubles. See *Pravda,* January 2, 1958, p. 1; *Pravda,* July 1, 1959, p. 2; and *Pravda,* March 1, 1960.

[22] Output per man-hour of course rises very rapidly in such a transition period. In 1961, output per man-hour in industry rose by 11 per cent.

that the authorities have been able to convince the workers that it is to their advantage to intensify their efforts within the shorter work week, the effects of the shorter hours on labor productivity may be mitigated. But it seems possible that the rates of increase in output per man-year may be slowed down perceptibly whenever the work week is shortened abruptly. In 1961 only a four per cent increase in output per man year was claimed. In other words, the overall increases in money wages and in annual output per worker were in precarious balance during this year of transition to the shorter work week.

In the consumers' goods market, there are also important elements making for potentially greater demand-pull inflation. The increase in the money earnings of workers in the lowest wage categories as a result of the minimum wage legislation added 3.2 billion rubles in additional purchasing power beginning in 1957, and is adding progressively more as the minimum wage is gradually rising from 27 to 35 rubles per month to 50 to 60 rubles per month by 1965. Between 1956 and 1961, total pension payments rose from three to 7.6 billion rubles.[23] The decision to eliminate compulsory bond purchases added still more rubles in current purchasing power after 1958 and the gradual elimination of the income tax has likewise been allowing more spendable rubles to end up in consumers' pockets, particularly in the pockets of those with relatively high propensities to consume.[24] Between 1953 and 1961, workers' money income from all sources, including wage increases, rose by 42 billion rubles or by 87 per cent.[25]

These increases in purchasing power should not result in inflation unless the planned expansion of consumers' goods, which

[23] See S. Ustiniuk and P. Tarasevich, *"Pravil'no naznachat' i vyplachivat' gosudarstvennye pensii"* (To Grant and Pay Out Government Pensions Correctly), *Finansy SSSR,* No. 7, 1962, p. 46.

[24] In 1959–60, 800 million rubles which would have been government revenue in the form of income tax ended up in consumers' pockets. See V. Garbuzov, *"Uspeshno vypolnit' biudzhet chetvertogo goda semiletki"* (To Fulfill Quickly the Budget of the Fourth Year of the Seven-Year Plan), *Finansy SSSR,* No. 1, 1962, p. 12.

[25] *Izvestiia,* June 1, 1962, p. 1.

on a per capita basis has been running around five per cent annually in recent years, fails to absorb these gains in disposable income. Thus, the success of the "new lands" policy is no doubt an important precondition for the continued disinflationary or stabilized price policy with respect to food. It is also possible that disinflation may be retarded by occasional important Soviet shipments of consumers' goods which may have to be made to Eastern Europe in an attempt to alleviate any dissatisfaction there, although United States farm surpluses seem to be reducing the need for such shipments to Poland or Yugoslavia by the USSR. The sharp increase in defense allocations announced in 1961 may also be limiting additional investment funds for agriculture and subsequent improvements in agricultural productivity. Thus in June, 1962, when the average prices of meat and butter were increased by 30 and 25 per cent respectively, this factor was given by the authorities as a partial explanation for the price hike.[26] Generally speaking, the Soviets seem to be going through a crucial period as far as their disinflationary price policy is concerned, and price stabilization is about the most that can be expected for the consumers' goods sphere. In the current Seven-Year Plan, very little has been promised in the way of further price reductions for consumers' goods, although continued cost and price declines for producers' goods should be possible.

Early accounts of the reform of producers' goods prices scheduled to take effect at the beginning of 1963 indicate that on average the price level for producers' goods will be reduced by three per cent at that time.[27] In actuality, this slight reduction in

[26] In addition, comparably higher procurement prices were announced for deliveries of meat and milk, supposedly as an incentive for greater productivity by farmers. In 1961, prices for agricultural machinery, parts, fuel and taxes were also reduced in an attempt to obtain greater agricultural productivity.

[27] Some prices will be increased, while others are to be reduced. Coal prices will rise by 30 per cent reflecting the fact that cost-push inflation is still operative in this industry. Iron and steel prices on the average will rise by 8.5 per cent, partly as a result of the higher coal prices. On the other hand, price reductions of 15 per cent will take effect for chemicals and electric power. An overall price decline of 10 per cent will be applied to machinery generally.

the producers' goods price level may represent a relative increase in the price level for heavy industrial products vis-à-vis the prices of consumers' goods as compared with 1955. At that time, the present prices for producers' goods were established more or less in line with their then current average production costs with allowance for a small planned profit of roughly five per cent. Since 1955, the average costs of producers' goods (in current prices) have apparently been reduced by almost 10 per cent.[28] If the same profit margin as was established in 1955 were provided in the new wholesale prices, an average price reduction of 10 per cent would therefore be in order. Thus it would appear that the new price level for 1963 must be designed to provide for somewhat higher planned profit rates as compared with the 1955 prices.[29] According to one source, the average rate of profit provided for by the new wholesale prices will be nine per cent. It is known, for example, that the new prices for electric power which are 15 per cent below the 1955 prices, will still provide for a rate of profit, in addition to turnover taxes, amounting to 40 per cent of production cost.[30] Nevertheless the price reform appears to represent a conservative approach to the problem of reforming the level of producers' goods prices.[31] Prices of producers' goods are still to be set roughly at the level of costs for the producer of more or less average efficiency, rather than at the higher

[28] *Narodnoe Khoziaistvo 1958*, p. 172; *1960*, p. 239.

[29] In ferrous metallurgy profits will amount to 12 per cent; in chemicals the profit rate will be eight per cent. In 1960, the rate of profit ranged from three to 32 per cent in heavy industry with an average rate of profit of 12.4 per cent. See G. Kosiachenko, *"Sovershenstvovanie optovykh tsen na produktsiiu tiazheloi promyshlennosti i tarifov na gruzovye perevozki"* (The Improvement of Wholesale prices on Products of Heavy Industry and Transportation Charges), *Finansy SSSR*, No. 12, 1961, pp. 17–21.

[30] See A. Bachurin, *loc. cit.*, p. 15.

[31] Some earlier proposals suggested roughly a doubling of the producers' goods price level in an attempt to equalize the distribution of the turnover tax collections throughout the economy. See M. Makarova, *"Eshche raz o probleme tsenoobrazovaniia"* (Once More on the Problem of Price Formation), *Promyshlenno-ekonomicheskaia gazeta,* March 24, 1957, p. 3. For a good account of some of these proposals, see Alec Nove, *The Soviet Economy,* Praeger, New York, 1961, pp. 271 *et seq.*

cost level of the least efficient plant or factory, as had been proposed earlier by some Soviet economists.

Further phenomena calling for clarification are certain symp-
toms of repressed inflation which chronically characterize the
operations of the Soviet economy. It is known, for example, that
collective farm market prices are frequently considerably above
the prices in the state and cooperative stores, and consumers'
queues have been observed at many times. With respect to the
fact that collective farm market prices are considerably above
the official state store prices, this is not exactly a new development, since the authorities have usually made it a practice to
establish the official prices below the freely determined prices on
the collective farm markets. In part, this price differential also
corresponds to the higher quality of collective farm produce with
respect to freshness as compared with the state and cooperative
store foods. In order to read any significance into these phenomena, one would have to show that the disparity between the
two sets of prices is growing, and there would seem to be little
evidence that this is so. The same can be said for queues. They
have also been a trademark of Soviet socialism since the inception
of the plans, and it is believed that they may be less prevalent
today than they were in the past.

In other noncapitalist-oriented economies, inflation after World
War II was a problem similar to that found in the USSR in
the thirties. These inflationary pressures were felt especially before 1954, and they were frequently accompanied by the formal
rationing of consumers' goods to insure greater equity. After
1954, price reductions have been the general rule in the Soviet
bloc, although mainland China, Poland, and Yugoslavia seem to
be exceptions in that they are apparently still plagued by rising
prices at various times.[32]

[32] For an account of Chinese inflation see "Inflation Spiral Worrying
Peiping," *New York Times*, January 14, 1962, p. 31. In December, 1961, the
Yugoslavian cost-of-living index was 16 per cent higher than it was a
year earlier. See Paul Underwood, "Yugoslavia Plans Public Price Curb,"
New York Times, February 11, 1962, p. 20. Bulgaria has also announced
substantial increases in the prices of meat and dairy products to finance
greater incentives for the Bulgarian farmers along the same lines as the

On January 1, 1961, a monetary reform (which will be discussed more fully in Chapter XI) provided for the moving of all decimal points in the price and wage system over one digit to the left. Since the price level for consumers' goods generally was about 10 times higher than it was in 1928, the current price level for consumers' goods is nominally pretty much on a par with that existing before the industrialization drive. For producers' goods, since their prices were only five times above the 1928 level, the nominal price level today is perhaps one-half of what it was in the late twenties.

Bulgaria has also instituted a similar monetary reform in their prices a year after the Soviet experience.[33] The chief impact of these reforms—which are basically modeled after an earlier French reform moving decimal points two places to the left— would seem to be one of obtaining greater convenience and easier calculation, accounting, and banking. In the Soviet case, it was also claimed that consumers would benefit from the rounding of prices to the tune of 10 million rubles. They also restored the meaningfulness of fractional coins—the Russian kopeck and the Bulgarian stotinka—allowing the use of metallic coins in their new automatic vending machines.

With the exception of the effects of the 1947 monetary reform —which will be discussed below—Soviet cost and price inflation can be largely explained in "real" or nonmonetary terms. If we were so inclined, we could undoubtedly show that there was a rather passive monetary side to the picture accompanying the inflation.[34] But since the Soviet economy has for all practical purposes been "demonetized," such things as the chronic small surplus planned for in the government budget—except during World War II—must be considered largely as vestiges of capitalist thinking rather than of any substantive importance in ex-

---

Soviet action in June, 1962. See "Bulgaria Increases Peasant Incentives," *New York Times,* July 30, 1962, p. 1.

[33] See Paul Underwood, "Bulgarians Jingle Coins Again Under Currency Revaluation," *New York Times,* January 28, 1962, p. 5.

[34] For an account of the monetary side of the picture, see the articles by Raymond P. Powell and Donald R. Hodgman in the reading list at the end of this chapter.

plaining the cause of disinflation or the control of inflation. However, this is not meant to imply that monetary authorities have no subsidiary power to check inflation in the noncapitalist-oriented economic systems. In the Soviet Union, beginning in 1954, the State Bank was ordered to restrict credits to enterprises failing to fulfill their production cost and profit plans. At the same time, the bank was permitted to extend supplementary credits to enterprises showing favorable qualitative indices.[35]

PRICE POLICY AND PRICE MOVEMENTS IN CAPITALIST-ORIENTED ECONOMIES

In recent Western economic thinking, there has been considerable disagreement regarding the appropriate long-run price policy for capitalist-oriented economies. Some Western economists have conceded that democratic governments of advanced capitalist-oriented economies will be forced to pursue policies permitting a certain amount of secular or long-run inflation, while others maintain that these governments should be able to adopt measures designed to insure general price stability in the long run. The late Professor Sumner Slichter of Harvard argued in widely read articles during the fifties that creeping inflation was not only acceptable but that it was almost inevitable. On the other hand, Professor Jules Backman effectively presented the case against

[35] See V. A. Bunimovich, *Sebestoimost produktsii i voprosy kalkulirovaniia v promyshlennosti SSSR* (The Cost of Production and Problems of Calculation in Industry of the U.S.S.R.), Gospolitizdat, Moscow, 1955, p. 35. Measures of labor productivity and production cost changes are classified as "qualitative indices" in the Soviet Union. The importance of the State Bank as a control lever is indicated by the fact that at present, its branches control the wage fund payments of 49,000 industrial firms; 9300 transportation units; 11,200 commercial establishments; 5600 municipal enterprises; 16,600 State Farms and other agricultural enterprises; and 341,000 budget and economic organizations. See L. S. Galimon *et al.*, *Kontrol' za raskhodovaniem fondov zarabotnoi platy* (Control over the Expenditures from the Wage Fund), Gosfinizdat, Moscow, 1962, p. 5.

secular inflation.[36] His reply, which probably represented the official—though not necessarily the private—view of most economists, was a flat rejection of the creeping inflation thesis. There is a third possible long-run price policy, namely one which would lead to long-run disinflationary price movements similar to those in the Soviet Union in the fifties, but Western advocates of such a policy have been rare birds.

In comparison with the Soviet record on inflation, our overall experience would indicate that runaway or hyper-inflation is certainly not one of the major problems facing advanced capitalist-oriented economies. This is especially obvious if we carry our look at the economic record back to the twenties, when our post-World War I prosperity was accompanied by little, if any, inflation. The contrast between our post-World War I and post-World War II years with respect to inflation is apparently to be found in the general ineffectiveness of our price controls during World War I and the resulting relative lack of pent-up consumers' demand after the war; the lack of any substantial postwar national defense establishment after World War I; and comparatively weak trade union activity allowing increases in labor productivity to generally exceed increases in money wages in the twenties.

Considering our more recent economic history, we find that during the thirties at a time when rampant inflation characterized all sectors of the Soviet economy, most of the efforts of the United States government were aimed at "reflating" our price level, which had declined sharply along with our GNP after 1929. Devaluation of the dollar, a generally easy monetary policy, and deficit financing all proved to be inadequate for the job. Prices were still almost 20 per cent below their pre-Depression level in 1940.

During World War II, our economy regained full employment and became the "arsenal for democracy" by running huge government budgetary deficits. The Treasury cash deficit reached over $50 billion a year at the peak of the war effort. Voluntary

[36] See Jules Backman, "Argument Against Creeping Inflation," *New York Times Magazine,* May 3, 1959, p. 15.

and virtually compulsory defense bond sales to our citizens were supplemented by the sales of government obligations to the Federal Reserve System, and repressed inflation was held in check by price controls. As a consequence of this deficit financing, our economy came out of World War II with a huge backlog of pent-up effective demand and most ample monetary reserves. With the lifting of our comparatively effective wartime price controls in 1946, the repressed inflation made itself felt in the steadily rising general price level as wages chased prices in the seller's market of that period.

The Korean War expenditures added some fuel to the inflationary situation, and the private capital expansion of 1955–56 may have further stimulated demand-pull inflation. But, by the end of the fifties, the Fed's rather consistently tight money policy had largely succeeded in bringing to an end the demand pull inflation and in replacing it with a cost-push on the gently rising price level, as higher unit overhead costs resulted from the steady growth of underutilized capital. By the early sixties it had become clear to all, and especially to those who had previously been hedging against secular inflation on the stock market, that relative price stability had been assured. The large underutilization of both capital and labor virtually guaranteed that the inflationary danger was a "dead horse," to be trotted out principally during periods of wage negotiations. The consumers' price index still continued to creep upward largely because of early year weights and the rising health and transportation components of the index, where productivity increases were sluggish and higher wages still had to be paid by transport authorities and hospital administrations to meet their competition in the labor market.

How does our inflation of the past thirty years compare with that taking place in the Soviet Union? Taking the comparable period from 1928 to 1960, the increase in the United States wholesale price index for all commodities, other than farm products and food, rose by a little less than two-fold. Even if we measure the increase from 1932 (the trough of the Great Depression) the price increase is only two and one-half times, compared with the five-fold increase in producers' goods prices in

the Soviet Union. Our price increase for iron and steel as measured roughly by the metals and metal products index was somewhat greater than the above-mentioned increase in the entire
United States wholesale price index, amounting to 2.4 times from
1928 to 1960 and 2.9 times from 1932 to 1960. But even this
increase in our prices is considerably below the roughly four-
fold increase shown by the Soviet price index for iron and steel
over the same period. Although the price inflation in the electric
power sector in the Soviet Union has been very inconsequential
relative to the price increases for other basic industrial products,
the prices of electric power in the United States have also behaved atypically in comparison with our industrial prices generally. The average prices of electric power for all services in
the United States declined from 2.66¢ per kwh to 1.64¢ per kwh,
or by over one-third between 1928 and 1956.[37]

Nevertheless, it should be pointed out that the relative price
movements in the two countries before World War II are chiefly
responsible for the smaller amount of overall inflation in the
United States. If we compare relative inflation in the two countries from 1940 to 1960, the results are the reverse of those mentioned above. The United States wholesale price index for commodities, other than farm products and food, rose almost 2.2-fold
from 1940 to 1960 compared with a 1.9-fold increase in the prices
of basic industrial goods in the Soviet Union. For iron and steel,
the United States price index, as measured by metals and metal
products, shows a 2.4-fold increase between 1940 and 1960 compared with only a 1.6-fold increase in Soviet iron and steel prices.

Generally speaking, this similar or even lower rate of increase
in Soviet prices since 1940 is brought about by the relative price
movements in the two countries since 1949. While prices in the
United States were still rising (in part due to the Korean conflict), prices in the USSR declined during the same period. The
basic reason for this disinflation in the Soviet Union was the
fact that wages were increasing by between two and four per

[37] United States Department of Commerce, Bureal of Census, *Historical Statistics of the United States, Colonial Times to 1957,* U.S. Government Printing Office, Washington, 1960, p. 510.

cent per annum while, at the same time, industrial labor productivity was rising by anywhere from five to seven per cent annually. These gains in productivity were also taking place in the consumers' goods industries and the net additions to the labor force employed in food processing and light industry were sufficient to permit the production of enough additional goods and services to absorb the additions to effective demand.

With respect to consumers' goods and services the price inflation in the United States since 1940 has been considerably greater than it was in the USSR, although for the entire period since 1928, the overall increase in these prices was considerably greater in the Soviet Union. From 1940 to 1960, Soviet consumers' goods prices in the state and cooperative stores rose by about 40 per cent, and the average price increase on the collective farm markets was negligible. In the United States, the consumers' price index more than doubled during these 20 years. Money wages in the Soviet Union have risen by 2.7-fold, while in the United States they have gone up 3.4-fold since 1940.

Since 1947–49, hourly earnings in United States manufacturing have risen by almost 70 per cent. At the same time, real product per man-hour in manufacturing has risen by roughly 35–40 per cent, or almost half as fast. In other words, there has been pretty much the reverse relationship between gains in productivity and money wages in the United States as compared with the USSR.

One important factor explaining the relative lack of inflation in the USSR after World War II was the currency reform at the end of 1947. During the war, collective farm market prices skyrocketed and many Russian peasants doubtlessly prospered, at least in monetary terms, much in the same manner as United States farmers and underdeveloped countries generally did during the war. These accumulated ruble savings of the farmers were virtually confiscated by the Soviet authorities when all outstanding ruble notes were called in and exchanged at the rate of 10 old rubles for one new ruble in December, 1947.[38] In the United States, on the other hand, the pent-up purchasing power

---

[38] Savings bank deposits and government bonds were also exchanged at somewhat more favorable rates to their owners.

inherited from World War II smoothed over the transition from a wartime to a relatively peacetime economy, and was useful in helping to overcome for a time our more normal tendencies towards inadequate effective demand. West Germany, which faced a capital reconstruction problem more like the one facing the Russians after the war, tended to confiscate wartime savings in much the same manner as the Russians did.[39] France and Great Britain, however, were more inclined to follow the United States example, although as a price for this conservatism, they were both forced to devalue their currencies at various times in the postwar years. France eventually "wiped out" the war and postwar inflation by moving all decimal points for domestic prices, including wages, two digits to the left.

ADVANTAGES AND DISADVANTAGES OF INFLATIONARY AND DISINFLATIONARY PRICE POLICIES IN VIEW OF BASIC PROBLEMS

There would appear to be a number of possible advantages to be derived from a disinflationary overall price policy in a maturing noncapitalist-oriented economy. In the producers' goods sector, falling prices may discourage abnormal inventory holdings, which are somewhat of a problem in the Soviet Union. Although there are official limits to the amount of working capital Soviet enterprises can legally tie-up in this form, it has been difficult to enforce these limitations in the past. It is possible that occasional monetary windfall losses sustained as a result of hoarding unnecessarily large inventories could act as a more effective control device.

In the consumers' goods sector, falling prices in noncapitalist-oriented economies will also discourage personal hoarding or

[39] Denmark, Norway, Holland, Czechoslovakia, and Austria also apparently carried out similar drastic monetary reforms. See Thomas Wilson, *Inflation,* Harvard University Press, Cambridge, 1961, p. 153.

speculative purchasing of goods, although lack of adequate storage space is probably a more effective deterrent here. It also seems possible that stable or falling price levels may stimulate the growth of voluntary savings in the form of savings bank deposits. The real rate of interest on savings accounts may in fact become rather significant with a declining price level for consumers' goods.

Since the basic problems of the United States economy are pretty much the reverse of those in the Soviet Union, a disinflationary price policy would be disastrous here. On the other hand, however, there might be certain economic advantages connected with a secularly rising price level. Inventory investment, one of our currently inadequate absorbers of full employment voluntary nonconsumption, would be stimulated by the prospect of windfall gains resulting from a gently rising price level.[40] Secular or creeping inflation discourages personal saving and encourages higher propensities to consume, inasmuch as it becomes costly to hold assets in the form of money. Since we also have a tendency for consumption to be inadequate relative to the amount required for full employment operations, we should benefit from this stimulant to consumption and penalty for saving. As long as savers are not covered by escalator clauses, this may be one way our economy might rather "painlessly" approach a falling real rate of return, or what Keynes called the "euthanasia of the rentier." [41] In times past, when capitalist-oriented economies were accumulating capital in the process of their early industrialization, the "money illusion" worked against

[40] The failure of businesses to build up their inventories since the 1960–61 recession as much as they did during previous postwar recessions has been partially attributed to the fact that prices are steady or falling in 1962. See Richard E. Mooney, "Analysts Weigh Inventory Role," *New York Times,* November 5, 1962, p. 47.

[41] J. M. Keynes, *The General Theory of Employment, Interest and Money,* Harcourt, Brace, New York, 1936, p. 376. Other more painful routes might be to do away with the money interest rate as has been suggested by Roy F. Harrod, *Towards a Dynamic Economics,* Macmillan and Co., London, 1948, p. 159; to eliminate rent as suggested a long time ago by Henry George; or to renounce dividends as has recently been suggested by a reputable Stanford economist, as discussed in the following chapter.

labor; now that labor is covered by escalator clauses and operates in an economy committed to full employment, it has been working against owners of capital in the postwar years.

An incidental benefit derived from secular inflation would be the possibility that a better relative price structure could be attained. There is a distinct reluctance on the part of businessmen when it comes to lowering prices in certain comparatively noncompetitive sectors of our economy. As a result, these sticky prices in "administered price" sectors may have a distorting effect on the relative price structure. However, if secular inflation could be attained, there would be no necessity for any sector to lower prices. Sectors which are more successful in increasing output per worker could have price increases which are nil or below the average price increase for the entire economy; sectors which are less successful in increasing labor productivity would have price increases above average for the economy as a whole.

As already pointed out in Chapter VII (p. 155), creeping inflation tends to foster a certain leveling in the wage structure of capitalist-oriented economies. To the extent that greater income equality is also achieved, there should be a generally higher propensity to consume and a lower propensity to save as a result. Considering all of these favorable economic effects produced by creeping inflation in the fifties, and the fact that Western Europe and Japan had been combining rapid rates of growth along with their secular inflation, it is not so surprising to find that second thoughts are being expressed concerning the desirability of price stability, now that it has been achieved in the United States along with stagnation and a growing underutilization of capital and labor.[42]

[42] See Richard E. Mooney, " 'Little Inflation' Called No Threat," *New York Times,* May 21, 1962, p. 53. According to Mooney, "some economists who have believed that adequate economic growth can and should be achieved without inflation admit to some doubts now. Others who have always believed that growth needs an inflationary stimulus are more convinced than ever."

Recommended Readings

BARAN, PAUL A., "Currency Reform in the USSR," *Harvard Business Review,* March, 1958, pp. 194–206.

BERGSON, ABRAM, *et al.,* "Prices of Basic Industrial Products in the USSR, 1928–50," *The Journal of Political Economy,* August 1956, pp. 303–328.

BORNSTEIN, MORRIS, "The Reform and Revaluation of the Ruble," *American Economic Review,* March, 1961, pp. 117–123.

**————, "The Soviet Price System," *American Economic Review,* March, 1962, pp. 64–103.

CAMPBELL, ROBERT W., "Accounting for Cost Control in the Soviet Economy," *Review of Economics and Statistics,* February, 1958, pp. 59–67.

GROSSMAN, GREGORY, "How the Soviets 'Plan' Their Prices," *Challenge,* January, 1958, pp. 22–26.

*————, "Industrial Prices in the USSR," *The American Economic Review,* Vol. XLIX, No. 2, May, 1959, pp. 50–64.

*HOLZMAN, FRANKLYN D., "Soviet Inflationary Pressures, 1928–57: Causes and Cures," *The Quarterly Journal of Economics,* May, 1960, pp. 167–188.

*HODGMAN, DONALD R., "Soviet Monetary Controls Through the Banking System," in Gregory Grossman, editor, *Value and Plan,* University of California Press, Berkeley, 1960, pp. 105–124, 130–131.

KASER, M. C., "Soviet Planning and the Price Mechanism," *The Economic Journal,* March, 1950, pp. 81–91.

*POWELL, RAYMOND P., "Recent Developments in Soviet Monetary Policy," unpublished paper presented to the Southern Economic Association, December, 1957.

TURGEON, LYNN, "Cost-Price Relationships in Basic Industries During the Soviet Planning Era," *Soviet Studies,* October, 1957, Vol. IX, No. 2, pp. 143–177.

WILSON, THOMAS, *Inflation,* Harvard University Press, Cambridge, 1961, especially Chapter 8, "A Note on Inflation in Russia."

IX ⤳ Managerial Decision-Making

WE HAVE BEEN CONSIDERING the underlying market forces operating within the contrasting economic systems. Now we turn to administrative decision-making—first, at the microeconomic level, where factory managers or corporation directors in executive positions attempt to obtain either the greatest output with given inputs or given outputs with the least input; and second, in the following chapter, we examine the macroeconomic level where central governments use their important powers to tax and to spend in an effort to insure the employment of resources required for their political and economic goals.

A visitor from another planet inspecting the day-to-day operations of an industrial establishment in the United States and in the USSR would undoubtedly discern many technical and economic similarities between the operations of the two organizations. Both productive operations are supervised by hired managerial personnel whose activities would seem to be at least superficially comparable. Labor and materials are combined using similar technological processes in both factories, and the end products are shipped either to other enterprises for further fabrication or to retail establishments. The transfer price in both systems generally exceeds the factory's costs of production as determined by their respective accounting departments, and the proceeds are then used to repeat the productive process, resulting in a more or less continuous circular flow between resources and money. The difference between the selling price and the cost of production is available for capital repairs and expansion of the enterprise or for government tax revenue. In the latter case, there will be either subsequent spending for capital expansion or communal consumption by the central government.

It is true that in capitalist-oriented economies, in contrast to the noncapitalist-oriented variety, there are bothersome owners of common stock who must be occasionally pacified with dividend payments, but these claims tend to have become relatively less important with the passage of time.[1] One imaginative professor of business administration has even gone so far as to suggest that the payment of increased dividends by a corporation in a capitalist-oriented economy is a sure sign of weakness—an indication that the firm has nothing better to do with its inner resources. Accordingly, he has suggested that a reduction of dividends, or better yet their complete elimination, should be regarded as a highly favorable development.[2] In connection with the "rollback" of steel prices by the Kennedy Administration in 1962, another economist who has made an exhaustive study of the steel industry suggested that, inasmuch as no major steel company had marketed new common stock during the past decade, high dividends were not needed to attract new capital and the reduction of these income payments might be an appropriate method to obtain any additional funds needed for capital expansion.[3]

One's overall evaluation of comparative management problems in the two contrasting economic systems would seem to be—at least, to some extent—a matter of taste. Certainly the

[1] Superficially it may seem that dividends as a percentage of corporate profits after taxes are growing. This reflects a tendency to write off depreciation in a more liberal manner. If we take dividends as a percentage of so-called "cash earnings"—that is, corporate profits after taxes plus depreciation—we find that they have declined from their postwar peak of 33 per cent to 30 per cent in 1961. See *New York Times,* August 4, 1962, p. 25.

[2] See "Better Off Without Dividends," a report of a talk by Professor James T. S. Porterfield of the Stanford Graduate School of Business, *New York Herald Tribune,* February 26, 1962, p. 25.

[3] See Harvard Professor Otto Eckstein's letter to the *New York Times,* May 10, 1962, p. 36.

sharp contrasts found in other areas of our comparison are less evident here. Those analysts who would emphasize the similarities of hired managers and their tasks in the two systems will tend to focus their attention primarily on the impersonal managerial bureaucratization of both advanced industrialized economies.[4] On the other hand, those who wish to stress the differences will be advised to compare and contrast our own managerial environment and behavior in the United States during World War II and at the present time. For, in many respects, the managerial problems and activities of directors of enterprises in noncapitalist-oriented economies are similar to those which plagued United States plant managers during the war.

ADMINISTRATION OF ENTERPRISE OPERATIONS IN NONCAPITALIST-ORIENTED ECONOMIES

The administrative apparatus above the plant or enterprise in the Soviet Union has varied considerably over time. In the early years of planning, the unrevolutionary sounding "trust" administered the operations of individual plants in an industry or region. The trusts were gradually replaced in the thirties by *glavki* or chief administrations, which in turn took orders from commissariats.[5] By the end of the thirties, most of the important industries had their own specialized commissariat. For example, there was a People's Commissariat of Ferrous Metallurgy, under which there were a number of glavki (such as the Chief Ad-

---

[4] See, for example, Erich Fromm, *May Man Prevail?,* Doubleday Anchor Book, Garden City, New York, 1961, especially pp. 77 *et seq.* In his interpretation, Fromm relies heavily on the interesting study of David Granick, *The Red Executive,* Doubleday, Garden City, New York, 1960.

[5] Trusts apparently still continue to be used in administering the coal mining and fishing industries. See N. A. Bulganin, *Tasks of the Further Development of Industry, Technical Progress and Better Organization of Production,* Foreign Languages Publishing House, Moscow, 1955, p. 49.

ministration of Special Steels) each giving orders to all plants producing a particular type of product, in this case special steels. The individual iron and steel combines or plants, each with their responsible director, were subordinated to the appropriate glavki.

The industrial commissariats officially disappeared in 1946, their functions being taken over by ministries. The number of ministries (or commissariats) tended to increase in periods of relaxation and to be reduced in times of stress. That is to say, power tended to be delegated more liberally in the former periods and, subsequently, to be withdrawn in times of uncertainty. For example, immediately after Stalin's death, the number of ministries was reduced in much the same manner as the number of commissariats had been cut during World War II.

Most of the industrial ministries were abolished in 1957, and 103 regional economic councils (*sovnarkhozy*) were created to administer and plan industrial and agricultural production on a regional basis. Many of the general functions of the defunct industrial ministries were acquired by departments of the all-Union state planning body (*Gosplan*) which bore designations similar to those of the erstwhile ministries: ferrous metallurgy, heavy machine-building, oil and gas, building materials, chemicals, etc. The central Gosplan coordinated and amended the draft short-term output plans (up to five years) submitted to it by the republican Gosplany. Longer term economic planning and research after 1960 was entrusted to an all-Union Economic-Science Council (*Gosekonomsovet*).

Ministries still remained after this administrative reorganization for some of the most crucial sectors: part of the defense industry (Ministry of Medium Machine-Building), foreign trade, merchant marine, transportation, transport construction, and electric power plants (later abolished at the end of 1958 only to be reconstituted in 1962).[6] This decentralization in the late fifties —if past reorganizations are any indication—would thus seem to have represented some delegation of power and therefore

[6] See "Soviet Electricity Industry Returned to Central Control," *New York Times,* September 27, 1962, p. 14.

to reflect a feeling of relative security on the part of the ruling Community Party.[7]

Instead of getting their orders from the ministry or glavk, most plants began to receive their planning directives from the local economic council or the Gosplan of the individual republics. In some cases, especially for commodities produced exclusively within a region, price setting powers were turned over to the regional councils.

A still further step towards recentralization—possibly as a reflection of growing insecurity—was taken in 1963 as a result of the meeting of the Communist Party Central Committee in November, 1962.[8] The more than one hundred *Sovnarkhozy* were consolidated into forty larger units. The Gosplan was abolished in its earlier form and replaced by a more powerful Union Council of the National Economy headed by V. E. Dymshits. The new Union Council will assume the Gosplan's role of implementing the Annual Plans, which will henceforth be drafted by the 15 constituent republics. The Union Council was also assigned "certain administrative powers" enabling it to make prompt decisions on resource allocation and other day-to-day problems of economic management. Formerly such decisions had to be submitted to a special committee of the Council of Ministers. At the same time, the long range planning agency (*Gosekonomsovet*) was rechristened as a new "State Planning Committee."

As we shall see more clearly when we come to the study of the Soviet budget in Chapter X, factories or enterprises in the USSR operate in some ways much like their United States counterparts. Unless substantial net investment is contemplated, a Soviet firm today may be run fairly independently of the gov-

[7] A very similar regional reorganization took place in Czechoslovakia in 1959. See M. S. Handler, "Czechs Announce 11 Per Cent Rise in Output," *New York Times,* November 20, 1959, p. 15.

[8] For a recapitulation of the changes in administration made at this meeting, see Harry Schwartz, "Khrushchev is Moving to Spur Soviet Economy," *New York Times,* November 25, 1962, Section IV, p. 46. Also, Theodore Shabad, "An Economic Czar Named in Moscow," *New York Times,* November 25, 1962, p. 1. For Premier Khrushchev's speech outlining these changes, see *Pravda,* November 20, 1962.

ernment budget from a financial standpoint. More than half of all economic activity in the USSR takes place without any dependence on the government budget. In Soviet parlance, the firm is said to be operating on the principle of *khozraschet,* or economic accountability. The Soviet firm brings together labor and materials; it manufactures some commodity or commodities out of these factors; and it sells the end product to another enterprise or to a marketing organization at a fixed price which is supposed to cover its production costs plus a relatively small planned profit margin, much of which is subject to government taxation. To finance these productive operations, the Soviet enterprise has its own supply of working capital and, if necessary, it may obtain supplementary working capital at roughly a two per cent rate of interest from the state banking system.[9] If the firm produces electric power, refined petroleum products, or most consumers' goods, turnover taxes will also be contributed to the central government's budgetary revenues at some stage before the end product is consumed.[10] If the operations of the firm are more efficient than planned, this results in the creation of so-called "unplanned profits," a small percentage of which also shows up on the revenue side of the government budget, the remainder being available for distribution among workers and management personnel in the form of various "carrots."

Soviet firms have not always been allowed to enjoy this relative financial independence. Before the universal application of the principle of khozraschet in 1929, many firms relied on the annual government budget, or the funds of their trust, for operating monetary resources. Later in the thirties and forties, rather substantial sectors of Soviet heavy industry were producing commodities at costs which chronically exceeded the fixed prices established by the state. As a result, direct subsidies from the

[9] Fixed capital refers mainly to plant and equipment; working capital may include both materials' inventories and monetary reserves out of which goods-in-process are financed.

[10] Turnover taxes have not been levied on producers' goods other than electric power or refined petroleum products since 1949. Before this, nominal turnover taxes were levied on all producers' goods, apparently as a minor control device.

government budget enabled many firms to meet their current wage and material obligations. Even today not all enterprises are operating at a profit and must therefore be subsidized in one way or another, although usually not out of the government budget. In 1960 over 20 per cent of Soviet enterprises, many of them in the coal mining sector, were planned to operate at a loss.[11] Before the dissolution of most ministries and the creation of the system of sovnarkhozy in 1957, the offsetting of profits and deficits was carried out by the glavki operating under the jurisdiction of the ministries. After the regionalization, the sovnarkhozy apparently offset losses with the profits earned by other enterprises under their jurisdiction.

The economic basis for these losses lies in the Soviet principle of setting the fixed prices of producers' goods somewhere near the average cost of production for the entire industry, as noted in Chapter VIII. Relatively efficient firms are therefore expected to make profits, while those enterprises with antiquated capital or poor natural resources at their disposal are planned to operate at a loss. There are very great variations in the production costs of the same product within the USSR, due in part of the universal practice of seldom replacing antiquated capital with the latest equipment within any given enterprise, or the failure to retire completely any relatively inefficient industrial operations for any reason whatsoever. In general, the modern Siberian plants, operating as they do on cheap fuel and power, are those with the lowest costs of production despite the fact that they are required to pay wages and salaries which are 20 per cent above those for workers and employees performing similar operations in the western areas of the USSR.

Soviet firms are chiefly dependent on the central government to the extent that they wish to expand their scale of operations—by increasing either their fixed or working capital. Most major additions to plant and equipment are provided for out of annual government budgetary allocations for the "National Economy,"

---

[11] See M. Volkov, *"Ukreplenie khoziaistvennogo raschet v promyshlennosti"* (Strengthening Economic Accounting in Industry), *Voprosy Ekonomiki,* No. 2, 1960, p. 46.

with the result that uncontrolled internal financing is comparatively rare in the USSR and other noncapitalist-oriented systems. Some small-scale investment may occur outside the Soviet budget on the initiative of the individual enterprise, but in general these decentralized expenditures constitute a relatively small percentage of the total net investment.

The enterprise in noncapitalist-oriented economies is also dependent on central or regional governmental organizations, either the Union Council of the National Economy or the sovnarkhozy, in the final determination of its planned targets for future production. Each year the enterprise submits estimates of what we might term its "production possibilities," or what it thinks it can turn out, given its existing productive capacity. Theoretically, at least, the determination of the production possibilities is a group decision with both trade union and management participation. When these initial draft plans have been studied by the central or regional planners, they are revised either on the basis of any new investment planned for the enterprise, or on the basis of comparable draft plans submitted by other enterprises. In examining the various production possibilities submitted by the enterprises, the central planners may feel that an enterprise has deliberately underestimated its potentialities, for reasons which we shall examine shortly. In general, the planners probably revise the draft plans upwards, but in some cases, the authorities may feel that the firm has been too enthusiastic in estimating its potentialities, in which case, they may trim the draft targets. The revised draft plan is then sent down to the enterprise as the new Annual Plan for the coming year, and it is this plan which the director of the enterprise is obligated to fulfill by the force of law.[12]

The Annual Plan consists of various goals or targets. In addi-

[12] The Annual Plan, although less widely advertised and imitated than the five-year variety, is undoubtedly of greater operational importance than the longer term plans. This seems obvious from the fact that the Sixth Five-Year Plan was "scrapped" at midpoint and a revised Seven-Year plan substituted some time later, yet the growth in output continued largely unabated. The Annual Plans are usually subdivided into quarterly and monthly subdivisions.

tion to the goal for overall production—which may be expressed in both physical and value terms—there may be an assortment goal, a labor productivity target, and a production cost objective. In the latter cases, the goal is ordinarily one of increasing labor productivity and reducing production costs. For some enterprises, the reduction of fuel and power utilized per unit of product, or an increase in the percentage of productive capacity being utilized, may also constitute important targets.

Responsibility for plan fulfillment in the early days of planning did not rest solely on the shoulders of the director or manager. Instead there was group responsibility, as formalized in the principle of the "factory triangle," until around 1937. The early factory triangle was composed of the plant director, the Communist Party secretary, and the trade union president. After 1937, however, the director has assumed sole responsibility for the efficient operations of the plant or factory, as well as for the fulfillment of the plan as finally handed down by the central planners. Since at present the vast majority of factory managers are also members of the Communist Party, the independent supervisory role of the party is probably less essential today than it may have been in the early days. In Eastern Europe, on the other hand, there is still a dearth of competent managers who are also politically reliable. As a result, technicians, rather than loyal party members, are apparently being moved into command posts in an effort to increase production.[13]

DIRECTORS AND THEIR PROBLEMS IN NONCAPITALIST-ORIENTED ECONOMIES

In many respects, the job of directing a plant in the Soviet Union resembles the position of a hired manager in the United States, say in the General Electric plant located in a small New

[13] See "Hungary and Rumania Seeking Managers for New Industries," *New York Times*, June 3, 1962, p. 14.

England city.[14] As in the case of our plant manager, the director of a Soviet factory has his price and output decisions largely determined for him in advance by the central management. His principal function therefore is to economize on the use of labor and materials in the production process, that is, to produce commodities at the lowest possible cost of production, and thereby to maximize his unplanned profits.

In contrast to the United States hired manager, however, the Soviet counterpart frequently has certain incentives to produce as much as possible in excess of his planned output goals. In so doing, the manager receives substantial bonuses attached to this overfulfillment. It seems obvious that there is some basic conflict between this quantitative goal of overfulfilling the physical or total value targets and the qualitative task of minimizing production costs or increasing labor productivity. Thus, unless bonuses are also linked to the improvement of labor productivity or the reduction of production costs, the director may be tempted to overfulfill the output or total value plan—by using overtime and other high cost labor—even though this means a higher cost and lower labor productivity than planned. In the past, particularly in the thirties and forties, this emphasis on the quantitative targets resulted in an excessive use of progressive piece-rates and overexpenditures of the plant's wage fund.

In other instances, the director may have attempted to overfulfill his output plan at the expense of his assortment plan. This can be done if several products are being turned out by a plant, each of which has a somewhat different price-cost ratio. If this is the case, the manager may direct the energies of his operations towards the production of those commodities with the greatest margin between price and cost since, in this way, he obtains the greatest total value out of given inputs. In other instances, the factory may be producing commodities with dif-

[14] For an interesting account of the development of managerial institutions in the USSR and their relationship to the regionalization of industry, see Harry Schwartz' article in the *New York Times,* June 2, 1957. An evaluation of the role of the director as obtained from post-Stalin fiction is given by George Gibian, "The Factory Manager in Soviet Fiction," *Problems of Communism,* March–April, 1959, p. 44.

ferent percentages of "value added" within the plant. If this is the case, output targets in value terms are more easily fulfilled by concentrating attention on those products with the largest percentage of materials purchased from other enterprises and thereby requiring the least value added by the plant itself. However, in the past, this advantage of relying on outside sources of supply was offset in some cases by the unpredictability of outside deliveries.

Generally speaking, the problems of Soviet managers are somewhat similar to those of United States managers during World War II, or within our defense establishment today—that is, they arise chiefly because of inadequate supplies rather than any lack of effective demand. Because of the material shortages, the managers may be forced to carry some *tolkachi* or "pushers" on their payrolls, although these expenditures may be disguised under such rubrics as "exchange of technical information," or "contract negotiations." [15] The procurer's function frequently consists of traveling, either with the purpose of locating scarce supplies, or in order to expedite shipments or orders scheduled according to existing contractual arrangements. To accomplish his task, the tolkach may frequently attempt to develop "influence" or *blat* with respect to his potential suppliers by showering them with lavish gifts (by Soviet standards) and entertainment. Thus, while there is no evidence that there has been any widespread manipulation of the official prices for producers' goods fixed by the central planners, the value of these "influencing" gifts and the salaries of any tolkachi should no doubt be added to the supply price of materials. [16]

Materials are obtained by plant managers in two principal ways. Some particularly scarce producers' goods, such as non-

[15] For a recent account of these practices, see "Soviet Sees Flaws in State Business," *New York Times,* April 19, 1959, p. 7. Apparently directors have been taking advantage of a decree of the Ministry of Finance in January, 1956, which made it unnecessary to give detailed accounts of expenditures for these "missions."

[16] See Joseph S. Berliner, "The Informal Organization of the Soviet Firm," *The Quarterly Journal of Economics,* Vol. LXVI, August, 1952, p. 352.

ferrous metals or rubber, are either "funded" or allocated centrally by the planners. However, other commodities are no longer allocated centrally and procurement of these products is decentralized. To obtain these materials, contracts are made by the using enterprise with the supplying firms. Penalties are extracted for failure to fulfill contractual obligations with regard to quality or delivery date. Even for commodities obtained as a result of "allocation certificates" (*nariady*) supplied by the supply-marketing (*snabsbyty*) departments of the Union Council of the National Economy, formal contracts containing detailed specifications, precise dates of delivery, etc., must be negotiated between buyers and sellers. These contracts constitute one important reason why the legal profession, although it plays a comparatively unimportant role in the USSR, does not seem to be exactly "withering away" under Soviet socialism. In addition, the successful manager attempts to overcome supply shortages by economizing on the use of materials—unless of course his physical goals are expressed in terms of weight in which case he may be inclined to be more extravagant.

Labor is also obtained by plant directors in two principal ways. Internally, increases in labor productivity release redundant labor for other operations. A manager may also be able to pare down his white-collar workers and thereby release labor for more "productive" uses. There is some evidence that the Russians have been comparatively successful since 1940 in reducing the relative numbers of administrative and office personnel.[17] Skilled labor may also be obtained internally by encouraging presently unskilled labor to take evening courses designed to lead eventually to a higher-skilled rating. Externally, the director may obtain new workers from the countryside or he may attempt to bid them away from other managers. Since the basic wage rates to be paid are fixed by the central planners, the director may be forced to use other "carrots" such as a higher percentage of

[17] In this connection, see David Granick, "Soviet-American Management Comparisons," in *Comparisons of the United States and Soviet Economies,* Part I, p. 146.

bonuses or premiums, as well as better housing, in order to entice workers from other factories.

As mentioned earlier, the goal of the Soviet manager has been one of overfulfilling his output targets. To attain this objective, substantial premiums or bonuses are available for directors and especially productive workers alike. Premiums may also be attached to other specific goals such as the following: economizing on the use of certain critical materials; reducing the volume of goods in process; producing goods from scrap; turning out spare parts; producing higher quality output; reducing costs of purchasing; evening out the production schedule; reducing spoilage; meeting obligations for delivery to other enterprises, particularly those outside the sovnarkhoz; keeping the plant clean and otherwise improving safety conditions; increasing labor productivity; economizing on fuel and materials.[18] Most of the premiums have arisen in response to certain malpractices developed by Soviet managers. For example, at one time there was a tendency for managers to avoid the production of spare parts since the production of these items was more time-consuming and interfered with ordinary output.[19]

Because large premiums frequently depend on only a small percentage overfulfillment of the overall goal, there has been a great incentive to "simulate" the overfulfillment of the overall targets, that is, to give an artificial appearance of successful accomplishment. There are a number of ways in which this simulation may take place. Outright falsification is fairly difficult to maintain in the long run, outside the agricultural sector, since each industrial enterprise operates on the principle of khozraschet. If nonexisting materials or commodities are reported, they

[18] See Joseph S. Berliner, *Factory and Manager in the USSR,* Harvard University Press, Cambridge, 1957, p. 27 and his "Managerial Incentives and Decisionmaking: A Comparison of the United States and the Soviet Union," in *Comparisons of the United States and Soviet Economies,* Part I, p. 365.

[19] For a recent change in these practices, see Max Frankel, "Soviet Revising Bonuses to Reward Cost Cutting," *New York Times,* December 18, 1959, p. 1.

cannot be sold or realized, so that the resulting financial loss will eventually show up in the subsequent auditing of the firm's accounts by the banking system. As an alternative, it may be possible in the short run to report materials-in-process as being completed units, even though they will not actually be finished until the following reporting period. However, operations in the subsequent period are handicapped by this practice, with the result that underfulfillment of the overall goal will almost certainly occur later on.

A better way to obtain premiums would be to allow for a certain "safety factor" when the original estimate of the plant's production possibilities estimate is drawn up. The hoarding of scarce materials may also help insure the continuous operations of the plant and the avoidance of work stoppages due to bottlenecks. Both of these practices are deleterious from the standpoint of the system as a whole, despite the fact that they do represent certain advantages to the individual factory manager.

Because the fulfillment of the plan is so important both to the directors and workers, production tends to be unevenly distributed over the month. The rate of production tends to be stepped up to a fever pitch as the end of the month approaches and the output goal appears to be incapable of fulfillment. As a result of this accelerated activity, which is referred to as "storming" in the literature, workers tend to be exhausted in the first part of the following month, so that storming again becomes necessary towards the end of the following period.[20] Thus, there would appear to be monthly cycles of economic activity under these conditions. Storming results in irregular deliveries and undoubtedly places unnecessary strains on the already overloaded transportation and distribution networks.

Because of the personal benefits attached to plan overfulfillment, there may be a certain understandable reticence on the part of conservative directors when it comes to the introduction of new techniques or to the production of new models, if such changeovers might conceivably result in a production slow-down

---

[20] For some interesting data on the lack of rhythmical operations in 1955, see N. A. Bulganin, *op. cit.,* p. 54.

due to transitional difficulties.[21] However, there is usually no problem caused by Soviet managers having a vested interest in withholding the introduction of a new machine because of its effect on existing capital values since the original plant and equipment is given in trust to the factory by the state. The only charge to the factory is the amortization deductions which figure as a cost item. If by some chance a piece of equipment were ever rendered useless by a new technique, depreciation or amortization charges would presumably cease on the old capital good and be replaced by depreciation charges on the new machine. In actuality, very little equipment is scrapped so that the problem of replacing old capital seldom arises. Instead, the addition of new equipment or plant occurs along side the old machinery and factory.

The backgrounds of Soviet managers are heavily weighted towards the technical or engineering side. Because of the fact that Russian top management is so completely dominated by the graduate engineer, one Western student of the subject contends that Soviet managers are more receptive to new technological ideas than their United States counterparts.[22] On the other hand, they may be less receptive to new ideas in accounting, procurement, marketing and finance because of their comparative lack of interest and training in these subjects.

In conducting their scientific research, Soviet practices would seem to be patterned on the European rather than the United States model.[23] A study of Soviet medical research institutes indicates that the Soviet director of research is hardly much more than a glorified clerk, while the scientists are more inclined to involve themselves in nonclerical aspects of administration, especially those connected with the effective conduct of research itself. In the United States, the director of a research

[21] *Ibid.*, pp. 17–18.

[22] See David Granick, *op. cit.*, p. 144.

[23] See Norman Kaplan, "Research Administration and the Administrator: USSR and United States," *Administrative Science Quarterly,* Vol. VI, No. 1, June, 1961, pp. 51–72. Although Kaplan's study was confined to medical research institutes, he believes that they are typical of the administration of scientific research generally.

organization is more frequently a scientist, but his role as a policy decision-maker affords him little time for research. As a consequence of these differences in approach to the administration of scientific research, it has been concluded tentatively that "there is probably less detail and bureaucratic red tape in the Soviet medical institute." [24]

We have discussed in Chapter VII the problems of labor mobility plaguing Soviet management. With respect to personnel practices generally, however, it would seem that the Russians manage to get by with relatively modest expenditures. Since there has been a chronic shortage of personnel relative to job opportunities, the screening of job applicants would appear to be rather superfluous.[25] The manager undoubtedly feels fortunate if and when the services of almost any laborer become available. By the same token, the practice of firing does not seem to be as time-consuming or as widespread as it is in the United States. In the event that firings take place in the Soviet Union, the worker may appeal to the Wages and Disputes Commission set up in each plant or institution, and composed of representatives of management and the trade union body of the plant on a parity basis.

As a matter of government policy, there has been a very rapid turnover of Soviet directors.[26] The authorities evidently felt that managers who remained at the same assignment for too long a time might be inclined to develop a "family atmosphere"—an apparatus designed to deceive the central planners. In creating this conspiracy, the chief accountant or bookkeeper would probably have to be the key figures involved. A new manager might

[24] See Norman Kaplan, *op. cit.*, pp. 62–63.

[25] The principal branches where hiring problems exist are those where seasonal labor is employed—especially in logging and peat extraction. There has been a tendency for seasonal employees to be replaced by full-time workers in both logging and peat extraction in recent years.

[26] The mobility of directing personnel seems to have been carried too far and to have resulted in adverse effects on production. In the coal mines, about 40 per cent of the managers and chief engineers of collieries and up to 50 per cent of the section managers are changed yearly. See N. A. Bulganin, *op. cit.*, p. 61. Also, David Granick, *Comparisons of the United States and Soviet Economies*, Part I, p. 145.

also notice areas for improvement which were not readily apparent to the former director. In general, the more successful managers tend to move up to positions in charge of larger plant operations, their base managerial salaries being largely determined by the scale of plant operation as well as the industry involved. By the same token, the less successful managers are frequently demoted to smaller-scale operations entitling them to less pay.

In selecting managerial personnel, as well as those available for technical training generally, the Russian would seem to be choosing from a relatively larger percentage of the total population than is the case in the United States. Discrimination based on race, sex, or economic background would seem to be much less prevalent in Soviet society.[27] While political and religious ideas might tend to limit the population out of which managerial talent is selected in the USSR, these are also limiting factors in the United States. In general, an economy operating under overfull employment conditions would seem to be able to afford less discrimination than one operating with chronic underemployment.

In recent years, there have been signs that overfulfillment of the quantitative overall target is assuming lesser importance as a "success indicator." Premiums are not usually paid unless the overall targets are met. However, in general they no longer rise with the percentage overfulfillment, unless the commodity is in particularly short supply. Instead, the qualitative targets are assuming greater importance, and premiums are being more frequently obtained as a result of the successful lowering of costs or increasing labor productivity.[28] There are even some commodities which must *not* be produced in excess of the planned goals since supplies of these products are already adequate.

[27] See Joseph S. Berliner, "Managerial Incentives and Decisionmaking: A comparison of the United States and the Soviet Union," in *Comparisons of the United States and Soviet Economies,* Part I, pp. 350–352.
[28] See Max Frankel, "Soviet Revising Bonuses to Reward Cost Cutting," *New York Times,* December 18, 1959, p. 1; Harry Schwartz, "Soviet Adopting 2 Western Ideas," *New York Times,* December 19, 1959, p. 2.

SOURCES AND ROLE OF PREMIUMS IN NONCAPITALIST-ORIENTED ECONOMIES

Premiums arise in two principal ways in the Soviet economy. A complex system of premiums constitutes a legitimate addition to the wages and salaries paid to managers and employees. These premiums are thus subject to comparatively strict regulations similar to those in effect for wages and salaries generally. At present, the upper limit to premiums amounts to about 50 per cent of the base salary.[29] In addition, some premiums come out of the margin existing between the fixed prices and the actual production costs of the commodities—from planned and unplanned profits. Depending on the industry, from one to six per cent of the planned profit and 20 to 50 per cent of the unplanned profit goes into the enterprise (formerly director's) fund, out of which certain premiums are paid. In addition, about 30 per cent of the unplanned profit is allocated to housing construction.[30]

Since the planned profit is established initially when the fixed prices are decreed by the planners at a level which is roughly five per cent above existing production costs, these minor contributions to the enterprise fund are fairly easily realized and do not constitute any particular incentive to workers or managers. But unplanned profits depend on improved economizing of

[29] Effective October 1, 1959, bonuses in the coal, oil, steel, and chemical industries were limited to 60 per cent of the base salary; in other industries, the upper limit was 40 per cent. In the postwar years, the percentage that premiums accounted for in the wage fund of engineer-technicians was lowered in machine building. See N. A. Maslova, *et al., Zarabotnaia plata i sebestoimost' produktsii v promyshlennosti SSSR* (Wages and Production Cost in Soviet Industry), Ekonomizdat, Moscow, 1962, p. 109.

[30] In the consumers' goods industries, 20 per cent is so allocated to housing; in mining and metallurgy, it is 50 per cent. See A. G. Zverev, *Voprosy natsional'nogo dokhoda i finansov SSSR,* (Problems of National Income and Finance in the USSR), Gosfinizdat, Moscow, 1958, p. 91.

labor and materials, and the initiative shown here by workers and managers does have an important bearing on the payment of premiums and the construction of housing. Since only about 10 to 25 per cent of these unplanned profits arising as a result of cost economies are deducted into the government budget, they do serve as a most important stimulus to workers and managers alike.

Soviet directors attempt to maximize their premiums or the amount of profits remaining for disposal within the enterprise they manage. But, in doing so, they must make sure they do not go overboard. If the plant is particularly successful in lowering production costs during the year, and thereby realizes a large amount of unplanned profits, the central planners will undoubtedly lower the factory's planned production cost target and raise the planned profit goal for the following period. As a result, it becomes easier to realize greater planned profit and the resulting minor contributions to the enterprise fund, but more difficult to realize unplanned profits and the substantial contributions to the fund out of which premiums are paid. Thus, the director of a Soviet plant, by not giving his "all," may possibly strive to maximize long-run premiums rather than the short-run variety.

In the case of an enterprise which is planned to operate at a loss—that is, a plant operating with expected average costs which are above the fixed prices for the product—premiums are based on a successful reduction of planned losses. In other words, if production costs are lower than planned, even though they are above the fixed wholesale prices, the cost savings become the basis for payments into the enterprise fund and eventually the source of premiums and other benefits.

The role of planned and unplanned profits in directing the flow of investment is virtually nonexistent in noncapitalist-oriented economies. Since profits are frequently higher in Soviet consumers' goods branches as compared with the producers' goods industries, we might expect that investment would somehow flow into the production of consumers' goods. Although some of the profits not ending up in the enterprise fund might be allowed to remain at the plant level to be earmarked for new investment purposes there, the bulk of the profits earned in consumers' goods industries is normally deducted into the budget where it is allocated to producers' goods branches and to communal consumption, including defense.

Since the earning of premiums is intimately connected with the lowering of production costs, we might consider the ways in which these cost economies might be attained by managers in noncapitalist-oriented economies. In so doing, we should first examine the nature of Soviet cost accounting procedures. Generally speaking, the principal components of production cost in the USSR are as follows: direct and indirect labor, including wages, salaries, and social security payments; [31] auxiliary and basic materials, including fuel and power; and amortization or depreciation. Although instances can be cited where differential rent and short-term interest payments for working capital are also included in the costs of production, rent and interest are largely omitted from Soviet cost calculations.[32] No charge whatsoever is made for interest on fixed capital in Soviet cost accounting procedures. While no formal charge is made for depletion as such, it might conceivably be argued that a heavy turnover tax is imposed on refined petroleum products with this factor in mind. The stumpage fees, which have at times been charged in connection with the exploitation of easily accessible timber reserves, may also be considered as depletion charges.

On the other hand, Soviet production costs sometimes include certain charges which are ordinarily not found in Western cost accounts. For example, expenditures for workers' housing are a component of the production costs of coal, peat, and wood. Some expenditures for workers' education are also generally included in Soviet cost accounts, while educational expenses may

[31] These deductions are figured as a percentage of the wages paid and they are turned over to the trade union for administrative purposes. The percentages paid into the social insurance fund vary from industry to industry.

[32] The fact that rent and interest are not charged on fixed capital does not mean that they do not exist in the Soviet system. They undoubtedly are concealed in the turnover taxes levied.

or may not be included in Western accounting costs. But in general it seems clear that the use of Soviet cost accounting practices results in nominal costs which are below the costs which would have resulted if Western accounting practices were employed under identical circumstances.

Russian managers study their cost accounts carefully and freely disclose this information to the central authorities who in turn widely publish the data. Soviet cost accounting procedures have been standardized since the middle twenties, and it is therefore possible to compare fairly meaningfully cost accounts for plants producing similar commodities. On the basis of these comparisons, the planners and managers can more easily pinpoint areas where slack or waste exist, at least to the extent that these costs bear at least some resemblance to factor scarcities.

Probably the most important source of cost economies has been that associated with the reduction of the labor required per unit of product, in other words, the increase in labor productivity. Since relative cost and productivity information is common knowledge in the noncapitalist-oriented system, it is frequently the subject of what the Russians call "socialist competition," in which factories challenge each other to produce more favorable qualitative indexes. To the victor in this competition goes a Red Banner and, incidentally, funds out of which bonuses are paid.

Material economies are also a possible source of lower costs and greater premiums. Although the prices of materials are fixed, the delivered price to users has in the past depended on the distance of the enterprise from the sources of supply. In the thirties, when the supply situation was extremely critical, there was undoubtedly much cross-hauling and unnecessarily high average transportation costs. In many cases, the managers did not care where they had to go for materials as long as they were able to obtain them. As pipe lines have become fuller in recent years, it has become more possible to order materials in a more rational manner. In addition, there has been a tendency for the government to establish the fixed prices of more and more producers' goods on a delivered price basis, including average costs of transportation. In such cases, it now becomes a matter of con-

232 THE CONTRASTING ECONOMIES

cern to the seller where he ships his products, and there is an incentive for producers to supply nearby consumers, if possible.

It also seems conceivable that the regionalization or decentralization of the administrative apparatus in the late fifties has produced a more rational distribution set-up and that the average lengths of haul and average transportation costs have been reduced. Between the first half of 1957 and the first half of 1958, for example, the average length of haul was reduced by 33 kilometers.[33] To a certain extent, the gains obtained from the reduction of transportation costs may be offset by what the Russians call "localism" or the preferential supplying of local enterprises within the sovnarkhozy, especially with respect to consumers' goods.

Improved technology has also been an important factor reducing the materials inputs required. Better technological methods of utilizing fuel, and the substitution of synthetics and light metals for more conventional materials, have also undoubtedly been used to cut costs and to increase premiums. The greater emphasis in recent years on the cheaper petroleum products as a source of fuel—rather than coal and peat—may also have been a factor in the reduction of production costs.

At one time, there was a tendency in the Soviet Union to deprecate the use of time and motion studies, and scientific management as pioneered by Frederick Winslow Taylor. But, along with the growing acceptance of Western technological ideas under Khrushchev, the principles of scientific management are increasingly being applied to plant operations in the Soviet bloc. This is especially true in Eastern Europe where United States college courses in business administration are even cited as models from which much valuable information can be learned.[34]

[33] For information on changes in the average length of haul for various producers' goods, see Iu. Kokdomasov, *"Ratsionalizdatsiia mezhraionnykh ekonomicheskikh sviazei v semiletnem plane"* (Rationalization of the Inter-Regional Economic Relationships in Plan VII), *Voprosy Ekonomiki,* No. 1, 1959, p. 28. Cement was the single product for which there was an increase in the average length of haul.

[34] See "Hungary Admires U.S. Management," *New York Times,* April 29, 1962, p. 10.

ADMINISTRATION OF CORPORATE
OPERATIONS IN CAPITALIST-
ORIENTED ECONOMIES

The typical economic unit in our industrial establishment is the large corporation controlling the activities of a number of separate plants or factories. Our business firm is an organization designed to make a profit, and profits constitute its principal "success indicator." Administrative control of the corporation rests largely in the hands of a board of directors plus the chief executive officers. Although outside interests may be represented on the board of directors, they are largely for "window dressing," the real power being exercised by professional managers whose interests and careers are completely associated with the corporation. Management of a large corporation in the United States is evidently an all-consuming task. Because of the complex nature of management problems at the level of the large corporation, there has apparently been a tendency for managerial subordinates to isolate top management from the outside world in the interests of greater executive efficiency.[35]

The top professional manager undoubtedly spends a good deal of time inspecting his various plants and operations, which may be widely dispersed geographically and therefore entail the use of a private plane. To the extent that the large corporation has diversified its operations, the activities supervised by top management may also cover a number of widely different fields of endeavor. Occasionally, very top management, such as Roger Blough of United States Steel, may pay a visit to the White House in an effort to improve the business environment. At regular intervals, top management is confronted with top labor in renegotiating a long-term labor contract. If there are insuf-

---

[35] For a good description of the isolated lives led by our top industrial management, see Clarence B. Randall, "Business, Too, Has Its Ivory Towers," *New York Times Magazine,* July 8, 1962, p. 5.

ficient internal reserves for capital expansion, management may have to contact the heads of the banking community, although this dependence on our monetary institutions is rapidly becoming less important as time goes by. In the postwar years, about two-thirds of all investment in the United States appears to have been financed via internal sources, and it seems safe to say that the percentage of internally financed investment is considerably higher in the large corporation.[36] Because of this internal financing, there is undoubtedly a high correlation between the creation of profit and the areas where our investment is taking place, in sharp contrast to the noncapitalist-oriented system.

Management is theoretically responsible to a body of stockholders and there is of course the ritual of the annual stockholders' meeting—complete with crackpots, little old ladies, and box lunches for all. But, for all practical purposes, the seven million small stockholders in the United States have little or no impact on policy making in the administration of corporate operations. In the words of a standard text on managerial economics, "dividends are paid largely to keep stockholders passive and management enthroned."[37]

In contrast to the almost universal engineering background of Soviet managers, a study of the biographies of the presidents of 200 large United States manufacturing corporations has shown that a very large number—between 20 and 25 per cent of the total—had a sales background. Almost as many had legal backgrounds, while about 10 per cent had financial backgrounds, other than banking. Only one-third of our top management had engineering backgrounds of various types.[38] According to one former steel executive, there has frequently been a denial of

[36] See Joint Economic Committee, *Variability of Private Investment in Plant and Equipment*, Part I, Investment and Its Financing, U.S. Government Printing Office, Washington, 1962, p. 32.

[37] Joel Dean, *Managerial Economics,* Prentice-Hall, Englewood Cliffs, N.J., 1957, p. 6.

[38] Leland Hazard, "Wage Theory: A Management View," in George W. Taylor, editor, *New Concepts in Wage Determination,* McGraw-Hill, New York, 1957, p. 35.

promotion on the basis of merit to members of minority groups.[39] Thus, while the technical backgrounds of our executives are more heterogeneous than those of Russian managers, our organizational men's social backgrounds would seem to be more uniform.

HIRED MANAGERS AND THEIR PROBLEMS IN CAPITALIST-ORIENTED ECONOMIES

Paradoxically, despite the generally greater openness of our society in relation to that of the Soviets, the actions of our hired managers would seem to be more circumscribed than those of their Russian counterparts. It would not be surprising if our managers felt that there are many more antithetical forces limiting their pursuit of profit than is the case in the Soviet Union. In general, we might classify these principal limiting forces under the headings of labor, government, and effective demand.

While the United States corporation manager has largely freed himself from any great dependence on the banking community in the period since 1929, he is now confronted with more powerful labor unions with considerable bargaining power. The interests of management and labor frequently come into conflict in a capitalist-oriented system. When the economy is expanding rapidly, both labor and management may be able to obtain larger absolute shares of the total pie, with the result that this conflict of interest does not appear to be as sharp. But in periods of sluggish business activity—as is the case in the United States in the sixties—increases in the absolute returns of one factor must frequently be at the expense of the other factor. Management's attempts to introduce new labor-saving technology under such circumstances may be frustrated by

[39] Clarence B. Randall, "For a New Code of Business Ethics," *New York Times Magazine,* April 8, 1962, p. 24.

featherbedding activities on the part of the unions. At times, our management may have considerable difficulty in firing certain technologically displaced individuals without long and drawn out negotiations and arbitration. To a United States hired manager, the activities of Soviet trade unions, designed as they are to stimulate their members' interest in increasing labor productivity, can only be envied.

There would seem to be pretty universal agreement among our managerial class that the scope of government activity should be limited as much as possible, unless of course an industry appears to be having economic difficulties. If the rate of return seems to be falling below what is considered "normal" by businessmen, it may occur to top management—sometimes working through their industry association—that lobbying in the state and federal legislatures might result in preferential tax rates, greater depletion allowances, or quotas limiting foreign imports. Such government regulating activities as exist in our antitrust enforcement agencies, the Food and Drug Administration, and the various congressional investigation committees undoubtedly limit to some extent the actions of the hired managers in their unfettered pursuit of profits. On the other hand, in addition to these activities designed to preserve competition and protect consumers, there are some governmental activities—largely spawned during the Great Depression—which have tended to restrain unbridled competition. In this connection, we might mention the Miller-Tydings Amendment to the Sherman Act permitting the states to pass their own "fair trade" legislation, or the Robinson-Patman Act designed to protect small business. In addition, our patent laws tend to restrict the free flow of technical information.

Probably the most important factor plaguing hired managers in the United States today is the growing lack of effective demand. Because of the limitations of the buyer's market, the corporation is forced to maintain an elaborate market research department which estimates the expected limitations of the market to absorb commodities during the coming period. It is for this reason that no plant manager would seriously consider producing in excess of the output which his market research department feels the market can absorb. In some cases, it has been possible to develop additional foreign markets, or to set up subsidiaries in Western Europe to take advantage of cheaper labor and the as yet unsatisfied demand in the growing Common Market. Because of this intense domestic competition, there is a tendency for price shading and cross-hauling to develop. Thus, in contrast to the situation in Soviet industry, the effective transfer prices for many products may be considerably lower than those published in the official price lists because of secret discounts or rebates.

The limitations of the market undoubtedly also make it seem advantageous for producers to attempt to create positions of monopoly power within the industry—whether these positions are based on patents, superior technology, or mere size. But the pressures of the buyer's market, a built-in source of countervailing power, would also seem to make these monopolistic positions comparatively unstable. At any rate, our economic history shows that there has been a constant erosion of monopolistic positions and increasing price and nonprice competition, unless, of course, government steps in to halt the process.[40]

Because of the lack of effective demand, and fluctuations in the rate of increase in consumption, production is more irregular in capitalist-oriented economies than it is in the USSR. At times,

[40] An example of state action to curb price competition is found in the control of milk prices by certain states. In 1962, two North Jersey milk distributors filed a motion in the New Jersey State Supreme Court asking that past and present orders of the State Office of the Milk Industry be declared unconstitutional. The concerns contended that they could make adequate profits by selling milk below the minimums set by the state. Pursuant to this court action, the Governor suspended all state controls over milk prices, which had been in effect for almost 30 years. However, a little more than a month later, the governor "in a surprise reversal of policy," offered bills to the state legislature which would permit a temporary resumption of price controls. Apparently these restrictions on price competition had become entrenched during the 30 year period. See "Two Milk Distributors Renew Jersey Suit for Lower Prices," *New York Times,* September 29, 1962, p. 25; and "Jersey to Suspend Milk Price Control," *New York Times,* October 19, 1962, p. 1; and "Hughes Returns to Milk Control," *New York Times,* December 1, 1962, p. 27.

waves of inventory investment and disinvestment may tend to accentuate these fluctuations in production. Output may also be accelerated when a strike is anticipated as has been the case with the steel industry in the springs of 1959 and 1962. When the uncertainty is resolved, there may be a sharp drop in the scheduled output—either to nil as was the case in 1959 or to 50 per cent of capacity as was the case in 1962. As mentioned earlier, in Soviet plants production cycles are generally on a monthly basis; in capitalist-oriented economies today, the irregularity of business activity is less predictable. However, businessmen have become so accustomed to having fluctuations in economic activity that they may actually plan for a recession every two or three years. In such cases, it is primarily the actions of government in attempting to avoid the recessions that become unpredictable.

In times past, a considerable amount of corporation activity was directed towards the stealing of the tightly-guarded research secrets of competitors. Here again, the openness with which the Russian managers share their technical information must seem strange to our managerial class.[41] In some cases, new technology may be deliberately withheld for a period of time in our economy in an attempt to protect existing capital values.

In its pursuit of profit, a great deal of the activity of the modern United States corporation is designed to avoid or at least postpone the payment of taxes to the state and federal governments. With a marginal tax rate of roughly 50 per cent, there is a great temptation to encourage or wink at employees' padded expense accounts, to create luxurious front offices and retreats for top management, to develop an impressive array of so-called "fringe benefits," and to press for faster write-offs of new capital equipment. There are also the stock option plans—since the

---

[41] This sharing of technical information should not be interpreted as an indication that there is no wasted effort in the area of invention in the Soviet Union. There is some indication that Soviet inventors and research organizations have been reluctant to make proper searches of the patent records before undertaking research activity. See Harry Schwartz, "Soviet Research Chided on Waste," *New York Times,* August 27, 1961, p. 6.

1950 Internal Revenue Act—which enable our corporation officials to avoid stiff tax rates while taking a free and tax-sheltered ride on the stock market.[42]

Although the rules of the game call for the maximization of profits, a great deal of corporate activity is directed towards the creation of a public image that at times would seem as though corporations were actually minimizing profits. In part, these activities which do not seem to represent profit maximization are designed to ward off any possible antitrust activities of the federal government. In some cases, the corporation may have a longer time horizon with respect to the maximization of profits than is the case with the individual small businessman. Thus, after World War II, our automobile manufacturers deliberately established suggested retail prices for new cars which were below the equilibrium level and thereby eschewed the exhorbitant profits which they might have received had they taken advantage of the seller's market of that time.

Among the firms which are heavily dependent on our defense establishment, there is a particular reticence to divulge information on profits by any meaningful measure. By employing extensive subcontracting, it is possible for the large firm engaged in defense production to show profits which are as low as two per cent of sales. By any meaningful measure of profits, such as profits as a percentage of value added, the rate of return (and incidentally also the wage payments to labor working in these areas) is undoubtedly higher here than it is in the non-defense sector.[43] In a recent investigation of profit pyramiding conducted by Senator McClellan, Western Electric representatives conceded that the rate of profit was higher in their defense activities than it was in their nondefense business, but pleaded that there was a greater risk involved in the former.[44]

[42] By 1957, 77 per cent of the largest manufacturing corporations in the United States had set up option plans. See Gabriel Kolko, *Wealth and Power in America,* Praeger, New York, 1962, p. 21.

[43] See James McCartney, "The Missile Markup," *The Nation,* May 5, 1962, pp. 392–395.

[44] See Hearings Before the Permanent Subcommittee on Investigations of the Committee on Government Operations, "Pyramiding of Profits and

EFFECT OF WORLD WAR II ON UNITED STATES MANAGEMENT PROBLEMS

During World War II, many of the prewar and contemporary problems of United States hired managers disappeared and were superseded by difficulties of a type similar to those presently bothering Russian directors. Our labor unions, operating in an over-full employment situation, were most happy to give up featherbedding and other restrictive practices, and worked long hours in excess of the normal work week—at time and a half, to be sure. Labor mobility became a serious problem and resulted in the freezing of certain skills in their places of employment. Discrimination against nonwhites and women was greatly reduced in the hiring, firing, and promotion practices of our businessmen.[45] Our federal government's antitrust activities were put in mothballs to insure the cooperation of big business in the war effort. Not only was there ample effective demand, but the price system was largely set aside to be replaced by formal rationing of many scarce commodities—in much the same manner as takes place with producers' goods in the Soviet Union. Advertising and the hard sell were greatly reduced for the duration, and salesmen were replaced by the "five-percenters"—our version of the Russian tolkach. Suppliers of our military establishment were reluctant to produce spare parts as called for in their contracts with the result that cannibalization of complete equipment was widely practiced in the field. As in the Soviet Union, the overall quality of our nonmilitary merchandise was low. Interest in foreign markets and protectionist sentiment against imports waned and the nation's gold supplies were usefully employed to obtain critical raw material imports from

---

Costs in the Missile Procurement Program," Part 2, U.S. Government Printing Office, Washington, 1962, pp. 440–441.

[45] Even today, the defense sector—one of the few seller's markets in our economy—appears to practice less discrimination than our economy generally.

abroad. Thus, while certain Soviet-type management problems were created by the war, other contemporary United States-type problems were greatly reduced or eliminated under conditions of overfull employment.

Recommended Readings

*BERLINER, J. S., "The Informal Organization of the Soviet Firm," *The Quarterly Journal of Economics,* August, 1952, pp. 342–365.

*———, "Managerial Incentives and Decisionmaking: A Comparison of the United States and the Soviet Union," in *Comparisons of the United States and Soviet Economies,* Part I, pp. 349–376.

DEAN, JOEL, *Managerial Economics,* Prentice-Hall, Englewood Cliffs, N.J., 1957.

GRANICK, D., "Initiative and Independence of the Soviet Plant Management," *American Slavic and East European Review,* October, 1951, pp. 191–201.

———, "Soviet-American Management Comparison," in *Comparisons of the United States and Soviet Economies,* Part I, pp. 143–150.

———, *The Red Executive,* Doubleday, Garden City, New York, 1960.

———, *The European Executive,* Doubleday, Garden City, New York, 1962.

*HOEFFDING, OLEG, "The Soviet Industrial Reorganization of 1957," *The American Economic Review,* Proceedings, Vol. XLIX, No. 2, May, 1959, pp. 65–77.

Joint Economic Committee, *Variability of Private Investment in Plant and Equipment,* Part I, Investment and Its Financing, U.S. Government Printing Office, Washington, 1962.

KAPLAN, NORMAN, "Research Administration and the Administrator: USSR and U.S.," *Administrative Science Quarterly,* June, 1961, Vol. 6, No. 1, pp. 51–72.

*LEVINE, HERBERT S., "The Centralized Planning of Supply in Soviet Industry," in *Comparisons of the United States and Soviet Economies,* Part I, pp. 151–176.

MILLER, J., "The Decentralization of Industry," *Soviet Studies,* July, 1957, pp. 65–83.

NOVE, ALEC, "The Soviet Industrial Reorganization," *Problems of Communism,* Vol. VI, Nov.–Dec., 1957, pp. 19–25.

*———, "The Problem of 'Success Indicators' in Soviet Industry," *Economica,* N.S. Vol. XXV, No. 97, February, 1958, pp. 1–13.

TAYLOR, GEORGE W., editor, *New Concepts in Wage Determination,* McGraw-Hill, New York, 1957.

X ∾ *Public Finance and Taxation*

HISTORICALLY THERE HAS BEEN A TENDENCY for capitalist-oriented governments to make increasing use of their taxing and spending powers, and, in so doing, to provide a greater range of consumers' communal services, to generate faster rates of growth, and to contribute to the stabilization of economic activity. In addition to the growth in the relative importance of government activity, there have also been changes in the types of activities involved. In the early years of economic development, public financing of the construction of social capital—canals, highways, school buildings, etc.—was a characteristic form of government economic activity, while today defense establishments are frequently responsible for a large share of government expenditures.[1] In the past, there has usually been some transfer of resources away from personal consumption in favor of social consumption or investment in social capital as a result of public finance. In recent years, however, the expanded activities of our government have not generally required any substantial transfer of resources away from personal consumption, but have rather been obtained from resources that in all likelihood would have remained to a great extent unemployed.

[1] For example, up to the Civil War, only about one-fourth of our canals were privately financed. See Carter Goodrich, editor, *Canals and American Economic Development,* Columbia University Press, New York, 1961, p. 6. In the United States, 59 per cent of the 1962 Federal Budget expenditures went for "major national security," while 70 per cent of all Federal employees were associated with our defense establishment.

In our relations with the outside world, government taxation of foreign imports was employed in our early economic development to encourage the growth of what were then "infant industries." Today the trend in government activity is away from tax protection for domestic industry and in the direction of greater use of taxes and subsidies to encourage investment of capital and employment-creating exports abroad. In other words, there has been some shift in the role of government from its function as a creator of domestic social capital and protector of domestic private investment to one of stimulating our foreign capital development and creating employment opportunities at home.

In the noncapitalist-oriented economies, the government budget is of considerably greater relative importance than it is under our type of system for two principal reasons: (1) a considerably higher percentage of total consumption is distributed communally through the government budget, as already noted in Chapter VI; and (2) a higher percentage of national income is devoted to investment and, of this total investment, a much greater share comes out of the government budget, rather than through internal financing or private financing by an independent banking system. In capitalist-oriented economies—with some notable exceptions—private enterprise is allowed to undertake a great deal of the health services and even some education is financed out of nongovernmental sources. Most investment is privately financed in the United States, although in Western Europe, especially in France, a somewhat greater share of total investment activity is undertaken by government. Traditionally, transportation and public utilities have more frequently been government operations in Western Europe in comparison with the United States, and even automobile manufacturing has been included in the government sector in some capitalist-oriented economies at different times. On the other hand, we ordinarily allow private enterprise to run our transportation and public utilities, albeit with some public control by regulating agencies and occasional subsidies, if necessary.

The scope of the Soviet budget is such that between 40 and 50 percent of GNP—depending on whether our or their concept of the pie is employed—is accounted for by their budgetary expenditures. If we include expenditures at all levels of government in the United States—which is necessary in order to obtain comparability, since the Soviet budget covers all-Union, republican, and local expenditures down to the lowly city or rural soviet—we find that federal, state, and local government purchases have been accounting for approximately 20 per cent of our GNP.[2] In other words, our combined budget is just about half as important, economically speaking, compared with the Soviet budget. This 20 per cent in recent years represents just about twice the percentage accounted for by these government expenditures before our Great Depression; but, even so, government expenditures in the United States are still relatively less important than they are in such well-developed European countries as West Germany, Austria, Finland, Norway, France, Sweden, Luxemburg, Great Britain, Netherlands, and Italy.

In addition to the varying importance of government budgets generally, somewhat different budget accounting practices are employed, even among the capitalist-oriented countries. In the United States, the administrative budget stems directly from the basic Budget and Accounting Act of 1921—an act which created a formal integrated budget for the entire Federal Government, thus ending the loose practices of government agencies and departments, which before this time sent separate appropriations to Congress. In contrast to European budgets, both current and capital outlays are lumped together on the expenditure side of the administrative budget, and our balanced budget addicts would require that incoming tax revenues cover both types of expenditures. In West European countries and the United Kingdom, on the other hand, it is customary to divide the budget into two parts: an operating budget, which frequently shows a surplus of receipts over expenditures; and a capital

[2] See Joint Economic Committee Print, "The Federal Revenue System: Facts and Problems 1961," U.S. Government Printing Office, Washington, 1961, p. 185. Most of the United States budget data cited below were obtained from this source.

budget (sometimes referred to as "below-the-line" payments) under which assets are created on borrowed money. Taken together, all government expenditures in Western Europe have generally exceeded the incoming revenue in recent years.[3] In Eastern Europe, including the USSR, the current and capital outlays are lumped together, and government revenues—sometimes with the assistance of compulsory bond sales—ordinarily exceed both types of expenditures, in much the same manner as Senator Byrd would have us do in the United States.

BUDGETARY EXPENDITURES IN NONCAPITALIST-ORIENTED ECONOMIES

In the USSR the annual government budget is usually presented to their Supreme Soviet in December, and is designed to cover the following calendar year.[4] The representatives attending the Supreme Soviet are allowed to give vent to their reactions to the government's document vocally—usually in the form of brief speeches complaining that the particular region they represent has been short-changed in the allocations of new investment, or that the resources earmarked for carrying out projects in their area are inadequate. There may be minor changes in the final document, but in general, it takes only about three or four days to confirm the wishes of the planners with the unanimous approval of the delegates. At the same time, a preliminary report is made by the head of the Union Council of the National Economy on the fulfillment of the past Annual Plan, which is

[3] If France kept its accounts along the lines of the United States administrative budget, it would show a deficit in each of the past 10 years. Great Britain would show a deficit in nine out of 11 years and West Germany would show one in each of the past four years. See *Business Week*, June 2, 1962, p. 72.

[4] Before the Khrushchev era, the budget meetings of the Supreme Soviet were held irregularly—sometimes as late as March of the fiscal year the budget was supposed to cover.

then followed by a presentation of the final goals for the coming year. It seems obvious that there is a very close connection between these two documents to the extent that the investment outlined in the budget is required for the fulfillment of the higher output targets for the new year.

The Soviet budget is designed to cover expenditures by all levels of government—All-Union, Union Republics, and local administrative units. In recent years, there has been a tendency for more of the actual expenditures to be made at the level of the Union Republic rather than at the All-Union or federal level. In 1940, three-fourths of all expenditures were dispensed by federal agencies, while in 1960 only a little over 40 per cent were expended by Soviet central administrative units. This growing importance of republican and local budgets reflects the transfer of control over and responsibility for many industries from a federal to a republican level soon after 1956.[5]

Relatively large government budgets have seemingly been traditional in Russia. Even before the October Revolution, state and local budgetary expenditures accounted for 20.6 per cent of national income in Russia, which was very high for that period, particularly in view of the fact that Russia was a backward and predominantly agricultural country.[6] The explanation for the relatively great importance of the budget in prerevolutionary times lies largely in the fact that railroads, postal and telegraph services, and the vodka monopoly were already included in the government sector.

According to Soviet calculations, total budgetary income amounted to over 50 per cent of their national income in 1960, as computed according to their concept of national income, which excludes many services. As a percentage of GNP—according to our own concept, that is, including depreciation and all services—their total budgetary income amounts to a little over

[5] A similar development has taken place in Czechoslovakia where about one-half of the national budget is now administered locally. See Paul Underwood, "Czechs Regroup Provincial Units," *New York Times,* July 8, 1960, p. 3.

[6] See R. W. Davies, *The Development of the Soviet Budgetary System,* Cambridge University Press, Cambridge, 1958, pp. 5–6.

40 per cent of the total pie. The remainder of almost 60 per cent consists largely of private consumption, depreciation, and some internally financed investment. In 1962 when budgetary expenditures were running around 80 billion rubles, we can therefore estimate that Soviet GNP must have amounted to about 200 billion rubles. At the official rate of exchange, this would be equivalent to a little over $220 billion, or about 40 per cent of our level of GNP.[7]

A breakdown of Soviet government budgetary expenditures at four different periods is given in Table X-A. The years selected were intended to represent a prewar government budget (1940); a typical budget of the Stalin era (1950); a Malenkov-Khrushchev budget (1955); and finally the planned expenditures in a recent year (1962).

1. *National economy.* The largest major subdivision of Soviet budgetary expenditures consists of those outlays designed to develop the "national economy." In the main, these expenditures represent the principal investment activities of the Soviet economy in the corresponding year. Among the activities included here are the expansion of both fixed and working capital, certain labor training, and some research and development. There seems to have been a tendency for this item to increase in relative importance over time. Such expenditures accounted for about one-third of the budget in the prewar period, and until 1962 they had been constituting over 45 per cent of the total budget. The decline in 1962 in the relative importance of these expenditures largely reflects the increased share going to the Soviet defense establishment. About half of all these expenditures for the national economy are assigned to industry and construction, of which the lion's share goes to heavy industry. In addition to the budgetary allocations for new investment, a considerable volume of investment is financed out of enterprise profits ear-

[7] At the official rate of exchange, consumers' goods tend to be overvalued while producers' goods appear to be undervalued, with the result that on average the new rate would seem to be a fairly realistic rate of exchange for the first time since the industrialization drive began. In this connection, see Morris Bornstein, "The Reform and Revaluation of the Ruble," *American Economic Review,* March, 1961.

marked for specific investment projects. Thus, in the 1962 budget over 40 per cent of all investment was expected to be financed from the internal resources of the enterprise at the specific direction of the central planners.[8]

The next most important claimant to investment funds is agriculture which ordinarily accounts for about 15 to 20 per cent of the total expenditures for developing the national economy. The tendency for this percentage to fall in recent years does not reflect any relative decline in overall investment in agriculture, but rather the fact that more of agricultural investment—instead of being assigned to the Machine Tractor Stations out of the government budget—is now internally financed independently of the budget by the collective farms out of their greater income resulting from higher procurement prices. Before the war and as recently as 1955, transportation and communications constituted the third most important category with respect to investment, but for the present, investment in housing and municipal services has taken over third place. In 1962, over four times as much government budgetary investment was planned for housing and municipal services as compared with 1955.

2. *Social and cultural services.* Social and cultural services are second in importance to the national economy as a major subdivision of the government's budgetary expenditures. Whereas the bulk of the expenditures for the development of the national economy could be classified as investment activities, the expenditures here represent basically collective or communal consumption.[9] There has also been a tendency for this major subdivision to grow relatively more important over time. In the prewar years,

[8] This internal financing is strictly controlled by the central planners. In fact, there seems to be some increase in the control by the sovnarkhozy over internally-financed investments. In 1962, 600 million rubles of formerly decentralized investment was expected to go through the government budget. See V. F. Garbuzov's budget speech, *Izvestiia*, December 7, 1961, p. 4.

[9] Obviously educational expenditures, unless they are a substitute for baby sitting or take place in a veritable country club atmosphere, might in a sense be properly classified as investment activities as well as communal consumption.

T A B L E X - A

Government Budgetary Expenditures in the USSR, Selected Years

	Year							
	1940		1950		1955		1962 (Plan)	
Type of Expenditure	(Billion rubles)	As % of Total	(Billion rubles)	As % of Total	(Trillion rubles)	As % of Total	(Billion rubles)	As % of Total
(1)	(2)	(3)	(4)	(5)	(6)	(7)	(8)	(9)
1. National Economy	5.8	33.4	15.8	38.1	23.3	43.2	32.5	40.4
Including:								
a. Industry and construction	2.9	16.4	7.9	19.2	11.0	20.4	14.8	18.4
b. Agriculture	1.3	7.0	3.4	8.2	5.1	9.4	5.1	6.3
c. Transportation and communication	.7	3.9	1.6	3.8	1.9	3.5	2.5	3.1
d. Housing and municipal services	.3	1.5	n.a.	n.a.	.9	1.7	3.8	4.7
e. Internal trade	n.a.	n.a.	n.a.	n.a.	.1	.2	1.7	2.1
2. Social and Cultural Services	4.1	23.5	11.7	28.3	14.7	27.3	28.7	35.7
Including:								
a. Education	2.3	12.9	5.7	13.8	6.9	12.8	12.4	15.4
b. Health and physical education	.9	5.2	2.2	5.3	3.1	5.7	5.0	6.2
c. Maternity grants	.1	.7	.4	.9	.5	.9	.5	.6
d. State social security	.3	1.8	1.3 }	8.4	1.7	3.1 }	11.3	14.1
e. Social insurance	.5	2.9	2.2 }		2.6	4.8 }		
3. National Defense	5.7	32.6	8.3	5.4	10.8	19.9	13.4	16.7

4. Administration	.7	3.9	1.4	3.3	1.2	2.3	1.1	1.4
5. Interest payments	.3	1.8	.5	1.2	1.4	2.6	.7*	1.0
6. Other (residual)	.8	4.8	3.6	9.1	2.6	4.8	4.0	5.0
Total expenditures:	17.4	100.0	41.3	100.0	54.0	100.0	80.4	100.0

Notes to Table X-A:

* Refers to 1960.

n.a. = not available.

Data were obtained from the following sources:

Narodnoe Khoziaistvo 1958, pp. 900 *et seq.*

Narodnoe Khoziaistvo 1960, pp. 844 *et seq.*

A. G. Zverev, *Natsional'nyi dokhod i finansy SSSR*, Gosfinizdat, Moscow, 1961

Budget speech of V. F. Garbuzov, *Izvestiia*, December 7, 1961, p. 4.

V. Lavrov, "Gosudarstvennyi biudzhet—vazhnoe orudie planovogo rukovodstva" (The Government Budget is an Important Lever for the Planned Leadership), *Planovoe Khoziaistvo*, No. 2, 1962, p. 46.

social and cultural services accounted for less than one-fourth of total budgetary outlays, while today they constitute around one-third of the total. The principal factor behind this relative growth of social and cultural services has been the increase in social security and social insurance expenditures. Expenditures for "science," which is thought to include nuclear research, are apparently included under education expenditures and have no doubt grown at a relatively rapid rate lately. At the present time, expenditures for education and various types of social security and social insurance each account for roughly 40 per cent of total expenditures in this major subdivision. Not all education outlays come out of the budget since about 25 per cent of the total expenditures for education come out of trade union funds, including the social insurance budget. The remaining 20 per cent of social and cultural service outlays is accounted for primarily by health and physical culture expenditures. Maternity payments to unwed mothers and to mothers of exceptionally large families constitute a relatively insignificant, though stable, share of the total expenditures under social and cultural services.

3. *National defense.* One of the most controversial items in the Soviet budget is the official budgetary allocation for national defense—the third most important subdivision of governmental expenditures and, in a sense, also a form of communal consumption. Although the figures in Table X-A indicate that these appropriations account for a declining percentage of total outlays, it should be noted that the percentage for 1962 (16.7%) represents a significant rise from 1961, when only 11.9 per cent of total expenditures was originally allocated to their national defense establishment. In July of that year, however, Premier Khrushchev announced that he was being forced to match the Kennedy Administration's sharp increase in defense expenditures by adding an emergency allocation of 3.1 billion rubles to the planned Soviet defense allocation.[10]

[10] In view of the magnitude of the increase in the defense allocation—roughly 44 per cent—it seems likely that this increase must have been calculated on an annual basis, and that the increase of 3.1 billion rubles

The Russians have been fond of pointing out that their defense expenditures constitute only a small and declining percentage of their total budgetary allocations in contrast to the level and development of the national defense sector in our budget. Our response has been that the budgets of the two countries are two entirely different "animals," so that any comparison of percentages between the two countries is virtually meaningless. Comparisons of budgets of the different noncapitalist-oriented economies would seem to be more meaningful, however.[11] Likewise, comparisons of defense budgets for capitalist-oriented economies would seem to be fairly rewarding, provided similar national accounting and budgeting practices are employed.

With respect to the declining share of defense allocations in

---

in 1961 was in all likelihood underfulfilled. Even in ordinary years, the Soviet defense establishment has somewhat the same problem as our own Department of Defense, namely one of contracting and spending all of the money appropriated by overly generous politicians. In recent years, only about 97 per cent of the total defense budgetary allocations have ordinarily been spent by the Soviet military. See *Narodnoe Khoziaistvo 1959*, p. 801. For the USSR as a whole, except the Arctic territories, the budget accounts are closed on December 31st, the unused appropriations being cancelled. In the United States, for certain types of contracts, our laws also require that the money appropriated by Congress be contracted for by the end of the fiscal year, June 30th, or else the appropriation is cancelled. The result of this legal requirement is that there is normally a flurry of defense contracts towards the end of the fiscal year, and the total awards in June are normally double those for other months. See Jack Raymond, "Pentagon Awards Half Billion in Two Days for Defense Work," *New York Times*, June 29, 1962, p. 33. As a result of the sharp increase in the defense appropriation, Khrushchev was forced to shelve his highly publicized troop reduction plans which originally called for a cutback in Soviet armed forces from 3.6 to 2.4 million men by the end of 1961.

[11] In 1959, for example, the Chinese planned to spend 11.2 per cent of all outlays for defense, compared with 12.5 per cent in 1958. See *New York Times*, April 22, 1959, p. 7. In 1962 the following percentages have been allocated to defense out of the total budgetary expenditures of the respective countries: Bulgaria—6.1%; Czechoslovakia—8.8%; Poland—8.0%; and Rumania—5.1%. See *East Europe*, February, 1962, pp. 41, 51, and 53; and April, 1962, p. 40. In 1960, Hungary allocated only 4.6 per cent of her total expenditures to defense, while in Albania the percentage was 7.9. See A. G. Zverev, *Biudzhety respublik i raspredelenie natsional'nogo dokhoda* (Budget of the Republics and the Distribution

their total expenditures (until 1962), we have attempted to explain away this phenomenon by claiming that the Russians are progressively concealing more of their defense expenditures, particularly research and development, in other-than-defense allocations.[12] But, if we accept a principle of "growthmanship" discussed in Chapter IV (see p. 62), it would seem that there may be a danger involved in carrying this argument too far. The over-all rapid rate of economic growth in the Soviet economy is *a priori* one reason why we should expect that the resources currently being devoted to military "hardware"—constituting as they do a drag on growth at this stage of Soviet development—might not be as great as supposed. The Russians could conceivably be devoting most of their investment resources to what we might call "near-defense"—investments in heavy industry which would produce a rapid rate of current economic growth, but, at the same time, which would provide a solid basis for some possible short-run future remilitarization.

If we were naive enough to accept Soviet budgetary figures at their face value, this would mean that only about seven per cent of Soviet GNP is currently being devoted to defense. Actually it is known that the investment in defense plant and equipment is included under the subdivision, national economy, and officers' military pensions are included under social and cultural services. Undoubtedly a good deal of the research and development for their defense establishment is also excluded from the defense budget *per se,* and included under the allocations for national economy and education. In the United States, we allocate about 10 per cent of our GNP to our defense establishment. While we also do not pay for investment in defense plant and equip-

---

of the National Income), Gosfinizdat, Moscow, 1961, p. 186. Apparently the Soviet Union is not relying on the Eastern European countries for very substantial additional military assistance, since these percentages are more or less in line with those prevailing in earlier years.

[12] A tantalizing question arises if we accept the explanation that the Russians have been progressively concealing defense expenditures in other categories. If this has been the case, why did the Soviet government not just continue this devious practice in 1962, but instead almost boastfully proclaim to the world that "anything you can do, we can do better."

ment directly out of our defense appropriation, research and development for defense is included in our defense figure.[13]

There are a number of reasons why comparisons of percentages of GNP devoted to defense are not too meaningful. For one thing, the Russians undoubtedly get relatively more value per defense ruble than we obtain per defense dollar. Generally speaking, the United States defense establishment—due to such institutions as cost-plus-fixed-fee contracting and higher wage and profit rates in the defense sector—probably does not get as much value per dollar expenditure in comparison with the non-defense sectors of our economy. There are undoubtedly many reasons for this, but perhaps the most obvious one is the fact that we do not generally rely on competitive bidding in this sector.[14] As a result, the margin between prices and costs is probably above average in this one sector of our economy where a seller's market prevails. The Russians, on the other hand, are believed to give a very high priority to their defense establishment. This higher priority is probably reflected in better manpower and resources generally being allocated to their defense sector. At least, there is no reason why the Russian defense establishment should be getting less than its money's worth, as is apparently the case in the United States.[15]

The general consensus in the United States seems to be that the Russians are spending about as much in absolute terms as we do for defense.[16] This finding seems to have originated in

[13] Of the total United States research and development in fiscal 1962, it is estimated that 48 per cent was financed by the federal government for security purposes. See Jack Raymond, "The 'Military-Industrial Complex': An Analysis," *New York Times,* January 22, 1961, Section IV, p. 4E.

[14] Of the $21 billion allocated for the procurement of military goods in the early sixties, 86.4 per cent is being handed out by military officers to industry without competitive bidding. See *New York Times,* May 21, 1961, p. 48.

[15] Senator Paul H. Douglas has estimated that our military wastes two to three billion dollars annually through "present practices and wasteful methods." For examples of waste and overcharges, see *New York Times,* August 3, 1960, p. 2; June 14, 1961, p. 12; and May 26, 1962, p. 29.

[16] Shortly after this was written, C. L. Sulzberger divulged the information that Arthur Dean, our principal Geneva negotiator, had indicated that our official position was that the Russians were only devoting 17

some work by our Central Intelligence Agency, and to have been divulged by its director, Allen Dulles, in 1959.[17] If the Russians are spending approximately $50 billion annually on defense with a GNP of roughly $220 billion, this means that they would have to be spending between 20 and 25 per cent of their GNP on defense. Professor Bornstein of the University of Michigan has made one of the most serious attempts to measure Soviet defense expenditures relative to those of the United States. His tentative conclusion was that the Russians were spending about 75 per cent of the absolute amount we were spending in 1955 when measured in rubles, or 94.3 per cent of our outlays when measured in dollars—or a geometric average of the two comparisons of 84.3 per cent.[18] However, Professor Bornstein, for reasons which are not entirely clear, backed away from these somewhat surprising conclusions and instead concluded that "because of the especially crude nature of both the initial national accounts estimate for Soviet defense expenditures and the ruble-dollar ratios for this end use, it seems prudent to allow for some understatement of the Soviet level both in rubles and in dollars and to consider Soviet defense outlays as approximately equal to those of the United States."

---

per cent of their GNP to defense—or a total expenditure that was only 72 per cent of our own. See C. L. Sulzberger's column, *New York Times,* July 25, 1962, p. 32. An earlier estimate by our State Department put Soviet national security expenditures at 14 per cent of GNP in 1957. See United States Department of State, "United States Versus Soviet Spending for Major GNP Categories," Intelligence Information Brief No. 87 (unclassified), February 24, 1959.

[17] See Dulles' speech before the Edison Electric Institute as reported in the *New York Times,* April 9, 1959, p. 8.

[18] Morris Bornstein, "A Comparison of Soviet and United States National Product," in *Comparisons of the United States and Soviet Economies,* Part II, pp. 385–389. Bornstein's finding would indicate that the Russians are spending 19 per cent of their GNP on defense which is still nearly two times the relative amount we spend. Bornstein's geometric mean is used as a basis for an interesting calculation by John Hardt, *et al., The Cold War Economic Gap,* Praeger, New York, 1961, p. 98. By taking this 1955 relationship as a starting point, the authors assume that the USSR has devoted 15 per cent of the increment in its GNP to defense and reach the somewhat improbable conclusion that five years

There are some additional indirect bits of evidence other than the rapid overall Soviet rate of growth which would lead an objective observer to conclude that the Russians might be cutting corners on defense.[19] It seems to me that the military posture of the Russians may also be somewhat cheaper to maintain than our own military position. Our posture, on the other hand, has developed out of the political vacuum left throughout the world in the wake of World War II, and consists of an extensive and expensive ring of foreign bases around the perimeter of what we might label "Fortress USSR."

There is also the apparent failure of the Russians to develop their missile and bomber capabilities to the extent which we thought possible.[20] Estimates which were made by our military experts in 1956 of Soviet production capabilities by 1961 with respect to ICBM's were apparently fulfilled by only 3.5 per cent, while their bomber strength increased to a level only 19 per cent of the estimated potential. The smallness of the Soviet nuclear delivery system, as reflected in their minimum deterrent strategy, would also be consistent with their position regarding inspection and disarmament, consisting as it does of a minimum of inspection and a maximum of disarmament. As Blackett points out, in the above cited source, "the Soviet fear of inspection may have been the more acute because there was so little to inspect."

4. *Administration.* Seemingly the Russians have managed to reduce their relative budgetary expenditures for administration. Before the war, these outlays constituted about four per cent of the total expenditures, but in recent years they have been

---

of Eisenhower "austerity" had allowed the Soviet military sector to overtake ours in absolute terms.

[19] There have been complaints that living conditions on Soviet military posts have been particularly poor, with inadequate bedding, unsanitary kitchens, and unappetizing and unvaried diet. See Theodore Shabad, "Army Poorly Fed, Russians Charge," *New York Times,* July 16, 1962, p. 10.

[20] See P. M. S. Blackett, "Steps Toward Disarmament," *Scientific American,* April, 1962.

accounting for only about 1.5 per cent of the total. Payments to administrators at all levels of government, including the dispensers of Soviet justice, come out of this appropriation. To some extent, this reduction in administrative expenses may reflect the elimination of government activities such as the Machine Tractor Stations, or the transfer of some governmental functions to a khozraschet basis. But it also seems probable that the chronic shortage of labor—and the resulting pressures to cut administrative staffs—may have paid off in a relative reduction in the governmental bureaucracy in much the same fashion as it has apparently reduced bureaucracy in the administration of factories—as mentioned in Chapter IX.

5. *Miscellaneous expenditures*. There is also a fairly large group of miscellaneous expenses, including payments to the late MVD or the successor internal security or police organization, the Ministry of Public Law and Order. Interest payments in connection with the sale and redemption of compulsory bonds were a comparatively important government expenditure item before the 1958 budget. This budget for the first time reflected the famous moratorium on interest and principal payments on the Soviet national debt.[21] An interest rate of three per cent is still paid on savings accounts in state banks, and these payments are indirectly reflected in the government budget. In addition, interest is paid on interest-bearing bonds which are now purchased voluntarily, primarily by citizens in the upper income brackets. Increases in the credit resources of the long term investment banks have also been included in this group of expenditures. Presumably the increased credits set up by the Soviet Union for the developing countries may be included here, although there is little concrete evidence to support this assumption.

21 The growing importance of debt servicing meant that government income from the compulsory bond sales was barely exceeding outlays of interest. From the government's standpoint, this taking revenue out of one pocket and putting it back into other pockets—and sometimes the same pockets—must have seemed a bit irrational.

BUDGETARY REVENUE IN NONCAPITALIST-ORIENTED ECONOMIES

The annually balanced budget, or preferably one showing a small budgetary surplus, is one of the quaint fetishes of both noncapitalist-oriented political economists and Senator Harry Byrd. According to one Soviet writer, "the most important premise and necessary condition for stability of currency and steadiness of monetary circulation is the stability of national finances brought about by an annual surplus of revenue over expenses in the national budget." [22] Even in the thirties, when inflation was rampant in the Soviet economy, Soviet budget-makers somehow managed to achieve a small surplus of receipts over expenditures year after year, and it was only during three years of World War II, when defense accounted for about 60 per cent of total outlays, that government revenues failed to cover expenditures. As with most monetary and fiscal institutions in the Soviet Union, the annual tiny budgetary surplus appears to play an essentially passive role in the Soviet economy.[23] The power of the Soviet government to regulate prices and their relationship to production costs would seem to insure the fact that profits (including turnover taxes) could always exceed the government expenditures for investment, communal consumption, and administration under normal operating conditions. As a matter of practice, the Soviet government in the past has also relied on direct taxes and tax-like compulsory bond purchases to cut present consumption and provide additional revenue, but these subsidiary sources of revenue seem to be on their way out.

[22] See A. Alekseev, *Voennye finansy kapitalisticheskikh gosudarstv* (War Finances of Capitalist States), Gospolitizdat, Moscow, 1949, p. 11.

[23] The annual tiny budgetary surplus in the noncapitalist-oriented economies would seem to be somewhat analogous to our ever-rising national debt limit. It may serve as something of a restraint on any spendthrifts in government.

A breakdown of the various sources of government revenue at the same four periods selected for study in Table X-A is given in Table X-B. In all periods, indirect taxation—either in the form of the profits deductions or the turnover tax—can be seen to account for between 60 and 70 per cent of total revenue. In this respect, the current Soviet regime has merely extended a practice existing under the Czar. In 1913, for example, 40 per cent of all government revenue was raised by indirect taxation, and if reinvested profits were included in the revenue of that period, the percentage of indirect taxation would probably approach its current relative importance.

1. *Turnover taxes.* The most important source of tax revenue since its introduction in the early thirties has been the turnover tax. Before World War II, the turnover tax was providing almost 60 per cent of all revenue, while in recent years it has still accounted for somewhat in excess of 40 per cent of the total budgetary revenue. According to a Soviet source, 93 per cent of the turnover tax originates in consumers' goods industries and only seven per cent is collected from producers' goods branches.[24] It has been estimated by Professor Holzman, our expert on Soviet taxation, that between 40 and 50 out of every 100 rubles spent on consumers' goods in state stores goes for the turnover tax.[25] The rates vary widely among different consumers' goods, largely depending on what is necessary to build up the retail prices of the individual consumers' goods to a level which will more or less ration the available supply. The turnover tax is largely concentrated in the price of 15 to 20 groups of commodities which account for about 85 per cent of total receipts from this source.

The chief advantage of the turnover tax lies in its flexibility. In contrast to the income tax, which is essentially a blunt instrument, the purchase or turnover tax can be used to adjust specific disequilibria in supply and demand. If consumption of some commodity or commodities lags and stocks accumulate, the rate

[24] M. Z. Bor, *Planovyi balans narodnogo khoziaistva SSSR* (The Soviet National Economic Balance), Gosplanizdat, Moscow, 1959, p. 23.

[25] See Professor Holzman's letter to the *New York Times,* October 6, 1959, p. 38.

of turnover tax on the object or objects can be reduced to stimulate consumers' demand and thereby to eliminate the excess supply at the old price. On the other hand, if the demand for some commodity increases beyond the readily available supply—or the immediate potentialities for increasing the supply—the tax rate and retail price can be raised for the specific commodity. An example of the latter development occurred on January 1, 1958, when the turnover tax rates on automobiles were increased sharply in connection with the rough doubling of car prices. On the other hand, when the prices of meat and butter were increased on June 1, 1962, the increase was apparently the result of higher procurement prices being paid to farmers rather than higher turnover taxes on these commodities.

2. *Profits.* The second most important source of revenue consists of the profits deducted into the budget. As explained in Chapter IX, these profits may be either of the planned or unplanned variety. The planned profits occur as a result of the government's policy with respect to planned price-cost relationships; the unplanned profits arise as the result of various economies effected by the enterprise. Whereas profits accounted for only about 10 per cent of all revenue as late as 1950, they now account for around 25 per cent of total budgetary income. In part this increased share of profits reflects the infrequency with which producers' goods prices have been changed in recent years. Since producers' goods prices were essentially unchanged from July 1, 1955 to 1963 and production costs were falling in between these years, it was inevitable that profits would rise as a percentage of total revenue. By the same token, if past experience is any guide, we should expect profits to fall somewhat as a percentage of total revenue after the wholesale price revision in 1963.

From a theoretical standpoint, the division of what must, to a certain extent, be labeled "surplus value" into two categories— profits and turnover tax—should be considered as arbitrary. The Russians could theoretically use either one of these indirect taxes to the complete exclusion of the other. As a matter of policy, the planners prefer to allow relatively small profit margins and com-

TABLE X - B

Government Budgetary Revenues in the USSR, Selected Years

Type of Revenue (1)	Year							
	1940		1950		1955		1962 (Plan)	
	(Billion rubles) (2)	As % of Total (3)	(Billion rubles) (4)	As % of Total (5)	(Billion rubles) (6)	As % of Total (7)	(Billion rubles) (8)	As % of Total (9)
1. Turnover taxes	10.6	58.7	23.6	55.8	24.2	43.0	32.5	39.7
2. Profits deductions	2.2	12.1	4.0	9.5	10.3	18.2	23.2	28.3
3. Tax on cooperatives, collective farms, and non-commodity operations	.3	1.8	.6	1.3	1.2	2.2	1.3	1.6
4. State loans	1.1	6.4	3.1	7.1	3.7	6.5	1.1	1.3
Including:								
a. Loans from population	.9	5.1	2.7	6.4	3.2	5.6	.1*	.1
b. Loans from savings banks (increase in savings deposits)	.02	.1	.3	.7	.5	.9	1.0	1.2
5. Direct taxes	.9	5.2	3.6	8.5	4.8	8.6	5.8	7.1
6. Income of MTS	.2	1.1	.4	.9	.6	1.0	n.a.	n.a.

7. Social insurance funds	.9	4.8	2.0	4.6	2.6	4.7	4.5	5.5
8. Other (residual)	1.8	9.9	5.0	12.3	9.0	15.8	13.5	16.5
Total revenue	18.0	100.0	42.3	100.0	56.4	100.0	81.9	100.0

Notes to Table X-B:
* Refers to 1960.
n.a. = not available because of demise of MTS.

Data were obtained from the following sources:

Narodnoe Khoziaistvo SSSR v 1958 godu, pp. 900 et seq.
Narodnoe Khoziaistvo SSSR v 1960 godu, pp. 844 et seq.
Budget speech of V. F. Garbuzov, *Izvestiia*, December 7, 1961, p. 4.

paratively high rates of turnover tax on the theory that to have the alternative relative high profit margins would encourage waste and a lack of economic discipline at the level of the enterprise. There is also the ideological consideration that profits and surplus value have also had a negative ideological coloration in the Soviet Union, so that the creation of a new label—the turnover tax—tended to obscure the economic fact that the consumption of current generations is in a sense being sacrificed for the benefit of future generations. Actually, since a great deal of the communal consumption must also come out of the turnover tax-profit mark-up, not all of the margin can properly be considered as "surplus value."

It now becomes evident that the incidence of the turnover tax is also fairly arbitrary. As a matter of practice, the Soviets have collected most of these taxes at the consumers' goods level. But they could just as easily distribute these collections throughout the economy—in producers' goods as well as in consumers' goods —as was suggested by some Soviet economists in the discussion of the impending wholesale price reform mentioned in Chapter VIII (see page 198). In such a case, consumers' goods industries would have to pay higher prices for their fuel and raw materials, but they would also pay lower turnover taxes so that the consumers' goods price level would remain essentially unchanged.

3. *Taxes on collective farms and other cooperatives.* These taxes on collective farms and other cooperative income have been a relatively unimportant, but stable, source of revenue, accounting for about two per cent of the total budgetary income. Recently 80 per cent of the kolkhoz income emanating from animal husbandry has been declared tax-free in an effort to stimulate collective farm activities in these areas. A tax on non-commodity operations—municipal laundries, baths, etc.—was formerly lumped together with these taxes, but it was eliminated in 1958.

4. *State loans.* Before the war, state loans were the third most important source of government revenue, and they were still of almost equal importance to direct taxes during the fifties until 1957. At that time, the compulsory bond sales which each year

took between two and four weeks' salary from most all workers were eliminated in connection with the moratorium on the outstanding government debt and its servicing. At present, there are some voluntary bond sales and, in addition, the net increase in savings accounts is loaned by the banks to the government budget where it is considered to be a component of revenue.

In 1962 a total of between 12 and 13 billion rubles was held by over 50 million Soviet citizens in the form of savings accounts. In 1940 only about 700 million rubles, or less than the annual increases in private savings in the sixties, were held by about 17 million persons in this form. Since the consumers' price level is only about 40 per cent above the 1940 level, it would appear that a considerably greater amount of voluntary saving is taking place today as compared with the prewar period. Undoubtedly a good deal of this saving is of a short-term nature. Since instalment credit has only recently become available and is as yet restricted to a relatively few commodities, this saving represents in many cases merely a safe way to accumulate funds required for large cash expenditures on automobiles or other consumers' durables.

5. *Direct taxes on the population.* These taxes appear to be on the way out along with the above-mentioned tax-like compulsory bond sales. The income tax which has always been only mildly progressive in relation to our rate structure is the principal form of direct taxation. For the ordinary workers and employees, the rates have ranged from 1.5 to 13 per cent of gross income. A few self-employed persons such as doctors or lawyers engaged in private practice pay a much higher tax rate, however. At present, those persons earning below 60 rubles monthly have been relieved of any responsibility for paying income taxes, while those individuals earning between 61 and 70 rubles monthly have had their income tax withholdings cut by 40 per cent. The direct tax on bachelors, single citizens and on small families was finally terminated on October 1, 1961. By 1965, according to Soviet plans first announced at the Twenty-first Party Congress in 1959, these direct taxes were to have been completely eliminated, after which

time most all government revenue would have been raised by indirect means.[26] The collective farmers pay an agricultural tax on their private holdings, though they pay nothing on their income from the collective farms.

6. *Machine tractor station income and social insurance.* After 1958 the income going into the budget from the Machine Tractor Stations has disappeared as a minor source of revenue, since the activities formerly performed by these organizations have been largely assumed by the collective farms. The income payments by the factories for social insurance are also included as a revenue item, although the Trade Unions are responsible for the administration of these funds.

7. *Stumpage fees.* Stumpage fees constitute still another minor source of revenue, particularly since 1949 when the rates were increased after a long period when only very minor fees were levied on the cutting of easily accessible timber. These fees have had a long history as a disincentive with respect to the exploitation of readily available timber, having originated sometime before the revolution. It is interesting to note that they were abandoned in 1930 shortly after the introduction of Plan I.[27] Apparently it was soon recognized by the planners that a conservation policy is more applicable to a society with some degree of affluence than it is for a frugal, developing one. At any rate, the easily accessible, cheap timber undoubtedly represented part of the surplus out of which Soviet economic development occurred.

8. *Other revenue.* There are a number of other minor sources of government budgetary revenue: net income of the state insurance fund, stamp duties, automobile registration fees, passport fees, entertainment tax, customs duties, and repayments of credits and interest on loans granted to developing countries, which are

---

[26] On September 24, 1962, *Izvestiia* announced a "temporary" cessation of their reductions in direct taxes because of "increased international tension." See *New York Times,* September 25, 1962, p. 3.

[27] For a history of Soviet stumpage tax policy, see W. Donald Bowles, "Pricing in Soviet Timber Sales," *Soviet Studies,* July, 1961, pp. 24 *et seq.*

included under "fees and miscellaneous non-tax revenues." Since insurance is a form of nonconsumption, it seems only natural that it should be encouraged in noncapitalist-oriented economies, and that the practice of purchasing insurance should not only continue but grow as more citizens can afford it. More Soviet tourism and private ownership of automobiles should also mean that these minor sources of revenue can be expected to be retained as control devices.

BUDGETARY EXPENDITURES IN CAPITALIST-ORIENTED ECONOMIES

In the United States, the administrative budget covering the fiscal year starting July 1 is sent to Congress each January, accompanied by a budget message on the state of the nation's economic health. During the ensuing few months, there is much discussion and study of the approximately 1,200-page document by the various congressional committees, but the budget allocations as finally passed by Congress six or eight months later bear a surprising resemblance to the original requests submitted by the executive branch.

Of all government expenditures in the United States, about two-thirds take place at the federal level; the state and local governments each take about half of the balance, with the local governments having a slight edge over the states. About one-third of governmental expenditures at all levels is being spent for major national security today. If we add in veterans' services and the interest paid on the national debt, most of which was contracted for during World War II, these military-oriented expenditures account for over 40 per cent of the consolidated expenditures at all levels of government. Government outlays for education, hospitals, health, sanitation, and public welfare are responsible for a little over 20 per cent of all our governmental expenditures. Highways, principally at the state and local level, account for about seven per cent of all expenditures. Other relatively minor governmental expenditures are made for such things as the preservation of our natural resources, postal services, police and fire protection, foreign aid, agricultural and other subsidies, and administration. The latter accounts for a little over two per cent of total expenditures, or somewhat more than the percentage claimed by the Soviets for their administration.

There is a growing awareness in capitalist-oriented governmental circles that there is a direct connection between a nation's budget and its economic health. Along with the growing disenchantment with respect to the effectiveness of monetary policy, there has been a gradual shift to a belief that fiscal policy is a more appropriate answer to our present economic difficulties. If there is a tendency for unemployment and stagnation to represent the principal problems facing the country, the pressures grow for lower taxes and/or greater government spending to get the economy rolling again.[28]

The Kennedy Administration has recently placed great faith in the use of tax-cuts to stimulate our lagging consumption and private investment. The new "consolidated cash" budget for fiscal 1964 proposes a $2.7 billion net reduction in tax revenue along with a $3.8 billion increase in spending, primarily for defense, space, and debt servicing. As a result, a $10.3 billion deficit is envisioned, although the promise is held out that by fiscal 1967, the nation will be able to operate once again in the black.[28a]

These pressures to cut taxes and/or increase government spending as counter-cyclical devices are felt chiefly at the federal level where spending is comparatively unlimited by incoming revenues. In practice, the power of the federal government to raise money by selling bonds to the central banking system—and thereby to add to the nation's national debt—is comparatively unlimited as we found out in World War II. The states and

[28] For a more extreme solution by the world renowned economist, Gunnar Myrdal, advocating both lower taxes and more spending, see Werner Wiskari, "Myrdal Terms U.S. 'Stagnant'; Urges Wide Economic Reform," *New York Times,* July 22, 1962, p. 38.

[28a] See "Budget in New Garb," *Christian Science Monitor,* January 18, 1963, p. 1.

localities, on the other hand, are less fortunate in this respect, and expenditures at this level tend to accentuate economic fluctuations by rising in prosperity as revenue rises, and falling in recessions as incoming revenue falls.

BUDGETARY REVENUE IN CAPITALIST-ORIENTED ECONOMIES

In the United States, individual income taxes at all levels account for about 40 per cent of all tax receipts. In all, 33 states levy income taxes at the present time and the number is growing rapidly. In some states, the income tax is withheld along with the federal income tax to insure collection and to minimize evasion. The official rates of income taxation are more progressive in the United States than they are (or were) in the Soviet Union. Here, they hit upper income groups progressively harder, rising to 91 per cent on additional income earned in excess of $500,000 per year. In actual practice, there are a number of legitimate ways in which individuals can minimize the progressiveness of the impact of these payments, with the result that our income tax is not as egalitarian or confiscatory as either its advocates or its enemies would have us believe.

The second most important source of government revenue is the corporation income tax which accounts for almost 20 per cent of all revenue. Third in order of importance is the property tax which accounts for about 15 per cent of total revenue, and which is levied exclusively at state and local levels, particularly the latter. Sales taxes of various types and other more specific indirect taxes on alcoholic beverages and tobacco products account for about 15 per cent of all revenue. Taxes on motor fuel and public utilities are important at the state and federal levels accounting for about six per cent of total revenues.

Customs duties are relatively unimportant today in contrast to our early economic history, accounting for less than one per cent of total revenues. Average rates on dutiable imports were 52 per cent in 1899, but only 11.9 per cent in 1955. As we have matured economically to the point where we are the most productive country in the world, we have become one of the chief proponents of free trade, in much the same manner—and for much the same reason—that Great Britain was in the vanguard for free trade in the nineteenth century. To the extent that we wish to protect some of our more inefficient industries, we are tending to do so either by means of quotas or informal agreements with foreign exporting nations to limit their sales in this country.[29]

Death and gift taxes account for about two per cent of our consolidated budget revenues at the present time. This represents something of a decline from the prewar years. To the extent that these taxes discourage saving and encourage consumption by elderly people, they would seem to play a useful role at the present time in making our economy function more efficiently. The Russians, on the other hand, do not levy inheritance taxes, although they do charge a legal fee of 10 per cent in the event that private property is transferred at death. From the standpoint of their basic problems, it would seem to make good sense for them to encourage saving via the institution of untaxed inheritance. However, a question has arisen recently concerning the possibility that children might be able to live idly on unearned income rather than contribute services "according to their ability." A recent legacy of 50,000 rubles, if deposited in a savings bank, would have resulted in 1,500 rubles annually, or more than the average industrial worker earns during the same period. At one time after the October Revolution there was a maximum legacy equivalent to 1,000 rubles, but all restrictions on the size of legacies were removed in 1926. At the time, the Russians quite frankly admitted that the frequent evasion through gifts and the need to encourage saving were the principal reasons for the removal of limitations.[30]

---

[29] Among the inefficient sectors which are still being protected by duties are the following: bicycles, watches, linen toweling, and dried figs.

[30] See Victor Zorza, "Unearned Incomes in Russia," *Manchester Guardian,* August 20, 1959, p. 5. It can be assumed that the evasion through

TRENDS IN PUBLIC FINANCE AND TAXATION AS REFLECTIONS OF BASIC ECONOMIC PROBLEMS

In the United States, there has been a trend towards greater use of the individual income tax and a corresponding decline in the use of excise taxes to obtain federal revenues. In 1939, the individual income tax accounted for 20.5 per cent of all federal budget receipts, while in 1962, it is estimated that over 55 per cent of total federal income will originate from individual income taxes. Excise taxes, which accounted for 37.2 per cent of all federal receipts in 1939 now account for less than 12 per cent of the total federal income.

World War II brought about a sharp increase in the relative importance of income tax collections as our tax system was converted to the requirements of a war economy—one which eventually required increased savings and a restraint on increases in consumption. As a result largely of the newly reintroduced withholding provisions, the number of income taxpayers increased sharply. In 1940 there were only about seven million taxable individual returns and by 1945 this figure had increased to over 40 million. Income tax exemptions were pushed down until most income receivers were taxable. Thus, what had formerly been a rather progressive tax—largely because of the exemptions and wide-scaled evasion at lower income levels—became much less progressive in the interests of diverting resources from consumption to the military effort. In the past and at present where withholding is not practiced, there has apparently been a similar evasion of state income taxes. Thus, when New York state income taxes were converted to a "pay-as-you-go" basis in 1958, it was soon discovered that more than a million additional persons sud-

---

gifts could have been eliminated through the imposition of a gift tax, as it has been in other countries, and that the principal reason for the lifting of limitations was that of encouraging saving.

denly began contributing taxes when their employers began withholding a share of their salary in April, 1959.[31]

After the war, there was some slight reduction in income tax
rates generally, but the Korean involvement again resulted in
higher tax rates which are still pretty much in effect. Thus, the
current income tax rate on the first $2,000 of surtax net income
is 20 per cent compared with 23 per cent in 1944, the highest
wartime rate. In addition, the withholding of income taxes has
remained and been accepted as a blessing by most taxpayers.
Because the withholding provisions have been applied only to
wages and salaries, the amount of tax evasion varies widely
among the different types of income. The National Bureau of
Economic Research has estimated that, whereas only five per
cent of wages and salaries go unreported for income tax purposes,
the following percentages of unreported income apply to other
income recipients: private entrepreneurs (doctors, gamblers, lawyers, call girls, butchers, confidence men, farmers, etc.)—30 per
cent; interest recipients—61 per cent; and dividend earners—13
per cent.[32] In 1962, when Congress was toying with the idea of
applying withholding provisions to interest and dividends, it was
estimated that the increased collections would have amounted to
1.24 billion out of a total of 12 billion dollars in dividend payments, and 2.52 billion out of a total of 11 billion dollars in
interest payments. In other words, over 10 per cent of dividend
income was (and is) untaxed, and over 20 per cent of interest
income was (and is) subject to income tax evasion.

The relative lack of progressiveness in our current overall tax
structure—particularly in comparison with the prewar structure
—has shown up in a number of studies. An investigation by the
nonprofit Tax Foundation of the entire tax burden, including taxes
levied at the federal, state and local levels, but excluding social
insurance taxes, indicated that the burden is approximately pro-

[31] See Warren Weaver, "State Checking 1,000,000 For Income-Tax
Evasion," *New York Times,* November 29, 1960, p. 1.

[32] In this connection, see John L. Hess, "The Gentle Art of Tax Avoidance," *The Reporter,* April 16, 1959. For percentages of unreported income
in 1957 which are approximately the same as these cited above, see
Gabriel Kolko, *op cit.,* p. 21.

portional to income for 80 per cent of our families in the income classes up to the $15,000 income per year level.[33] If social insurance taxes are included, our entire system is actually regressive for these families. Incomes under $2,000 pay 28.3 per cent of their incomes in taxes, while those between $10,000 and $15,000 pay only 24 per cent of their income in taxes of all types. Even at the higher income levels, there is little evidence that income taxes account for any substantial redistribution of incomes today. In 1959, the top 20 per cent of the income recipients took in 45.7 per cent of total personal incomes before taxes and they still had 43.8 per cent of the total personal income remaining after taxes.[34] Thus, it would seem that the share of this highest income group was scarcely cut down at all as a result of the higher tax rates to which they were theoretically subject.

In Western Europe, where there has traditionally been a tendency to favor indirect taxation over the income tax, there are indications that purchase taxes and other indirect or turnover taxes are growing at the expense of the income tax in the postwar years.[35] The British purchase tax, which was introduced as a wartime measure in 1940, continues to exist more than 20 years later.[36] To the credit of the British, however, they have at least adapted it as a counter-cyclical device. Whenever consumer demand lags in Great Britain as it did in 1959, the government

[33] See "Study Shows Taxes Took $1 of Each $4 of Income in 1958," *New York Times,* May 16, 1960, p. 47.

[34] Peter L. Bernstein, "Paradoxes of Taxation," *The Nation,* March 24, 1962, p. 261. Gabriel Kolko, *op. cit.,* pp. 34–35, cites statistics indicating that the income distribution by tenths after Federal income taxes is practically the same as the distribution before taxes. For a similar conclusion based on the effect of income taxation on the net incomes of the top five per cent of the population, see Herman P. Miller, "Is the Income Gap Closed? 'No!' " *New York Times Magazine,* November 11, 1962, p. 50.

[35] In Great Britain, 45 per cent of federal revenue is obtained through income taxes, while in West Germany 40 per cent of total income comes from this source.

[36] The aggregate revenue obtained from the purchase tax is ordinarily less than that obtained from alcohol taxes. See Ursula K. Hicks, *British Public Finances, Their Structure and Development, 1880–1952,* Oxford University Press, London, 1954, p. 79.

reduces the purchase tax in an effort to stimulate consumption.[37] While there may be some reduction in total government revenue as a result of the tax reductions in the short run, there should be a stimulus to consumption and eventually to private investment, derived as a result of the operation of the acceleration principle. As a result, increased corporation tax revenue and more income taxes from rehired workers may more than compensate for the decline in purchase tax collections.

France, Denmark, and Sweden have also recently begun to shift towards even greater use of indirect taxes at the expense of the income tax. In 1961 France announced a slight easing of the income tax burden as a cautious start to a three-year fiscal reform.[38] The 10 per cent increase in income taxes instituted in 1956 was reduced to five per cent in the hopes that an expanding economy and greater tax revenue would make up any losses caused by the lower tax rates. In 1962, Sweden increased their sales tax introduced in 1960 from 4.2 per cent to 6.4 per cent.[39] As a result, direct taxes on income were replaced as the government's top source of income. In 1963, direct taxes are expected to account for 42 per cent of the Swedish revenue, while indirect levies such as sales, excise, and customs duties will now account for about 48 per cent of the total revenue. Furthermore, the Finance Ministry has indicated that the "reduction of direct income taxes will continue." Apparently the old evolutionary socialist phi-

---

[37] Unlike the United States, there does not appear to be any great bias in favor of a balanced budget in Great Britain. In 1959, the Conservatives planned to reduce purchase taxes despite the fact that the budget deficit would have run to about one billion dollars in the absence of a tax cut. As a consequence, a two billion dollar deficit was planned. The actual deficit was below one billion dollars or even less than originally expected, due to increased revenues derived from added employment. See *New York Times,* April 20, 1959, and April 5, 1960, p. 6. In November, 1962, the British Conservatives again attempted to stimulate the lagging British economy by cutting the purchase tax on automobiles by almost 50 per cent. See Seth S. King, "Britain Cuts Auto Purchase Tax Almost 50 per cent," *New York Times,* November 6, 1962, p. 5.

[38] "French Will Pay Less Income Tax," *New York Times,* October 2, 1960, p. 3.

[39] Werner Wiskari, "Swedes Receive Tax Rise Calmly," *New York Times,* January 28, 1962, p. 7.

losophy of using income taxes as a means of redistributing income is becoming passé. Beginning on August 1, 1962, Denmark imposed a purchase tax of nine per cent on wholesale prices of all goods and products except food, fuel, farm equipment, pharmaceutical articles, gasoline, and electricity in an effort to check growing inflation prior to her entry into the European Economic Community.[40]

In both the United States and in Western Europe, there is increasing use of the tax system to encourage lagging private investment activity. The favorite device in this regard is one of allowing accelerated depreciation, which in effect permits a business to reduce its current tax payments to the extent that its recorded depreciation costs are higher than they would otherwise be. The current government revenue is thereby lessened as a result of these provisions unless there is additional revenue resulting from added investment activity stimulated by the rapid write-offs. The treatment of depreciation varies considerably from country to country in Western Europe, but in almost all cases these governments are more liberal in their allowances than we are in the United States.[41] In effect, these rapid depreciation devices give businesses interest-free use of capital, thereby stimulating internal financing of new investment.

In general, in capitalist-oriented economies there seems to be a growing dissatisfaction with the progressive income tax and an increased use of indirect taxes in the prosperous postwar

[40] "Economic Overhaul Slated by Denmark," *New York Times,* June 3, 1962, p. 18.

[41] For a description of the different European methods used to stimulate private investment, see Edwin L. Dale, "Europe is Liberal on Depreciation," *New York Times,* July 15, 1962, Section III, p. 1. The most liberal allowances of all are apparently to be found in Sweden where corporations can write off machinery almost as rapidly as they want, up to a limit of 30 per cent a year for combined assets. A variation on these measures designed to stimulate investment consists of the liberal tax deductions resulting from new investment by manufacturers. In Great Britain, these now amount to 30 per cent for new investment in plant and machinery and 15 per cent for new buildings. For an account of this recent increase in investment incentives in Great Britain, see Seth S. King, *loc. cit.*

years. While the trend towards the use of indirect taxation is less evident in the United States, the metamorphosis of the progressive income tax into something which is only slightly progressive seems to have accomplished the same thing. All of these trends seem to indicate that any redistribution of income through the tax structure is either no longer needed or else out of the question. John Kenneth Galbraith in his *The Affluent Society* makes the point that the use of the sales tax should be extended, not only because it is easy to collect, but also because it may force consumers to cut personal consumption of what he considers to be nonessentials in favor of much needed communal consumption (better roads, schools, etc.). This proposal, however, would only make sense if we got back to something resembling full employment since at present there would seem to be no serious competition between personal and communal consumption for the same resources.

The use of indirect taxation, because of its ease of collection, undoubtedly seems attractive to modern governments, especially when the economy is growing rapidly. But as unemployment and creeping stagnation develop into serious problems for capitalist-oriented economies generally in the years ahead, it would seem possible that income redistribution in an attempt to stimulate consumption and discourage savings may yet become an active issue of our time.

As already noted, the trend towards the use of indirect taxation has reached its ultimate extreme in the Soviet Union, where such taxes may soon account for virtually all government revenues. In the Soviet case, however, the interesting question is not so much why they are eliminating the income tax, but why they ever bothered with one in the first place. Considering the need for inequality to stimulate productivity and to cut relative consumption (which we have already discussed in Chapter VII), it did not seem to make much sense to turn around and redistribute income more equally via a progressive income tax. The explanation for the use of the income tax under Soviet conditions must have had an ideological rather than an economic basis. There has been a strong Marxist bias favoring the use of progressive income taxes since the *Communist Manifesto* advocated the wresting of capital by workers from the bourgeoisie in advanced capitalist countries via a heavy progressive or graduated income tax.[42] Since the progressive income tax had only been introduced in Russia in 1916, apparently after some pressures from the Bolsheviks themselves, it might have appeared to be rather awkward for the Communists to dispense with it once they had attained power. It is interesting to note that the top tax rate for workers and employees during the years of Soviet power was almost the same as that originally enacted in 1916. Another reason for the past use of direct taxes, such as the income tax and compulsory bond purchases, has undoubtedly been the fact that such taxes more dramatically emphasize the personal contribution of the individual to economic development and thereby involve him psychologically in the government's effort, whether it be a war or industrialization drive.

There is an interesting contrast between the attitudes of capitalist and noncapitalist-oriented governments with respect to growth in general and budgeting in particular. Government fiscal policy in capitalist-oriented economies (as in the case of Japan) is frequently directed towards slowing down an "overheated" boom, largely because of the fear of inflation and its deleterious effect on the balance of payments problem. Thus, when the Chancellor of the British Exchequer presented the 1960–61 budget to Parliament, it was claimed that the budget would slow down the economic expansion.[43] By 1961 the British Government attempted to increase the present level of unemployment from the then existing 1.5 per cent to one of about 2.5 per cent, in an effort to keep wages from rising so fast.[44] In noncapitalist-oriented economies, on the other hand, the chronic policy is one of "full steam ahead" as

[42] See Karl Marx, *Selected Works,* Vol. I, International Publishers, New York, 1933, p. 228.

[43] See Thomas P. Ronan, "Britain's Budget Raises Taxation," *New York Times,* April 5, 1960, p. 1.

[44] See Edwin L. Dale, "Britain Is Seeking Employment Cut," *New York Times,* August 28, 1961, p. 33.

far as the budget is concerned. Larger budgets are looked upon by planners and population alike as an indication that the economy is growing and that greater welfare will ensue.

The tendency to pare government budgets and reduce deficit spending is also apparent in Latin American countries, where such policies are encouraged, if not actually dictated, by our monetary experts in charge of economic development financed by the World Bank and the Alliance for Progress.[45] On the other hand, the Australian budgetary deficit for 1963 reflected the government's determination to follow through on its expansionary program until the national economy was operating at the highest possible level of activity.[46] In Vietnam, too, a rigid balanced budget policy is being replaced by a large-scale program of deficit financing aided and abetted by United States officials on the spot and supported by substantially increased United States economic assistance.[47]

Another difference between the contrasting tax systems has to do with the complexity of the system and its enforcement. In capitalist-oriented economies where taxes, once levied, are seldom eliminated, there is apparently a trend towards a growing patchwork of taxes, greater complexity, and difficulties of enforcement requiring the services of large numbers of specialized tax lawyers and accountants to detect legitimate loopholes, as well as government agents to uncover illegitimate evasions.[48] The noncapitalist-oriented economies, on the other hand, seem to be simplifying their tax system and saving labor at the same time by adopting

[45] See "Colombia Curbs Deficit Spending," *New York Times,* May 20, 1962, p. 36; Edward C. Burks, "Uruguay Plans Revised Economy," *New York Times,* June 18, 1962, p. 10.

[46] "Australian Budget Calls for $259.6 Million Deficit," *New York Times,* August 8, 1962, p. 6.

[47] Jacques Nevard, "Vietnam To Begin Deficit Financing," *New York Times,* August 20, 1962, p. 2.

[48] The present patchwork of special provisions and preferences tends to distort economic judgments and channels an undue amount of energy into efforts to avoid tax liabilities, according to President Kennedy in his address before the Economic Club of New York, *The National Observer,* December 17, 1962, p. 14.

the simplest and most easily collected tax of all—the sales or indirect tax.

Recommended Readings

DAVIES, R. W., *The Development of the Soviet Budgetary System,* Cambridge University Press, Cambridge, 1958.

GOODRICH, CARTER, editor, *Canals and American Economic Development,* Columbia University Press, New York, 1961.

HOLZMAN, FRANKLYN D., *Soviet Taxation: The Fiscal and Monetary Problems of a Planned Economy,* Harvard University Press, Cambridge, 1955.

*———, "Financing Soviet Economic Development," in Moses Abramovitz, editor, *Capital Formation and Economic Growth,* Princeton University Press, 1955, pp. 229–287.

———, "Income Taxation in the Soviet Union: A Comparative View," *National Tax Journal,* June, 1958, pp. 99–113.

———, "The Soviet Bond Hoax," *Problems of Communism,* Vol. VI, Sept.–Oct., 1957, pp. 47–49.

———, "The Burden of Soviet Taxation," *The American Economic Review,* September, 1953, pp. 548–571.

———, "The Soviet Budget, 1928–1952," *National Tax Journal,* September, 1953, pp. 226–249.

———, "An Estimate of the Tax Element in Soviet Bonds," *American Economic Review,* June, 1957, pp. 390–396. Cf. "Comment," by Bornstein and "Reply" by Holzman, September, 1958, pp. 662–667.

KOLKO, GABRIEL, *Wealth and Power in America,* Praeger, New York, 1962.

"The Federal Revenue System: Facts and Problems 1961," Materials assembled by the Committee Staff for the Joint Economic Committee, Congress of the United States, U.S. Government Printing Office, Washington, 1961.

XI ∾ The Uses of International Trade

THE THEORETICAL PURPOSE OF FOREIGN TRADE is to allow countries to specialize in the production of those commodities in which they enjoy the greatest productive efficiency. The factors determining whether a country has a so-called "absolute" or "comparative" advantage in the production of a commodity are both natural and man-made. In terms of underlying natural resources, we have already seen that agriculture in the United States has an edge over farming in the Soviet Union. On top of our better soil and climate, we have added a manmade advantage—relatively more capital equipment per worker or cultivated acre. As a result of these two advantages, we have seen that in terms of labor, our agriculture is perhaps about four times as productive as their farm sector.

It seems likely that the United States has an absolute advantage over the Soviet Union—that is, produces at a lower real cost—in the cultivation and manufacture of almost all products, with the possible exception of mass-produced machine tools, caviar, balalaikas, and crabmeat. However, if there were no political factors inhibiting trade between the two countries, it would pay for the United States to specialize only in the production of commodities on which it enjoys the greatest absolute advantage. By the same token, the Soviet Union should specialize in the output of commodities where they are at the least absolute disadvantage, or where their real costs of production lag least in comparison with the United States.

There are powerful benefits to be derived by both sides as a result of each country's specializing in the production of those goods in which they have a comparative advantage and trading these products for goods in which the other country has a comparative advantage. These advantages of international specialization and the subsequent exchange of products have been well known to economists since the writings of Ricardo in the early nineteenth century. The desirability of free trade happens to be one of the few things upon which most reputable economists have agreed for some time and have been consistently teaching in their classrooms for many decades.[1] Even the United States Chamber of Commerce and most of the spokesmen of our business community have finally become convinced since World War II of the disadvantages of protectionism and the merits of free trade.

Capitalist-oriented governments have also been actively working for greater world trade. Beginning with the Export-Import Bank of Washington during the thirties, our government has taken an active role in attempting to stimulate our exports. After World War II, the principal Western governments—largely influenced by the ideas of the late Lord Keynes—established two important international institutions, the International Bank for Reconstruction and Development (World Bank) and the International Monetary Fund, in an attempt to smooth and accelerate the postwar development of world trade. In view of the widespread agreement among all concerned, as well as the measures which have already been taken, it may come as somewhat of a surprise to note the historical tendency for the share of foreign trade in national income or output to fall as countries become more industrialized.[1a]

---

[1] At the time of the passage of the Smoot-Hawley bill in 1930, for example, over 1,000 American economists and teachers of economics protested in the *New York Times.* For a reprint of this statement see Reuben E. Slesinger and Asher Isaacs, *Contemporary Economics,* Allyn and Bacon, Boston, 1963, pp. 441–442.

[1a] This failure of foreign trade to expand as fast as the growth of output was predicted by Sombart who felt that the future belonged to nationalism. See Karl W. Deutsch and Alexander Eckstein, "National Industriali-

There are a number of possible explanations for this disconcerting phenomenon. As economies mature the relative growth of the service sector, which except for tourist services is largely not exportable, may be an important factor in explaining this tendency. Periodic wars, threats of war, and depressions have also encouraged protectionist policies in the name of national defense and the creation of domestic jobs. On the other hand, the exhaustion of critical natural resources should force industrial economies to rely on imports of certain raw materials to a greater extent. But one of the most important factors explaining the relatively slower growth in international trade may be the fact that, as capitalist-oriented economies mature, they all eventually attempt to use foreign trade for a rather irrational purpose—that of creating employment by exporting more than they import. As more and more economies reach this stage in their development, they all attempt to do the same near-impossible thing— to export as much as possible and import as little as they can get away with. This growing international buyer's market in the West results in a situation in which "the world's exporting nations are swiftly being pushed into a global sales war to rejuggle their share of a world trade market that the import-limiting schemes are helping to keep from growing very fast." [2]

Fortunately, all countries are not at this stage in their development today and some areas would probably prefer to do the opposite, namely, to import more than they export, just as our United States economy generally did before 1873. In the early stages of development, when so-called "young debtor" countries are obtaining credits from more advanced countries, imports of goods can normally be expected to exceed exports. By the same token, when a country is recovering from war devastation—as was the case in Western Europe after World War II—there is no need

---

zation and the Declining Share of the International Economic Sector, 1890–1959," *World Politics,* January, 1961, for a discussion of this phenomenon.

[2] See Frank K. Linge, "Global Sales War," *Wall Street Journal,* July 13, 1962, p. 1. As a result of these developments, free world exports rose by only 4.2 per cent in 1961 compared with an 11.4 per cent increase in 1960.

for it to create employment by exporting more than it imports. Indeed our Marshall Plan insured that the opposite would take place, thereby accelerating West European economic recovery and capital rebuilding.

In addition, the noncapitalist-oriented economies operate in a perpetual seller's market with most commodities in short supply. As a result, when they conduct their overall foreign trade through state monopolies, they first look around abroad for what they need to import, and then decide what they can afford to part with in order to pay for the required imports. If possible, they would like to get as many of their imports as they can on credit, but, failing this, they may have to part with certain commodities that are in comparatively plentiful supply. In the event that they are unable to export enough useful commodities, either because of pressing domestic needs or foreigners' reluctance to buy, they may be forced to dispose of a portion of their gold supply.

Logically there should be no reason for any country to prefer imports over exports, or vice versa. If all countries were at the same stage in their development, we might even say that trade is a two-way street or that the real benefits from trade are obtained by *importing* goods more cheaply than they can be produced domestically. But the fact remains that countries where capital is in short supply would prefer to import more than they export, a reflection of their present need for foreign loans to finance their industrialization. On the other hand, countries where capital is plentiful may find it attractive to export more than they import, not only because of the stimulating effect on employment, but also because this export surplus reflects the lending of capital at higher rates of return than can be obtained internally.

The necessity for foreign trade, particularly with respect to import requirements, also varies with the size of the country. A large country such as the United States or the USSR usually finds that most raw materials are available in some geographic area of the country, and they can therefore rather cavalierly pursue a policy of autarky or self-sufficiency. As a result, imports or exports of commodities in large countries such as the United

States or the USSR may normally account for only three to five per cent of GNP at any one time. A smaller country such as Great Britain or Poland, on the other hand, is much more dependent on imports of crucial raw materials not available within her borders, with the result that a fairly large share of their economic activity may depend on foreign trade.[3]

An important factor affecting the real benefits of foreign trade consists of the relative prices obtained for exports as compared with the prices paid for imported commodities. In this respect, there is frequently a situation in the international markets which is similar to the internal "price scissors" affecting farm and non-farm prices, as discussed in Chapter V. The prices of agricultural products and raw materials generally seem to be more competitively determined than the prices of manufactured goods so that the terms of trade frequently work against the developing countries of the world.[4] This handicap disappears under wartime and immediate postwar conditions when the demand for agricultural products and raw materials is high and prices reflect temporary relative scarcity. On the other hand, the blades of the international price scissors tend to open widely in a period such as the Great Depression.

FOREIGN TRADE POLICY IN NONCAPITALIST-ORIENTED ECONOMIES

Although the noncapitalist-oriented countries are currently emphasizing and promoting the expansion of international trade,

[3] Exports or imports represent about 15 per cent of the GNP's of France, West Germany, and Italy; for Belgium and the Netherlands, the figure is between 25 and 35 per cent. See Ray Vicker, "West Europe's Boom," *Wall Street Journal,* July 27, 1962, p. 8.

[4] Dr. Raul Prebisch, adviser to the United Nations Economic Commission for Latin America, argues that from the 1870's until World War II, the price relations or terms of trade have turned against the primary producing countries. See U.N. Economic Commission for Latin America, *The Economic Development of Latin America and Its Principal Problems,* United Nations Department of Economic Affairs, Lake Success, E/CN, 12/89/Rev. 1 1950, p. 8.

both within and outside their own bloc, there was a tendency for the Soviet authorities to pursue a calculated policy of autarky in the thirties with the result that Soviet foreign trade declined drastically, along with world trade generally. It can be estimated that Soviet exports accounted for less than one per cent of their total GNP by 1938. Since the amount of Soviet foreign trade was very limited at this time, 1938 makes a good base to use whenever Soviet propagandists wish to exaggerate the relative success of their more recent policy of encouraging foreign trade as a basis of peaceful coexistence. According to official Soviet claims, their volume of foreign trade expanded 10-fold between 1938 and 1961, compared with a 7.4-fold expansion of their industrial output.[5] However, if Russia's foreign trade in 1913 is used as a basis for comparison, it can be seen that the Soviet experience is certainly no exception to the overall tendency for foreign trade to grow more slowly than either industrial production or GNP. Although industrial output is probably between 10 and 15 times higher than it was in 1913, the volume of foreign trade in 1960 was less than double the prerevolutionary figure. At present exports and imports are each running a little more than five billion rubles annually, which would imply that foreign trade, even after their 10 years' campaign to expand international trade, still accounts for no more than three per cent of their national income, as calculated roughly in Chapter X.

1. *Changes in structure of foreign trade.* The changes in the structure of foreign trade can be seen from data presented in Table XI-A. Before the revolution, grain constituted about one-third of all Russian exports, but by 1928 this exportable surplus had virtually disappeared, partly as a consequence of the internal "scissors crisis." Collectivization of agriculture once again gave the government control over the agricultural surplus and grain resumed its previous role as the single most important earner of foreign exchange, accounting for about one-fifth of all exports in 1938. There has been a relative decline in grain as an export

[5] See G. Rubinshtein and M. Baksht, *"Razvitie sovetskoi vneshnei torgovli"* (Development of Soviet Foreign Trade), *Vneshniaia torgovlia*, No. 4, 1962, p. 6.

TABLE XI-A

STRUCTURE OF SOVIET EXPORTS AND IMPORTS, SELECTED YEARS 1913–1960
(Percentages)

Item (1)	1913 (2)	1928 (3)	1938 (4)	1950 (5)	1955 (6)	1960 (7)
EXPORTS						
Machinery and equipment	0.3	0.1	5.0	16.3	17.5	20.5
Fuel, raw materials and other materials	42.8	63.1	57.7	50.7	57.4	n.a.
Including:						
Coal	0.1	0.6	1.0	0.3	1.4 ⎫	16.2
Petroleum and oil products	3.3	13.5	7.8	1.5	6.2 ⎭	
Ferrous and nonferrous metals	0.6	0.8	1.6	12.6	15.0	19.5
Lumber	6.3	6.8	14.1	2.0	3.3 ⎫	5.5
Other wood products	4.5	5.1	6.0	0.9	1.5 ⎭	
Cotton	n.a.	n.a.	1.9	11.7	11.5 ⎫	6.4
Fiber-flax	6.2	3.1	1.7	0.5	0.2 ⎭	
Furs	0.4	15.1	9.4	3.3	1.4	n.a.
Chemicals, paints, and fertilizer	n.a.	n.a.	3.8	n.a.	2.0	2.5
Grain	33.3	3.3	21.3	18.5	10.5	8.4
Food and raw materials for food processing other than grain	13.8	17.4	8.1	5.6	1.5	5.0
Including:						
Meat, milk products and eggs	12.0	13.1	0.3	4.6	0.3	n.a.
Sugar	1.8	4.3	2.5	1.0	0.8	n.a.
Nonfood consumers' goods	n.a.	n.a.	7.4	n.a.	3.0	2.8
Including:						
Textiles	3.0	6.5	4.8	2.7	1.6	n.a.
IMPORTS						
Machinery and equipment	15.9	23.9	34.5	27.1	35.3	29.8
Fuel, raw materials and other materials	63.4	67.8	60.7	56.6	44.6	n.a.
Including:						
Coal	5.5	0.1	—	2.3	3.4 ⎫	4.2
Petroleum and oil products	0.4	—	1.2	5.5	3.4 ⎭	
Ferrous and nonferrous metals	6.8	13.7	25.9	9.3	5.2 ⎫	15.3
Ores and concentrates	0.1	—	2.6	1.7	4.1 ⎭	
Natural rubber	2.9	2.5	3.5	3.8	0.8	3.2
Cotton	8.3	16.3	1.8	0.2	0.5 ⎫	6.5
Other textile raw materials	10.0	10.3	7.9	5.5	5.6 ⎭	

T A B L E X I - A (Continued)

Item (1)	Year					
	1913 (2)	1928 (3)	1938 (4)	1950 (5)	1955 (6)	1960 (7)
Consumers' goods	20.7	8.3	4.8	16.3	20.1	29.3
Including:						
Meat, milk products, and eggs	0.7	—	0.3	1.9	4.4	n.a.
Sugar	—	0.1	—	3.8	3.3	n.a.
Fruits, vegetables	2.8	1.8	1.9	1.0	1.6	n.a.
Foods and raw materials for food processing	n.a.	n.a.	12.7	n.a.	20.2	12.1
Nonfood consumers' goods	n.a.	n.a.	1.0	n.a.	4.8	17.2

Notes to Table XI-A:
n.a. = not available; "—" = nil.

Sources of data: Percentages for 1913 through 1955 are for the most part obtained from *Narodnoe khoziaistvo 1956*, pp. 239–240.
Percentages for 1960 are obtained from G. Rubinshtein and M. Baksht, *"Razvitie sovetskoi vneshnei torgovli"* (Development of Soviet Foreign Trade), *Vneshniaia torgovlia*, No. 4, 1962, pp. 8, 11. For rubber imports, see *Narodnoe khoziaistvo 1960*, p. 747. In some cases, percentages in the different sources do not agree. This is particularly striking for 1938. The percentage for foods and raw materials for food processing from Rubinshtein and Baksht is much larger than the percentage for consumers' goods given by the 1956 handbook.

item since 1950, although the absolute quantities being exported are still higher than they were in 1938. In 1960, grain accounted for less than 10 per cent of total Soviet exports, and almost three-fourths of this was shipped to noncapitalist-oriented countries within their own bloc. Total exports of grain by the USSR are averaging somewhere between 10 and 15 per cent of their total domestic grain output in the early sixties.

Lumber was another traditional Russian export that was responsible for a large share of the foreign exchange required to finance the industrial expansion of the thirties. In 1938 lumber was about two-thirds as important as grain and second only to grain in relative importance as an export item. Petroleum and oil products reached great relative importance as an export category in 1928, but declined thereafter until by 1950 they accounted for only 1.5 per cent of all exports. During the late fifties, petroleum output had generally risen faster than planned, permitting petroleum and oil products to regain once again their earlier relative importance as an export item. The USSR now exports over 22 per cent of their domestic output and Soviet exports accounted for 11.4 per cent of the world's petroleum exports in 1959, including 8 per cent of the total oil consumption in Common Market countries.

Furs were also an important item for export in 1928, but their economic significance has been reduced steadily, reflecting the secular decline in the demand for natural furs throughout the world. Exports of meat, dairy products, and eggs were of considerable significance before the revolution, but they too had virtually disappeared as exports by the middle fifties.

The greatest relative gains as export items have been made by machinery and equipment. This export category was virtually non-existent both before the revolution and in 1928, but now accounts for about one-fifth of all goods shipped. There has been a sharp expansion in the shipments of machinery and equipment to developing areas—in some cases no doubt because of political motivations. Between 1955 and 1960 the share of these countries in total Soviet machinery exports rose from two to 13 per cent. There has been a steady growth in ferrous and nonferrous ores and metals as earners of foreign exchange. These metallurgical products were also negligible as exports in both 1913 and 1928, but today account for another one-fifth of the total outflow of commodities. Raw cotton was scarcely exported before the war, but in the early fifties was accounting for over 10 per cent of all exports.

In general, the trend among Soviet exports seems to have reflected the growing comparative advantage of their economy with respect to the products of heavy industry where investment has been lavished during the industrialization drive. On the other hand, products from sectors where the Soviet Union suffers a comparative disadvantage—especially agricultural products, other than cotton—seem to have declined in relative importance as components of their exports.[6]

Among Soviet imports, machinery and equipment has been an important item fairly consistently since 1913, frequently accounting for over one-third of all incoming goods. Cotton was a principal import both before the revolution and in 1928. But with the development of their own cotton growing regions in Central Asia, it has virtually disappeared as an import. Occasionally the Soviet Union may do a political favor for a country such as Egypt and import some of her surplus cotton. Recent Soviet purchases of natural rubber may also be partly political in motivation judging by the fact that natural rubber imports almost vanished in 1955. However, Soviet synthetic rubber seems to be produced at high cost so apparently there are economic as well as political advantages connected with these imports.[7]

Consumers' goods accounted for about one-fifth of all imports before the revolution, but these products declined greatly as an import item in the thirties, as a reflection of the sharp drop in consumption levels at that time. In the postwar period, there has been a rapid expansion of consumers' good imports, especially in nonfood consumers' goods. Two food import items have also experienced unusual growth in recent years, primarily because of political factors. The import of cocoa and coffee increased five or six times between 1958 and 1960, and this development has no doubt contributed to the greater economic well-being of both Ghana and Brazil.[8] Tea imports have de-

[6] Most Soviet cotton is irrigated and, as a result, their qualitative indices with respect to cotton are fairly high in relation to our own. See D. Gale Johnson and Arcadius Kahan, "Soviet Agriculture: Structure and Growth," in *Comparisons of the United States and Soviet Economies,* Part I, pp. 211–215. For evidence of greater Soviet attention to the principles of comparative advantage in their foreign trade transactions, see Robert Loring Allen, "Economic Motives in Soviet Foreign Trade Policy," *Southern Economic Journal,* October, 1958, pp. 189–201.

[7] As a result of Soviet purchases of rubber from Ceylon, world rubber prices were pushed to an eight-year high in 1960. See "Soviet Offers Oil at Cut-Rate Price," *New York Times,* June 25, 1960, p. 24.

[8] For an account of the problems of cocoa-producing countries and Soviet efforts to establish amicable relations by purchasing large quanti-

clined concomitantly to a level which is now only somewhat higher than that for coffee. Imports of raw sugar from Castro's Cuba increased almost 10-fold in 1960 in comparison with the previous year. Since sugar from cane is much cheaper to produce than the beet sugar characterizing Soviet domestic production, Cuban cane sugar imports by the USSR represent some movement in the direction of using the principle of comparative advantage. As a matter of fact, Cuban sugar exports to the Soviet Union began to increase substantially in 1955 under the anti-Communist Batista regime so that these increased sugar imports are apparently not entirely political in motivation. While political factors seem to be fairly important in determining the structure of Soviet imports, particularly from the developing areas, there are undoubtedly also economic gains based on the law of comparative advantage associated with this trade.

2. *Balance of trade.* In the thirties, the Soviet Union was comparatively unsuccessful in obtaining credits from abroad, and it was necessary for the Russians to balance their purchases of machinery and equipment from the advanced capitalist-oriented economies by exporting grain, timber, oil, furs, alloy materials, etc. Thus, from 1933 through 1937, total Soviet exports slightly exceeded their total imports, presumably as a reflection of repayments on their external debt, which had been largely acquired in 1931.[9]

---

ties of cocoa, see George Auerbach, "Prices of Cocoa at 11-Year Low," *New York Times,* March 5, 1961, Section III, p. 1. Brazil, which is chronically burdened with a large coffee surplus, entered into this bilateral trade with the idea of obtaining equipment for her state oil and electric enterprises, for which United States credit was withheld as a matter of policy. See Juan de Onis, "Brazil Will Test Market in Soviet," *New York Times,* November 14, 1959, p. 33. The resulting agreement provided for the receipt of oil, oil equipment, and wheat in exchange for coffee. See "Soviet and Brazil Sign 200 Million Trade Pact," *New York Times,* December 10, 1959, p. 15.

[9] The external debt reached a maximum of 1.4 billion rubles measured in the exchange rate of the time by the end of 1931. This compares with a total capital investment during Plan I of about 52 billion rubles. Most of this credit was of a short-term nature and tended to be paid off via an export surplus during the years of Plan II. See A. M. Smirnov,

In recent years, there does not yet appear to be any general tendency for Soviet merchandise exports to exceed imports as has been the case in the United States in the twentieth century. Between 1955 and 1960, total Soviet exports exceeded total imports in three years. However, in their trade with the members of the Soviet bloc, the tendency ordinarily seems to be for the USSR to export more than they import. In only two out of the last six years have the total imports from these countries exceeded Soviet exports to them. Likewise, it can be assumed that the Soviet Union generally will be exporting more to the developing areas than she takes in return, although the reverse is the case thus far. In both cases, the export surplus no doubt reflects extension of credit or deliveries on obligations to supply credit by the USSR. In their trade with Western Europe, on the other hand, it is usual for them to have a reverse balance—to import more than they export. This import surplus is financed by West European extensions of short-term credit to the Soviet foreign trade monopoly, and also by the annual outflow of approximately $200 million worth of gold each year.[10]

It seems possible that the increase in Soviet exports relative to imports in 1957 reflects the response of the Russians to the Hungarian uprising, since it is known that large quantities of consumers' goods were shipped to Hungary in 1957, primarily on loan. In general, Soviet assistance to Eastern Europe increased

Mezhdunarodnye raschety i kreditnye otnosheniia vo vneshnei torgovle SSSR (International Accounts and Credit Relations in the Foreign Trade of the USSR), Vneshtorgizdat, Moscow, 1953, pp. 224, 226.

[10] In 1961, our diplomatic sources estimated that these trade credits might approach the billion-dollar level, the largest share coming from Great Britain, the next largest from West Germany and significant amounts from both France and the Netherlands. See Kennett Love, "Zellerbach Says Some in NATO Are 'Lending a Knife' to Soviet," *New York Times,* February 10, 1961, p. 6. For an account of nongovernmental credits to the Soviets for West German pipe, see Sydney Gruson, "U.S. Voices Concern to Its Allies Over Private Credits to Red Bloc," *New York Times,* July 27, 1960, p. 6. There have evidently been some long-term credit offers of up to five years by West German, Belgian, French, and Italian bankers to the Czechs. See M. S. Handler, "West Europe Banks Offer Czechs Long-Term Credit," *New York Times,* December 11, 1959, p. 1.

after the uprisings there. But the burden of increased Soviet assistance to Eastern Europe was alleviated somewhat by Chinese repayments for earlier Soviet aid. In 1957, the Chinese export surplus with the Soviet Union was about $200 million.[11] In other words, for a time mainland China was shipping more goods to the USSR than they were receiving in return.[12] The more recent agricultural difficulties of the Chinese have no doubt reduced China's export possibilities and either reduced or eliminated this export surplus to the Soviet Union.[13] On balance, it would seem that current Soviet assistance to members of her bloc and the developing areas is an economic burden reducing some of the immediate overall gains from foreign trade obtained as a result of the principle of comparative advantage.

Although the Soviet Union ordinarily more or less balances its imports with exports, they would undoubtedly prefer to import more commodities than they export, that is, they would like to receive credits from abroad. This was particularly true in the thirties and it was also true after World War II when Stalin unsuccessfully sought to obtain a postwar loan from the United States.[14] Until recently the Soviet regime has been pretty much boycotted in the international money markets. As a result, the imports of machinery and equipment necessary for industrialization had to be paid for by exports of food and raw materials, despite the fact that the population was generally ill-fed. The relative price movements on the international markets during the Great Depression further complicated the situation from the

[11] See Richard Moorsteen, "Economic Prospects for Communist China," *World Politics,* January, 1959, p. 201.

[12] According to figures published by the United Nations, between 1955 and 1958, the Chinese export surplus amounted to over $247 billion at the official rate of exchange. See Kathleen McLaughlin, "Soviet in Deficit in Chinese Trade," *New York Times,* April 5, 1960, p. 51.

[13] In 1961, however, China apparently shipped $185 million worth of goods in excess of what they received in return from the Soviet Union. See Tad Szulc, "Peiping's Economic Woes Said To Demoralize People," *New York Times,* August 8, 1962, p. 1.

[14] For an account of Soviet efforts to obtain a postwar loan from the United States, see Albert Z. Carr, *Truman, Stalin and Peace,* Doubleday, Garden City, New York, 1950.

Soviet standpoint. Since machinery and equipment import prices were comparatively sticky during the thirties, in contrast to the prices of exported raw materials and foods which dropped sharply, the Soviets were adversely affected by these terms of trade and were forced to tighten their collective belts still further in order to meet their obligations abroad.

Today the Soviet Union would still also probably prefer not to export any more than is absolutely necessary, since virtually all commodities are in general short supply internally. But since foreign credits have not been forthcoming in any great amount, certain commodities are being exported to earn foreign exchange and pay for the required imports of machinery and equipment. The items selected for export to the West are probably commodities which are in least critical short supply. Quantities of Chinese tin in excess of domestic requirements have been accepted by the Soviet Union in payment for earlier loans to mainland China and some of this tin has apparently found its way into Western markets via the Soviet Union.[15] The output of aluminum, in which the Russians have apparently developed a comparative advantage, has been expanding at a very rapid rate and for a time had been one of the principal Soviet exports, much to the initial consternation of the Western aluminum cartel. Petroleum output, which has also risen faster than planned, is also being used increasingly as a means of payment for required imports, and will probably be exported in even greater quantities as soon as Russian pipe lines—partly imported from Italy and West Germany—have been extended to Eastern Europe and the Baltic. The only development which might conceivably slow down or restrict Soviet oil exports would seem to be for the Western oil producers to admit the Soviets into their international club and allocate the Russians an export quota similar to those already in effect for other raw materials.

In the years after World War II, the USSR was no doubt im-

---

[15] According to United Nations data, Soviet imports of Chinese tin amounted to $56 million in 1955 and $51 million in 1957. See Kathleen McLaughlin, "U.N. Issues Data on Soviet Trade," *New York Times*, January 18, 1959, p. 2.

porting more than they were exporting to Eastern Europe, principally under the guise of reparations. The instrument for this import surplus was frequently the joint stock company which will be discussed below. Since the uprisings in Eastern Germany in 1953 and in Poland and Hungary in 1956, the joint stock companies have been liquidated and on balance more goods are currently being shipped to Eastern Europe than are being sent to the Soviet Union from this area. Czechoslovakia, which is the most industrialized member of the bloc, emulates the Soviet Union by tending to have an export surplus with the less developed noncapitalist-oriented and neutralist countries.

The pattern of trade within the bloc varies from country to country. The USSR exports capital goods to the more underdeveloped areas (Bulgaria, Rumania, and to a lesser extent Hungary). At the same time, raw materials from these areas flow to the Soviet Union. On the other hand, machinery is shipped to the USSR from East Germany, Czechoslovakia, and to a certain extent Poland, in exchange for Soviet food and raw materials.

The Soviet Union will also probably have to export capital goods to mainland China if they honor their existing long-term agreements for more trade and assistance.[16] Raw materials and food are the principal exports with which the Chinese can be expected to pay for their capital imports. To the extent that the Russians wish to play politics in the developing areas of the world, they are no doubt going to export increasingly more commodities, especially capital goods, to these areas compared with what they will receive in return. To the degree that the Russians export capital goods and have an export surplus, either within or outside their bloc, their internal capital expansion and rate of development should be retarded, for reasons which we have already noted in Chapter IV (see p. 61).

3. *Soviet trade policy outside their bloc.* The prices the Russians pay for the raw materials they accept in return for capital

[16] See Harry Schwartz, "Peiping Official Hopes Soviet Will Increase Economic Help," *New York Times,* February 19, 1961, p. 5.

goods exports to the developing countries are ordinarily some-what above existing world market prices, which undoubtedly adds an attractive fillip to this trade from the standpoint of the exporting countries, particularly if the raw material is in over-supply as is frequently the case. On the other hand, the Russians are generally forced to shade their prices on the items they ex-port in order to enter and compete on the world market. Thus, the entry of the Russians into world markets may tend for some time at least to close the blades of the international price scissors.[17]

Although the Russians have had to shade their prices initially in order to make their exports attractive to Western importers, they have also been more than happy to enter into restrictive Western cartels. As a result, they receive a quota of commodities which they can export at higher prices and thereby earn greater foreign exchange than could be obtained in the absence of such agreements. At the present time, aluminum, tin, and diamonds are subject either to export quotas or marketing arrangements designed to obtain the highest possible prices. At a luncheon given by Cyrus S. Eaton in New York in 1960, Premier Khru-shchev indicated that the principle of establishing export quotas for the Soviet Union should be extended to other goods.[18] The Soviets have also pledged to restrict their exports of zinc and lead to their 1961 level, to help the major nonbloc producers ease their market glut.[19]

It has sometimes been argued that since the Russians do not

[17] A report of the Food and Agriculture Association of the United Nations concludes that Soviet purchases or sales have acted as a stabilizing element in global exchanges. See Kathleen McLaughlin, "Communists Gain in World Trade," *New York Times,* June 18, 1961, Section III, p. F-11.

[18] See Harry Schwartz, "Khrushchev Backs Export Pact," *New York Times,* October 8, 1960, p. 27. The Soviets have also endorsed the idea of a code of fair trade practices, such as that proposed by Governor Rockefeller and the International Chamber of Commerce. See Harry Schwartz, "Russians Favor Trade-Code Idea," *New York Times,* May 8, 1960, p. 26.

[19] "Restrictions in Output of Zinc Are Pledged by Soviet Union," *New York Times,* June 2, 1962, p. 23. The title of this article is misleading since the Russians only promised not to increase their exports. Other parties to the agreement did agree to reduce their production.

need to make a profit in their foreign trade transactions, we are faced with a prolonged period of cutthroat competition in which the Soviets will dump indiscriminately and thereby ruin our stabilized price structures.[20] It is true that there is no necessary connection between the internal cost of production and the price which must be realized on the export of a product from the Soviet Union, and in this respect the Russians no doubt have considerable flexibility in the operations of their foreign trade monopoly. If the Soviet economy ever developed into a buyer's market, there might be some grounds for these fears. But, as we shall see in the concluding chapter, there is no theoretical reason to expect this development, and therefore there is no reason for the Russians to part freely with useful commodities produced with their scarce inner resources. In any event, if they were ever so foolish, we should rationally welcome this windfall.

In assessing the magnitude and effectiveness of the Soviet foreign assistance program, a number of things should be kept in mind. First, the Russians frequently set up credits for fairly long periods of time, while our Congress and President are ordinarily faced with the problem of meting out our foreign aid program on a year-to-year basis. Thus, the impressive credits set up by the Russians for their assistance only become a drain on their economy when the materials, equipment or technicians leave the USSR, in some cases a number of years later.[21] As a result, their program tends to look superficially more impressive than is actually the case. In addition, their assistance is ordinarily in

[20] A typical viewpoint along these lines is held by our former Under Secretary of State, Chester Bowles, who fears and expects that the Soviet Union will probably increase rather than reduce its economic warfare against the West by underselling in the world markets for political reasons. Bowles concludes that the Western nations may be forced to counter such moves, by creating national or allied export controls. See James Reston, "Kennedy's Solutions To Problems May Prove Radical in Long Run," *New York Times*, January 20, 1961, p. 1.

[21] There is some evidence that the later deliveries of machinery and equipment may be delayed. For example, Soviet officials have already informed the Indian government that they will have to back down on a promise to deliver electrical equipment. See "Russians Disappoint India on Machinery," *New York Times*, August 6, 1962, p. 2.

the form of a loan at a nominal interest rate of about 2.5 per cent, rather than being an outright gift as is frequently the case with our assistance.

Soviet aid also usually takes the form of a complete plant or capital project (dam, road, oil refinery, steel mill) which will serve as a reminder to the people of their Russian benefactors for a long time to come. Since the Russians are themselves still in the process of developing economic complexes from scratch in their eastern regions—rather than modifying existing capital stock as is frequently the case in the United States—it seems possible that the Soviets may enjoy a comparative advantage in this field of endeavor. There is also less attention paid by the Russians to the economic feasibility or "profitability" of a project as long as it is wanted by the developing country. At the same time, there is no Soviet ownership—or even partial ownership—of capital in the developing countries, with the result that the endless repatriation of profits which is a by-product of our private investment does not arise as a source of local irritation. Although the Russians may occasionally give food in the case of a national calamity, they do not ordinarily give much assistance in the form of food or raw materials, possibly because of their own agricultural difficulties, but also because the obvious effect of such assistance is not too long lasting.[22]

Soviet foreign assistance outside their bloc tends to be concentrated in a few key countries—India, Indonesia, Egypt, Cuba, Afghanistan, Iraq, Ghana, Syria, Ethiopia, Yugoslavia, and Guinea—so that on balance they seem to have reaped considerable good will with a minimum of effort. The Soviet Union and other Communist bloc countries which have been extending aid commitments to non-Communist countries only since the middle fifties had provided by 1960, credits and grants valued at only about $4.5 billion, of which the highest total aid extended in any one year was $1.4 billion.[23] A great deal of Soviet assistance takes the

[22] For further information on Soviet foreign assistance, see Joseph S. Berliner, *Soviet Foreign Aid,* Praeger, New York, 1958, especially Chapter 7, "Soviet Economic Gains from the Aid Program."

[23] For a digest of a book by H. J. P. Arnold, *Aid for Developing Countries,* giving these data, see "West Far Ahead of Soviet in Aid,"

form of the dispatch of technical experts, 8500 of whom have been sent together with their assistants to the developing areas.[24]

4. *Soviet imperialism.* One of the frequent charges made by both sides in the cold war is that the opposition is imperialistic. Although there are undoubtedly many aspects of imperialism, we shall consider here only some of the economic manifestations. What is the basis of the charge that the Russians have acted in an imperialistic fashion? Perhaps one of the most damaging Soviet institutions supporting this charge was the joint stock company, which was utilized to varying degrees after World War II until well after Stalin's death. Generally speaking, this form of exploitation was confined to countries or areas which had fought on the German side during the war—Hungary, Rumania, Bulgaria, and East Germany. Under joint stock arrangements, certain key industries (including petroleum, chemicals, aluminum, uranium) were developed jointly by the Russians and the local Communist governments with the lion's share of the commodities being produced syphoned off to the Soviet Union. In some instances, such as was the case with coal from the new Polish areas which had formerly been part of Germany, the products were simply sold to the Russians at very low compulsory delivery prices. The Russians undoubtedly rationalized this exploitation on the grounds that people from these areas had engaged in plundering the Ukraine and RSFSR during the war, and hence reparations were in order.

Since the revolutionary uprisings in Eastern Europe in the

New York Times, May 20, 1962, p. 53. In 1962, new commitments were running at an annual rate of $500 million, off from the $1 billion of 1961. Actual deliveries by the Soviet Union, however, were running around $500 million compared with total deliveries of $300 million in 1961. See *New York Times,* September 26, 1962, p. 3.

[24] See "Red Bloc Steps Up Aid For Neutralist Nations," *New York Herald Tribune,* March 14, 1962, p. 13. Also, Felix Belair, Jr., "Soviet Foreign Aid is Plagued By Many Obstacles, Study Finds," *New York Times,* April 15, 1962, p. 1. An earlier sensational report had indicated that there were 600,000 Communist-bloc experts on duty in the underdeveloped countries in the middle of 1960 and that the number would be doubled by 1962. See M. S. Handler, "Reds' Foreign Aid Put at 3 Billion," *New York Times,* March 5, 1961, p. 6.

mid-fifties, the joint stock companies have been completely liquidated and the result has been a fairly steady improvement in the level of living in these areas. In Czechoslovakia, where joint stock companies were never utilized inasmuch as this was German-occupied country during World War II, the level of living was less affected by the forced industrialization after 1948. On the other hand, recent large-scaled capital exports by the Czechs seem to be creating some economic difficulties for their economy.[25]

Since about three-fourths of Soviet foreign trade is with the East European bloc countries, we should inquire into the nature of the prices at which these exports and imports are valued. It is believed that world market prices, sometimes those existing in 1938, have been used in valuing commodities entering into intra-bloc trade. To the extent that these prices reflect the international price scissors, the Russians would seem to be exploiting the agricultural areas (Bulgaria, Rumania, to a certain extent Hungary, and until recently Albania), while at the same time the USSR is being exploited by East Germany, Czechoslovakia, and Poland. However, the Russians apparently have recognized the unfairness of relative prices reflecting the international price scissors, and have therefore adjusted upward the prices they pay for certain agricultural crops. In 1958, for example, prices on Bulgarian exports to the Soviet Union were 15 per cent above world market prices while prices of Bulgarian imports from the USSR were five per cent below world market prices.[26]

There have been a number of studies comparing the relative prices used in transactions between the Soviet Union and the members of the bloc, with the prices at which commodities ex-

[25] See "Sausage and Strippers," *Newsweek,* July 23, 1962, pp. 21–22. Also, Paul Underwood, "Czechs Cheerful Despite Problems," *New York Times,* November 4, 1962, p. 16.

[26] See M. N. Savov, *"O tovarnykh otnosheniiakh mezhdu sotsialisticheskimi stranami i tsenoobrazovanii na mirovom sotsialisticheskom rynke"* (About Commodity Relationships Between Socialist Countries and Price Formation on the World Socialist Market) in Akademiia obshchestvennykh nauk pri TSK KPSS, *Dve mirovye sistemy khoziaistva* (Two World Economic Systems), Izdatel'stvo VPSH i AON pri TSK, KPSS, Moscow, 1961, p. 153.

change between the USSR and West European countries. According to one of these studies, the overcharges by the Soviet Union on exports and undercharges on imports from the bloc amounted to five billion dollars between 1955 and 1960.[27] The calculation also indicates that the peak price discrimination was attained in 1960 when over 1.5 billion dollars worth of exploitation occurred.

These findings, as well as those of an earlier study by Horst Mendershausen, have been challenged by Professor Holzman who contends that these losses are simply a reflection of bloc autarky as pursued in Eastern Europe, and the advantages these countries forego by not trading with the West European countries.[28] While foreign trade is relatively unimportant as far as the Soviet Union is concerned, it is more important for the other bloc countries. As a result, this bloc autarky would seem to hurt the smaller East European countries more than it does the Soviet Union. There are a number of indications that some of the East European countries—with West European cooperation, if not also their initiative—are changing their pattern of trade in favor of greater trade with West European countries.[29] If so, this should tend to reduce the losses resulting from bloc autarky.

[27] For an account of the study by Aleksander Kutt, an Estonian refugee, see "Exile Group Accuses Moscow of Exploiting East Europeans," *New York Times,* April 10, 1962, p. 8. Kutt's method of calculating the discrimination is based on an earlier study by Horst Mendershausen, "Terms of Trade Between the Soviet Union and Smaller Communist Countries," *Review of Economics and Statistics,* May, 1959, pp. 106–118.

[28] Franklyn D. Holzman, "Soviet Foreign Trade Pricing and the Question of Discrimination: A 'Customs Union' Approach," *Review of Economics and Statistics,* May, 1962, pp. 134–147. For an exchange of views between Holzman and Kutt, see *East Europe,* August, 1962, pp. 55–56.

[29] For example, see M. S. Handler, "Rumania Forges Links with West," *New York Times,* January 2, 1962, p. 23. The new Rumanian agreements with France, Italy, and Austria run from 3 to 5 years in length. See also Paul Underwood, "Rumania's Trade with West Rises," *New York Times,* March 25, 1962, p. 24. Since 1958 the share of the Soviet bloc in Rumanian foreign trade has dropped from 75 to 63 per cent. This growing trade between the two blocs would also seem to serve the needs of Western Europe as their postwar seller's market evolves into the more normal buyer's market.

The Russians claim to be using "world market" prices in their intra-bloc trade transactions. If this is so, then it will have to be assumed that the exchange prices in Soviet trade outside the bloc are different from these so-called "world market" prices: below this world market price level in the case of exports and above this level for Soviet imports. The reason for this is obvious. No one is too anxious to trade with the Russians unless a little sweetening is added in terms of lower prices on Soviet exports and higher prices paid for their imports. Thus, the differential shown by Mendershausen and Kutt is at least partly a reflection of higher profits for West European importers and exporters as a result of this lucrative price discrimination in their favor.

In recent years, the USSR has made loans to the noncapitalist-oriented economies of Eastern Europe at low rates of interest, which may have helped reduce some of the hostility among the satellite peoples. Generally speaking, these loans would seem to slow down the internal rate of growth in the Soviet Union and accelerate the development of the borrowing countries, thus tending to even up the different degrees of industrialization found in Eastern Europe.[30] Between 1957 and 1961, the rate of growth in industrial production in all members of the Soviet bloc—with the single exception of the German Democratic Republic—was higher than it was in the USSR.[31]

In contrast to the charge made against Western imperialism, which will be discussed presently, there has been little effort made to stifle heavy industry in any of these areas of Eastern Europe, particularly while Stalin was alive. In fact, some economists would no doubt say that the Russians should have vetoed the construction plans for iron and steel plants in Bulgaria or

[30] According to Felix Belair, *loc. cit.,* Soviet aid to their bloc since 1959 totaled six billion dollars. A figure of $2.8 billion is calculated by Stanislaw Skrzypek, "Soviet Aid: A Balance Sheet," *East Europe,* August, 1962, p. 6.

[31] See N. Silvianov, *"Razvitie i ukreplenie ekonomicheskogo sotrudnichestva sotsialisticheskikh stran"* (Development and Strengthening of the Economic Cooperation of Socialist Countries), *Voprosy Ekonomiki,* No. 8, 1962, p. 4. To some extent, these results may be affected by the prices used in weighting these indexes, as well as the size of these economies.

Hungary, for example. In the early years after World War II, each satellite attempted to become self-sufficient and division of labor within the Soviet bloc was minimized.

In recent years, however, intra-bloc specialization has been pushed by an overall planning agency—the Council for Economic Mutual Aid, sometimes referred to as "Comecon"—with the result that each satellite is now supposed to specialize in the production of particular types of capital and consumers' goods. If successful, intra-bloc trade should expand as a result of this planned international division of labor. As a result of increased specialization, intra-bloc trade was expected to grow seven-fold between 1956 and 1965.

The most ambitious goal thus far has been the decision to unify the electric power grids of Eastern Europe. Since 1959, when the decision was made by Comecon, Czechoslovakia has been linked up with Poland, East Germany, and Hungary. A transmission line also connects the Soviet Union and the Polish parts of what was formerly East Prussia, and construction is under way linking up Rumania and Czechoslovakia. The Ukraine is now linked to Hungary and the decision was made in 1962 to establish a central dispatching office to coordinate movements of power between national grids.[32] A policy of encouraging joint investment projects by two or more members of the Soviet bloc was adopted at the June, 1962, meeting of Comecon.[33] Among those joint investment projects already in the process of being fulfilled is a cooperative tractor and copper production effort

[32] See Theodore Shabad, "Red Bloc Pushes Unity on Power," *New York Times,* July 27, 1962, p. 3. For an account of the earlier meeting, see Harry Schwartz, "Red Bloc to Unify Electric Power," *New York Times,* May 27, 1959, p. 27. At this earlier meeting, the production of cable-manufacturing equipment was assigned to East Germany and Hungary; the production of forging installations and oil refining and processing equipment will be concentrated in the Soviet Union and Rumania. Hungary, which is comparatively lacking in raw materials, is hoping to become the "Switzerland" of Eastern Europe. See Paul Underwood, "Hungary to Slow Some Industries," *New York Times,* June 12, 1959, p. 4.

[33] See Harry Schwartz, "Red Bloc Pushing Projects Jointly," *New York Times,* August 6, 1962, p. 5.

by Poland and Czechoslovakia, and a Czech-East German agreement to create facilities for producing potassium products.

Most serious charges against the Russians with regards to the practice of economic imperialism arise in connection with their relationships to the Yugoslavs. In this area, Soviet foreign policy has alternated between friendship and bitter hostility, with the result that trade relations have alternately expanded and contracted sharply between Yugoslavia and the Soviet bloc. The Yugoslavs experienced considerable economic difficulty after the rupture of close economic relationships with the Soviet world in 1948, but their economy eventually recovered and even exceeded its previous rate of growth. Since 1948 Yugoslavia has had a certain amount of success in playing the neutralist game, that is, in obtaining assistance from both sides of the street. In 1962, however, the annual rate of industrial expansion in Yugoslavia had slowed down to only four per cent, despite the fact that the Yugoslavs have been obtaining assistance from both the United States and the Soviet Union.

With respect to the neutralist world, the Russians have thus far apparently behaved in a rather exemplary anti-imperialist fashion, although they have certainly made some mistakes in executing their aid program.[34] Their economic assistance is usually granted without any specific strings attached, while their technical personnel usually keep to themselves and avoid local politics. It is somewhat ironic to note that Russian aloofness is frequently cited as one of the unfavorable characteristics of Soviet technical assistance.[35]

5. *Valuation of the ruble.* It has been Soviet policy to set unilaterally a value of the ruble in terms of gold, and, in so doing, to establish a relationship between the ruble and currencies of

[34] For a good list of some of the mistakes connected with Soviet foreign aid, see Felix Belair, Jr., "Soviet Foreign Aid Is Plagued by Many Obstacles, Study Finds," *New York Times,* April 15, 1962, p. 1.

[35] *Ibid;* also, Jay Walz, "Egyptians Speed Dam at Aswan; Coexistence Cool With Russians," *New York Times,* February 17, 1962, p. 2; Harrison E. Salisbury, "U.S. Lead is Seen in Aid to Afghans," *New York Times,* November 26, 1961, p. 30.

other countries. Until January 1, 1961, when all decimal points affecting their internal economy were moved one digit to the left, it was the practice to set a foreign exchange rate which greatly overvalued the ruble in relation to other currencies. The creation of a foreign trade monopoly and the planning of both exports and imports meant that there was no way to test the officially declared value of the ruble in open competition with other currencies. As a result, the Russians could and did set any artificial value they desired on the ruble. Until 1961 the overvalued ruble meant that prices abroad looked very attractive to Soviet import organizations in relation to the domestic price for the same commodity. On the other hand, at the overvalued ruble exchange rate, it appeared that the Russians were getting relatively little for their exports. The paper "profits" on imports tended to be offset by "losses" on their exports.

Their "heavy" ruble is officially defined in terms of its so-called gold content, which has consisted of 0.987412 grams of pure gold since January 1, 1961. Since we define our dollar in terms of 0.888671 grams of pure gold, the Russians thereby established the rates of exchange between the ruble and the dollar and other foreign currencies defined in terms of gold. In this case, one ruble was declared to be equivalent to $1.11, or one dollar equaled 90 kopecks.[36] We have seen in Chapter VI that this new foreign exchange rate still tends to overvalue their currency with respect to consumers' goods.[37] At the same time,

[36] It is sometimes claimed by Soviet propagandists that the Russian ruble is "more valuable" than the dollar. By the same token, the British might claim that their pound was more valuable than both the dollar and the ruble since it takes only about one-third of a pound to equal a dollar or ruble. Or any other country might move its decimal points over a number of places and achieve the same result. There would be some basis for Soviet claims if they are able to maintain their overall price stability or disinflationary policy, while at the same time Western countries continued to experience secular inflation.

[37] These comparatively high prices for domestically produced consumers' goods make it attractive for Soviet tourists (and sailors) to obtain as much foreign currency as possible before they leave the USSR in order to buy consumers' goods very cheaply abroad. As a result, a "service industry" has developed with Soviet citizens buying and selling foreign currency at higher than official rates of exchange.

producers' goods seem relatively low priced in relation to ours when conversion is made at the new official rate, so that on the average the new rate seems for the first time to be a realistic expression of the overall purchasing power of the ruble.[38] The fact that consumers' goods seem comparatively expensive and producers' goods seem relatively cheap at the new rate of exchange is a reflection of the fact that Soviet investment policy for the past 30 years has resulted in the Russians having developed a comparative advantage with respect to producers' goods, while they are at a comparative disadvantage with regards to the production of consumers' goods.

Before the recent revaluation of the ruble, the Russians maintained two rates of exchange: the official rate of four old rubles to the dollar, and the so-called tourist rate of exchange, which made it possible for Western tourists to spend profitably some of their excess dollars, entitling foreigners to 10 old rubles for each dollar exchanged. Had the government simply moved over the decimal place on the official rate of exchange one digit leftward, the new foreign exchange rate would have been 40 kopecks to the dollar, while the ruble and dollar would have been on a par for tourists. By setting the new exchange rate of 90 kopecks to the dollar for both the official and tourist rates, the Russians were in effect "devaluing" the official rate and revaluing upward the tourist rate. This devaluation was entirely different from the type of devaluation practiced by Western countries, when they suffer from growing unemployment or more-than-average inflation, and devalue their currency in order to stimulate exports to create domestic employment and thereby rectify their balance of payments deficit. The Russians merely stopped being unrealistic about their official exchange rate, and at the same time, decided to get a little more out of capitalist tourists and the diplomatic colony in Moscow.

There have been hints that the Russians are preparing the way for some sort of convertibility of the ruble as a result of

[38] See Morris Bornstein, "The Reform and Revaluation of the Ruble," *American Economic Review*, March, 1961, pp. 117–123.

their revaluation.[39] They may also be planning to use the ruble price structure to value their foreign trade transactions, since it undoubtedly irritates them to have to use capitalist market prices in their trade agreements. However, the proposed revision of producers' goods prices in 1963 does not seem to be adding a great deal to the production costs of producers' goods so that these commodities will undoubtedly still seem to be bargains to any country fortunate enough to have their imports of capital goods from the Soviet Union valued at these Russian internal prices. In effect, the internal Soviet price structure can be described as a sort of "reverse price scissors," with industrial product prices on the lower blade and food and consumers' goods on the upper blade. It would seem that the use of such a relative price system to value items entering into foreign trade might tend to provide a windfall gain to developing countries—both within and outside the bloc—in much the same manner that the present world market price structure creates hardships for the developing areas.

An interesting question arises concerning the reason why the Russians should consider it necessary to declare that gold is the theoretical backing for their currency, and, furthermore, that the ruble is thereby strengthened as a result of this currency backing. For example, when the Soviets decided to revalue the ruble in terms of gold on January 1, 1961, Finance Minister Garbuzov claimed that "our Soviet ruble is today the only currency whose gold content has increased compared with the gold standard

---

[39] A hint that the ruble would become fully convertible was made by Deputy Premier Mikoyan, according to William Benton who predicted that there would be a "death grapple between the ruble and the dollar" designed to drive the dollar out of world trade. See "A Soviet Revolution in Finance Foreseen," *New York Times,* April 9, 1959, p. 3. See also Harry Schwartz, "Q. and A. on the Ruble," *New York Times,* November 20, 1960, Section IV, p. 6E. A leading Soviet economist, K. V. Ostrovitianov, vice president of the Soviet Academy of Sciences, also predicted at the Twenty-first Party Congress that the ruble would become an international currency and begin to supplant the dollar in foreign trade. See Harry Schwartz, "Ruble Envisioned As Top Currency," *New York Times,* February 17, 1959, p. 2.

period when banknotes were exchanged freely for gold." [40] At times it even seems as if Soviet conservatism in this respect is greater than that of some of our leading banking executives.[41]

Soviet respect for gold as a backing for currency probably goes back to Marx's writings on the subject. In the nineteenth century, gold was an important full backing for currencies generally and gold discoveries, as well as the operation of the gold standard, meant that gold flows between countries frequently had an impact on the supply of money and to some extent on domestic price levels. Writing in this environment, Marx treated money and its basis, gold, as he would any other commodity, its value being determined in accordance with the labor theory of value. So-called commodity theories of money are now considered old-fashioned by most Western economists since the value of gold is determined primarily by the United States' willingness to purchase and store unlimited quantities at $35 per ounce.[42] Furthermore, modern governments are unwilling to link seriously their money supply to gold. In the United States, for example, the gold reserve requirement behind the Federal Reserve Banks note and deposit liabilities was reduced from 40 down to 25 per cent during World War II, and could easily be eliminated entirely with no repercussions.

[40] *Pravda,* November 16, 1960.

[41] Consider, for example, the speech before the first full convention meeting of the Investment Bankers Association by Henry C. Alexander, chairman of the Morgan Guaranty Trust Company, in which he said that sound money stemmed not from gold reserves, but from efficient production. See Paul Heffernan, "25% Gold Backing of Money Scored," *New York Times,* November 29, 1960, p. 51. The ideas of Roy Reierson, senior vice president of New York's Bankers Trust Company, would also seem liberal in comparison with the official Soviet position on gold and money.

[42] In the absence of the monetary demand for gold and the "gold fetish," the price of gold would no doubt be but a fraction of its current price. For an amusing fable concerning what would happen should gold be abolished from the world's international money system, see the London *Economist,* December 24, 1960. Here it is estimated that the price would eventually fall to $2.50 per ounce. For a brief account of this fable, see Edwin L. Dale, Jr., "Cure Offered for Ailing Dollar: Make Gold Just Another Metal," *New York Times,* December 25, 1960, p. 1.

FOREIGN TRADE POLICY IN
CAPITALIST-ORIENTED
ECONOMIES

In the United States, foreign trade has also expanded irregularly during the past 60 years. As in the case of Soviet trade, the thirties witnessed a sharp decline in our volume of international trade, primarily as a consequence of the worldwide depression and the prevalent "beggar-thy-neighbor" policies of the time. While our exports were over 17 times as high in 1957 as they were in 1900, the nation's output (in undeflated or current prices) was 25 times higher than it was at the turn of the century.[43] Exports of merchandise, which averaged around five or six per cent of our GNP in the early 1900's and also in the twenties, fell to around three or four per cent of GNP in the thirties, and now account for between four and five per cent of our total output. As in the Soviet Union, there has apparently been a tendency over time for our foreign trade to expand more slowly than our total product. Our net export surplus of goods and services, which is considered as part of the investment component of our GNP, has been running around four or five billion dollars yearly. Exports of goods and services in both 1900 and currently seem to be running around one third above imports. In other words, although we might like to increase our relative export surplus and thereby create greater employment opportunities, we have apparently been unable to do so to any great extent. We now consider various aspects of our foreign trade which have already been examined for the noncapitalist-oriented Soviet economy.

1. *Structure of foreign trade.* At the beginning of the twentieth century, the United States was largely independent of foreign

---

[43] See U.S. Department of Commerce, *Historical Statistics of the United States, Colonial Times to 1957,* pp. 562–563. Although the data are not deflated, the relative lag in the growth of foreign trade is not affected since both foreign trade and total output data should be inflated by approximately the same extent.

raw material supplies. At present, however, materials imported into the United States in crude or semi-manufactured forms, comprise well over half of our total imports. Among the individual commodities for which ratios of imports to total supply ranged from 80 to 100 per cent in 1955 and 1959 were the following: tin, nickel, manganese, industrial diamonds, chromite, cobalt, platinum, titanium, carpet wool, and natural rubber.[44] Of increasing importance as import items are: long-staple cotton, copper, jute, burlap, asbestos, mica, newsprint, aluminum and bauxite, tungsten, lead, zinc, iron ore, and petroleum products. As our low cost domestic supplies are becoming depleted, we are increasingly looking for cheaper imports. Such developments as the present import restrictions on the importation of inexpensive foreign oil, or the import quotas on lead and zinc, seem to be contrary to our overall trends in this connection.

With respect to exports, finished and semi-finished manufactures are looming larger over time until now they account for about three-fourths of all merchandise exports. The largest drop in exports has been felt by crude materials, which now comprise only a little over 10 per cent of our total exports. As we have matured, our comparative advantage with the rest of the world (excluding the USSR) seems to have shifted to capital-intensive products and away from labor-intensive ones, in much the same manner as is the case in the Soviet Union.

2. *Balance of trade.* The United States was a debtor nation before World War I. Although we tended to export more commodities than we imported after 1873, interest and dividend payments on early British and European investments in United States securities and mortgages more than balanced the account. Gradually we too began to invest in such less developed economies as Canada and in Latin America. Since World War I, our investments abroad have generally exceeded foreigners' investments in this country. Partly as a result of this net investment abroad, merchandise exports have generally continued to exceed merchandise imports by large amounts. In the early sixties, these

[44] *Statistical Abstract of the United States, 1961*, p. 720.

exports were running around $20 billion while imports totaled about $15 billion. Our export surplus amounts to about one per cent of our GNP, and about five per cent of our total investment. Although this seems to be but a small addition to our investment sector, it is the same as domestic investment from the standpoint of income-determination, and this export surplus also produces important secondary or multiplier effects on our economy as a result of further spending and respending.[45]

3. *United States trade policy in developing areas and Western Europe.* Following our assistance to Western Europe in the rebuilding of their war-damaged economies, we have turned increasingly to the task of assisting the developing countries, no doubt stimulated in part by Soviet activities in some of these same areas.[46] In comparison with the Soviet assistance program, our aid program seems much more impressive. Between 1946 and 1960, the United States supplied economic aid to underdeveloped countries valued at about $20 billion and private investment of about eight billion dollars.[47] In addition, the West European nations have also received $26 billion in economic aid.

One of our chief assets in assisting the developing areas is our agricultural surplus. Since some sort of agricultural surplus seems to be a precondition for industrial development, countries which are unable to provide their own surplus may be able to rely on the bountiful nature of our agricultural sector to feed and clothe workers engaged in capital accumulating projects. Because Soviet agricultural produce is still required to feed her own people, as

[45] A multiplier effect is also exercised by the intangible items in our balance on current account. In recent years, these intangible imports, arising primarily because of the activities of our tourists abroad, have exceeded our intangible exports and reduced the employment effect of our merchandise export surplus. Our government efforts to stimulate tourism in the United States by foreigners—as a result of the creation of the U.S. Travel Service in 1961—is designed to rectify this leakage.

[46] As H. J. P. Arnold indicates, "is it not possible that, in the absence of the 'cold war' the less-developed countries would have received less aid?" See "West Far Ahead of Soviet in Aid," *New York Times,* May 20, 1962, p. 53.

[47] *Ibid.*

well as people within the Soviet bloc, they are unable to match our efforts in this respect.

In some cases, our commitments to the developing countries have been more conservative and our political demands more exacting than those of the Russians. For example, our refusal to go along with Colonel Nasser's beloved Aswan Dam was justified by the fact that the project was uneconomic in scope. Our governmental loans for capital expansion are frequently limited to certain areas where private investors will not invest. The United States executive branch is also forced to follow an especially cautious line in selling agricultural produce or making loans to countries which are either in the Soviet bloc (Poland) or in the neutralist camp (Yugoslavia or Ghana) since our Congressmen are apparently unable to distinguish between the many shades and gradations of socialism and communism. Frequently our assistance is given to these countries only after a great debate, much of which undoubtedly alienates the recipients. Thus, when Ghana sought financial assistance with her Volta River Project, there was a long investigation of Nkrumah's politics. Our final financing is to be in stages, with the possibility that our aid might be withdrawn should Ghana fail to live up to our expectations.[48]

Since the recovery of Western Europe from World War II and the restoration there of stable capitalist-oriented economies, a great deal of our foreign trade policy has been aimed at shutting off or restricting the shipment of critical materials to the Soviet bloc. In this connection, it is apparently hoped that the Common Market will provide enough trade within the West European countries to make greater East-West trade less tempting.[49] It is certainly possible that in the process of creating a

[48] See E. W. Kenworthy, "U.S. Annoyance Defers Ghana Aid," *New York Times,* September 23, 1961, p. 8.

[49] The development of a unified Western trade policy within the framework of the Common Market in an attempt to stop the profitable trade with the Soviet bloc, is specifically advocated by Samuel Pisar, who accompanied Senator Jacob K. Javits on a trip to the USSR in 1961. See Felix Belair, Jr., "Trade With Reds Scored at Inquiry," *New York Times,* December 9, 1961, p. 19. For an attempt to use the mechanism of the Common Market to restrict the imports of Soviet oil to 10 per cent of the European

large free trade area in Western Europe, certain economies of large-scaled production and greater specialization within this area will stimulate investment activities, at least in the short run. Whether it will provide rates of return which are comparable to those currently being earned on trade with the Soviet bloc is somewhat conjectural however.

If and when the Common Market is finally organized, it would seem to be only a question of time before the United States joins—either as a full or associate member. The high priority which the Kennedy Administration assigned to the Trade Expansion Act of 1962 (H.R. 9900) is indicative of the direction in which our trade policy with respect to Europe is rapidly moving.[50] This act will empower the President to cut all tariff rates by as much as 50 per cent during the next five years. The Administration's policy is to bargain down the Common Market's external tariff by offering mutual concessions so that the United States can sell to Europe on a competitive basis. In tying in our economy to the rapidly expanding European economies, it is hoped that some of their full employment and growth will rub off on us. Since they have relatively full employment and adequate effective demand and we have superior productivity and lower costs, it stands to reason that we should on balance be able to create some additional employment for ourselves as a result of our effective entry into this free trade area. Among the reasons given by Secretary of Commerce Luther H. Hodges in his testimony supporting the bill was the claim that several million jobs would be created for workers in this country—many times the number likely to be wiped out as a result of our concessions.[51] As a result of the expected increase in our exports of several billion dollars, our balance of payments difficulties would also be lessened.

Economic Community's total oil requirements, see J. H. Carmical, "Market to Study Importing Oil," *New York Times,* September 30, 1962, Section III, F 1.

[50] For a good digest of the Administration's arguments, see John D. Morris, "Kennedy Drives for Trade Bill," *New York Times,* March 18, 1962, Section IV, p. E-5.

[51] This employment effect was also stressed in President Kennedy's message of January 25, 1962. For a criticism of this "advantage" of the

4. *United States imperialism.* According to some authorities on the subject, capitalist imperialism describes the economic relationships that develop between advanced capitalist economies on the one hand, and underdeveloped countries on the other.[52] The general pattern which supposedly results from this highest stage of capitalism is one in which the advanced country regards the underdeveloped countries as being: (1) a source of raw materials; (2) an outlet for capital investment; and (3) a market for its manufactured goods. As the inner contradictions under capitalism become intolerable, the foreign economic relations between the advanced capitalist countries and the more backward areas develop along the indicated lines. As far as the underdeveloped country is concerned, this means that heavy industry is generally not allowed to get started and their economy is frequently unduly dependent on the export of a few crucial raw materials to realize foreign exchange. This dependence on several raw materials is sometimes limited to a single crop in which case it is usually referred to as "monoculture." The frequent oversupply of certain raw materials thus presents the problem of inadequate and widely fluctuating sources of foreign exchange for the country that is dependent on a single export crop.

While there is undoubtedly considerable suffering today in the underdeveloped countries throughout the world, it seems at least debatable to attribute this hardship to economic imperialism, particularly the type of economic imperialism supposedly pursued by the United States.[53] Economic development in these overpopulated, undernourished lands is not an uncomplicated task, and it seems possible that the suffering might be even greater had not the United States exported capital—including

bill and an interpretation that this claimed advantage had somehow escaped the red pencil of President Kennedy's advisors, see Seymour E. Harris, "United States Trade and the Common Market," *Current History,* August, 1962, p. 70.

[52] For a contemporary Marxist view of imperialism, see Paul M. Sweezy, "A Marxist View of Imperialism," in *The Present As History,* Monthly Review Press, New York, 1953, p. 79.

[53] The results of our colonial imperialism are on display in both Puerto Rico and in the Philippines. While levels of living in these two countries are certainly not high by our standards, they are higher in both countries

technical education—into these areas. We know from experience that the process of capital accumulation has involved sacrifices in most economies in which it has taken place, and to the extent that some of the capital is provided from abroad, the burden of economic development should be lessened, and the rate of development accelerated.[54]

This is not meant to imply that only good can come from these economic relationships between developed and underdeveloped countries, since the international price scissors undoubtedly seriously reduces some of the benefits of our capital exports. For example, it seems likely that the decline in the prices of Latin America's raw materials between 1953 and 1961 may have wiped out most of the gains attempted by the Alliance for Progress program in the first year of its operation.[55] On the other hand, the occasional expropriation or confiscation of capital investment by the developing countries probably tends to even the score somewhat. For example, many United States loans to Latin America in the twenties were defaulted in the early thirties.

---

than they are in nearby underdeveloped countries. In Puerto Rico, for example, per capita net income has almost doubled in the past decade and its level of about $700 is now among the highest in Latin America. See "Puerto Rico's Economy Sets Record for Growth," *New York Times,* September 30, 1962, Section III, p. F 12.

[54] The sacrifices were most evident in Great Britain during the first half of the nineteenth century and in the USSR in the thirties. Certain natural advantages in our own development—including foreign investment and bountiful natural resources—undoubtedly lessened the burden on our citizens. This advantage of capital exports was apparently recognized by Lenin who claimed that "the export of capital greatly affects and accelerates the development of capitalism in those countries to which it is exported." See V. I. Lenin, *Imperialism, The Highest Stage of Capitalism,* International Publishers, New York, 1939, p. 65.

[55] According to Brazil's Ambassador to the United States, Roberto Campos, the average price of Latin American exports to the United States declined by 20 per cent between 1953 and 1961, while the prices of United States exports rose by 10 per cent. See Juan de Onis, "Lags in Alliance for Progress Scrutinized at Brazil Parley," *New York Times,* August 9, 1962, p. 11. Colombia's Finance Minister, Jorge Palacio, claims that his country had lost 2 to 3 times as much foreign income from falling prices as it had received in Alliance for Progress credits. See Juan de Onis, "Latins Criticize Washington Aid," *New York Times,* April 24, 1962, p. 1.

Examples where considerable benefit was obtained from the seizure of foreign investments by the developing areas are the nationalization of the Suez Canal by the UAR, the nationalization of Mexican oil, Bolivian tin, and Brazilian electric power plants, and the seizure of most everything foreign-owned that Castro's Cuba could get its hands on.

The impact of recessions in mature capitalist-oriented economies on the primary producing countries is also unfavorable. As a result of the decline in prices of their export products and the concomitant stickiness in the prices of imports, the primary producing countries' loss in both real income and the capacity to import was estimated by the United Nations at two billion dollars during our 1958 recession.[56]

One of the first impacts of penetration by developed countries in the underdeveloped areas is usually a sharp reduction in infant mortality, since sanitary conditions must be improved before technical personnel from advanced economies can be induced to come into these areas. This improvement in health conditions usually reduces infant mortality, increases population pressure, and a food shortage frequently develops. Thus, countries which were formerly self-sufficient are often compelled to import food for the first time. Social capital or public utilities such as transportation, electric power, and communications are also developed by the advanced countries, at least those facilities required to remove the inexpensive raw materials. These facilities are also frequently subject to nationalization or controls in the event of a revolution. Generally speaking, the underdeveloped areas have in the past relied on the developed capitalist-oriented economies for imports of such things as iron and steel products, chemicals, and machinery. But they are increasingly developing their own heavy industries as a result of capital assistance from both the Western and Soviet blocs.

5. *Value of the dollar.* The value of currencies, including the dollar, is determined and maintained by the actual, as opposed to the potential, productiveness of the respective economies. In recent years, however, there has been a great deal of worry about

[56] See *New York Times,* May 26, 1959, p. 3.

the so-called "weakening" of the dollar in the eyes of our international bankers due to our chronic balance of payments deficit and the resulting outflow of gold.

In this connection, it is sometimes argued that we have priced ourselves out of world markets by allowing our money wages to rise faster than our labor productivity resulting in rising unit labor costs. Yet in recent years wage increases in our economy have been among the smallest and our price level is perhaps the stablest in the Western world, while West European wages and prices are both rising by significantly greater amounts each year. It may be true that productivity is also rising faster in Western Europe than it is in the United States, but studies of comparative costs in Europe as compared with the United States still show that we have generally lower production costs than either the West Europeans or Japanese in the vast majority of industries. Thus, there would seem to be a sound economic basis for our annual export surplus of roughly five billion dollars worth of goods.[57]

Despite this so-called "favorable" balance of trade, we have been running a balance of payments deficit for some time. This is due to the fact that our income from the goods and services we sell falls short of the dollar outflow for our merchandise imports, tourism, foreign aid and investment, and military outlays. The basic factors underlying this condition would seem to be more political than economic. In the postwar years, when we spread out into the international political vacuum of the time, we tended to overcommit our resources both politically and militarily. Now that the developing areas are growing more restive and demanding more assistance, the combined demands of our military and foreign aid requirements are chronically exceeding our surplus of exports over imports. The problem has become one of getting the now thriving West European economies to share more of our current and future burden—both for foreign aid and military outlays.

There are a number of things which are being done to reduce

[57] Even if we exclude exports financed by foreign aid, our commercial trade shows a surplus of three billion dollars. See *New York Times,* September 21, 1962, p. 6.

our balance of payments deficit and restore the wavering confidence of the international banking community. Our military outlays which constitute an important source of the difficulty, are
being pared.[58] Unnecessary bases abroad are being closed; de-
pendents of servicemen remain in the United States rather than
join their husbands where they in effect would become permanent tourists draining our foreign exchange supplies. More
military supplies are being procured within the United States
rather than being bought from foreigners, despite the fact that
the cost of our supplies is thereby increased. The merchandise
that tourists from the United States can bring into the country is
being limited and a U.S. Travel Service was established in June,
1961 to encourage visitors from abroad.[59] With respect to
foreign aid, more provisions are being made to require the
countries being assisted to buy their capital goods in the United
States, regardless of whether or not we offer the lowest price. In
other words, although our overall interests are served by freer
trade, our overextended military and political commitments are
forcing us to become more restrictive in an effort to reduce our
balance of payments deficit.

USES OF FOREIGN TRADE AS
REFLECTION OF BASIC
PROBLEMS

Noncapitalist-oriented economies approach foreign trade from
much the same standpoint as we did during World War II.
Because of the seller's market for most products, our merchandise
export surplus (excluding Lend-Lease and Reciprocal Aid) dis-

[58] See James N. Wallace, "Pentagon Presses Drive to Cut Outlays
Abroad, Curb Outflow of Gold," *Wall Street Journal,* July 27, 1962, p. 1.
[59] In the first four months of 1962, visitors from overseas increased by
16 per cent in comparison with the same period in the previous year,
before the first official effort to attract tourists. See "Foreign Tourists on
the Rise in U.S.," *New York Times,* August 3, 1962, p. 25.

appeared and we imported more than we exported between 1942 and 1944.[60] Our exports of crude foodstuffs, which had accounted for over eight per cent of our total outflow in 1938 dropped to less than one per cent of the total in 1942. Gold, which before the war was flowing in so rapidly that it had to be "sterilized," became a valuable asset to pay for needed imports under wartime conditions. The large gold inflows in 1939 and 1940 dwindled and were replaced by large gold exports towards the end of the war. In 1944, a new record outflow was recorded when over $800 million worth of gold was shipped out, presumably to pay for more useful commodities from abroad.

As long as advanced capitalist-oriented economies are willing to accept gold in exchange for useful commodities exported to the Soviet bloc, or will consider giving credit for Soviet bloc purchases, the basic complementarity of the two types of economies should insure a continued expansion of East-West trade in the long run. The buyer's market of the West and the seller's market of the East would seem to fit together like the proverbial hand-in-glove.

Recommended Readings

ALLEN, ROBERT LORING, "Economic Motives in Soviet Foreign Trade Policy," *The Southern Economic Journal,* October, 1958, pp. 189–201.

———, "An Interpretation of East-West Trade," in *Comparisons of the United States and Soviet Economies,* Part II, pp. 403–426.

ALTMAN, OSCAR L., "Russian Gold and the Ruble," International Monetary Fund, *Staff Papers,* April, 1960, pp. 416–438.

AUBREY, HENRY G., "Sino-Soviet Economic Activities in Less Developed Countries," in *Comparisons of the United States and Soviet Economies,* Part II, pp. 445–466.

[60] See *Statistical Abstract of the United States 1944–45,* pp. 525, 534, and 537.

BERLINER, JOSEPH S., *Soviet Economic Aid,* Praeger, New York, 1958, especially Chapter 7, "Soviet Economic Gains from the Aid Program."

GRANICK, D., "The Pattern of Foreign Trade in Eastern Europe and Its Relation to Economic Development Policy," *The Quarterly Journal of Economics,* August, 1954, pp. 377–400.

HOEFFDING, OLEG, "Recent Trends in Soviet Foreign Trade," in *The Annals of the American Academy of Political and Social Science,* January, 1956, pp. 75–88.

HOLZMAN, FRANKLYN D., "Some Financial Aspects of Soviet Foreign Trade," in *Comparisons of the United States and Soviet Economies,* Part II, pp. 427–444.

MENDERSHAUSEN, HORST, "Terms of Trade Between the Soviet Union and Smaller Communist Countries," 1955–57, *Review of Economics and Statistics,* May, 1959, pp. 106–118 and follow-up paper in May, 1960.

NOVE, ALEC, "Soviet Trade and Soviet Aid," *Lloyd's Bank Review,* January, 1959, pp. 1–19.

SCOTT, N. B., "Sino-Soviet Trade," *Soviet Studies,* October, 1958, pp. 151–161.

———, "The Organisation and Technique of Soviet Foreign Trade," *Soviet Studies,* Vol. X, No. 4, April, 1959, pp. 393–400.

STOLT, RICHARD G., editor, *The Western Economy and Its Future as Seen by Soviet Economists,* International Film and Publications, Montreal, 1958, pp. 37–42. An interview given by N. S. Khrushchev to Eric Ridder and Heinz Luedicke of the *Journal of Commerce.*

TURGEON, LYNN, "The Significance of Soviet Trade Policies," *Illinois Business Review,* July, 1961, pp. 6–8.

XII ∾ The Roads to Affluence

IN THE PRECEDING CHAPTERS, an attempt has been made to show that a mature capitalist-oriented economy such as that of the United States in peacetime and noncapitalist-oriented economies generally are in many respects mirror-images of each other—in much the same fashion that our World War II economy differed from our peace-time economy. What is an asset or advantage for the one becomes a liability or disadvantage for the other. Each country would no doubt relish the idea of having to put up with the other country's problems for awhile. We could use a little more of their ample effective demand and they could certainly make good use of our growing labor and materials surplus.[1]

At the same time that we have stressed the complementary nature of the two types of economies and their diametrically opposite problems, we have also attempted to show that our own contemporary economic problems are to some extent different from those which we faced in the nineteenth century. In fact, in

[1] To some extent, the same comparison could be made in the early sixties between the United States and some of the West European countries. In commenting on President Kennedy's statement that he had a problem of 25,000 new workers to employ each week, a European economist is reported to have said, "I wish we had them. The United States seems to have got twisted. It regards as a problem its greatest asset: more machines and more labor. If we had more of both, particularly more machines, we might catch up to you." See Edwin L. Dale, Jr., "Trouble for U.S., Boon for Europe," *New York Times,* February 25, 1962, p. 3.

many respects the present problems of noncapitalist-oriented economies *were* our own problems a half century or more ago. This is also true for the underdeveloped capitalist-oriented economies. Their economic difficulties today in some respects resemble those problems which we faced a long time ago, as well as those confronting Soviet planners before the industrialization drive began in the late twenties. It is therefore not surprising to find that the educated leadership in these hopefully developing areas is studying both Soviet and United States developmental experience in search for some key to the door leading to their "take-off" and eventual success in overcoming abject poverty.

To the extent that the leaders in the developing areas wish to emulate either the United States or the USSR—or develop a synthesis of the two approaches—certain policy implications would seem to be self-evident. It should be borne in mind, however, that what we might consider an ideal economic policy may be inconsistent with the political realities of the situation.[2] We might recapitulate briefly some of the problems and institutions which seem to have developed—or failed to develop—under what we may loosely term our nineteenth century or capital accumulating conditions.

In the agricultural sector, we have seen that the creation and extraction of an agricultural surplus is a necessary precondition for industrial development—unless of course this surplus can be obtained abroad. In developing this surplus, it would seem that there may be certain advantages to both large-scaled farming operations and the intense utilization of available agricultural machinery. Thus, when developing countries are considering the break-up of their large estates as a result of some sort of "land reform," they should make certain that they do not reduce

---

[2] An obvious example of this conflict between the economically desirable and the politically feasible occurred in British Guiana in 1962 when an eminent British economist, Nicolas Kaldor, drew up an austerity budget designed to get British Guiana's development started. However, the announcement of the budget resulted in a general strike that culminated in two days of rioting and damage estimated at $30 million. See Seth S. King, "Riots Are a Familiar Story to Tax Economist," *New York Times,* February 20, 1962, p. 13.

agricultural productivity in the process of obtaining greater equity. The problem of extracting the surplus would seem to be best handled through the operation of some sort of internal price-scissors—allowing either market forces or compulsory deliveries of agricultural products at nominal prices to work against the immediate interests of the farmers. Certainly there is no necessity for any agricultural price support or subsidy program at this point. If the large estates are broken up, some sort of arrangement for the pooling and cooperative use of scarce agricultural machinery under government auspices would also seem to be a minimum requirement.

With regard to levels of living, it is an accepted maxim among development economists that substantial increases in current consumption must be foregone in order to achieve significant economic growth. However, levels of living are not only determined by consumption of goods. Improvement in health standards and education are also indicators of rising levels of living. In the process of restricting increases in consumption in order to plow back resources for future benefits, it is possible that the allowance for a certain amount of inflation may tend to force the required savings out of the population with less damaging effects on morale than would be the case with more orthodox methods. If there are questions of equity as a result of the inflationary process, these might be better answered by instituting formal rationing rather than by the government's attempting to pursue deflationary or "tight" monetary policies. This is particularly true in situations where strong labor unions have developed as they have in Argentina, if the chaotic events there in 1962 are any indication. Such institutions as a highly developed advertising sector, market research activity, and consumers' instalment credit should be avoided if possible. If there is ever a time when Say's Law—that supply creates its own demand—works, it is during periods of capital accumulation. Advanced social security programs—particularly unemployment insurance, old age pensions, limitations on the length of the work week, etc.—should be kept to a minimum, although some sort of public health program may be necessary, especially where an undernourished populace exists. In the absence of the puritan ethic, some type of austerity campaign may be required to limit the hedonistic appetites of the population.

In obtaining the necessary supply and cooperation of labor, fairly large wage differentials may be useful in stimulating productivity, encouraging personal investments in technical education, and at the same time acting as somewhat of a brake on increases in current consumption. Incentives to attract woman power into the labor force may be created by allowing the real wage of the principal breadwinner to decline. Western-type trade unions, to the extent that they direct their efforts towards greater wage equality and resistance to the use of piecework, may actually play a negative role in the early stage of economic development. Certainly there is no place for Wagner Acts, child labor laws, or minimum wage legislation in the early stages of industrialization.

In the area of management, production-oriented engineers would seem to make more satisfactory administrators as compared with sales-oriented business administration types. High rates of return to capital should be tolerated, if not actually encouraged. In this connection, it seems clear that there is no point in having government antitrust activity under such conditions.

In the field of public finance, greater government activity in the construction of social capital, even if a budgetary deficit results, would seem to be called for. Military expenditures, on the other hand, should be kept to the minimum conducive to domestic tranquility. As for taxes, regressive taxation and the resulting encouragement of saving and investment by private individuals would seem to be called for; progressive income taxation, inheritance taxes, and capital levies should be avoided. Mass subscriptions to government bonds, on the other hand, may be of some use in giving workers a feeling of participation in the development of social capital projects.

With respect to the flow of trade, an import surplus or so-called "unfavorable" balance of trade, particularly if the loans it reflects can be financed at low rates of interest, would seem appropriate in the early stages of development. Restrictive tariffs, or import controls of some sort, rather than free trade would be desirable to allow specific infant industries to get started. If there is a danger that the entrepreneurial profits of business may be "wasted" through the importation of symbols of conspicuous consumption, or on luxurious foreign travel or education, strict government foreign exchange controls may become imperative.

It would seem that our economic institutions that developed largely without any conscious planning in the nineteenth century were highly useful in facilitating our capital accumulation. On the other hand, as our twentieth century institutions have developed, they have tended to reflect something other than the need for more accumulation. Questions of equity become more urgent, as well as more feasible, after a period of intense capital accumulation. Such institutions as strong trade unions, progressive income and inheritance taxes, farm subsidy programs, and social security programs and other institutional developments commonly associated with the mature capitalist-oriented welfare state become not only possible but necessary.

As the potentialities for more than mere human existence increase, questions naturally arise concerning *where* this is all going to lead; *what* we want to do with our tremendous productive potential; *when* we can expect to reach a stage of comparative affluence for all; and *how* this will all transpire. Soviet ideologists, basing their work to some extent on the writings of Marx and Engels, have been thinking in vague terms about these questions for a number of decades, even though the possibilities for implementing their answers must have seemed remote indeed. We first examine their comparatively well-reasoned outline for future development along their road to affluence, and then look at our initial response to the growing Soviet challenge.

GOALS FOR NONCAPITALIST-ORIENTED ECONOMIES

In the USSR—which at present must be classified as a relatively frugal economy—the goal of all goals is communism, their somewhat austere version of the affluent society.[3] According to the official Soviet ideology, what are some of the economic characteristics of this goal?

1. *Absolute abundance*. First and foremost, there will be such an abundance of goods and services that it will become possible to supply *all* of the needs of all of the members of society.[4] In most economies today, including the Soviet economy, there are a few elite individuals who, for all practical purposes, have already attained this goal. As time goes by and productivity increases, more and more members of society should be admitted to this presently exclusive club.[5]

2. *Mental and physical labor*. Ultimately there would also be no distinction between mental and physical labor. At present there seems to be a universal preference for mental as opposed to physical labor. Gradually more and more people can be expected to receive technical training permitting them to design, construct, and maintain the machines performing man's more

[3] For an up-to-date version of this theoretic goal, see Premier Khrushchev's speech at the Twenty-first Party Congress as translated in *The Current Digest of the Soviet Press*, March 11, 1959, p. 13. Cf., also, *Problems of Economics*, Vol. I, No. 9, January, 1959, pp. 46–67. The latter is an account of a meeting of the Social Science Departments of the USSR Academy of Sciences held in Moscow in June, 1958. For a more recent version, see Premier Khrushchev's two-volume report of the Central Committee of the C.P.S.U. to the Twenty-second Party Congress of October 17, 1961, Crosscurrents Press, New York. The latter contains goals for the Twenty-Year Plan giving more concrete details of expected developments along the road during the sixties and seventies. See also Harry Schwartz, "What's Communism? Does Russia Have It?" *New York Times Magazine*, October 15, 1961.

[4] The range of commodities and services envisaged by the Soviet ideologists would still probably not be as great as that currently available in our country.

[5] If there were an absolute abundance of goods or an absence of scarcity, money and prices, including wages, would appear to be redundant—as well as a good many jobs which owe their existence to conditions of scarcity. Among the economies of communist distribution, we might mention the elimination of the following activities: billing, dunning and repossessing; banking and credit; guarding property (ticket-takers, checkout librarians, night watchmen, and much of the legal superstructure); and (alas!) most economists.

arduous work. Automation is undoubtedly expected to play an important role in the eventual elimination of physical labor. Closely connected with the above characteristic of communism is the changing nature of people's attitudes towards work. At present most individuals experience some disutility in connection with their jobs, either the nature of the job itself, or the number of hours of work required since they may obtain some positive utility from the first few hours at their job. As time goes by, the required number of hours of labor will probably be shortened gradually until eventually some people may be working voluntarily in excess of the minimum. According to Krushchev, three or four-hour days and 15 or 20 hour weeks seem to be within the realm of practicality. If realized, Marx's prediction that labor would some day become a "prime necessity of life" might seem to hold true.

3. *Rural and urban living.* There would also be no difference between rural and urban living. The objective of society would be to raise rural levels of living up to the higher urban level. Small agricultural communities with apartment-type housing plus urban cultural facilities would presumably develop something along the lines of Premier Krushchev's abortively-suggested agrogorods, as described in Chapter V.

4. *Role of the state.* Finally, there would be a "withering away of the state." National armies would be unnecessary, although the "administration of things" would still be required. During the Stalinist era, the Soviet ideologists claimed that there were as yet no signs of this development because of the hostile capitalist encirclement. Consequently, the state was becoming stronger rather than weaker. In November, 1957, however, Premier Khrushchev began to talk about the state withering away to the degree that socialism was moving towards communism. Apparently the decentralization of industrial management earlier that year, as well as some success that had been achieved in cutting administration costs, might have given Khrushchev the idea that the long-awaited withering process was at last beginning. The subsequent reductions in the Soviet armed forces

in the late fifties might have also been cited as harbingers of things to come. However, the increased defense appropriations of the Kennedy Administration, the Soviet response, the growing crisis over Berlin, coming as they did on the eve of the Draft Program seem to have postponed any firm ideological commitment by the Communist Party with respect to the present withering away of the state.[6]

Given the above capsulized version of the ultimate communist goal, the Soviet theoreticians profess to see their collective dreams being gradually fulfilled as a result of the following developments: the catching up with and overtaking of the most advanced capitalist economy in per capita production and eventually in per capita consumption; the growing importance of technically trained personnel in the composition of their labor force; the substantial reductions achieved and planned for the compulsory work week; the narrowing of the differences between collective farmers and urban proletariat via the substitution of guaranteed and sometimes advance wage payments for the currently predominant cooperative division of agricultural income; the relative growth of state farms resembling their industrial counterparts, the factories; the reduced inequalities in the wage and salary structure; and the decentralization of certain administrative decision-making.

At the present time, the Russians distribute much more of their social product free of charge than we do in the West, particularly in the United States. As times goes on, they plan to expand the range of commodities and services which are distributed without prices. According to Soviet calculations, about one-fourth of the current incomes of workers is distributed "on the basis of need," and by 1980 roughly one-half of their then much larger real incomes will be so distributed. In addition to most medical and educational services, which are at present distributed freely, the Soviet government will supply without prices all transportation, housing, and public utilities. The mid-day meal, which is the

---

[6] See Myron Rush, "After Khrushchev, What?," *East Europe*, July, 1962, pp. 2–7. As Rush points out, there is no mention of the withering away of the Communist Party under any circumstances.

backbone of the Soviet workers' diet, will also be supplied without charge by 1980.

After World War II, some Soviet theoreticians were advocating the introduction of the free distribution of bread, thinking that this would be an encouraging sign of the promised land.[7] As it turned out, the price of bread fell so low in the early fifties that some suburban livestock raisers began feeding bread to their animals with the result that the government was forced to issue specific legislation against such presently uneconomic practices.[8] Another school of thought apparently feels that children, who are already something of a privileged class in the USSR, may become the first recipients of free food, clothing, and toys.

Still other Soviet writers saw the successive lowering of the price level between 1947 and 1954 as eventually leading to the introduction of communist or free distribution. During this relatively brief period, the prices of most products were at least cut in half. But since then, the government has apparently decided that other things are more important than lower prices. As a result, the price level before the monetary reform of 1961 was still about the same as it was in 1954.

Things which have been given precedence over further price cutting include the following: the revision of the wage structure and norms, which has been accompanied by above-average increases in money wages in the sectors where it has taken place; the improvement of the relative economic position of the Soviet farmers; the provision of economic assistance to the underdeveloped socialist and neutralist countries;[9] the improvement of pensions for elderly members of Soviet society; the elimination of compulsory bond purchases for all persons; and the disappearance

[7] See Ts. A. Stepanian, *"O nekotorykh zakonomernostiakh perekhoda ot sotsializma k kommunizmu"* (About Several Regularities of the Transition from Socialism to Communism), *Voprosy Filosofii* (Problems of Philosophy), No. 2, 1947, p. 34.

[8] A decree of July, 1956, provided for 500 ruble fines for persons caught feeding bread, flour, groats or potatoes to their cattle.

[9] This decision to give economic assistance to the neutralist countries, incidentally, may have precipitated the demise of the so-called "anti-party" group (Kaganovich, Molotov, *et al.*) and is probably at the root of the subsequent disagreements between the USSR on the one hand, and China and Albania on the other.

of income taxes for certain low income groups. All of these measures have either increased the amount of money income in the hands of Soviet citizens or reduced the supply of goods available for domestic consumption, both of which lead to a postponement of further price reductions. It seems clear that any further substantial reductions in the price level will not take place until after 1965 at least; if the plans for increasing communal consumption in the Twenty-Year Plan are carried out, the price level should remain more or less as its present position in relation to the level of money wages until 1980.

Since the reduction of the compulsory work week in the late fifties, the Russians have been making detailed investigations into the way people have been utilizing their time away from work. These findings indicate that the benefits thus far have been largely realized by male workers who are inclined to be European in their approach to shopping, work around the kitchen, and household responsibilities generally. As a result, there has been pressure from the distaff side for more precooked meals, child care facilities, and self-service shopping so as to permit Soviet women to enjoy some of the benefits from the shorter work week.[10] It seems obvious that such studies of the uses of leisure will have increasing relevance if the Russians are serious about moving towards a 15 or 20-hour work week.

GOALS FOR CAPITALIST-ORIENTED ECONOMIES

The impressive success of the noncapitalist-oriented economies in fulfilling their planned targets in the postwar years has appar-

[10] In this connection, see Margaret Miller, "The Problems of Leisure: the Soviet View," *The Listener,* April 13, 1961, p. 641. For an interesting account of these studies, see G. Prudensky and B. Kolpakov, "Questions Concerning the Calculation of Non-Working Time in Budget Statistics," *Problems of Economics,* Vol. IV, No. 12, April, 1962, pp. 29–33. According to this source, there has been a decline in the gap between the free time available for men and women since 1923–24. Nevertheless, Soviet men still have almost twice as much free time as Soviet women.

ently stimulated considerable thinking in the United States about whether or not planning is consistent with the paramount goal set forth by our founding fathers—to guard the rights of the individual, to insure his development, and to enlarge his opportunity.[11] Although we seem to have developed a built-in bias against government planning outside our own defense establishment, it is becoming increasingly evident that some sort of economic guide-lines or goals are going to become more commonplace in the United States, as well as in other capitalist-oriented economies.

There are already a number of schools of thought on the subject of growthmanship and the proper role which government can play in stimulating growth. According to the consensus of the President's Commission on National Goals, "the economy should grow at the maximum rate consistent with primary dependence upon free enterprise and the avoidance of marked inflation." There was also general agreement that increased investment in the public sector was compatible with this goal, although the report is rather vague as to whether this increase should be of a relative or absolute nature—or where and for what purposes this investment in the public sector would take place. Although it was concluded that an annual increase in our GNP of 3.4 per cent was possible in the sixties without extraordinary stimulating measures, there were a number of dissenters who felt that we should shoot for four or five per cent increases in our pie each year. It should be noted, however, that even the lower rate of increase is considerably above the rate of increase that has been achieved by our economy in the years since our involvement in Korea.

This projected growth rate was considered essential in order to absorb approximately 13.5 million net new additions to our labor force expected in the sixties. Although our average rate of unemployment was 4.5 per cent during the fifties, it was felt that this rate could be lowered below four per cent without risking

[11] The most impressive inquiry into this problem was that undertaken by President Eisenhower's Commission on National Goals and published as a Spectrum paperback, *Goals for Americans,* Prentice-Hall, Englewood Cliffs, N.J., 1960.

any serious inflationary pressures. Thus, the overall employment goal for the sixties involves the creation of something in excess of 13.5 million additional jobs by 1970.[12]

The recommended measures which can be taken to improve on our recent growth and employment record seem conventional enough since they merely call for high levels of demand brought about by "adequate" monetary and fiscal policies. An overhaul in the tax system, including greater depreciation allowances, would be designed to improve the climate for new investment. In general, those "growthmen" who are willing to settle for a lower rate of growth of between three and four per cent are unwilling to expand the relative size of the government investment sector to any great extent; those who advocate aiming for a growth rate of five per cent or more are ready to accept a considerably greater role of government in our investment activity.[13]

Those "minimalists" who accept the lower rate of growth as a satisfactory goal recognize the fact that the relatively greater growth of the service sector which seems to characterize all mature capitalist-oriented economies is a factor which can be expected to bring about lower overall rates of growth over time. These growthmen are also concerned about the effect that greater relative government expansion might have on the climate for private investment. Some of those "maximalists" who advocate the higher rate of growth are more willing to have government investment cut into personal consumption or leisure, while others, such as George Meany, feel that the high rate of growth is necessary in order to avoid cutting into workers' consumption and leisure.

[12] A more recent ten-year projection extending into the seventies reaches a figure of 12.6 million on the assumption that there will be a greater decline in labor force participation rates by young and old men. See Sophia Cooper, "Interim Revised Projection of U.S. Labor Force, 1965–75," *Monthly Labor Review*, Vol. 85, No. 10, 1962, pp. 1089–1099.

[13] For a good exposition of the "minimalist" position, see Howard C. Peterson, "Soviet Economic Growth and U.S. Policy," in *Comparisons of the United States and Soviet Economies*, Part II, pp. 517–527. The "maximalist" position is represented by the earlier Rockefeller Brothers Fund study and also by Harry Schwartz, "Reflections on the Economic Race," in *Comparisons of the United States and Soviet Economies*, Part III, pp. 609–616.

There would seem to be considerable disagreement over the fields where government investment and consumption activity is acceptable. Everyone agrees on investment for and consumption by the Defense Department; most everyone agrees on investment in outer space activities, especially if they are connected with the national prestige or defense considerations; nearly everyone agrees that research and development can be a legitimate field of government activity, particularly if it can be squeezed into the National Defense budget; the vast majority agree that investment abroad is desirable if it preserves presently capitalist-oriented economies; investment in National Defense Highways is fairly certain to win Congressional approval; even education seems to be a proper government investment activity when it comes under the auspices of the National Defense Education Act. Considerably less Congressional enthusiasm and presumably public support can be obtained for domestic nondefense government investment in such needed activities as urban redevelopment or medical research.

When the Kennedy Administration took office, one of the first steps of the Council of Economic Advisers was to set a GNP target of $570 billion for the following year which would be consistent with a balanced budget. However, since the forthcoming private investment activity was disappointing, the recovery was less robust than anticipated and the deficit more ample than planned. As a result, a cut in taxes in the form of increased depreciation allowances and lower income tax rates generally seems to be high on the agenda of government actions designed to get our economic machine moving off its plateau of high level stagnation in 1962. Another innovation of the Kennedy Administration was the informal rule that wage increases be held within the gains in labor productivity or between 2.6 and 3.5 per cent per annum. Here the aims of the Administration were largely achieved since the average wage increase amounted to 3.2 per cent during the first half of 1962, indicating substantial compliance with this new guidepost.[14]

The trouble with many of these developments is that they are

[14] See *New York Times,* July 31, 1962, p. 11.

essentially *ad hoc* answers to short-term problems, as pointed out by the world-renowned political economist, Gunnar Myrdal.[15] In all Europeon economies, on the other hand, the government authorities "make an analytical forecast of what a greater growth rate for five or ten years implies." It seems clear that the impact of the Soviet experience in government planning on capitalist-oriented economies increases as one moves away from the United States and nearer to the USSR. In Japan, for example, targets have been set by the government for the entire decade of the sixties providing for annual increases of 7.8 per cent in their national income; 8.2 per cent for fixed capital investment; and 7.6 per cent in personal consumption. Only slightly less impressive are the goals of the French Four-Year Plan, which is itself being studied intensively by the British Conservatives.[16] The fourth French Four-Year Plan since the end of World War II aims at an annual growth rate of 5.5 per cent. All major industries are involved in drawing up the investment targets of the plan. Most of the detailed work is done by industry committees with a small government planning staff in charge of such things as input-output tables. The British are reportedly considering some modification of the French formula as a result of the formation of a national council with representatives from labor, management, and government to advise on policy. The British are also going ahead with their plan to establish a National Incomes Commission to review trade union demands for wage increases in an effort to achieve greater economic expansion.[17]

In general, these West European moves are all somewhat

[15] See Werner Wiskari, "Myrdal Terms U.S. 'Stagnant'; Urges Wide Economic Reform," *New York Times,* July 22, 1962, p. 38. Myrdal urges the United States to set its sights on achieving a steady growth rate of five to six per cent a year by increasing government spending *and* cutting taxes. He warned that economic stagnation, with its creeping unemployment, could menace the prospects for accelerating the American Negro's progress towards economic equality.

[16] See Edwin L. Dale, Jr., "France Prepares New Four-Year Plan," *New York Times,* August 21, 1961, p. 31; "Britons Explore Economic Plans," *New York Times,* August 24, 1961, p. 39.

[17] "Britain Spurs Plan for Board on Wages," *New York Times,* August 9, 1962, p. 3.

reminiscent of the planning by our own industries as a result of the N.R.A. in 1934. At that time, it was the crisis of the Great Depression that caused us to abandon competition; today it is the Soviet challenge which seems to be moving capitalist-oriented economies away from workable competition and in the direction of greater government and industry planning.

Thus far, not a great deal of attention has been paid to the qualitative aspects of Western economic growth. It is true that the report of President Eisenhower's Commission on National Goals recommended that basic research should be aimed at creating new products and that our economy should become less dependent on superficial changes in style. But it is apparently assumed by both the West Europeans and the Japanese that the pattern of life already established by the near-affluent Americans will eventually prevail. In Western Europe, particularly, there are many signs that they are progressing along essentially the same road as the one we have taken.[18]

The transformation of Western Europe into a durable goods economy has only just begun as indicated by the fact that in Britain only 20 per cent of the blue-collar workers own cars and 35 per cent have washing machines. Nevertheless, their progress has been rapid as judged by the fact that Europe's vehicle population increased by 2.8 million in 1960 compared with our 2.1 million net increase. Along with this growing "Americanization," the British automobile industry is beginning to plan obsolescence along the same lines as Detroit. The age of instalment credit has hit Europe although outstanding debt in Britain is still only about one-fifth of our per capita indebtedness. In 1960 instalment credit rose by 21 per cent in West Germany and by 50 per cent in France. West German advertising also rose by 15 per cent in 1960, while British commercial TV shows a

[18] See the following articles by Edwin L. Dale, Jr., "Europeans Greet Era of Affluence As Mixed Blessing," *New York Times,* December 24, 1959, p. 1; "Europe At Dawn of Affluent Age," *New York Times,* July 16, 1961, p. 15; "Italy Enters the Age of Affluence But Continues to Battle Poverty," *New York Times,* September 18, 1961, p. 1; and " 'Affluence' Begins to Affect Europe," *New York Times Magazine,* January 28, 1962, p. 12.

similarlity to our advertising that, according to one observer, is "breathtaking." The production and sale of comparatively ridiculous consumers' goods is certainly not confined to the United States market. In Great Britain, for example, it was possible to spend the equivalent of roughly $400 for a nailfile with a diamond abrasive surface.[19] Sperry and Hutchinson Company, the largest United States Trading Stamp concern, is about to introduce S&H Green Stamps in the United Kingdom and eventually plans to introduce these stamps in the Common Market countries.[20] Even in Italy, where levels of living are below those in Britain, France, and West Germany, there are signs that the age of affluence has dawned. The consumption of durable consumers' goods, the ultimate badge of affluence, approximately doubled between 1953 and 1960 in Italy.

Occasionally we hear an isolated complaint from people like Vance Packard or J. K. Galbraith that perhaps we should begin to look at the structure of our GNP. Along these lines, A. A. Berle has suggested that we abandon "the style racket in cars and household appliances which organize waste rather than provide honest service."[21] But in general these isolated voices are drowned out by the roar from Madison Avenue.

Although there is general agreement at present that our work week will not be reduced, the continued presence of considerable unemployed labor—coupled with the gradual lowering of the official Soviet work week—will undoubtedly bring greater labor pressure on both government and management for shorter hours at the same rate of pay.[22]

[19] See Thomas P. Ronan, "Thriving Britain on Buying Spree," *New York Times,* December 24, 1959, p. 3. It was almost possible for Mrs. Krobo Edusei, wife of Ghana's Minister of Industries, to purchase a golden bed for the equivalent of $8,400 in London until her husband put his foot down in response to a protest march by the women of Accra. See "That $8,400 Gold Bed Goes Back to the Store," *New York Herald Tribune,* April 4, 1962, p. 2.

[20] See "Invasion of Europe With Green Stamps, Set by S&H," *Wall Street Journal,* August 6, 1962, p. 8.

[21] See "Berle Asks End of Auto Style Racket," *New York Post,* March 8, 1960.

[22] See John D. Pomfret, "Goldberg Fears Plea to Cut Hours," *New York Times,* August 3, 1962, p. 1. In this respect our electricians, who

When asked to look ahead for the next 25 years, notable United States figures were considerably more pessimistic and cautious than their Soviet counterparts.[23] President Kennedy has set the tone for this inquiry by warning that there will be risks, burdens and hardships ahead. The threats to freedom, chaos, and crises of the sixties show no signs of lessening. Our goals consist principally of hopes that we will have learned to use our wealth wisely by the end of this period.

CONVERGENCE OR NONCONVERGENCE?

As presently constituted, the Soviet economy can be described as suffering from supply problems emanating from the chronic seller's market for goods and services, including labor power. Is there a possibility that the Russians may eventually solve their supply problems and then be faced with problems of effective demand and chronic buyer's markets similar to the ones that we are now experiencing? In other words, suppose the Soviet leadership somehow felt secure enough so that they could reduce the frantic pace of their development and begin to plan for fewer resources going into defense and heavy industry, thereby releasing more investment resources for consumers' goods industries. They might also set their overall targets so as not to overcommit their resources quite as much as they are doing at present.[24] As a result

---

are pushing for three or four-hour work-days, would seem to be in the vanguard.

[23] See special issue of *Look*, "The Next 25 Years," January 16, 1962, a project that apparently was stimulated by the Soviet Twenty-Year Plan.

[24] Some Soviet economists asserted prematurely during Plan V (after Stalin's death) that the USSR already had a highly developed heavy industry, and as a consequence, they advocated identical rates of development for both heavy and light industry, or even a higher rate for the latter. See N. A. Bulganin, *op. cit.*, p. 10. At a reception in the spring of 1961, Premier Khrushchev is supposed to have said: "Now we consider our heavy industry as built. So we are not going to give it priority. Light industry and heavy industry will develop at the same pace." However, the new 20-Year Plan targets show that, while the growth rates in heavy

of this policy change, fuller pipe lines in the producers' goods sector as well as consumers' goods inventories at the retail level would undoubtedly develop.

If the time ever came when this were possible, the turnover tax would constitute a remarkably effective instrument to reduce the amount of capital investment or economic "roundaboutness" required. In other words, as goods accumulate at the retail level, the logical step would be to reduce the price level and the over-all gap between prices and production costs via reductions in the turnover tax rates. As aggregate revenue from the turnover tax is reduced, the financial source of new investment is automatically cut, but to no one's chagrin, since this is exactly what is required by the new decision, that is, a lower rate of investment, an increased rate of consumption, and a slow-down in the overall rate of growth. Since the turnover tax is so very important as a source of revenue and investment funds—and no one can be seen to have any vested interest in its continuation—its theoretical elimination provides considerable flexibility with respect to the Soviet's eventual adjustment to their affluent stage and their ability to "taper-off" the capital accumulating process. As we have mentioned in Chapter X, the line drawn between planned profits and the turnover tax is arbitrary so that the same flexibility applies to this other form of government income.

When we discussed management problems in Chapter IX, we noted the importance of unplanned profits, out of which some of the bonuses are paid. This would seem to be the only component of what we might call surplus value which anyone would seem to have a personal vested interest in maintaining. In the same manner that no one should object to reductions in prices and the gap between the wage and price level, no one should object to reductions in the compulsory work week. If the Soviet economy ever approaches affluence, the compulsory work week may even be lowered without the proviso that the same output

---

and light industry will become closer during the sixties, they are scheduled to widen again in the seventies with heavy industry enjoying about the same priority that it had in the fifties. See *New York Times,* July 31, 1961, p. 2.

be turned out in the shorter time. It would seem therefore that the lowering of prices, the resulting smaller margins between prices and costs, and a shorter compulsory work week at similar rates of pay would constitute important safety valves preventing problems of inadequate effective demand from ever arising in noncapitalist-oriented economies.

If there is no logical reason for problems of inadequate demand to ever arise in the Soviet economy, then too there is no logical reason to expect that Western contemporary institutions and practices reflecting the problems of inadequate effective demand should ever develop to any great extent in noncapitalist-oriented economies. Hard-sell advertising, aggressive time-payment selling, trading stamps and other "give-aways," huge sales forces, market research departments engaged in forecasting downturns in business activity, artificial product obsolescence, output restrictions or government stockpiling to maintain profit rates, and economic pressure to create employment by exporting either capital goods or surplus consumers' goods—all would theoretically never develop to any great extent in such an economy.

On the other hand, the trends in our own economy are all in the direction of increasing the relative importance of those wasteful and/or irrational institutions. In the last analysis, these institutional developments all seem to be designed either to stimulate artificially consumers' effective demand, hold back the realization of our productive potential, or have as their principal purpose the creation of employment rather than useful goods and services.

If we can venture the hope that both sides in the cold war refrain from mutual annihilation, it seems possible that in the long run both the United States and the USSR may both successfully solve their present scarcity problems and be legitimately described as being relatively affluent societies.[25] The main dif-

[25] According to Professor Kenneth Boulding, it is likely that we will reach what he calls "capitalist communism" before the Russians reach their "socialist communism." For a report of his speech before the National Conference on Social Welfare, see Emma Harrison, "End to Poverty Is Held Possible," *New York Times,* May 16, 1961, p. 44.

ference between the principal economies of the two worlds will then be that the Russians will have a somewhat less frivolous affluence with a bare minimum of economic waste, while we will have our more exciting affluence despite the existence of a good many wasteful institutions.

Recommended Readings

BALINKY, ALEXANDER S., "Has the Soviet Union Taken a Step Towards Communism?" *Social Research*, Spring, 1961, pp. 1–14.

**BARAN, PAUL, "National Economic Planning," in *A Survey of Contemporary Economics*, Vol. II, Richard D. Irwin, Homewood, Illinois, 1952.

DEUTSCHER, ISAAC, *The Great Contest, Russia and the West*, Oxford University Press, New York, 1960, especially Chapter 4, "East and West: Implications of Coexistence."

Goals for Americans, The Report of the President's Commission on National Goals, A Spectrum Book, Prentice-Hall, Englewood Cliffs, N.J., 1960.

KHRUSHCHEV, N. S., *Report on the Program of the Communist Party of the Soviet Union*, Vols. I and II, Crosscurrents Press, New York, 1961.

MILLER, MARGARET, "Problems of Leisure: the Soviet View," *The Listener*, April 13, 1961, pp. 641–643.

**NOVE, ALEC, "The Pace of Soviet Economic Development," *Lloyd's Bank Review*, April, 1956, pp. 1–23.

PETERSON, HOWARD C., "Soviet Economic Growth and U.S. Policy," in *Comparisons of the United States and Soviet Economies*, Part II, pp. 517–523.

**ROSTOW, W. W., "Summary and Policy Implications," in *Comparisons of the United States and Soviet Economies*, Part III, pp. 589–607.

SETON, FRANCIS, "The Tempo of Soviet Industrial Expansion," *Bulletin of the Oxford University Institute of Statistics*, No. 1, February, 1958, pp. 1–27.

VARGA, EUGENE, "Everything is Fine in Russia," *Fortune,* July, 1957, pp. 119, 218–227. This is an answer to "The Crisis of Soviet Capitalism," *Fortune,* February, 1957.

WILES, PETER, "Soviet Russia Outpaces the West," *Foreign Affairs,* July, 1953, pp. 566–580.

———, "Don on Rostow," *Encounter,* December, 1959.

Glossary

AGROGORODS. Agricultural cities. Residential communities for collective farms to provide urban-type apartments and cultural facilities.

BLAT. Influence or "pull" exerted at many levels in Soviet society (see TOLKACHI).

GLAVKI. Chief administrations, which in the thirties replaced the "trusts" as units administering industries or sectors of in-industries.

GOELRO. State Commission for Electrification, established in 1920 to prepare an electrification plan for the whole country.

GOSEKONOMSOVET. All-Union Economic-Science Council. Established in 1960 with the responsibility for long range (more than five years) economic planning and research. Rechristened as "Gosplan" in reorganization at end of 1962.

GOSPLAN. State Planning Committee, of which there were two kinds: the All-Union or central Gosplan and the Gosplany for each of the 15 Republics of the USSR. The central Gosplan coordinated and amended the draft short-term output plans submitted to it by the republic Gosplany. Replaced by more powerful Union Council of the National Economy in reorganization at end of 1962.

KHOZRASCHET. The principle of economic accountability, instituted in 1929, as a result of which Soviet firms operate

343

independently of the government budget, without relying on the central government for operating monetary resources unless substantial net investment is contemplated.

KOLKHOZY. Collective farms, accounting for bulk of agricultural production in USSR.

MESTNICHESTVO. "Localism," the nonfulfillment of obligations to deliver specified goods to other regions that depend on them. Instead goods are disposed of locally to save on transportation costs and to "take care of one's neighbors" with an expectation of reciprocity.

NARIADY. Allocation certificates issued by the supply-marketing departments of Gosplan (or Union Council of the National Economy after the end of 1962) for centralized distribution of certain commodities.

NEP. New Economic Policy, period from 1921–26 characterized by temporary encouragement of small private enterprise in trade and industry in an effort to attain pre-Revolutionary output levels.

RSFSR. Russian Soviet Federal Socialist Republic, largest of 15 Soviet Republics. Others include: the Ukrainian, Byelorussian, Uzbek, Kazakh, Georgian, Azerbaijan, Lithuanian, Moldavian, Latvian, Kirkhiz, Tadjik, Armenian, Turkmen, and Estonian Soviet Socialist Republics.

SMYCHKA. Union or alliance between the working class and the peasantry, urged by Lenin, in an attempt to secure peasant support for working class leadership.

SNABSBYTY. Supply-marketing departments of the Gosplan (or Union Council of the National Economy after the end of 1962).

SOVKHOZY. State farms, organizations of agricultural output along same lines as industrial plants in USSR.

SOVNARKHOZY. Regional economic councils, established in 1957 to administer and plan industrial and agricultural production on a regional basis. Reduced from over 100 to about 40 in number at the end of 1962.

TOLKACHI. Expediters or "pushers" clandestinely employed by Soviet factory managers. Their function is to travel about exercising "blat," and thereby locate scarce supplies or speed shipments of existing orders.

ZADRUGA. Yugoslav farmers' cooperatives. Ownership of land is private. The zadruga provides credit for seed, markets the harvest, and sells supplies to the peasants. In some cases, it provides mechanical equipment for cultivation and harvest of crops.

ECONOMIC TERMS

ABSOLUTE ADVANTAGE. The ability of a country to produce a commodity at a lower cost than that of another country.

ACCELERATED DEPRECIATION. Tax incentive granted to corporate enterprises in capitalist-oriented economies enabling them to write off depreciation costs at a rapid rate, thereby reducing current taxes and supposedly stimulating investment.

ACCELERATION PRINCIPLE. The tendency, under certain circumstances, for changes in the consumption and output of consumers' goods to stimulate much greater proportional changes in the output or inventories of producers' goods.

ADMINISTERED PRICE POLICY. Rigidity to price change exhibited by monopolistic enterprises and/or unions, which has retarded a decline in price and wage levels in the United States, despite the recent growth of underutilized capital and labor resources.

AGRICULTURAL CIRCLES. Voluntary organizations in Poland enabling peasants to participate in the cooperative use of agricultural equipment, while maintaining their private ownership of land.

ASSORTMENT PLAN. The production goals for specific products, included in the total output or production plan. Frequently violated by over-fulfillment of the targets for some products, while the quotas for other products are under-fulfilled.

AUTARKY. Economic self-sufficiency or near self-sufficiency, attained by discouraging imports, developing substitute commodities for imports, and maintaining strict controls over foreign trade.

AUTHORS' CERTIFICATES. Certificates issued to Soviet workers, entitling them to receive compensation and certain privileges, as a result of their inventions.

BUYER'S MARKET. Sellers searching for scarce buyers. Characteristic of advanced capitalist-oriented economies in peacetime with problems of inadequate and slowly growing effective demand relative to rapidly growing productive capabilities.

CANNIBALIZE. To combine a number of broken pieces of equipment, in order to produce one which works.

CAPITALIST-ORIENTED ECONOMIES. Economies characterized by a predominance of private ownership of the means of production and distribution, possibly accompanied by substantial but relatively frozen sectors of public ownership.

COMECON. Council for Mutual Economic Aid, composed of Soviet Union and East European members of Soviet bloc. Engaged in regional planning, especially the planned international division of labor.

COMMISSARIATS. Soviet administrative units controlling specific industries, for example, the People's Commissariat of Ferrous Metallurgy. Replaced by Ministries after 1946.

COMMISSION TRADE. Sale of commodities by Soviet farmers to consumers' cooperatives at prices which are approximately 10 per cent above the official state and cooperative retail trade prices, and 25 per cent below the collective farm market prices.

COMMUNAL CONSUMPTION. The practice of governmental provision or distribution of certain goods and services without prices, for example, free education, medical care, and national defense.

COMMUNE. Agricultural institution in which the members of the farm work and share returns collectively. In mainland China the members also frequently live in a common building.

COMPARATIVE ADVANTAGE. The general principle upon which the net gain from trade rests. A country utilizing this principle should export products of industries in which it is most efficient (or least inefficient) and import products of industries in which it is least efficient (or most inefficient).

COMPULSORY LEISURE. Involuntary unemployment.

CONSTANT DOLLARS OR RUBLES. Current prices adjusted with price indexes to eliminate effects of fluctuations in the purchasing power of respective currencies.

CONSUMER PRICE INDEX (CPI). A weighted average of prices for selected commodities and services commonly purchased by consumers. Prices for any period are expressed in terms of their relationships to prices existing in a base period, which are assigned a value of 100. Our index is published regularly by the Bureau of Labor Statistics of the Department of Labor.

CONSUMERS' SOVEREIGNTY. The principle that consumers through their consumption or nonconsumption vote for the goods that are to be produced as well as when they will be consumed.

CONSUMPTION-INVESTMENT DECISION. Decision as to how much of present income will be diverted from present consumption to capital accumulation. These decisions tend to be made centrally in noncapitalist-oriented economies, without much concern for consumers' wishes. In capitalist-oriented economies, they are made independently by individual investors and governments with greater regard for present-day consumers.

CONVERGENCE. The theory that the United States and the USSR, as industrialized or industrializing economies, are developing increasingly similar institutions to deal with common economic problems.

COST-PUSH INFLATION. See WAGE-PUSH INFLATION.

DEFLATION. Falling prices which are accompanied by increasing unemployment and declining national income.

DEMAND-PULL INFLATION. Increases in the price level resulting from excessive demand relative to available supplies.

DISGUISED UNEMPLOYMENT. Poorly utilized manpower, particularly in the agricultural sectors of underdeveloped countries.

DISINFLATION. Generally falling prices, accompanied by relatively full employment and rising national income.

EFFECTIVE DEMAND. Sufficient desire and ability to purchase goods and services.

ENGEL'S LAWS. Consumer behavior patterns at successive income levels—more particularly the declining proportion of income expenditures for food as income rises—noted by the nineteenth-century statistician Ernst Engel.

ENTERPRISE FUND (formerly Director's Fund). A fund in Soviet factories arising from 1–6 per cent of the planned profit and 20–50 per cent of the unplanned profit, out of which premiums and other incentive benefits are paid.

ESCALATOR CLAUSE. A contract provision providing for price or wage adjustments to offset changes in money costs or in the general price level as reflected in the CPI.

EVOLUTIONARY SOCIALISM. A set of economic measures providing for a gradual transfer of the means of production and distribution from private to social ownership. Sometimes referred to as "creeping socialism."

EXTERNAL ECONOMIES. The term describing a favorable effect on the productivity of one or more firms that emanates from the action of a different person or firm, or the state.

FACTORY TRIANGLE. Administrative structure composed of the Soviet plant director, the Communist Party secretary, and the trade union president, who until 1937, shared responsibility for plan fulfillment. Since 1937, responsibility has rested solely with the plant director.

FAMILY ATMOSPHERE. Relationship developed between factory managers and chief accountants, which planners fear would lead to glossing over of poor plant operations. Remedied by periodic turnover of Soviet management personnel.

FASCISM. An economic system characterized by the retention of private ownership of the means of production and private profit under centralized governmental controls.

"FAVORABLE" BALANCE OF TRADE. Mercantilist evaluation of trade balance describing the condition in which the money value of exports exceeds the money value of imports.

FISCAL POLICY. The use of government revenue, expenditures, and general budgetary policies to achieve desired economic objectives.

FIVE-YEAR PLANS. The periods for each of the Soviet Five-Year Plans are as follows: Plan I—1928–32; Plan II—1933–37; Plan III—1938–42; Plan IV—1946–50; Plan V—1951–55; Plan VI—1956–60 (abandoned in midstream); Plan VII—1958–65 (Seven-Year Plan).

FIXED CAPITAL. Durable goods used repeatedly in the process of production, and subject to depreciation.

FRICTIONAL UNEMPLOYMENT. Unemployment resulting from job shifts within the labor force in response to changing employment opportunities. This type of unemployment exists even when the economy is at full, or overfull employment.

FULL EMPLOYMENT VOLUNTARY NONCONSUMPTION. A concept reflecting the resources voluntarily released by consumers for investment-type or communal consumption activities under conditions of full employment, sometimes referred to as "ex ante saving" at full employment.

FUNDING. Physical allocation or rationing of producers' goods by the Soviet central planners, rather than by the price system, which tends to allocate available consumers' goods.

GROSS INDUSTRIAL PRODUCTION (GIP). An index of production in the USSR, which omits agricultural activity and includes double-counting of materials transferred between reporting units.

GROSS INVESTMENT. Additions to capital stock plus allowances for replacement of depreciated capital during a given accounting period.

GROWTHMANSHIP. A preoccupation with comparative rates of growth stimulated by the rapid increases in the Soviet economy and our need to project a competitive image to the growth-starved areas of the world.

HEAVY RUBLES. Soviet rubles after January 1, 1961, when the currency revaluation moved all decimal points one digit to the left, and defined the gold-content of the ruble as 0.987412 grams of pure gold.

IMPROVEMENT FACTOR. Increases in labor productivity which unions in capitalist-oriented economies partially rely on in negotiations for money wage increases.

INCOME REVOLUTION. Supposed trend towards greater wage and income equality taking place in the United States during World War II and in the Soviet Union since 1956.

INNOVATION. The introduction of new methods or devices, designed to improve quantitative or qualitative indexes.

INSTALMENT PLAN-IN-REVERSE. The purchase and sale of goods in which the price is to be paid in regular and fixed amounts, over time, and delivery takes place after payments have been completed.

INVESTORS' SOVEREIGNTY. The tendency for the aggregate consumption-investment decision to be the result of investors' decisions in capitalist-oriented economies.

JOINT-STOCK COMPANY. Post-World War II Soviet and East European institution, as a result of which certain industries (petroleum, chemicals, aluminum, uranium, etc.) were developed jointly by the USSR and those East European nations which had fought on the side of the Germans during World War II. Most of the commodities produced were syphoned off as war reparations by the Soviet Union. All joint-stock companies were liquidated after the uprisings in Eastern Europe during the mid-fifties.

LABOR-DAYS. Units measuring the quantity and quality of work put in by Soviet collective farmers, which provide the basis for differential payments after the harvest.

LABOR PRODUCTIVITY. Output per unit of labor input. Changes in productivity result from changes in the technical skills of workers and/or increases in the mechanization of the productive process.

LAW OF VALUE. A Marxist concept describing the functioning of free market forces in a capitalist-oriented economy, as a result of which there is supposedly a tendency for products to be exchanged at prices reflecting their labor content.

LOCALISM. (See MESTNICHESTVO.)

MACHINE TRACTOR STATIONS (MTS). Soviet and Eastern European agricultural institutions which rented the services of agricultural machinery and operators to the collective farms, facilitating the intensive utilization of scarce capital resources and insuring the political reliability of the farmers. Established in the late twenties. In 1958, their machinery was sold to the Soviet collective farms and the MTS were converted to repair stations.

MACROECONOMICS. The study of economic aggregates of public and private consumption and investment and their impact on the economy's level of employment, incomes, and prices. The study of how the economy answers the basic question, "How much will be produced?"

MARGINAL DISUTILITY OF LABOR. The difference in discomfort attendant upon increasing one's labor by an additional unit. The basis of the supply curve for labor, reflecting man's inherent distaste for work which must be overcome in order to attract additional labor to the labor market.

MARGINAL VALUE PRODUCT. The value that an additional worker adds to the employer's total revenue, assumed to underlie the demand curve for labor in Western economic theory under perfectly competitive conditions.

MAXIMALIST GROWTHMEN. Those economists who advocate efforts to increase our GNP by five per cent or more per annum. They agree that the relative size of the government sector should be increased in order to stimulate such growth, but disagree as to the fields in which government investment and consumption activity is acceptable.

MICROECONOMICS. The study of market pricing and output decisions in such individual economic units as the firm or industry. The study of how the economy answers the questions, "What is produced? How is it produced? For whom is it produced?"

MINIMALIST GROWTHMEN. Those economists advocating efforts to increase our GNP by three to four per cent per annum. Generally, they are unwilling to expand the relative size of the government sector, in attempting to stimulate such growth.

MIXED SYSTEMS. Economic systems in which a combination of public and private economic institutions coexist.

MONEY ILLUSION. Tendency of workers or investors to think of income in money rather than real terms.

MONOCULTURE. The dependence of an underdeveloped economy on the export of a single crop or raw material in order to realize foreign exchange. An economy practicing monoculture is sometimes referred to as an "exposed economy."

NET INVESTMENT. Net additions to existing capital stock. Obtained by deducting depreciation costs from gross investment.

NONCAPITALIST-ORIENTED ECONOMY. An economy which is consciously progressing with the socialization of industry and/or the collectivization of agriculture.

OVER-COMMITMENT. Description of the basic problem of the Soviet economy, which is reflected in consistent attempts to invest more of their resources than has been warranted by readily available manpower and capital.

PEOPLE'S CAPITALISM. An attempt to describe the evolution of the capitalist system into a stage providing greater equity.

PLANNED PROFITS. Profits arbitrarily established by the central planners in the Soviet Union, ordinarily amounting to about five per cent of the planned production cost.

PRICE SCISSORS. The peacetime relationship between industrial prices (the upper blade) and agricultural prices (the lower blade). Applies within economies as well as in international markets.

PRODUCTIVITY. The amount of output relative to the use of any factor of production.

PROGRESSIVE PIECE-RATES. Payments per unit made at increasingly higher rates for output in excess of norms.

PROGRESSIVE TAX. A stated tax which takes a higher percentage of income as income increases.

PROPORTIONAL TAX. A tax which takes a fixed percentage of all incomes.

REGIONALIZATION. Breaking up of the Soviet Ministries in 1957, thereby decentralizing some of the decision-making process.

REGRESSIVE TAX. A tax which takes a lower percentage of income as income increases. Opposite of progressive tax.

RESERVE ARMY. Marxist term describing chronic existence of un-employed labor in capitalist-oriented economies.

RUBLE-DOLLAR RATIO. The relationship between the price of a given commodity (or the average price of a group of commodities) in the Soviet Union as compared with the price of the same commodity (or the average price of a group of similar commodities) in the United States.

SAFETY FACTOR. Margin by which a Soviet plant's production possibilities are deliberately under-estimated, in order to avoid under-fulfillment due to unexpected bottlenecks in the production process.

SECULAR EXHILARATION. A long period characterized by rapid technological development and an excess of investment opportunities relative to full employment voluntary non-consumption.

SECULAR STAGNATION. A long period characterized by the growing inadequacy of investment-like activities to utilize fully the resources released by full employment voluntary nonconsumption.

SELLER'S MARKET. Buyers searching for scarce products or labor. A characteristic of noncapitalist-oriented economies, and wartime capitalist-oriented economies with chronic conditions of inadequate supply relative to effective demand.

SIMULATION. Practice by factory managers in the USSR of presenting an artificial appearance of over-fulfillment of goals, in order to earn the attached premiums.

SOCIAL CAPITAL. Capital assets frequently developed by governments, for example, transportation facilities, power plants, schools, etc.

SOCIALIST COMPETITION. Competition between Soviet factories to produce higher quantitative and qualitative indices, with premiums and honors awarded to the winner.

STAKHANOVITE MOVEMENT. Movement of workers in the Soviet Union, beginning in 1935, designed to increase productivity by encouraging workers' initiative in the rationalization of the process of production. Composed of those workers who had made substantial achievements, entitling them to be ranked as Stakhanovites and to be awarded special bonuses.

STORMING. Acceleration of the rate of production towards the end of the month in Soviet factories, in order to achieve output goals and premiums.

STUMPAGE FEES. Depletion charges levied on the exploitation of easily accessible timber reserves.

SUBSIDIES. Government grants extended to assist and encourage the development or maintenance of a branch of industry or agriculture.

SURPLUS VALUE. According to Marx, the difference between the labor costs of a commodity and the value of the product, the basis of the price of the commodity. That difference includes rent, interest, profits, or dividends.

SYNDICALISM. A theory which gives to trade unions the central role in a revolutionary struggle. It opposes political action, preferring the use of such weapons as sabotage and the general strike, in order to achieve a decentralized brand of common ownership and control, with the trade unions as the future organs of administration.

TAX AVOIDANCE. Escaping the payment of taxes by taking advantage of discrepancies or loopholes in the tax law.

TIGHT MONEY POLICY. A policy of the Federal Reserve System to reduce the amount of excess reserves held by member banks, thereby discouraging loans and investment by banks, making credit more difficult to obtain, and restraining growth in the money supply.

TRUST. Early Soviet administrative unit which was responsible for the operations of individual plants in an industry or region. Still used in administering the coal-mining and fishing industries.

TURNOVER TAX. A huge indirect or sales tax levied largely at the consumers' goods level in the Soviet Union. Also employed in both Eastern and Western Europe.

UNDER-COMMITMENT. Description of the basic problem of the United States economy as reflected in our under-utilization of available manpower and capital.

UNION COUNCIL OF THE NATIONAL ECONOMY. Soviet administrative organ, established at the end of 1962 to replace the old Gosplan. It is responsible for the coordination and amending of the draft annual plans of the 15 Republics as well as for the prompt allocation of scarce resources.

UNPLANNED PROFITS. Extra profits emerging from economies effected in the process of production in noncapitalist-oriented economies.

VIRGIN LANDS. Area in Siberia and Kazakhstan opened up in the fifties as part of Khrushchev's program to expand agricultural production. Previously not utilized because of severe climatological conditions.

WAGE FUND. Monies set aside for factory managers to permit the payment of wages and salaries during a planning period in noncapitalist-oriented economies.

WAGE-PUSH INFLATION. Increase in price levels during periods of under-utilization of labor and capital attributed to wage increases in excess of productivity gains and resulting in rising unit labor costs. Also referred to as "cost-push" inflation, although this may result from rising unit overhead costs.

WAR COMMUNISM. Term used in the Soviet Union to denote the policies of severe rationing and egalitarianism, prevailing during the protracted civil war period of 1918–21.

WELFARE STATE. Capitalist-oriented economy with large and growing communal consumption sector.

WORKERS' COUNCILS. Yugoslav institution which affords trade unions a role in the management of industrial enterprises. Adopted in modified form in Poland after October, 1956, but quietly abandoned since 1960.

WORKING CAPITAL. Materials, supplies, and stocks of semi-finished and finished goods included in the assets of a factory. Also referred to as "circulating" capital.

Index

SUBJECT INDEX

* Hereafter abbreviated as "n.c.o.e.";
capitalist-oriented economy = c.o.e.
g = glossary; n = note; t = table